INTERNATIONAL DISPUTES: THE POLITICAL ASPECTS

INTERNATIONAL DISPUTES

THE POLITICAL ASPECTS

F. S. NORTHEDGE
Professor of International Relations in the University of London

and

M. D. DONELAN
Senior Lecturer in International Relations in the London School of Economics and Political Science

audi partem alteram

Published for
The David Davies Memorial Institute of International Studies
by
EUROPA PUBLICATIONS: LONDON

EUROPA PUBLICATIONS LIMITED
18 Bedford Square, London, W.C.1

ISBN: 0 900 36236 7
Library of Congress Catalog Card No. 70-149885

Printed and bound in England by
STAPLES PRINTERS LIMITED
at The Stanhope Press, Rochester, Kent

Foreword

In 1966 the David Davies Memorial Institute of International Studies published the report of a study group, with Sir Humphrey Waldock as chairman and rapporteur, on the legal aspects of the peaceful settlement of international disputes.[1] The report was well received and aroused wide interest. The Institute considered that a companion study of the political and economic aspects of such disputes would also be valuable. The project was discussed with Mr Kenneth Younger, Director of the Royal Institute of International Affairs, who agreed to make available to the Institute the results of some tentative work which they had done on the subject. At this point the Institute approached us and asked us to act as co-chairmen of a Study Group consisting of: Professor Max Beloff; Sir Eric Berthoud; Dr D. W. Bowett; Professor G. L. Goodwin; Professor L. C. B. Gower; Dr Max Habicht; Professor F. H. Hinsley; Lord Hodson; Professor R. Y. Jennings; Professor W. N. Medlicott; Lord Shawcross; Lord Strang; Lord Trevelyan; Sir Francis Vallat; Sir Ernest Vasey; Professor Sir Humphrey Waldock. In addition to the members of the Group we have also had advice and help from other experts.

The role of the Group was to be the general direction of the study. Individual members undertook to give help and advice, both on the academic side and on that of actual practical experience as diplomats and advisers on policy. Our first action was to appoint Professor F. S. Northedge and Mr Michael Donelan to be authors of the study. They were given a completely free rein, subject only to comments, suggestions and criticisms from members of the Group.

During the course of the work the authors paid a visit to Washington and New York and were fortunate enough to talk with: Mr Dean Acheson; Chief Simeon O. Adebo; Dean Willis C. Armstrong; Mr Charles G. Bolte; Dr Aron Broches; Mr McGeorge Bundy; Lord Caradon; Mr Henry Darwin; Sir Patrick Dean; Professor T. J. Farer; Professor A. B. Fox; Professor W. T. Fox; Mr William Gleysteen; Mr Arthur Goldberg; Professor Leon Gordenker; Professor Charles Hermann; Professor Roger Hilsman; Mr J. N. Hyde; Mr Elmore Jackson; Mr Joseph E. Johnson; Mr Andreas Lowenfeld; Mr Abraham Lowenthal; Professor P. E. Mosley; Professor Robert Osgood; Mr Robert Owen; Ambassador Richard E.

[1] David Davies Memorial Institute, Report of a Study Group on the Peaceful Settlement of International Disputes, London, 1966. This will shortly appear in a revised edition.

Pederson; Dr John Plank; Mr David Popper; Mr K. J. Reddington; Mr Oscar Schachter; Professor Harold Sprout; Mr C. A. Stavropoulos; Mr Donald B. Straus; Dr M. Rafael Urquía; U Thant; Professor Oran Young and Mr Ralph Zacklin. They also talked with Lord Avon, Lord Harlech and Sir Alec Douglas-Home in London and with Mr Averell Harriman in Paris.

As explained, the Study Group was composed both of scholars, jurists, and other students of international affairs, and of certain individuals who had had practical experience of, and responsibility for, the formulation and execution of policy. All the members of the Group were unanimous in thinking that the completed work would be of great value both to the "academics" and to the "practitioners" and they, and we the co-chairmen, have no hesitation in recommending this book to all those interested, from whatever angle, in the study of international affairs.

Finally, the Institute's thanks are due to the Social Science Research Council and the Foreign and Commonwealth Office, without whose financial support the work could not have been successfully carried out. We are deeply grateful for the encouragement and assistance which we have received from the Foreign and Commonwealth Office at all levels throughout the study, but would stress that the views expressed in the study are the responsibility of the authors and the Group, and of them alone.

Caccia
Inchyra

Authors' Acknowledgements

FOUR years ago, Miss Mary Sibthorp of the David Davies Memorial Institute, combining charm with the authority of Kitchener in the famous poster, persuaded us to accept a piece of work on international disputes involving, she said, "just the collation of a few documents". Since then, we have never ceased to wonder at how the project grew and at how her organising work and help and encouragement to us grew with it, and to be deeply grateful to her.

For our appointment and for standing advice and criticism, we thank the Institute and the Study Group under Lord Caccia and Lord Inchyra. We hope that we shall be seen to have benefited from the opportunity to talk with them and with the many other statesmen and scholars, named or referred to in the Foreword. We can at least say, as could anyone who does this kind of work, that it was a relief and a pleasure to be able to turn sometimes from books, documents and papers to living learning, living history.

We thank also Mr Michael Banks, Miss Hazel Fox, Miss Muriel Grieve and Mr Ronald Higgins who each wrote a specialist paper for us at our request. They are not responsible for any views we have expressed, only for providing very helpful material. Mr Banks's and Miss Grieve's papers are cited in connection with Chapters 1 and 10 (pages 24 and 228). Miss Fox's paper on "The settlement of disputes by peaceful means and the observance of international law – African attitudes" assisted us at numerous points in Chapter 14 and Mr Higgins' paper on "Policy-Making by Disputants", at numerous points throughout the book.

Mr Peter Fielder and Miss Hélène Warning were our research assistants for three years, doing the spade work on studies of fifty international disputes, answering innumerable miscellaneous questions, arguing with us about what we proposed to say. We hope that they enjoyed the experience as much as we valued their assistance and that they are not too dissatisfied with what has grown from their labours.

We have a special fellow-feeling for Miss Esme Allen who, like us, hammered out every word and comma that we wrote and, unlike us, did it perfectly.

F. S. Northedge
M. D. Donelan

January 1971

Contents

Abbreviations

CENTO	Central Treaty Organisation
COMECON	Council for Mutual Economic Assistance
ECSC	European Coal and Steel Community
EDC	European Defence Community
EEC	European Economic Community
EFTA	European Free Trade Association
IAPC	Inter-American Peace Committee
IAPF	Inter-American Peace Force
ICJ	International Court of Justice
IMF	International Monetary Fund
NATO	North Atlantic Treaty Organisation
NFD	Northern Frontier District
OAS	Organisation of American States
OAU	Organisation of African Unity
PCIJ	Permanent Court of International Justice
PLO	Palestine Liberation Organisation
SEATO	South-East Asia Treaty Organisation
UNCTAD	United Nations Conference on Trade and Development
UNEF	United Nations Emergency Force
UNFICYP	United Nations Peace-Keeping Force in Cyprus
UNOGIL	United Nations Observer Group in the Lebanon
UNSCOB	United Nations Special Committee in the Balkans

Introduction

In all human history the problem of how dissimilar groups, whether social classes, races, religious communities or the like, can live together in harmony and in the same confined space has been a major concern of mankind. Since the First World War the question of peace between the different nation-states has assumed primacy of place within this problem owing to the revolution in arms technology, transport and communications. With the advent of nuclear weapons and their incorporation into the armouries of the major Powers it is now a question of whether man can afford any longer to run the risks of living in an international system which lacks a central authority to suppress violence and in which the member-states are still to a large extent judges and juries in their own cause. The replacement of the present international system, however, seems as yet far from being within the scope of practical politics and hence the question of how international relations can be managed without civilised life being destroyed by international conflict will continue to rank as the major problem of mankind. But even if it is assumed that the sheer dread of nuclear war will somehow succeed in averting that catastrophe, it will remain both a duty and interest of the world that disputes between nations be settled with the least friction and waste of resources. The notion that disputes can somehow be eliminated from the international system by better education, better communication or better means of settling those disputes seems to us utopian. To dispute is inherent in the human situation. The most that men can do is to learn more about how to manage the inevitable clashes in outlook, policy, and interest between states more efficiently and with less risk to the continuance of organised life on this planet. That is what the present study aims at.

In the twentieth century the means available for the peaceful settlement of disputes are many and varied; some of the chief examples are set down, for instance, in Article 33 (1) of the United Nations Charter which commits Member-States to seek a solution of any dispute which is likely to endanger international peace and security "by negotiation, enquiry, mediation, conciliation, arbitration, judicial settlement, resort to regional agencies, or other peaceful means of their own choice". The question inevitably arises, therefore, as to why more effective use is not made by states of these means and this issue was posed by the earlier Davies Institute study *The Peaceful Settlement of International Disputes: The Legal Aspects* when it reported that "the extreme reluctance often shown by one or both Governments (in any dispute) to contemplate the introduction of an impartial third element into the negotiations as a catalyst to dissolve hard positions which they have taken up is undoubtedly the principal cause of the all too frequent failure to settle international disputes".[1] The problem may be formulated in a slightly different manner and, as such, has been the dominant preoccupation of the present study, namely, what are the conditions, political, economic, military or other, which facilitate or, as the case may be, militate against the peaceful settlement of international disputes?

Disputes and Situations

There is, of course, a vital distinction to be drawn at the outset between an international dispute *per se* and a "situation" or "situation of friction", from which a dispute or disputes may later develop. The distinction is referred to, without being elaborated, in Article 1 (1) of the United Nations Charter which defines one of the Organisation's purposes as being "to bring about by peaceful means . . . adjustment or settlement of international disputes or situations which might lead to a breach of the peace". Article 11 (3) of the Charter authorises the General Assembly "to call the attention of the Security Council to situations which are likely to endanger international peace and security", while Article 34, amongst other references in the Charter to this distinction, permits the Security Council "to investigate any dispute, or any situation which might lead to international friction or give rise to a dispute, in order to determine whether the continuance of the dispute or situation is likely to endanger the maintenance of international peace and security".

In the practice of the United Nations and the writings of commentators on the United Nations Charter no absolutely clear distinction has been drawn between these two concepts. States have referred what we would call "disputes", as defined below, to United Nations bodies while describing them as "situations" and some writers regard the distinction as "academic". Bentwich and Martin, in their commentary, go somewhat further and write that situations may be classified under two heads, one class consisting of states of international relations "which might lead to international friction" and the other of conditions "which might give rise to a dispute in the technical sense of the term".[2] We may perhaps generalise the meaning of the word "situation", as understood by such commentators, to imply a state of potential conflict, where all the ingredients of a dispute exist but where the dispute has neither been formulated nor crystallised. This allows us to define the term dispute quite simply as a formulated

[1] P. 35. [2] N. Bentwich and A. Martin: *A Commentary on the Charter of the United Nations*, London, 1951, p. 80.

difference of opinion as to matters of law, fact or justice arising in the mutual relations of states.[3]

Such a distinction still leaves out of account, however, yet another type of "situation", from which disputes may develop and the understanding of which is essential to the understanding of the nature of international disputes. The point may be put as follows. An international dispute may develop within a context of otherwise friendly relations between nations, as for instance the dispute about Gibraltar between Britain and Spain or the dispute between Britain and Iceland concerning fishing rights in the seas surrounding Iceland. In such instances it may be presumed that settlement of the determinate dispute will generally be sufficient to cause relations between the parties to revert to friendliness. A "situation" or "situation of friction", on the other hand, may be described as a diffuse condition of tension or potential tension between two communities, which may co-exist within the same state, and as such may arise from deeper incompatibilities of culture, ideology, psychology, or historical experience than those ordinarily present in a dispute or "situation" as defined in the limited sense of the above paragraph. If a dispute, in the sense of a formulated difference of view on a determinate issue, develops in a situation of this kind, it may be regarded as a consequence or symbol of the underlying tension rather than its cause; and if the dispute is settled without the fundamental bases of tension being alleviated, the possibility is that further disputes will arise in future. The classic situation of tension between Slavs and Teutons in Eastern Europe and the latter-day frictions between Greeks and Turks in Cyprus, or Arabs and Israelis in the Middle East are obvious examples. In including "situations" in this wider sense within the purview of the United Nations, the Charter appears to us to mark a striking step forward from the Covenant of the League of Nations, in which the dominant assumption seemed to be that wars and less serious ruptures of diplomatic relations arose from unsettled disputes. No doubt the experience of the 1930s convinced the framers of the United Nations Charter that, in dealing with revolutionary or nihilistic regimes like Nazi Germany, it was not enough merely to work for a settlement of outstanding disputes between those regimes and other nations. There was a total conflict of basic values to be faced.

In this study we have from first to last borne in mind the distinctions between these three types of international experience – the dispute *per se*, the "situation" defined in the limited or technical sense of a state of affairs from which a formulated dispute may later emerge, and the "situa-

[3] *Ibid*, p. 80, where a dispute is defined as a "conflict between states in which the contesting parties have formulated definite claims, defences and possibly counter-claims".

tion" in the sense of a diffuse condition of wide-ranging tension of which disputes, if they develop, are rather the symbol than the cause – though naturally some overlap is bound to occur. We have, where convenient, differentiated between methods of alleviating each which experience has shown to be more or less relevant, although for purely verbal convenience the single word "dispute" has generally been used to describe all three conditions where the same point about each needs to be made.

Reverting to our initial question – why are some international disputes pursued peacefully or why do they fade from the agenda of diplomacy without the peace being broken while others involve a resort to armed force? – it seemed to resolve itself into four basic subordinate questions. Firstly, what are international disputes and what essential common attributes may be said to distinguish them? Secondly, how do they arise and what can be done to mitigate their occurrence? Thirdly, how do they develop or, in the contemporary jargon, escalate, and how may their development or escalation be controlled? Fourthly, and finally, how are disputes resolved and under what conditions are they resolved by non-violent procedures? The successive parts of this book are attempts to throw such light as study and reflection provide for the answering of such questions.

The Systemic Approach

In seeking an approach to these four questions we might have focused on what may be described as the "systemic" approach to international politics. That is to say, we might have reviewed the general development of the international system since the Second World War and considered the general causes of international conflict during these past twenty-five years. The relevant themes to be considered here would be the consequences of the defeat of the Axis Powers in 1945 and the break-up of the great wartime coalition which wrought that defeat; the resurgence of China under the Communists; the momentous revolution in world affairs known as decolonisation; and the legacy of territorial problems left to the successor states formed from the old European empires. Most of the leading disputes since 1945 have sprung in one way or another from these events. It would also have been necessary in such a systemic approach to consider other developments affecting the international system, notably economic problems, financial and commercial changes and the revolution in technology, especially in the production of weapons. It would then have been essential to go on to try to define the conditions, in the world as a whole, or in any particular region, which are conducive to the initiation, development and violent pursuit of disputes and which, contrariwise, make for their prevention, limitation and peaceful resolution.

The Sociological Approach

Alternatively, the focus of study might have been the sociological. In this case we would have investigated the social circumstances prevailing within a state which dispose it to erupt in civil war in such a manner as to endanger international peace, or which cause it to embark upon external policies which lead to friction with other states. In this case our aim would have been to formulate generalisations about the kind of internal conditions within states which cause them to dispute with other states and to use violence in the resolution of these disputes, whereas conditions of a different order might induce them to avoid disputes or to settle them in a peaceful manner whenever they arise.

Statecraft

The central approach which we have in the event adopted is neither of these, though it incorporates substantial elements of both. Perhaps it can best be described as that which is focused upon statecraft, or the skilful management of relations between those social units called states within the global system which they now collectively constitute. In the chapters which follow we shall take account of the systemic approach; we shall discuss the various patterns of power and interests among the different states, the influence of ideas and norms in the world at large and the growth of international organisations whether world-wide or regional in scope. Again, although we are sceptical as to whether research has so far thrown much light on the internal circumstances which may dispose states towards quarrelling and violence, we shall have much to say in what follows about relevant internal factors bearing on the external conduct of states and conditions engendering the kind of internal conflicts within states which have disturbing effects on the relations between them. Nevertheless, our preferred approach throughout is basically political and within that term centres upon the statecraft of the antagonists in dispute. We shall seek to show what it is that governments and peoples do in their conduct of policy that leads to the outbreak of disputes, to their development and enlargement, to violence and war; and conversely what they do or can do which prevents disputes, limits them and leads to their peaceful resolution.

We must never forget, however, that statecraft is not practised in a vacuum; no country can handle its foreign relations without being at all times influenced, even if its actions are not determined, by factors beyond its control. We shall try to bear in mind in this book, in other words, not merely the political management of international affairs, but also the entire complex of external forces, in so far as we are able to understand them, which favours or conspires against the management with the minimum of friction and waste of such disputes as occur in the international system.

It may seem a drawback of all the three approaches that they traffic, as they must, in generalities. The systemic approach can at best arrive at generalisations about conditions in the international system and its various sub-systems which stimulate or discourage disputes, as the case may be. The sociological approach can at best provide broad statements concerning critical stages in the internal development of states which are likely to lead to internal or external breaches of the peace. Similarly, in our stress on statecraft in disputes we can offer the reader nothing more than what can be said in general about the conduct of states engaged in disputes. We cannot, within our terms of reference, go into great detail, as the historian does, about what a particular state did in a particular dispute; or argue the detail of what it might have done.

But this is not in fact wholly a drawback. Human intelligence is sometimes measured in terms of its capability for distinguishing between superficially similar objects, but it is also surely a constructive and habitual function of the human animal to generalise from its experience. In the course of our research for this book we have frequently met with diplomats or practising politicians who would deny the existence of similarities between different international situations such as would make possible generalisations about desirable ways of handling them. But this denial may well conceal and overlay the continuous, though unconscious, application of rules and generalisations intuitively acquired. As observers of international affairs, we feel bound to probe into the unstated assumptions of governments and their diplomatic agents which communicate a certain general stamp, or style, to their conduct of affairs. Indeed it may be better for all concerned if the unconscious general wisdom of the practitioners of statecraft were given an articulated and precise form.

Taking full account, therefore, of both the limitations and the possibilities of the generalising bent of the scholarly mind, it seems to us that the approach we have chosen has certain advantages. The study of international relations is often described as a social science and rightly so, but it is also in our view one of the humanities, the *literae humaniores*. Reflection on the behaviour of nations in handling disputes between themselves or, as we prefer to call it, their statecraft, leads to knowledge which is to be valued in its own right, that is, as the understanding of human performance under certain determinate conditions. Beyond this, we believe that the approach which we have adopted has a further value in assisting governments and people to prepare themselves to face and handle with somewhat less friction and waste the disputes which inevitably occur in the international system.

But what kind of assistance can this be? In the years since 1918 the academic study of international relations has grown rapidly and voluminously in some of the leading countries of the world. Obviously, the principal reason for this has been the increased risks to civilised life in an ungoverned system of world politics fraught with all the dangers implicit in vast strides in weapon technology. Nevertheless, confusion has sometimes prevailed as to the kind of assistance academic study can give to the practical management of human affairs. Our view is that that assistance is, and must be, more theoretical than practical.

The Academic Contribution

Academic study can provide a theoretical framework for analysis and for the critical examination of the premises of thought of the practitioner; a deeper understanding of the historical roots of this or that dispute; some tentative generalisations, drawn from the study of actual experience, about how states behave under different conditions, why they adopt certain policies, how and why they are able to resolve their disputes peacefully in certain kinds of circumstances and why they fail to do so in others; and occasionally new – because detached – insights into familiar problems. To that extent academic study can assist those whose duty it is to grapple with the practical, ever-changing problems of this world. But its function is essentially analysis and explanation, not policy prescription or its execution; it cannot lay claim to prescribe in detail what practitioners should do in a determinate situation. The practitioner in international affairs, perhaps in other human affairs, too, tends to suffer from what may be called the "illusion of uniqueness" and the academic from the "illusion of similarity"; the idea, on the one hand, that each and every situation is *sui generis* and on the other that all situations are divisible into general categories. Though there are dangers in both thought patterns, we would insist that the scholar has a vital function to fulfil in acting as a "remembrancer", an instrument for the orderly storage of the accumulated experience of mankind.

Informed Statesmanship

Accordingly, in this book we do not presume to offer a detailed catalogue of technical rules for statesmen and the general public in dealing with the disputes and situations which will confront them in future years. What it is to be done will depend on the particular facts of the particular matter in hand; techniques of handling such matters cannot be prescribed in a detailed or general way in advance; there must be, each time, a creative action in a given situation. We have in mind a rather more diffuse and at the same time perhaps more fundamental kind of assistance of which statesmen and the general public stand in need. We seek to enlarge somewhat their general understanding of what international disputes are and of what experience and reflection can contribute towards their practical resolution. We do so in the belief that deeper general understanding can have some influence for good on the actions of states in particular situations. The crux of the practical problem of international disputes, as we see it, is the presence or absence in states of informed statesmanship, a combination of practical flair in handling human situations and the distilled experience of the past. Academics cannot presume to dictate to the practitioners of diplomacy what good statesmanship will require in the as yet unknown crises of the future. They can invite them to reflect, on the basis of ordered historical experience, what good statesmanship is and what it is not.

Fifty Case Studies

Turning now to the methods we have adopted in writing this book, our bedrock raw material has been case studies which we have made of fifty of the most important international disputes since the Second World War. We hope to have these published later as a separate volume and a list of them will be found as an appendix to this book. We cannot claim that these fifty disputes constitute anything in the way of a statistical sample of all international disputes since 1945; we have merely tried to include in our list the major disputes which have figured on the diplomatic agenda of the international community since the war and which have received prominent publicity. One or two of them, as for instance the civil war in Nigeria from 1967 to 1970, have been resolved since the work for this book was completed; others, perhaps of equal importance to the fifty, have been omitted. But we claim that the selection is large enough for valid conclusions concerning the nature, genesis, evolution and resolution of disputes to be drawn, and that these conclusions would not have needed substantial modification had a larger or different selection of case studies been made.

We have used the fifty case studies as our raw material in different ways. In the first place, we continually put forward propositions about human nature, the concerns of states, the nature of conflict and the manner in which conflict unfolds. The case studies have served as a means of testing and shaping these propositions. Secondly, we use the case studies to illustrate and pinpoint the propositions we present. Thirdly, and notably in the final part of our book, which deals with the solution of international disputes, we use the case studies in a rather more statistical way in order, *inter alia*, to estimate the effectiveness under varied conditions of the different existing methods for the settlement of international disputes.

The case studies, as stated earlier, all derive from the past twenty-five years. However, the propositions we are putting forward about disputes are not bound to any particular period of history. In so far as they have any validity, they belong to the perennial nature of human politics and group conflict. This is worth saying, especially from the standpoint of the next few years. The accustomed forms of international disputes may be changing. Bilateral disputes focused upon a certain piece of territory may become fewer; multilateral disputes concerned with the entire organisation of world politics and the distribution and consumption of the world's income and resources may bulk larger. But the basic nature of disputes and their manner of development, as we have tried to describe them in this book, will remain the same.

We would emphasise finally that this is essentially a preliminary study. The reason for this is simply the absence of scholarly works encompassing the politics or statecraft of international disputes. Had such a study already existed, the case for writing the present book would obviously have been less urgent; but, try as we might, we have been unable to find any work which adequately fills this gap. Hence we have sought above all else to provide a first basic map of this subject – making a division into the nature of disputes, their origins, development and solution, giving within each section the broad heads of analysis, the various forms which disputes may take, the different elements in the motivations and attitudes of the contending parties. Each of these is in itself a whole programme for further study.

Explanatory and analytical studies of the past and current operations of the international system, such as this, are at present somewhat under a cloud cast by the advent of "behaviouralist" theory which purports to work out "scientific" laws of political activity which have the regularity and precision of the laws of natural science and the same predictive value. We attempt in the following pages to extract as much insight into our subject from such theorising as we are able. But we remain unconvinced that human behaviour, individual or collective, lends itself to precisely the same kind of intellectual treatment as, say, the inanimate world. There is such a thing as wisdom concerning human performance in politics, which relies upon a general understanding drawn from history, reflection upon the relevant social and psychological forces operating in the political community, and developing insight into the human condition, as well as scientific or quasi-scientific knowledge. We believe that political studies must be pursued in a scientific spirit, however far they may fall short of providing the basis for predictive sciences; but that there is much else in those studies besides scientific method. It is on these assumptions that this book is written.

1. *Past and Present Thought on International Disputes*

RESEARCH into any subject must take as its starting point the existing state of thought and knowledge on that subject and then seek to extend the frontiers of that thought and knowledge. We shall, therefore, try in the present chapter to survey the existing literature on international disputes and in subsequent chapters try to make our own contribution to the understanding and control of those disputes at the point at which we believe the present state of thought to be deficient. There are, however, two considerable difficulties confronting us at the outset. One is that the relevant literature is very extensive indeed; we have virtually to take account of all that has been written on international politics since man began to speculate about it. Hence there must be in this chapter a good deal of selection and broad generalisation. However, it should be pointed out that we are concerned here with *thought* about international disputes and less with the experience gained by governments and diplomats in the practice of international relations. The latter we shall be concerned with in later chapters.

The second difficulty is that while volumes have been written on war as an international phenomenon, and only somewhat less on international conflict, meaning the continuing struggle between states for the achievement of certain values or protection of interests, less attention has been paid to the narrower subject of international disputes and situations of friction as we have defined them in the Introduction.[1] This relative lack of concern with disputes in the literature is in one sense fortunate in that it somewhat reduces the sheer volume of writing on international relations which we must handle in this chapter. On the other hand, writers have not always been very precise in the dividing lines they draw between such concepts as dispute, conflict, tension and so on and hence it is not always easy to distinguish writing on disputes as such from writing on those other related conditions of international affairs. However that may be, we propose to divide the present chapter into three parts. In the first (I) we shall discuss very briefly some of the well-known historical accounts of the nature of international strife. In the second (II) we shall concern ourselves with writing, mainly in the first half of the twentieth century, on

[1] *Supra*, pp. 2–4.

the better ordering of international relations so as to produce a less dispute-prone world, while in the third section (III) we shall be more interested in the findings of research in the last decade or so on the subject of disputatious conditions of international relations. The concluding remarks in section IV merely seek to summarise the three previous sections.

I

Realists and Idealists

Throughout the greater part of man's history thinkers have tended to fall into one or other of two broad groups in their attitudes towards disputes and conflicts between the contemporary political units of mankind, be they Greek city-states, multi-racial empires like the Persian or Roman, or modern nation-states. On the one hand are those who may be called "conservatives", meaning writers who regarded international strife as inevitable, perhaps even desirable. At the other extreme are the "abolitionists" or "reformers", those who considered conflict undesirable and wasteful, and believed it could be eliminated or substantially reduced by suitable social or political arrangements. Broadly speaking, we might be inclined today to identify these two groups as "realists" and "idealists" respectively.

The thought of the ancient world was on the whole biased towards the "conservative" pole. Heraclitus of Ephesus, for example, represented a common attitude in ancient Greece when he taught that throughout nature conflict was the "father of all and king of all". Nothing could exist, according to Heraclitus, if strife between the different elements in human society and nature were ended; "all things come into being and pass away through strife". There is nothing, similarly, in the writings of Plato and Aristotle to suggest that conflict between the city-states of their day was regarded as anything other than part of the order of nature. Only in periods like that of the demoralisation of the Greek world produced by the later stages of the Peloponnesian war did anything resembling modern pacifism or internationalism enter into the writings of social critics such as Euripides and Aristophanes.

The Just War

With the advent of Christianity, however, the problem arose – and it is still with us today – of the contradiction between, on the one hand, Christ's seeming injunction to his followers that they should abjure violence and not defend themselves if attacked and, on the other hand, the all too obvious fact of conflict, often violent and ruthless, as for instance between the rulers of the Christianised Roman and Byzantine Empires and their enemies. It was partly from reflection on this contradiction that there stemmed in time the celebrated medieval Catholic conception of the Just War. St Thomas Aquinas, Dante and the Spanish theologian, Francisco Suarez, held that, while peace should be the normal object of state policy, there were certain kinds of conflicts in which natural law allowed sovereigns to participate. Aquinas (*Summa Theologica*, III, ii, 40, 1) defined three criteria of Just War: when it is declared by the public authority of the state, when its cause is just and when the intention of the belligerent is right. Later thinkers, Suarez, for example, added the condition that to be just a war must also be moderate in the manner in which it is waged and the peace concluding it must be moderate, too. The problem of the Just War also preoccupied the seventeenth-century "father of international law", Hugo Grotius. He held that force could only be used justly in the process of settling an international dispute if it was a matter of the enforcement of rights and if applied within the bounds of law and good faith.

The importance of speculation about the Just War is that it finds a distant echo in much latter-day thinking about international order and its collective enforcement in the international system. In the League of Nations Covenant, for example, there was the principle that war was legitimate in situations in which the belligerent had complied with the existing procedures for the settlement of international disputes and these had effected no solution. In the United Nations Charter of 1945 there is a somewhat similar recognition that the lawful use of force against the territorial integrity or political independence of any state is only possible when it is resorted to by the Security Council acting on behalf of the Organisation as a whole, or in individual or collective self-defence within the meaning of Article 51 of the Charter, or when consistent with the purposes of the Charter. Nevertheless, when considering the problems raised by international disputes, we are always confronted by the fact that a dispute can generally be "resolved" by the imposition of overwhelming force by one or other of the parties. Yet this is not the kind of "settlement" which most people have in mind when they call for a reduction in the incidence of unsettled disputes. We must always keep in mind the question whether the method of settling international disputes is "just", as well as effective, before approving of it as a solution.

The Sovereign State

We must now take account of the impact of the development of the nation-state on speculation concerning the nature of international disputes and their settlement. In the Middle Ages, before the advent of the idea of national sovereignty, when European rulers considered themselves, in theory at least, as brotherly agents in the government of Christendom, it was assumed, again in theory, that quarrels between them should in the last resort be subordinated to the will of the Supreme Pontiff, or at least the local Church or Bishop. It was they who must ultimately determine whether engagement in a particular dispute was just or in accordance with doctrine on the Just War. The advent of the theory of national sovereignty, however, in the sixteenth and seventeenth centuries, as expounded by such writers as Niccolò Machiavelli and Jean Bodin, appeared to establish that it was for the monarch, or sovereign people as the case may be, to determine the legitimacy of his or its cause in a foreign quarrel. If one assumed, with Machiavelli, for instance, that the sovereign state was solely dependent upon itself for its survival in a violent world, then it, or its chieftain, alone had the right to determine the lawfulness of its position in disputes with others.

The conflict inherent in the principle of sovereignty between the oecumenical world order represented by the Catholic Church and the secular needs imposed by the idea of *raison d'état* appeared to be resolved – though the tension continues between the two until today – in favour of the latter with the growth of the nation-state in the seventeenth and eighteenth centuries and the advent of nationalism in the late-eighteenth and nineteenth centuries. Nationalism had a twofold impact on thought about the handling of international disputes. First, it substituted for the medieval notion of a universal natural law the new conception of the nation-state as a moral entity bound by moral laws exclusive to itself; it was but a small step from this to the idea that what was good for the nation was good for all mankind. The effects in terms of nationally based political morality as expressed, for instance, by German writers like G. W. F. Hegel, Treitschke or Bernhardi, need no elaboration. Secondly, the fact that the nation now comprised millions of human beings who had nowhere but their own government to look to for the defence of their rights in a violent world meant that inter-state disputes now became, not rivalries about prestige or power between paternalistic monarchs, but clashes between organised interest-groups each of which generally had some right, in the sense of the legitimate claim of a community to live and prosper, on its side. Once whole nations are locked in conflict over values which each deems to be precious to itself, it is no longer as easy as it was to allocate moral praise or blame to one side or the other. This is in one sense a vindication of the "conservative" position, since it can be inferred from the nature of struggle between nations that no nation will easily abandon a conflict when the stakes in terms of the security or welfare of millions are, or are thought to be, so high.

Turning now to the "abolitionist" conception of international conflict, evidently it is relatively modern compared with the "conservative" position. No doubt the mounting cost of modern war, especially after the Industrial Revolution, and the increasing interdependence of nations during the last two centuries had much to do with this. The only parallel one finds in the ancient world to the common modern idea that international strife is wasteful and eradicable is the Stoic creed of the Roman Empire; the burden of this was the unity of all mankind which was affronted by war and conflict. When, however, Stoicism was embraced by the Roman Emperors themselves, this pacifist tone was muted. The same may be said for the early Christian teaching of non-violence after Christianity had been adopted by Constantine and his successors.

The Idea of Permanent Peace

Apart from occasional protests against the wastefulness of international conflict voiced by such humanists as Desiderius Erasmus, mankind remained untroubled by it until speculation about the possibility of permanent peace and international order developed in Europe in the seventeenth century. The important factors in contributing to this were no doubt, on the one hand, the growth of international commerce and, on the other, the sense of the need for one final united effort on the part of the European nations to expel the Turks from Europe. Accounts of these seventeenth-century peace plans, many of which owed their inspiration to Pierre Dubois' scheme for the reunification of Europe in his *De recuperatione terrae sanctae* (1305–07), are available elsewhere.[2] They range from the "Grand Design" for uniting the Christian world which was probably compiled by the Duke of Sully, the chief minister of Henri IV of France, in the 1630s to schemes of European integration like those of William Penn (*An Essay towards the Present and Future Peace of Europe*, 1693) and the Abbé de Saint-Pierre (*A Project for Settling an Everlasting Peace in Europe*, 1713). Many of these plans were given a new lease of life in the eighteenth century during the French and German Enlightenment. Jean-Jacques Rousseau, for instance, took the peace project of the Abbé de Saint-Pierre and applied it to the Europe of his own day in *A Project of Perpetual Peace* (1761). Rousseau insisted that unless the proposed central authority for Europe was strong enough to overawe all the constituent states the proposal would fail; in any case Rousseau entertained no great hope that the plan would ever be adopted. A similar scheme for a new European system was that of Immanuel Kant whose *Perpetual Peace* appeared in 1795. Kant's recipe for international order is distinguished by its claim that it was conditional upon the attainment of constitutional

[2] See F. M. Stawell, *The Growth of International Thought*, London, 1929, and F. H. Hinsley, *Power and the Pursuit of Peace*, Cambridge, 1963, Part I.

government in all the constituent states. Kant, too, regarded the implementation of his project as a very distant prospect.

These visions of an ordered European system declined rapidly after Rousseau among serious thinkers; they were followed by the great phase of liberal advocacy of practical institutions for the peaceful settlement of international disputes. The nineteenth century represented in many ways the high water-mark of belief in the rational adjudication of international differences and the development of international law and diplomacy. While peace between the European Great Powers was maintained through a variety of political, economic and social forces, the optimistic mood engendered by the immense expansion of the European economies in the last century suggested to many thinkers that there was nothing inevitable about international conflict, nor anything in international conflict which could not be alleviated by suitable legal or diplomatic machinery. Among the English Utilitarians, for example, writers like Jeremy Bentham, James and John Stuart Mill, it came to be accepted almost as dogma that just as economic studies had apparently disclosed a harmony of interests between the different parties to the wealth-producing process, so internationally there was no essential conflict between the interests of one nation-state and another. Given better state practice and the development of international law, interests could be reconciled and solutions found of mutual benefit to the parties.

The culmination of this optimistic philosophy of international disputes could be seen in the theme developed by Sir Norman Angell in his widely influential book *The Great Illusion* (1908) in which he prophesied that the violent solution of disputes through war would prove so ruinous to the interests of all prospective belligerents in the economically interdependent world of the 1900s that they would have more sense than to embark upon it. The effects of that view could be seen, too, in the puzzlement and dismay of many liberal-minded people after the First World War, when they could not imagine how great nations could have been so shortsighted as to slither so easily into that catastrophe. It was noted after the First World War, however, that the period preceding it, say from about 1870 until 1914, had been a time in which *pari passu* with the rationalist liberalism we have been referring to, there developed in Europe a species of atavistic nationalism, the *sacro egoismo* which writers like Bernhardi in Germany and D'Annunzio in Italy fulsomely praised. The conclusion, therefore, tended to be reached among liberals after 1918 that the international order had broken down in 1914 partly because the existing machinery for settling international disputes had not been strong or subtle enough, and partly because of the power of a blind, irrational, herd-like nationalism. This conclusion struck the note for speculation about international conflict among liberal schools of thought after the First World War. The two main needs seemed to be, first, to construct and develop, within the broad framework of the League of Nations, appropriate international agencies for settling international differences, and, second, to train the minds of rising generations in the necessity and value of these institutions, and so to inoculate them against any retrogression into the tribal nationalism which had plunged Europe into war in 1914.

II

After 1918

The study of international relations after the First World War drew many and heterogeneous writers in Europe and the United States into an examination of that catastrophe and the means of avoiding its recurrence; all in all, however, these added little that was new and restricted themselves to the re-statement, in ever more passionate form, of older internationalist ideas. The literature of international relations during the 1920s refurbished the liberal optimism, in the Anglo-Saxon countries, at least, of pre-war times. Its tenets were that international disputes, especially of the kind which lead to war, are either unnecessary or become as serious as they do because of man's defective understanding. Nationalism was really the chief evil, a heady drink blinding nations to their real interests and needing replacement by some wider commitment to the international community.

Was, then, any change in the incidence of international conflict possible without some fundamental change in the international system or even its conversion into a world state? In giving a negative answer to this question, G. Lowes Dickinson, for example, contended in *The International Anarchy* (1929) that the urge for power was so strong within states that there was a natural tendency for a balancing process to develop in order to curb the power of the more aggressive state or states. Yet this balancing process was inherently unstable since the object of any balance-of-power policy pursued by any particular state is not merely to equal the power of a rival state but to exceed it, and hence there could be no freedom from international conflict so long as the present international system existed. "It is hardly possible", Lowes Dickinson continued,

> that the relations of states should be determined by anything but a balance of advantage and power. For that reason those relations change, like the figures in a kaleidoscope, and even though they may for a certain period assume a certain permanence, yet there is no guarantee of perpetuity, for they are based not on natural sympathy and community of purpose but on considerations of temporary advantage. One

thing and one thing only is permanent: to any given nation it is always clear that all the right is on its side and all the wrong on the side of the Power that for the moment is the enemy.[3]

Peace Through Democracy

Leslie Buell in his textbook *International Relations*, published in 1925, argued for as far-reaching a change in the structure of international relations if disputes were to be brought under control, but this referred rather to the structure of power *within* the various states than between them. His view was that since the broad mass of the people as a whole have nothing to gain from war and conflict, the solution lay in the progressive democratisation of the different states. Buell was also in the main stream of thought characterising the 1920s in Britain in his call for the abolition of secret diplomacy and the opening up of international negotiations to the widest possible publicity in order that ordinary people could see what was being done by governments in their name. But the public needed to be educated in order to be able to take an international rather than a narrowly national view of their disputes with other nations. The international intercourse of ideas, Buell contended, was even more important to harmonious international relations than freedom of trade. "If mankind lacks the intelligence and the imagination to handle the political aspects of the problems of the world", he wrote, "the will to peace will never be converted into a reality".[4]

Viscount Cecil, one of the outstanding British champions of the League of Nations, took a similar view of the prime importance of a sound and informed public opinion in the rational handling of international disputes. Looking back on his experience in *The Great Experiment* (1941), he writes how he regarded the League as essentially a machinery for the prevention of war; the *roots* of war, in the sense of international disputes which, unless attended to, might precipitate an armed conflict, he proposed to deal with by the existing machinery of negotiation, arbitration and international conference. Meanwhile, he considered it vital that the nations should labour together for the common interest, thus building up something in the nature of a working world community through the use of international machinery for the settlement of outstanding political or economic grievances. It will be remembered at this point that it was a peculiar characteristic of the British approach to the building of world order in the 1920s that it placed the greatest emphasis upon the removal of grievances within the existing international system. In this respect the British attitude towards the League of Nations differed markedly from that,

[3] *Op. cit.*, Chapter I, pp. 36–7. [4] *Op. cit.*, Chapter I, p. 27.

for instance, of France and the successor states of 1919. British foreign policy in the 1920s and even until late in the 1930s was strongly tinged by the belief that the rooting out of grievances before they had time to develop was the soundest method of making the international order secure.

The Need for World Government

With the coming of the 1930s and the repeated failure of the League of Nations to prevent or halt the aggressions of the three Axis Powers, a more dour and Hobbesian note began to insinuate itself into the easy-going belief in the English-speaking world of the 1920s that an international community already existed and that all the world had to do was to draw the necessary psychological conclusions from that fact; in other words, to feel and act as their world environment now required. Bertrand Russell, for example, in his *Which Way to Peace?* (1936), was confident that the League lacked the necessary executive power and so could not compel its members to co-operate. Collective security, he considered, could not succeed as a method of preventing war unless there existed an international armed force acting under an international authority. So long as there is sovereignty, Bertrand Russell repeatedly insisted, war was likely. But no such central authority could be created, capable both of putting down aggression and of securing economic and social justice between the nations, unless there is first a change in the climate of world opinion. "Most of the civilised nations", Russell contended, must "have become persuaded that unrestricted national sovereignty involves disaster".[5] A similar view was reached by Lionel Curtis in *World war: its cause and cure.* The fatal defect of the national commonwealth, according to Curtis, is that it inspires supreme loyalty to itself and not to the commonwealth of man. There can be no cure for that until the whole of human society has been organised as one commonwealth. Nation states, Curtis wrote, have had their day and this fact must be brought home to the public opinion of the day by those with responsibilities for educating the masses. "If Leviathan" (that is, the nation state) "is the idol democracies worship", Curtis concluded, "they are dooming their children to the fires of war".[6] A similar line of argument was adopted by Salvador de Madariaga in *World Government. Dream or Necessity?* (1946) in which he advocated nothing short of the root-and-branch conversion of the international system from a congeries of self-contained units into a united political structure completely transcending the national state. Madariaga's argument may be summed up in the statement that "the only way to solve these root causes" (that is, of international anarchy) "is to so reorganise the world that it will be possible to

[5] *Op. cit.*, Chapter IV, p. 84.

[6] *Op. cit.*, Chapter II, p. 4.

solve all international problems not from the point of view of any one nation but from that of the world in general – that is, to put international politics on a co-operative basis".[7]

Perhaps the most explicit of what may be called the "root-and-branch" reforms of the international system, however, was that spelled out by Lord Davies in his monumental work, *The Problem of the Twentieth Century*, first published in 1930. Lord Davies took as his starting point the fundamental distinction between municipal (or intra-state) and international society, namely, that in the former justice is meted out by the courts to litigants without regard to their relative power or influence in society – or should be so meted out – whereas in international affairs any decision by a judicial or arbitral body must either take into account the relative strength of the parties or run the risk of being ignored by the stronger party if the decision is unfavourable to him. The only remedy, Davies considered, was to back such decisions and judgments by the same kind of force as implemented judicial decisions within the state: in other words, by an international police force. "The League (of Nations)", he wrote,

> falls far short of the standard which human experience has dictated as the minimum in the sphere of municipal law. It runs the risk of a catastrophe at any moment unless steps are taken to ensure that the administration of international law is fortified by the provision of sanctions, unless force is "put behind international peace".[8]

It is interesting to see that the "Executive" proposed by Lord Davies for setting in motion the international police force, besides echoing the scheme unsuccessfully proposed by M. Léon Bourgeois to the 1919 Paris Peace Conference, bears a strong resemblance to the Security Council embodied in the United Nations structure designed fifteen years after Davies' book was first published. In brief, it was to consist of a core of Great Powers assisted by a group of lesser states, each graded according to four criteria: "their sacrifices to the cause of peace, their standards of civilisation, the size of their populations, and their ability to govern".[9] The notable difference, however, was that in the Davies scheme there would be no room for a veto on the Executive, or, in UN terminology, the Security Council; Davies was quite adamant that "any Executive whose decisions are to be strained through the sieve of the unanimous vote is foredoomed to impotence".[10] This would mean, of course, that any Great Power would run the risk of having military sanctions applied against itself or one of its allies.

[7] *Op. cit.*, p. 11. [8] Third Edition, 1938, p. 10. [9] *Ibid.*, p. 516.
[10] *Ibid.*, p. 526.

It should be remembered that these proposals seem to run counter to the fundamental problem which the world faced when the UN Charter was drawn up in 1945: namely, how, short of a world war, a world Power could be forced into an international court on an issue which involved what it considered as a vital national interest or be compelled to comply with the court's judgment if unfavourable to itself. Lord Davies' reply was that, if his scheme were adopted, such a state would already have substantially disarmed, relying for its security on the international police force. Such a change, however, would no doubt demand a degree of trust and moral consensus among the Powers which has not been conspicuous in recent years and which, if it existed, would make our present inquiry unnecessary.

These brief references to writings on international relations in the inter-war period indicate a certain progression of ideas: namely, from reliance upon better intelligence and greater awareness of the existence of a world community of interests to the Hobbesian demand for a superior authority to overawe the separate states. It is noticeable, moreover, that in this literature of international relations it is war and peace rather than international disputes which occupy the centre of attention. It is true that in the 1930s a great deal of study of means for the settling of disputes, peaceful change and the improvement of existing machinery for restoring cordiality between disputing states was carried on, particularly, for instance, by the International Studies Conference organised under the auspices of the League's Organisation for Intellectual Co-operation. Here, too, however, a predominantly rationalist philosophy prevailed. The general assumption appeared to persist that a solution could be found for any international dispute given patience and rational discussion.

A New Age of Realism

The fact that man's thinking about international affairs tends to follow rather than precede actual historical developments in those affairs is evident when we remember how thinking on this subject immediately after the Second World War was powerfully influenced, first by the phenomenon of the Nazi regime in Germany, and later by the seemingly ruthless pursuit by the Soviet Union of her security and ideological interests in the late 1940s. There thus began an age of "realism" in international thought, which was in fact a revival of an older tradition of conservative thought. Expressed by such writers as H. J. Morgenthau, E. H. Carr and Georg Schwarzenberger, it took the form of certain propositions focused on power as the central reality in international, and indeed in all human, relations. First, there was the argument that what international politics is all about is the pursuit of national interest, conceived, as Morgenthau put it, "in terms of power"; second, that there was an inherent tendency in the state to expand and entrench upon its neighbours' interests unless restrained by countervailing forces such as an effective balance of power; third, that moral considerations or the belief in a new order of justice and peace waiting to be born could delude mankind as to the true meaning of international politics and generally acted as rationalisations serving to disguise the real goals of state activity; and fourthly, that international conflict, save for its most trivial forms, could not be restrained by appeals to reason or majority voting in organs such as the UN General Assembly, but only by business-like negotiations between the parties based upon hard-headed calculations of what one side could afford to demand in the light of its strength and what the other side had to yield in the light of its weakness. The relevance of this for international disputes was that the self-justificatory arguments built up by each side could be dismissed as explanations of its real motives; that every dispute reflected a conflict of concrete interest which both sides promoted with all the power at their command; and that any solution must rest less upon principles of justice or welfare than upon crude ratios of military strength and diplomatic skill.

This Machiavellian conception of international relations held sway in much of the world during the intense phases of the Cold War in the 1950s. Underlying it, among Western states, was the determination not to be deluded a second time by the fair-sounding promises of dictators but to stand on guard, fully under arms and resolved to maintain a favourable relation between commitments and power. The value of this thinking was that it threw doubt, in so far as events themselves had not already done so, on the easy-going Anglo-Saxon idea of the inter-war years that international conflict could be cleared away to the satisfaction of both parties by rational discussion of the facts of the case. The realist school also made its contribution by drawing attention to the concept of "national interest", or the aggregate of the claims which a state makes on its international relations by reason of its historical experience, geographical situation, internal economic, social and political forces and of everything in fact which makes the state what it is. National interest cannot be brushed aside as a mental aberration of authoritarian states, nor can the fact that national interests, with the best of wills on both sides, sometimes conflict so that if one is served the other must be frustrated. A conservative state, satisfied with the *status quo* may ignore these facts, but not so those countries which feel that at every turn their foreign relations operate to their own disadvantage.

Turning now to the weaknesses of the realist school, it is clear that with it the pendulum has swung too far in the opposite direction. In the first place, history shows that states very often have aims to pursue very different from national interest, if that term means anything more than merely doing what one wants; states will, for example, make quite considerable sacrifices in "real" or economic terms on behalf of some ideological goal or ambition which is only very remotely related to their actual welfare. Secondly, it is clear that, with decolonisation, some fifty or sixty new states have come into existence which are not militarily strong enough to engage in "power politics" as traditionally understood; they are obliged to conduct their foreign policies on bases other than that of power, if the latter is defined in the crude economic or military sense. And thirdly, it soon became evident, with the harnessing of nuclear energy to weapon technology, that the time-honoured "struggles for power" could be infinitely dangerous with weapons of this kind lying about. Hence states in the nuclear age were bound to consider whether they had better not strive to create a more peaceful world by co-operative rather than competitive means. It is still too early to say whether this is likely to become a rule among the giant Powers.

Behaviouralism v. Realism

From these criticisms of the "realist" school sprang certain new approaches to the study of international relations which are now frequently classified together under the heading of Behaviouralism. It will take time for the more fanciful theories often grouped under that heading to be separated from those of more permanent value. Nevertheless, the Behaviouralists, true to their claim to be "scientific", have done rather more than earlier students to single out the different possible types of international disputes from the wide-ranging category of international conflict. Consequently they deserve a place in this necessarily brief review of thought on the subject of international disputes.

While not purporting to give a complete account of Behaviouralism, we may take note of the fact that one of its most common premises is that the infinitely varied phenomena of human behaviour, including international relations, can be converted into a subject matter which is not only capable of being studied *in a scientific spirit*, but is in fact the raw material of a *science*, with all the regular paraphernalia of objective laws with predictive value, to be derived from the testing of hypotheses constructed after the scrutiny of the various data of human behaviour. There is also a second and rather more tacit premise of Behaviouralist thought which would appear to relate it to thinking on international relations in the West during the 1920s; and that is the assumption that international conflicts are mainly the result of poor understanding on the part of, or poor communications between, the conflicting parties. The Behaviouralist appears to think that the mastery which science has given man over nature could be extended to the social and political spheres. It is, of course, not suggested that the science-like analysis of politics can provide a yardstick of *values* for the better ordering of human affairs; merely that such analysis can better our understanding of the options available to us.

The findings of a good deal of Behaviouralist research on international conflict may strike the more traditionalist student as the revival of old ideas or familiar assumptions shrouded in pseudo-scientific language; commonsense, in other words, made difficult. Nevertheless, considering the hold which this approach now seems to have acquired over the social sciences, especially in the United States, it is necessary to round off this account of international thought by some attempt to summarise it. Again, the risk of superficiality through over-simplification and condensation is great, but it seems better to include some such account than to omit it altogether. Hence, for the purpose of this summary treatment, Behaviouralist thought and research may be classified under four heads, the gist of each of which will be summarised in the paragraphs which follow. These four heads are (a) general systems analysis; (b) structural-functionalism; (c) communications theory; (d) decision-making analysis.[11]

General Systems Analysis

The basic postulate of general systems analysis is that man exists within a large number of social systems, that is, interrelationships of certain determinate units which together form a single but complex whole.[12] These varied systems are similar to one another (or "isomorphic") in certain respects; for instance, valid comparisons may be drawn as to how the parts are related to each other in a number of social systems. The diplomatic or inter-governmental system, however, is only one of the many systems in which individual men and women live. Now it is in the nature of things that when international disputes are taken in hand, they are predominantly so through governments or the representatives of governments. We ourselves in fact in the present book are studying the handling of these disputes by the diplomatic community, that is, the world's governments. But it is conceivable that the inter-governmental level is not necessarily or always the most desirable level at which a given dispute should be treated; for some disputes it may be the least desirable – governments, for instance, tend often to be actuated by considerations of

[11] The sections which follow are freely based on an unpublished paper commissioned for this study, by Michael H. Banks, of the London School of Economics, entitled "Conflict: behavioural approaches and their relevance to the settlement of international disputes".

[12] For a well-known example of this approach see C. A. McClelland, *Theory and the International System*, 1966.

power and prestige which may hamper a rational and judicious approach to the question at issue. It is, therefore, suggested by some of the proponents of systems analysis that lines of communication should be established between the peoples involved in a given dispute at other than governmental levels of relationship. In Cyprus, for example, it may be argued that if social, economic, religious, artistic or other bonds of association could be forged between the two peoples in an entirely non-political context, the dispute might be easier to solve. It is when the dispute is entangled with considerations of power and prestige, such as characterises the diplomatic-system level of human relations, that the path to a *modus vivendi* is obscured.

It will be seen, as is so often the case in Behaviouralist thinking, that much of this echoes the old-fashioned liberalism of the early days of the League of Nations, when it was held that international disputes should as far as possible be depoliticised and that a growing nexus of international contacts should be formed between nations at other levels than the intergovernmental.[13] Again, during and immediately after the Second World War there was a good deal of support for the idea of functional co-operation, that is, the formation of non-political organs of international co-operation in which considerations of power and prestige would have no place and from which co-operative habits built up over a period of years would "spill-over" into the political realm.[14] For some time after 1945 the rigid control of transnational activities by governments of East and West undermined the hopes of functional co-operation during the most intense years of the Cold War. As the international climate between the Communist and non-Communist worlds improved during the 1960s, however, the credibility of the old nostrum of depoliticisation revived. It is, nevertheless, still true that belief in its efficacy remains after all a matter of faith rather than of tried and tested theory.

Structural Functionalism

The second main body of ideas which we wish to consider under the heading of contemporary theory, namely functionalism or structural functionalism, must not be confused with the kind of functional co-operation which was discussed in the previous paragraph. Functionalism actually considers the extent to which international conflict and, by the same token, international disputes, may be said to have a positive role to play in the international system as at present constituted.[15] That it has a negative role, or in the modern jargon is "dysfunctional", is all too clear;

[13] See H. R. G. Greaves, *The League Committees and World Order*, 1932.
[14] See David Mitrany, *A Working Peace System*, 1946.
[15] For works on this approach, see Oran Young, *The Intermediaries*, 1967; L. A. Coser, *The Functions of Social Conflict*, 1956.

the conducting of a dispute with another country is presumably consumptive of time and energy on the part of Ministers and officials which could be put to better use, and moreover any such dispute may jeopardise relations with the other country, or with third countries, which carry with them definite benefits to the state concerned. Functionalists have, however, considered the extent to which conflicts or disputes positively confirm or maintain the present system of international relations, and it is evident that they do by *inter alia* contributing to the internal cohesion and stability of the state-members of the international system. Clearly, the sense of sharing certain common bonds, interests and values which characterises modern nationalism is very largely based upon a feeling of difference from and even antagonism towards other nations. It is also easier for a community to define for itself what is "normal" and what is "deviant" behaviour by reference to patterns of action in other groups.

Communications Theory

In contrast to the functionalist's view that international conflict may be either functional, dysfunctional or both, depending on circumstances, the third main group of ideas in contemporary theory, namely communications research, has a tendency to assume that conflict is always dysfunctional in so far as it is a symptom of some disarrangement of or interruption in the communication flows which are constantly at work in the international system. Basing itself on the analogy with modern electronic devices such as the computer, communications theory holds in its central focus the unending flow of communications between one government and another, between governments and other organised forces working within the individual state, and even within the brain of the single human individual.

Communication is, however, more than the mere transfer of a message, an intention, an idea or a feeling; it is also a response to the response made by other parties to the political process to previous acts or communications from oneself. This is the process known as "feed-back". Clearly, if the international system is characterised by communication and feedback between the different parts of the system, the likelihood of conflict in any one part of that system, or in other words some stoppage in the communication network, can be detected by looking at the state of communication flows in other parts of the system. Communications theorists have therefore tried to work out a "meteorology" of international relations, which may presumably be used to forecast "good weather" or "bad weather" in the international system. This could be done, for instance, by examining large numbers of such indices as stock market prices, the direction and volume of international trade investment, and the actual movement of communications, private as well as inter-governmental, from one country to another, in order to determine whether there is any co-variation between these and the incidence of international conflict. Much of this work remains, however, for the present inconclusive.[16]

Another concern of communications theorists is with the question whether the channels of communication within the international system may not become clogged or "overloaded", thus destroying the ability of the human agents to cope with the communication flows with which they have to deal. It is often remarked in the history of international relations that at this or that point there was a "loss of control" or that "events took over from men". We are to visualise in such a situation responsible Ministers or diplomats throwing up their hands in despair and yielding to the pressure of forces which they have lost the power to control or even to understand. The German Foreign Minister, Gottlieb von Jagow, asked Chancellor Bethmann-Hollweg in August 1914 how the war machines could have been launched against each other, and he recalls the Chancellor answering in a dull tired voice, "Oh, if I only knew". It is in the hope of preventing this kind of situation that communications analysts have proposed the opening of new forms of communication between disputing nations at other than the governmental level, an echo, it might be pointed out, of the systems theorists' ideas. The new school of "conflict management", for instance, believes that better understanding between disputing states can be achieved by initiating a dialogue between nationals from these states away from the political context, as for example in a university seminar. We have to consider this technique as somewhat resembling group psychotherapy. The subjects are encouraged to talk freely about their wishes and fears, which have such a large part to play in conditioning their attitudes towards the issues between their states, and hence are able to distinguish between the objective and the subjective factors in their quarrels.[17] Again, as in our consideration of structural functionalism, our natural disposition is to say that there may be some truth in this, and that when states are as much at each other's throats as, say, Israel and the Arab states today, almost any kind of communication, at almost any level, is better than none. Nevertheless, it must be said that no substantial evidence exists as yet that such methods of group psychotherapy actually produce results in the sense of a measurable reduction of friction between the states concerned.

[16] For some representative writings on communications theory see Karl Deutsch, *The Nerves of Government; Models of Political Communication and Control*, 1963, and Robert North, "The Analytical Prospects of Communications Theory" in James C. Charlesworth (ed), *Contemporary Political Analysis*, 1967.

[17] See J. W. Burton, *Systems, States, Diplomacy and Rules*, Cambridge, 1968, and *Conflict and Communication*, London, 1969.

Decision-making Analysis

Communications form an essential part of the decision-making process through which states define their attitudes towards disputes. We assume that decision-making by responsible governments is also responsible in the psychological sense that it represents a considered and carefully thought out reaction to the different issues raised in a particular dispute. All governments, of course, must pay some heed to irrational demands, wishes and fears of their own people, and to some extent of people in other countries. Nevertheless, we are apt to assume that no government would adopt a policy position, especially on a matter of major importance, without a rational scrutiny of the pros and cons of the various possible courses of action and the likely consequences, in so far as they can be anticipated, of the adoption of one or other of these courses. But need this be so? Responsible Ministers and officials are human like the rest of us, suffer from much the same sorts of prejudices, fears and hopes, tiredness and laziness, and often live more stressful lives than most people. And however hard they try to see the world "as it really is", they can never do so; for the complexity of the world is such that all of us, however well-trained, can only "see" the world in terms of a partial selection from its multifarious reality. H. J. Laski called this unconscious selection our "inarticulate major premises"; contemporary theorists call it, more simply, the "image". Can these biological or psychological factors play a part in affecting the rationality with which a particular government determines its policy in an international dispute in which it may be involved?

Students of the decision-making process, our fourth and final category of Behaviouralism, declare in their discussions of conflict that this may indeed happen.[18] Central to their thinking is the nature of perception. How far can failure to see what the other state wants, or why it should want what it wants, mislead governments in handling a dispute with that state? We have seen, at least in the public pronouncements by leaders on both sides in the Cold War, a certain narrowing of the frames of perception on the two sides which is the consequence, according to the contemporary theorists of this school, of attempting to cope mentally with complicated matters in which, as it happens, powerful emotions are engaged. The result is a tendency towards stereotyping, or classing all the traits of one

[18] Some examples of studies of subjective factors in decision making are the following: Robert Jervis, "Hypotheses on misperception" in *World Politics*, XX, 3 (April 1968), 454–79; H. C. Kelsen (ed), *International Behaviour*, 1965; R. Stagner, *Psychological aspects of international conflict*, 1967; O. R. Holsti, Richard Brody and Robert North, "Measuring affect and action in international reaction models. Empirical materials from the 1962 Cuban crisis", in *Journal of Peace Research*, 1964, 3–4, 170–90.

side under one simple and highly emotionally-toned heading; projection, or the unconscious transfer to the other side of desires or fears which actually exist in oneself, but which, for a variety of reasons, one is reluctant to admit to harbouring; and the closure of the mind to other possibilities of settlement than the time-honoured methods of conflict and perhaps war. The decision-making students may admit that the different nations cannot deal with this problem by having their leaders periodically psychoanalysed. But it is as well, they say, to be aware of these hidden factors in the development of international disputes, as we should also be aware that they generally tend to exist on each side and, in doing so, exacerbate each other.

This is not the place to attempt an evaluation of this more recent work in the study of international conflict. The whole question whether the subject matter of international relations will ever lend itself to the same kind of scientific investigation and precision as man's physical environment is also not one which we wish to pursue here. Nevertheless, it has been argued that what the Behaviouralists have done is to introduce into international studies some of the intellectual rigour distinguishing the natural sciences, and the effects of this sometimes compare favourably with the rather subjective writing which tended to pass as academic treatment of international relations in the inter-war period. Their critics, on the other hand, contend that by loose analogies with the natural sciences the Behaviouralists have made the subject woollier than it need be. In our view it is doubtful whether as yet the Behaviouralists in their different schools of thought have done much more than present us with a set of speculations about international conflict, and many of these turn out on examination to be much older ideas dressed up to look like modern science. Prominent among these ideas we would place the notion of different levels of international intercourse, apart from the diplomatic or inter-governmental, on which it seems that the resolution of international conflict must proceed; the idea of conflict being inherent in the present international system because it seems to serve certain sorts of social needs; the importance of adequate and well-controlled communications throughout the whole of the system and within the individual states; and the role of psychological processes of a non-rational character in the decision-making situation.

These are ideas we should do well to keep in mind in considering any particular dispute. But this is far from agreeing that the Behaviouralists have established, or are likely to establish, their claim to reduce knowledge about international relations to a congeries of natural-science-like laws which would enable us to predict what forms of international dispute are likely to occur in future or which kinds of disputes will respond to which kinds of treatment. In fact, the scientific theorists themselves have now recognised that the bulk of their work to date has added only to the body of speculative and intuitive understanding of world politics. To progress further in the direction of empirical understanding much more work will be required in the fields of measurement, testing and comparison of existing theories. Recent work has been moving in this direction.[19] Until the results of this work provide the proof of the more extreme Behaviouralist claims, it seems that we must move ahead using commonsense and judgment, while recalling the Behaviouralist principle that it is the *scientific* and not the subjective appreciation of international facts which interests us.

Conclusion

It would be wrong to attempt here anything in the way of a concluding summary of this brief outline of the development of man's thought on his international relations and the conflicts of will, interest and emotion which occur in those relations. There are, however, one or two salient threads which are worth emphasising. One is that there is a tendency for thought on these questions to follow events; man may reflect upon the problems of his own day and believe that the ideas which he forms about them to be valid for all time, but in practice his studies inevitably have to make a leap forward, sooner or later, when a new world comes into existence necessitating fresh thinking. We have seen, for instance, how in the Middle Ages the fact of international conflict forced Catholic scholars into formulating distinctions between just and unjust causes of conflict which have been sources of controversy ever since. In the same way, the catastrophe of the First World War created a new problem by giving fresh urgency to the question whether man could afford to continue trying to make do with an international system, in which the lack of effective law and order threatened everything he understood as civilisation. At the same time, we have noted a certain oscillation in thinking about international relations between what may be called the optimistic and the pessimistic poles, or between what we have described as "abolitionism" and "conservatism" respectively. The debate had existed, if latently, in past thinking but was intensified in the twentieth century. Optimism (or abolitionism) held sway after the First World War, only to be followed by the more dour and Hobbesian pessimism of the late 1930s and the 1940s, largely owing to the problems created for democratic states by the expansionism of the Fascist, and later the Communist, states. With the advent of a kind of *détente* in the East-West relations in the early 1960s,

[19] J. David Singer (ed), *Quantitative International Politics*, 1968.

optimism seems to have resumed its sway once more, as exemplified by the vogue amongst Behaviouralists for peaceful change, for functional co-operation, and for regarding conflict as in some way the result of the imperfect adjustment of men's minds to their real circumstances. It seems as though, certainly in the twentieth century and among liberal democratic states, there is a gravitational pull towards optimism, which shines forth like a will-of-the-wisp as the first portent, real or misleading, that the clouds of international conflict may be passing away.

Although, however, we may recognise that actual events shape thought on international affairs, there is equally no doubt that the kind of theory about international conflict which man entertains has a marked effect on his mental approach to conflict. It is clear today, for instance, that the predominantly humanitarian and rationalist thinking which the League of Nations aroused, especially in Anglo-Saxon countries, bore some responsibility for the credulity and lack of realism which these states showed towards the dictators in the 1930s. If, as internationalists often believed, conflict could be removed by "sweet reasonableness", the dictators seemed willing to allow the democracies to indulge in that "sweet reasonableness" while they themselves were making off with the loot. The reverse seems to have happened in the post-Second World War period. Here, as many Behaviouralists argue, the East-West conflict was possibly made more bitter and intransigent than it need have been owing to the uncompromising "realism" which each side applied in its dealings with the other; and this "realism" stemmed from ideas on international conflict which had been engendered on both sides through experience of Hitler's Germany. There is operative here what the Behaviouralists call "the self-fulfilling prophecy": that is to say, if you postulate a gulf of irreconcilable hostility between yourself and your rival, he is as likely as not to take your view of the situation at its face value and to react by becoming precisely the kind of person you falsely assumed he was. The rule, as we have said, works the other way, too; by postulating the impossibility of an Anglo-American war in the 1890s, despite much American offensiveness, Britain seems to have created a special relationship. It remains true, however, that much of this is in the realm of plausible hypothesis rather than that of attested knowledge.

The third and final point we would make is that attitudes towards international disputes are part and parcel of attitudes towards the entire international political system in which these disputes occur. Behind any statement or theory about international disputes there lurks a philosophy of international affairs as a whole, and it is this in the final resort which determines what our attitude towards disputes will be. Ultimately, as the Behaviouralists are never tired of pointing out, we can say nothing about international disputes without dragging into the light of day some particle of that wider conception of international relations which all of us carry around with us amid our mental furniture. That is why in this book we shall be concerned with the more far-ranging implications of disputes as functions of the international system rather than with the *minutiae* of these disputes. We are looking, as far as possible, for generalisations rather than for statements about concrete historical issues, and as we proceed we shall be aware that in discussing disputes we shall in effect be unfolding our whole conception of international politics.

2. *The Nature of Disputes*

We are accustomed by harsh experience to think of international politics in terms of conflict, and yet without always recalling the full extent to which this is true. The whole of human life moves by conflict of some degree. In our personal affairs, in our work, in the internal politics of the nation, we set opinion against opinion, interest against interest, and in this way, thought and action develop. International politics share this character throughout. The everyday work of diplomacy is a matching of the interests of one state against those of another, not merely in great affairs but right down to the least. The most friendly discussion of the smallest point between the representatives of two states involves conflict of a sort as surely as does the greatest clash of armies in battle.

If this is so, how are we to define the kind of conflict that matters? It would be easy to do this roughly. We might say that it is the conflicts of the great powers. But, though there is obvious sense in this, we have no grounds for assuming that the conflicts of the great powers are different in kind, as opposed to significance, from those of lesser powers, with which in any case they are closely intertwined. We might say that the conflicts which matter are those which involve war. But again, we have no grounds for assuming that these are different in kind, as opposed to degree, from those which merely involve lesser forms of pressure.

It would be equally easy to pursue scientific precision. We might say that conflicts which rise to a certain level on empirical indices are to be distinguished from conflicts which do not. These indices might be the diplomatic communications which pass, the newspaper column inches written, the shots fired, the physical damage done and the like. But reflection suggests that the empirical data of a human activity, such as an international conflict, can never be established with the precision of the data of the natural sciences and that, in consequence, dividing lines thus drawn between conflicts must inevitably remain arbitrary. Moreover, it is scarcely conceivable that the physical phenomena of a conflict are in a fixed relationship to those aspects of it which are most interesting, its origins, development and manner of ending, and can throw any light on them.

A plausible starting-point in distinguishing one kind of conflict from another is the experience of the United Nations. Since 1945, the Organisation has had many conflicts brought before it in the name of its responsibility for international disputes or situations which might lead to a breach of the peace. Admittedly, this group of conflicts may be an entirely arbitrary group, having nothing in common except the mere chance of being considered by the United Nations. Much effort has been devoted at the United Nations and elsewhere to seeking definitions of a situation of friction and a dispute, but in practice it seems clear that the United Nations has simply been prepared to consider any conflict which a sufficient number of its members thought it ought to consider. Practice has not followed definition but reasonably enough, definition has had to follow practice. Yet, from this a further thought follows. It is surely possible, even likely, that states seek to bring only a certain kind of conflict to the United Nations. It is possible, in other words, that conflicts which were brought to the United Nations or which, it seems to us, might have been brought had it suited the states concerned to do so, have some characteristic in common which, despite their diversity, marks them off from others. Let us agree to reserve for such conflicts the name "dispute" and let us try to see what this characteristic is.

One point is no doubt obvious. We often speak of a great conflict in the world since 1945 between the United States and the Soviet Union as in earlier times between France and Austria, Empire and Papacy, Rome and Carthage, Athens and Sparta. But these were not disputes; rather, they were accompanied by disputes or embraced many disputes or came to a head in disputes. A dispute itself is a comparatively narrow affair, a formulated difference of opinion on some particular matter.

This point does not, however, take us very far. Many a conflict meets these conditions without being a dispute. States are constantly, day by day, formulating precise differences of opinion and engaging in hard argument over them without being in dispute. Perhaps then, a dispute is a conflict on a particular matter which has remained unresolved for a long time or one between enemies or one which threatens violence? But this too is inadequate. The conflicts between Chile and Argentina over their border and between Britain and Iceland over their territorial waters, two friendly pairs of countries, be it noted, were disputes from the first moment that the opposing opinions were precisely formulated. The clash of these opinions never represented an ordinary conflict. A vague conflict can turn into a precise one and equally a vague conflict can turn into a dispute; but when it does so, some other factor than the passage of time is responsible.

Perhaps a dispute is a conflict on a matter of the highest importance? But the conflict between Britain and France in the 1960s on whether or not Britain should be permitted to join the European Economic Community was a matter of the highest importance, but it was not a dispute. It was not at all the kind of affair that states have brought before the

United Nations. No doubt a direct challenge to the vital interests of a state will usually cause a dispute but, on the other hand, there are many disputes in which vital interests are not at stake, at least in the most obvious sense of the phrase. The smallest strip of worthless borderland or the most trifling commercial debt can give rise to a dispute, but these are vital interests only in the sense that states are vitally concerned to defend anything, however insignificant in itself, which they consider to be theirs.

Disputes as a Conflict of Justice

With this point, we seem to come to the heart of the matter. The distinguishing characteristic of a dispute is that it is a conflict not of mere will but of justice or of truth. In the most common form of dispute between states, one or both of them believes that the thing at issue is not something that they merely want but something that is "theirs". The conflict is not simply one of interest but one of justice.

In all human affairs, we distinguish between two kinds of conflict. The one is a clash of opinions or interests. The other is a clash of opinions or interests which we believe to have behind them a sanction higher than our own personal will. To take small examples, we disagree with a newspaper's opinions but we dispute its account of the facts. We debate an historian's interpretation of the past but we dispute with the propagandist who disregards truth. We argue against a man's judgment on what is to be done; but we dispute with him if we think his views perverse and irrational. We disagree over moral and religious questions if we believe that morality and religion are matters of personal choice; but the conflict is altogether different in temper or, to use our chosen word, we dispute over these issues if we believe that they are matters of objective truth.

The same distinction arises in conflicts over activities and possessions. Here the sanction that stands above the personal will of the parties is the social conception "ours" and "theirs". Two companies in a business transaction disagree over the price to be paid for a thing and argue and bargain as best they can. But they dispute if one of them subsequently accuses the other of breaking the price agreement. In the one case, they are saying "this is what we want"; in the other, they are saying "this is ours, this is our due".

Most relationships in a society, personal, commercial, political or any other, are governed by rules of some sort establishing what is ours, or due to us, and what is theirs, or due to them. The rules lay down what is and is not allowed in pursuit of interests. A thing may be done or acquired thus but not so. The rules, in other words, form for each relationship in society an area of permitted conflict. Within that area we disagree and compete as we choose; beyond it or concerning what it should be, we dispute.

Society as a whole may be seen in the same way. It is both a process of continual conflict of opinion and interest, and a structure of rules which sets bounds to what otherwise would be chaos. When this structure is held to have been infringed, there is a dispute. When the very structure itself becomes a matter of conflict among the members of society, there is a dispute on a still more momentous scale.

We should add, however, that in this picture the detailed concepts, "rules", "process" and "structure", are not the main focus. The distinction between process and structure, which we shall use continually in this book, is only a metaphor, and if pressed too far, inevitably breaks down. Far more important, rules, whether laws, customs or conventions, are only the elaboration of more fundamental beliefs by which things are divided into ours and due to us, theirs and due to them. Disputes are not in the last resort conflicts about rules, though within states that is the usual form, but conflicts about justice.

If this broad description of two kinds of conflict in human affairs is acceptable, we must now try to trace it in greater detail in politics within states and between states. In each case, we must first give some further account of ordinary conflict; and second and principally, some further account of disputes. In doing so, we are in effect involved in giving a picture of the whole of the politics of states, and yet without supposing that we shall achieve anything more than the crudest outline of some of its more prominent features.

Conflict within States

A society, as we have said, can first of all be seen as a process, and the most obvious feature of this process is its endless diversity. Nonetheless, we can single out three aspects as having special significance for politics. We can see, that is, that men are concerned for three things on behalf of themselves and those that they like or love which day by day bring them into conflict with their fellows.

First, they each have many interests in the form of activities which may or may not be directed to some particular result but which in any case, they like doing just as such. These may include their jobs as artists, builders, civil servants, doctors, politicians or whatever these may be; the affairs of their households; their sports and pastimes; and so on endlessly. The first point of conflict is that an activity of one may preclude the same or a different activity of another. Moreover, some activities, notably jobs and positions within a job, are intrinsically more interesting than others, and yet, in the nature of society, only a few among many can have the opportunity to do them.

Second, men want possessions, whether as such, like works of art or land in one of its aspects; or as a means, like money or machinery or land in another of its aspects; or in the sense in which we speak of a composite of people, activities and things as being a possession, like a village or an oil company. Possessions are scarce, either naturally or in the nature of society or in the particular situation of a society. This is the other main point of conflict of interests.

Third, men want many kinds of sentiment from their fellows but, simply as members of a society, the most important of these is honour. They like the esteem that comes from possessions and from doing an admired activity well. They like to outdo others in esteem, ranking higher than them in these things. Especially among politicians, we often speak of a desire for power, but a liking for having others at one's disposal is usually only part of the matter. The wider desire observable in every line of life, is to be more successful than others and so to enjoy more honour than they do. This is the third main point of conflict.

In the ordinary way, conflict about these things runs within limits, is legitimised and, so to say, tamed and called competition Let us now look at disputes where men are not simply competing but are saying "this is ours".

Here the things contended for are exactly the same, activities and possessions and the honour that springs from them; but wider issues are also at stake and further feelings are aroused. When something that is his is seized or something due to him is denied, whether or not it has any value in itself, a man feels that a blow has been struck at his honour at the deepest level, his dignity as a person. Seizure of one thing also makes him fear for the security of all else that he has. On this account alone, he is determined to assert his right and to defend the laws or the personal reputation for power on which he relies. When something belonging to a neighbour is seized, love or expediency ensures that he has similar anxieties. Feelings of a supernatural kind are also stirred and deeply when some great injustice is seen or suffered. It is not simply an offence against particular men but against the entire order of creation.

Though all disputes involve these further issues, they do so in very different degrees because they are of different kinds. First, and for our purposes least important, there are legal disputes where the issue is simply to find what the law is at some doubtful or novel point. Next, and most common, there are disputes in which particular individuals or groups or sides of some sort are in conflict about a particular thing. Most such disputes of sufficient size are decided by the application of laws, though some are not. Most can be called private disputes, though all in some way or other have a public significance.

The momentous disputes within states are those in which groups within the society are in conflict over how activities or possessions shall be allotted between them. Typically, they take the form of a struggle to make or change a rule delimiting the scope of the groups. Most of these disputes do not run deep; only one interest of the members of the groups is at issue, counter-balanced by all the other interests in life which divide them and link them with their opponents and with other members of the society. Some of these disputes, on the other hand, those which will concern us in this book, involve most of the interests of the members of the groups. The distribution of land does not give the poor their due. The social system gives unequal scope to men who are equal. The constitution does not allow the citizens the political activity that is rightly theirs. In multinational states, the constituent agreement is held to cheat the interests of one of the communities. In empires, the governmental and social system is held to profit one nation at the expense of the others. In all such disputes, the basis of the society is challenged and it is in danger of violent disintegration, perhaps threatening the peace of other states.

Conflict between States

Let us now turn to the world of international relations. Here we see the same human characteristics at work; the same things wanted; the same distinction between competition for these things in which states, however keenly they compete, do not deny the legitimacy of the actions of other states, and disputes in which they assert that something that is theirs or due to them, is being taken or denied.

International relations consist, in the first place, of a great flow of dealings between individual citizens and groups of the different states. These are the extension abroad of their home activities and we can leave them aside except in so far as they are a matter of state interest. As regards states themselves, they are either effectively individuals, as in the case where an autocrat is concerned only with his own interests, or quasi-individuals as in the case of nation states. In either case, they have the same three basic political concerns as do ordinary individuals on behalf of themselves and of other states to which they are tied by sentiment.

In the first place, the foreign policy of states is determined by leading individuals who like political, military and related activities and whose liking does not suddenly cease at the borders of their state, but extends as far as may be. In the case of nation-states, policy is also determined by a wider public which derives vicarious satisfaction from these activities. They do not themselves do these things, but at least they are done by representatives of their nation and in the name of their nation. Historically, much of this enjoyment of action abroad has, inevitably, involved disputes, as in the creation of empires and the fascination with warfare and conquest. But there is also a legitimate involvement in the fortunes of other states and in shaping the affairs of the world and a legitimate liking for it and rivalry between states about it.

The second point of competition concerns possessions. States value territory in itself and as the ground for every kind of activity of life, cultural, economic, political. At the present time, increased territory and new subjects are of little interest to most states. The most prominent form of competition for possessions is in national economic growth and in the commercial activities and possessions abroad which result from it and assist it.

The last point of competition is the desire to be more successful than other states in whatever activities and forms of possession are esteemed at that time by the international community. States do not compete in this respect to the same degree with all others. They have their particular set of competitors, states of comparable scale and extent of activities. If their competitor is active in the affairs of some other state or of a region or of the world generally, they must be more active and exercise more control than it does. If their competitor's economy is growing fast, theirs must grow faster. Much of this competition is in parallel but often it is competition for the same particular thing. The desire in either case is for higher honour in the world.

In such discussions as this, the usual next step is to draw a distinction between the vital and secondary interests of states. Some things are more valuable than others; the defence of things at home is more important than their extension abroad; and so on. But another distinction comes first, that between competition and dispute, between the desire for something and the conviction that it is "ours". It is with this in mind that states weigh the importance of a thing and how much they will sacrifice for it. A thing may not be worth a moment's competition and yet be worth bitter dispute. For at very least, national honour is at stake. At very least, a challenge has been made which must be resisted for fear for the security of all else.

When we consider the affairs of the world at any given time, much can be understood as competition between states in the things we have mentioned. When we consider the great volume of day by day international transactions, most of it consists of ordinary conflict. We see states engaged in a continual round of diplomacy in which they confront one another with their opinions and interests, and bargain for the best outcome they can get. They do this in commercial and financial affairs, social affairs, alliance politics, military talks and negotiations on armaments, and whatever it may be. If we were to fix exclusive attention on the great issues of international history or on the headlines of newspapers, we would get the impression that all dealings between states involve bitter dispute, but on closer consideration, this is clearly not so. Most dealings between states, however keen the conflict of opinion and interest, go forward without either side denying the legitimacy of the actions of the other.

Yet, at the same time, much of this day to day activity is in the end in furtherance of those special conflicts, great or small, which are the focus of a state's foreign policy and of world politics. The business of involvement in other states, of winning control of affairs regionally or world-wide, of extending protection, of running military and diplomatic alliances, is to a greater or lesser extent directed towards security from dispute and towards the successful conduct of the disputes in which the states concerned are engaged. In the world since 1945, the greatest of these have been, in Europe, the German question; in the Far East, Taiwan; in South Asia, Kashmir; in the Middle East, Palestine. Disputes are not the usual type of dealing between states any more than between individuals; but they are the dominant type in the different conditions of international society, overshadowing its whole life.

In our effort to understand inter-state disputes, we are concerned in this early chapter only to notice that they are of various kinds and that, whatever their kind, they are not about mere wants, nor yet simply about law, but are essentially a clash of convictions about "ours" and "theirs".

First then, as within states, there are disputes which may be called legal disputes. The states concerned have, for example, made an agreement; they are willing enough to keep it; the issue is merely to establish some doubtful point in it. In other disputes, the states concerned well know what the agreement is but one of them does not wish to keep it because this no longer suits its wishes or because it believes that the agreement cheats it of something that is its due. The dispute which then arises may partly take the form of argument about the terms of the agreement but, in substance, the dispute is not about the agreement but about the things dealt with in it and whose they should be.

In most of the great inter-state disputes since 1945, agreements have been involved in one way or another; in some of them prominently, for instance, the Anglo-Iranian Oil Company and Suez Canal disputes; in others, such as those just mentioned over Taiwan, Kashmir and Palestine, more marginally. But in either case, the antagonists did not believe that rights to the thing in question had been acquired in the past or could be decided in the present solely, or even mainly, by a recorded agreement or that the fundamental issue was the breach of that agreement.

We should notice here the basic similarity between inter-state disputes and those of individuals in domestic society. The disputes of individuals are, it is true, determinable by the application of law, but the similarity is that neither the individual nor the state believes that the thing in question is theirs because custom or the law may say so. An individual believes that a thing is his on more fundamental grounds which may or may not be reflected in custom and law. Similarly, states continually speak of things as theirs whether or not there is any enforceable positive law governing the matter. The belief in a right to a thing prior to the laws or in the absence of laws has sometimes been said to be a delusion; that is a matter to be raised later. Meanwhile, we should simply notice that Communists and Nationalists say, not "we want Taiwan" but "Taiwan is ours". Indians and Pakistanis say, not "we want Kashmir" but "Kashmir is ours". Arabs and Israelis say, not "we want Palestine" but "Palestine is ours".

In the same way, the United States in 1945 did not simply want equal control with the Soviet Union over the whole of Germany; nor yet did it simply believe that it was entitled to this by virtue of the Yalta and Potsdam Agreements; it believed that equal control was due to it as a matter of right on more fundamental grounds, of which the agreements were only an elaboration and a record.

The United States also frequently asserted at that time a similar kind of right in less exceptional cases and it is this that we must next consider.

Within states, all the members of society have a concern with the private disputes of their neighbours but they can usually entrust this concern to the authorities. In international society, states pursue this concern actively for themselves. The great powers in the world at large and, to some extent, the smaller powers within their regions believe that they are charged with a degree of responsibility for the maintenance of order and, above all, equal responsibility with their fellows.

Great powers tolerate the competition of their rivals but what they will not tolerate is that their rival should engage in a serious dispute or intervene in a dispute in some part of the world and, in doing so, completely disregard them. They may, or may not, have particular interests at stake in the dispute but, at very least, such unilateral high-handed action is a denial of their equal standing, a blow to their dignity and to their reputation for power. The United States in 1945, for example, might or might not have disliked a slow, unforced achievement by the Soviet Union of a position on the Dardanelles and an oil concession in Iran. What it would not accept was that its views should simply be ignored in an abrupt international crisis in which the Soviet Union dealt unilaterally with these states.

Beyond the jealous sense of right to participate lies another of still greater consequence. Great powers are concerned that their rivals should not over-ride the rights of small states for fear of the danger of this to their own. Turkey and Iran believed in their disputes with the Soviet Union that they were struggling for something which was theirs to grant or not to grant and which should not be coerced from them. The United States agreed with them in this and believed, in consequence, that something which was its own was also threatened. It had some particular interests in these countries but this, in itself, was not the point. The point was that it believed that all its interests, whether in these countries or in neighbouring areas, or in the world at large, or ultimately even in its home territory, were endangered by a great power which showed that it would not respect what belonged to others. There could be no knowing where such a state would strike next, and to live with it and to submit to its acts was to live in continual fear.

It was on these grounds that Britain and the United States had fought with Germany and Japan in the first and second world wars. The competition of these states in world affairs was one thing, but their ever-increasing disregard for the rights of weaker states was quite another and could not in the end be tolerated. It is sometimes said of Britain, in particular, that its constant concern in the politics of Europe was to maintain a balance of power and that in this cause it from time to time went to war. But, though the principle of balance of power is of extreme importance in the conduct of disputes, it is superficial as an explanation of why states dispute at all.[1] They dispute with another state, not just when its power is rising but whenever this involves the seizure of what belongs to other states, and thus threatens, sooner or later, what is theirs.

In resisting unilateralism and the over-riding of the rights of small states, the great powers have always in effect insisted upon certain rules in their dealings with one another, certain limits to legitimate competition. They were not engaged in deliberate, abstract rule-making. They spoke of "the peace of Europe" or of "international order" but they did not set out to construct it directly. Their concern was with the Eastern Question or the Dardanelles or the Iran dispute or whatever it might be. Nonetheless, in the very course of these disputes, they were in fact defending and re-asserting the nearest thing that international society has to a constitution for its political affairs.

The United States and the Soviet Union were also attempting in the course of their disputes to promote a constitution for mankind in a much more advanced sense. Like the imperial powers in the past, though in a different form, they held vigorous views on the rules by which men

[1] It is superficial, that is, when interpreted as a mechanistic equilibrium of power rather than in terms of the maintenance of rights, cf. Friedrich Gentz, *Fragments Upon the Balance of Power in Europe*, English translation, London 1806.

ought to live both as regards inter-state politics and the internal structure of states. In dispute after dispute in the late 1940s, the United States was not merely resisting the unpredictable, unilateral thrusts of the Soviet Union against the *status quo*; it was defending the rules of the Charter of the United Nations. In dispute after dispute it was not merely protecting the independence and other rights of small sovereign states; it was defending the free way of life of peoples. The Soviet Union, on its side, was not simply taking the steps that it thought desirable to it as a state; it was furthering the spread of Communism.

We shall try to assess the effect of this ideological element in the disputes between the great powers in a later chapter. Here we need only remark once again that this element, like all others in disputes between states, concerns not what they merely want but what they consider due to them or to all states or to all men. We need only add for the sake of bringing our discussion back to its beginning, that at this point disputes about justice sometimes become indistinguishable from the other great category of human disputes, disputes about truth. It is so within states whenever the existing political and social structure is held to have the mandate of heaven. It is so between states whenever their ideological views are founded on religious or secular authority, as was to some extent the case in the disputes between the Soviet Union and China in the 1960s. Then the antagonism is redoubled.

The Practical Contrast between Kinds of Conflict

In this discussion, we have not mentioned all the kinds of disputes between states. We have dwelt on disputes between particular states about a particular thing and on the consequent interventionary disputes of the great powers. There is another kind which corresponds to the great public disputes within states and which is about how things should be allotted between the states of a region or of the world. However, unless we accept notions of world affairs as a grand struggle about the structure of human society, such disputes are still rare and we may leave a brief mention of them to a later chapter.

For the moment, certain final questions arise. Throughout the discussion, our purpose has been to point to the distinction between two types of conflict in human affairs, domestic or inter-state: the one in which the two sides want something; the other, a dispute, in which one or both say, it is ours or due to us or to all men or all states. The one is about the pursuit of interests and honour; the other is about the pursuit of interests and honour conceived as rights, that is, on the level of justice. We must now ask, what is the practical significance of this distinction?

Let us first give a summary answer. The practical difference between the two situations in politics is this. In the one case, in which individuals or groups or states say that they want something, they propose to give something in return. In the other case, in which they demand what is theirs or due to them, they do not. In the one case, neither side stands to lose; there is to be, at most, an exchange. In the other, one side stands to gain and the other to lose; there is to be an absolute transfer.

In the competition of men and states, the two sides may be competing in parallel with one another. Two states may be competing in the rate of growth of their economies. Here, it is true, one may lose supremacy and therefore honour and the other gain it; still, there is at least no loss of interests and no unrequited transfer of these. At other times, the two sides are competing for what is at the bestowal of a third, a business contract, for instance, or an economic aid relationship, or an alliance or the like. In such cases, the successful side must give something in return for what it wins and the unsuccessful loses nothing which it had, only what it would have liked to have. At yet other times, one or both sides are struggling to make a bargain with the other in furtherance of interests. Britain, for instance, is seeking to enter the European Economic Community; the United States and the Soviet Union are seeking to make an armaments agreement with one another. On such occasions, if a bargain is made, neither side loses; there is an exchange.

In disputes, on the other hand, matters are entirely different. One side or both claims that a piece of property, or the enjoyment of a contract, or a piece of territory, or the right to form a government is theirs; they will make no return; it is theirs. They claim that the present distribution of wealth, the laws governing education and jobs and property, the existing constitution, the disposal of a defeated state, the unilateral decision of great international issues, the trampling on the rights of small states, cheats them of what is their due or threatens them in what is their own; once again, they will make no return for an alleviation of this; it is their due. They may say this cynically when the reality is merely that they want to get or keep the thing and believe that they have the power to do so. Or they may say it because they believe that it should be theirs in justice. In either case, the effect is the same. There is a demand to get or to keep something without return.

The significance of this for those in charge of policy is readily apparent. In competition or dispute, the statesman is in two very different situations, raising different problems, requiring different skills. Let us suppose that his side is taking the initiative. In the one case, behind him is a public which wants something and sees the necessity of giving something in return. Facing him is a group in the community or a foreign state to whom he is prepared to make an offer.

In the other case, he has behind him a public which demands something and sees no necessity to give anything. He is faced with a group or a state to whom he is putting a sheer demand. Or let us suppose the converse when the statesman is dealing with an initiative. In the one case, an offer is being made to his people. In the other, a demand is being made which threatens an absolute loss in interests and honour.

So, India and Pakistan demand Kashmir; China, Taiwan; the Arabs, Palestine. The United States demands that the Soviet Union co-operate in the common administration of Germany and allow free elections there; that it permit the Polish and Czechoslovak peoples to have a government of their choice; that it cease its pressure on Turkey and Iran. There is no question here of an offer in return for something wanted. It is an absolute demand. The thing is due as a matter of right. In the vast, diverse business of international politics, states do not ordinarily demand things of each other. They bargain. In disputes, they do. If the demand is not accepted, the Indians, Chinese, Arabs, Poles, Czechs, Americans or whoever it may be, feel cheated of their due. Their adversary, for his part, is faced with a demand for absolute capitulation with nothing in return. The emotions and the enmity aroused on both sides are unparalleled in the ordinary competion of states.

To say that disputes involve an absolute demand, is to speak of their essential nature or, in practical terms, of their starting-point. As the dispute goes on, men or states sometimes come to recognise that what they thought at the outset ought to be, is not in fact just; more often, they are forced to recognize that what they still think ought to be, is not in fact possible. The pursuit of justice is not some quixotic crusade; if it were, there would be no ending disputes, no solving them, no limit to the bloodshed of mankind; it is about the promotion of interests and honour on the highest level, and what is possible and at what cost rightly temper the calculation. So, after a shorter or longer term, the antagonists often come to compromise or to offer some return for what they claim or to forget their quarrel in some greater common interest.

On the way to this, nonetheless, disputes show that special character which comes from demand. We need only mention here the outstanding aspect of this, their danger. Whenever in the course of politics, the cry is heard "this is ours", "this is due to us", it is an unfailing sign of the possibility of the use of force. It is a testimony to the validity of the concept of justice that even the most ambitious men and states take trouble to deck their demands with a clothing of justice. States, whether cynically or sincerely, rarely make war saying "we want this" but rather "this is our due". Disputes, conflicts of justice, are the kind of conflict that states think worth bringing before the United Nations in a search for support in their cause; and rightly so because these are the conflicts that are in every way of social concern and especially in that they can endanger the peace and security of the world.

The Concept of Justice

There remains a final question which we must raise, however inadequately, the question of the validity of the conceptions involved in a dispute, of the beliefs which men and states have that something is "theirs", "due to them", required by "justice".

According to an old European tradition of political and legal thought, these beliefs have no final validity at all. They are an illusion which the realist statesman should no doubt take account of, but which are ultimately groundless. The concepts "ours", "theirs", "due", "just" only have meaning as a result of established laws. Only when these have been established by the will of the lawmaker does society and, therewith, justice come into existence. When laws themselves are at issue or when new laws are being made for some new contingency of life or when, above all, as in inter-state affairs, there are no genuine laws at all, these concepts are meaningless. The conflict is one of sheer will. The eventual decision is a matter, not of justice, but of will. Politics is a conflict of will.

This tradition of European thought is less plausible after the experience of the Nazi triumph of the will, whose victims were driven to the conviction that it represented not a mere crushing of their own personal will, but was an affront to something universal. The other great tradition of European thought, that society and its laws are not the outcome of will but, on the contrary, express the urge to set limits to the will, that laws can be just or unjust, that there is justice and injustice even in the absence of laws, that politics is fundamentally about justice, nowadays has renewed vigour and carries greater conviction.

Yet, at the same time, even among many who are attracted towards this conviction, there remains doubt and despair as to whether it is tenable. The cause of this is not so much that political life is replete with men and states who manifestly care nothing about justice. It is rather that when all sides are convinced that something is "theirs", how can "justice" between them be done? When there are no laws, is not one opinion of what is "just" as good as another? Is not the outcome, therefore, necessarily and not merely as so often in practice, a matter of the pressures of power?

These doubts, which afflict all, plainly owe much to the scientific mood of our time. Whatever cannot be proved, as justice cannot be, has only shallow grounding. The concept of "a right" to a thing must be abandoned to the lawyers; the concept of "justice" to the speechmakers. Our doubts owe still more to the fact that justice has in the past been elevated out of existence by some of its own champions. Some claimed to be able to discover by abstract reason a vast and universal system of detailed rules for doing justice in any given circumstances. Others equated justice with the pursuit of a naive legalistic and moralistic code. Others have perorated about justice in their speeches in a manner so pretentious, so self-righteous and sometimes so plainly at variance with their own policies as to discredit justice altogether as mere hypocrisy. These various champions of justice, each in their own style, have in effect claimed that men cannot merely see something of justice, but everything. The inevitable reaction is the belief that since men plainly cannot see everything of justice, they can see nothing.

Others, however, throughout history, have not thought of justice in either so inflated or so abject a manner. They have been concerned with it as a practical problem, encountered and more or less satisfactorily dealt with daily. Men are confronted with the task of doing justice whenever they are faced in their affairs with the problem of deciding between two or more who say that they want a thing, not for a return, but because they merit it or need it. Men are seeking to do justice whenever their aim is not simply to assert their own will but to grapple honestly with the problem of what the respective merits and needs are.

In the present climate of opinion in much of the Western world, many who are concerned in making foreign policy would be ashamed to say that they were seeking to do justice or would even repudiate any such notion. They would claim that their only concern was to promote the interests of their country. But much of the time they are engaged in the conduct of disputes. And much of the time, they are concerned not only to calculate the power of their country's and their opponent's desire, but to examine the opponent's motive and to assess its arguments of merit or need. It is in this light that they advise how their country should act, either to make concession, or to resist with force and to go on in honest argument with the opponent for as long as need be. They are in all this speaking the language not simply of interests but of justifiable interests. If this is indeed how they try to act in a dispute and if this is indeed their approach to promoting the interests of their country in it, then like Monsieur Jourdain and his famous prose, they are all the time seeking to do justice without knowing it.

The business of assessing merits and needs is necessarily one of uncertainty and the conflict of many opinions. Politics is an endless discussion of justice. Disputes are the debate of justice. Those which we shall consider in this book are, for the most part, the very greatest, far exceeding the ability of anyone to see the solution. The outcome of any dispute at all can never be one of satisfaction that absolute justice has been done, only of more or less, of nearer or further. There can never be absolute assurance for the statesman that either he himself or his adversaries are entire in their dedication to justice. On the contrary, it is certain that this will not be so and that their concern for justice will be shot through with desire to assert their own will and that of the people they represent. But, though all this is true, it still also remains true that men know the difference and can tell it between more and less, nearer and further, the assertion of will and the concern for justice. On these grounds, they can be confident that, obscure as justice is, they are engaged in a real, not an illusory task when they try to discover and to do it.

PART ONE: ORIGINS

3. The Origins of Disputes Within States

SOME of the most serious international disputes of the past twenty-five years have been disputes within states or, at least, have begun as such. Nation has fought against nation in federal states and empires. Faction has fought against faction in unitary states in a manner which has involved external intervention. The ever-increasing interconnection of human society ensures that very rarely does a great dispute within a state have purely domestic significance.

The causes of disputes within states, as of all others, are twofold. First, there is the issue of justice. One or both sides believes that through the ambition of the other, it is being deprived of what is due to its interests and honour. Second, there is the issue of power. Before launching into a dispute, the two sides, at least in principle, consider not merely their ambition or their grievance, but whether they have the power to assert it successfully. We shall consider these two causes in turn.

Beyond this, there is the fact that disputes have both a static and a dynamic aspect. We can ask of a dispute "what was it about?" but we can also ask "how did it come about?" A dispute is in practice not logical but historical, it is a growing thing. Ambitions, grievances and power develop over time. In a long chain of events, they are always present as the basic guide to what is to be done, and yet what is done also depends on how the pattern of action and reaction develops, on circumstances and on chance. This aspect also of the origin of disputes will have to be considered in conclusion.

The Issue of Justice

We begin then with the issue of justice, and first between rulers and subjects. The right relationship between them has been very differently formulated in different societies in different times and places, and yet, even when the religious sanction for rule was strongest, there has always been, whether crudely or in some highly developed political theory, a relationship of mutual demand. The ruler shall enjoy obedience; the subject shall benefit. Sometimes, little benefit has been expected; perhaps only that the rulers should spend as much time in fighting the oppressors of the people as in oppressing the people themselves. Sometimes, it has been expected that they should be lucky in war, or that they should keep the customs and enforce them, and so on up the scale to the most optimistic formulae of contemporary Western societies according to which governments shall promote the expressed interests of the people, as in representative democracy, or incarnate the real will of the people as in messianic totalitarianism.

The basic idea that subjects shall benefit has often been disregarded, still more often disappointed but rarely explicitly denied. The ordinary process of politics among rulers consists, together with personal rivalry, of conflict on how best to achieve whatever is expected to the required extent. In a nation at large when all citizens participate in politics, it consists of the continuous conflict of opinion on public policy. This process includes from time to time the replacement of rulers where custom or the constitution allows this, for the sake of the fuller satisfaction of expectations or the more competent handling of public policy. An electoral contest is not a dispute and neither necessarily is a contest which leads to a *coup d'état*. The rulers are doing what they ought to do but not as well as others could, and should be replaced. Disputes, on the other hand, begin when it is claimed that they are not doing what they ought to do.

Historically the most momentous form of this is when the entire system of government no longer satisfies the expectations of the subjects. A struggle begins to change from monarchy or oligarchy to democracy or some other more popular form of government. In one of the most archaic countries of the world, Yemen, such a struggle became manifest in the late 1950s and came to a head in the *coup d'état* of 1962. Four years previously, the Imam had formed an alliance with Egypt whose support he sought in his claims to what was at that time a British colony and protectorate and later became South Yemen. This action led to a new influx of foreign modernising influences, particularly from Egypt, to an increase in the number of foreign-educated Yemenis, and to a sharpening impatience with the governmental structure of the country. When later the Imam fell out with Egypt, the demand was especially loud for the restoration of the alliance. The background to this was the general sentiment of Arab solidarity throughout the Middle East and also the belief in Egypt as the centre of political and social modernisation in the region. Hand in hand with desire for modernisation went resentment at the monopoly of political activity by the Imam and the traditional oligarchy. The new Imam who succeeded in 1962, while himself wishing modernising reform, could not accept sweeping change in the governmental and social structure, nor the role of Egypt as the centre of reform, nor control by it over Yemen's foreign policy. Behind him in this, he had the convictions of the traditional section of his people.

In a more modern state, in Hungary in 1956, many of the original dissidents were simply exasperated by the incompetent handling of the affairs of the country in recent years, particularly economically, and on these grounds wished governmental and policy changes. What inflamed a sense of injustice in the population at large was the conviction that their government was ruling in economic affairs and in all else, not in the interests of the nation but of foreigners, that is, the Soviet Union. The close alliance with the Soviet Union, anyway in so far as it involved subjection, must be ended. More than this, many wanted to alter the entire constitution prevailing in the country. Some wanted the complete downfall of a socialist pattern of society. Most were at least certain that whether or not according to doctrine the Communist Party expressed the real will of the people, they wanted to express their own views of their interests themselves. Furthermore, it was unjust that there should be such restrictions on freedom as then prevailed and that only some, the Communist Party faithful, by an intolerably arbitrary discrimination, should have liberty of political activity and of many other activities as well.

Sometimes a dispute arises in a state, not exactly between rulers and subjects, but over the distribution of benefits between groups within the state. However, this is often related to the governmental or constitutional question. The privileged form the government or, even if they allow the less privileged to form it, retain the power to make or break it. So they retain their privileged position.

An obvious contemporary case of this issue is the land question in many Latin American countries. The rich, for a variety of reasons, have been able to retain ultimate power even in relation to apparently popular governments and often to prevent programmes of land reform. Not just land in itself is involved. From land spring many of the other interests of life both for the peasantry and for the rich whose social and political position is closely linked with their landed wealth.

On both sides in these disputes, those active on behalf of the peasantry and the landowners, there is a powerful sense of injustice; injustice in the existing distribution of land, injustice threatened by redistribution. The reformers see the extreme poverty of the peasantry, the place of land reform in helping to change it, and the failure of the privileged to generate ideas for curing the ills of society generally. The poverty in wealth of the poor is matched by the poverty in imagination and leadership of the rich.

The landowners, for their part, frequently concede the necessity in principle for some measure of land reform, as they did, for instance, in two of the first major disputes since 1945, in Bolivia and Guatemala in 1952, but they challenge the extent and practicality of many of the schemes. Above all, in so far as the break-up of the old order of society is portended, they have no confidence that anything more just will succeed it. They see only that they will be deprived of what they have; they have no assurance of countervailing benefits for themselves or anyone else. The reformers, as they see it, have no coherent picture of a new economy in which reformed land holding will take its place and no coherent vision of a new society generally. In so far as they do have this, it is a vision which draws on the abhorred theories of Marxism. In these countries, in short, neither side has confidence in the leadership of the other. The one side is accused of inertia, the other of extremism. Each demands justice; neither has a conception of society which seems to offer justice to the other.

Against this general background, each land reform dispute has its own special and crucial features. A case of particular interest is that of Guatemala in 1952 to 1954. The landowners made their own modest proposals but they had no confidence in the Land Reform Bill proposed and ultimately enacted by the President, Colonel Arbenz. They mistrusted the personality of Arbenz himself. They mistrusted his associates, that is, his heavy reliance from the outset on the comparatively few vigorous officials, the Communists. They feared that his measures were only the beginning of a limitless sequestration. Above all, they saw no compensation for themselves whether in straightforward payment terms or in terms of a transformed economy in which losses would be balanced by new opportunities.

The main special feature of the situation was that the leading landowner was foreign, the United Fruit Company of Boston, USA. The company had an additional sense of injustice in that they believed that the President's programme was in large part inspired by an arbitrary enmity towards them as foreigners. They could cite as additional evidence the encouragement by the government of labour unrest in their concerns. The whole affair was an effort, in sheer, unjustified xenophobia, to repress their activities and perhaps drive them from the country.

The nationalist conviction in this, as in many another dispute, was that the foreign company could not disclaim the position of representative of a foreign nation which had acted oppressively in the past in a manner now to be revenged. In particular, the foreign companies had accepted help and protection from their own country in the past; they could therefore justly expect the penalty now. They had acted as foreigners; they should be treated as foreigners.

More than this, the foreign company was in itself oppressive in that it held a dominating position in the national economy, not only as regards the land but in most other significant areas, in a manner which was unjust to the interests and honour of the inhabitants. They were treated as unequals in the most significant activities of national life. The foreign companies often felt the injustice of this in as much as, without their efforts, there would often have been no national economy at all worth speaking of for anyone to dominate. But the nationalist reply was that foreign domination had forestalled and prevented development by the inhabitants themselves.

Even if this was not so, a poor economy which gave them their due honour was preferable to a developed economy which did not.

Other disputes within states involve not rich against poor, foreigners against natives, but religious or ethnic communities as the groupings for the defence and promotion of interests. These groups are to some extent foreigners to each other and, in one degree or another, there is continual watchfulness for any sign of discrimination and injustice.

In Lebanon in the years after independence from France in 1943, relations between the Muslim and Christian communities were governed by a series of understandings reached at that time, designed to protect ultimately all the interests and honour of each in relation to the other. Notably, it was agreed that the Christian community should have a majority in the legislature and that the President should always be a Christian and the First Minister always a Muslim. The Christians would not invoke the intervention of the Western powers nor seek to make treaties with them. The Muslims would abandon efforts towards the union of Lebanon with Syria or its subjection to external Arab influence.

These understandings and the principles underlying them were jeopardised in the mid-1950s by the ferment in the Middle East against the Western powers. In March 1956, the Muslims suspected that the Christians wanted to bring Lebanon into the Baghdad Pact. In the Suez crisis of the autumn, the Christians mistrusted the Muslim demand for a breach of diplomatic relations with Britain and France. In March 1957, the atmosphere became still more bitter with President Chamoun's endorsement of the Eisenhower Doctrine, a statement aimed against the expansion of the Communist powers into the vacuum created by the Anglo-French *débâcle* but which seemed to Arab opinion an attempt by the United States to step into the old imperialist shoes. The final issue was the accusation by the Muslims that the President had manipulated the elections of June 1957 as part of an effort to arrange for himself a further term of office in defiance of the constitution, in order to maintain his pro-Western policies.

In this protracted crisis in Lebanese affairs which extended throughout the following year, it was always uncertain whether either side had actually broken the agreements on which their society was based or had ever intended to. They had been brought into collision by inevitably sharing in the great wave of enthusiasm and fear which swept the Middle East at that time. They were not so much in dispute as in an intense state of mutual suspicion and consequent enmity. These facts were to have a crucial bearing on the success of the United States intervention in the summer of 1958 and on the ultimate resolution of the affair.

The position is very different in certain other cases where communities confront each other in concern for their interests and honour. To take an outstanding example, the policies pursued by the Afrikaners in South Africa and the laws passed by them from 1946 onwards seemed to an increasingly significant group in the Asian, coloured and black communities, a clear breach of justice. As usual in such disputes, much of the issue could be expressed in terms of the problem of equality. For the Afrikaners, equality is just only for those who are equal. To concede equality to Asian, coloured and black people in some simple fashion as though they were in no way different would be unjust to the white community. Their solution was the policy of "separate development" in so far as this was possible and, for the rest, discriminatory laws. As usual also, these feelings of principle were charged with other, more particular sentiments. They feared not merely reduction to straightforward equality, but eventual reverse discrimination against themselves. They also believed that they were not foreigners in southern Africa. The country was no less their rightful possession, indeed more so, than the possession of other immigrant peoples from Asia and northern Africa. They retained a powerful Biblical faith in the righteousness of their rule in the land and in the preservation of the culture they had founded there.

Their opponents, for their part, were convinced that the Asian, coloured and black communities were equal to the white in fact or in potential. They therefore demanded, as due to them in justice, equal opportunity for all activities from the accumulation of wealth to the pursuit of education and the enjoyment of political activity. The policy of *apartheid*, they dismissed as both unjust and impractical. It denied them their share in the high level of development which South Africa had already achieved and offered them only comparatively trivial assistance in developing something equivalent afresh on their own. Absolute or even extensive *apartheid* was, furthermore, impossible without destroying the entire working of the society. The Afrikaners well knew this and, accordingly, their programme was a mere fiction, designed to solace their own consciences and to appease the naive among the black community. To match the sense of righteous possession of the land of the Afrikaners, the leaders of the black community believed that it was to be seen essentially as part of Africa in continent and in culture and that the white peoples were, here as elsewhere in the continent, invaders.

The same human interests and the same concern for honour, are also at issue, though in a different manner, in disputes over the federal constitution of a state. Does it give what is their due to the constituent groups, tribes or nations? In the Congo in 1960 with the departure of the Belgians, the country exploded into disorder and for several years thereafter suffered the travails of establishing the constitution under which it should live. One of the greatest disputes was that between the tribes of the province of Katanga and those which controlled the central government. The issue was the degree of autonomy of Katanga, different in its culture, different in its degree of developed wealth. The issue had arisen shortly before the departure of the Belgians and they had suppressed a movement towards separatism. But the federal constitution left by the Belgians could not be the last word. Conflict on what was just to the whole and to the part continued violently for the first four years of the country's independence.

An aspect of the dispute of particular interest is Katanga's declaration of secession in the midst of the disorders immediately after independence. Interpretation of this, like most other events of the dispute, must be uncertain. It may have been a real secession; or a response to the collapse of order in the country at large; or a bargaining move in relation to the centre; or a way of arousing wider international sympathy for Katanga's attitudes to the centre with the emotive cry of independence; or several of these.

Whatever the intention was, Katanga's secession sprang less from bitter experience in the past than from hopes and fears regarding the future. This may be contrasted with the case of the Ibo of Nigeria some years later. In Nigeria, since independence from the British, the process of political conflict had always had a strongly tribal character, but this went beyond all former limits in the *coup d'état* of January 1966, the intention of which, as the opponents of the Ibo suspected, or at least the likely effect of which, was to place the Ibos in a commanding position in the affairs of the state. Then followed a counter *coup d'état* and finally in September, widespread massacre of Ibos. At this point, their leaders determined to secede from the federation. The difference of background to this secession from that of Katanga was very great and was the decisive reason why the Katanga secession could readily be ended by force by the United Nations, once they had determined on it, whereas the Ibo secession could not be readily ended by force by the remainder of the federation.

The final kind of dispute to be considered is that within empires. Such disputes are not merely of historical or even contemporary interest. Situations in which several nations combine to form one integrated state, and in which one nation threatens to dominate the rest, will no doubt recur in the future.

One of the oldest imperial relationships to come into dispute in the years after 1945 was that between China and Tibet. This relationship had been tighter or looser over the centuries depending upon the fortunes of China, but the enduring basis of it was that Tibet acknowledged the suzerainty of China and for the rest enjoyed its own customs. After the Communists had attained authority in China in 1949 and had asserted it in

Tibet in 1950, they reached an agreement with the Tibetans in 1951 which expressed in detail once again this historic, basic relationship. In the following years, however, the Chinese showed increasing determination, as they saw it, to liberate the Tibetans from an obsolete social structure. They sought, in particular, to impose new educational, agricultural and tax laws and to restrict the status of the Dalai Lama. The result was increasing hostility, at first from the most unruly and elusive of the tribes and later from the Tibetans generally. This reached a crisis in the spring of 1959 and though the Chinese were able to crush the resistance at that time, thereafter they were confronted with the usual dilemma, either to do justice or to spend resources on repression.

The declaration of secession and independence by the secular and some of the religious leaders of the Tibetans in the crisis of 1959 is to be seen less as a determination to achieve international sovereignty than as a traditional defiance of an unjust suzerain, expressed in the modern terms needed to evoke international sympathy and support. The disputes within the Western empires, on the other hand, were attempts at secession in the fullest sense; or rather, they were still more than this. The overseas nations in these empires were not merely rejecting continued society with the metropolitan nation on the grounds of injustice done to them, but denying that such society had ever existed at all at any time in their common history. They had from the beginning been in bondage and were now determined not on secession but on liberation.

The imperial structures developed by the metropolitan nations can be seen in the first place, as they were exclusively seen by many, in terms of the promotion of the metropolitan's own interests. The imperial structures promoted their activities in relation to the overseas territories and the activities of their settlers in these territories, and in consequence exalted the honour of both. The nations of Europe, above all else, derived honour in relation to one another from their empires. In very recent years, a country such as Portugal bitterly regretted the loss of what was in terms of interests so trivial a possession as Goa because its empire and the memory of its greatness and this small territory most of all, epic *senhora de todo o Oriente*, gave it, a small nation, a sense that it counted in the world. As to the colonists who went to these territories, they had the satisfaction of superiority over the people who already lived there.

At the same time, the metropolitan nations believed that the empires were just. The imperial structure did justice not merely to their interests but to those of the overseas peoples as well. So far as these peoples were concerned, they were given by the empires in relation to each other and to all citizens of the empire, equality of redress before the law. If they did not enjoy political and social equality, this was because they were in fact unequal. They had the opportunity for such equality and they could take it. In political terms, as in the case of the French and Portuguese empires, they could make their way into the highest ranks of the imperial government, or, as in the case of the British empire, they could make their way collectively towards independence. In either case, the imperial structure created the conditions in which the overseas peoples could advance themselves.

Even if the leaders of the overseas peoples were prepared to admit, as they sometimes were, the nobility of the imperial ideal, they came in time to deny its reality. They, the leaders, manifestly equal in capacity and in culture, were still made to feel, by virtue of their race, social and political inequality in practice. In so far as their areas of the empire were backward, for instance, economically, they were not given an equal chance to develop according to their interests but were controlled in their development as suited the metropolitan country. To the extent that their people themselves were backward in culture, they were not given that unequal, greater assistance which was their due. They were the object only of a patronising, "civilising mission". For all these reasons, in order to achieve equality in the promotion of interests and in honour with the metropolitan states, they must have their own governments. The imperial structures must be destroyed.

It is often said that the empires were destroyed by nationalism. Though this is true, it is not as though nationalism was fundamental as a force in human affairs. Nationality is a grouping along with oligarchy against democrats, rich against poor, Muslim against Christian, Catholic against Protestant, white against black through which ambition and the passion for justice are expressed. Moreover, by whose nationalism were the empires destroyed? On the one hand, the overseas peoples were geographically, ethnically and culturally separate and this inevitably created feelings of national separateness. On this they built much nationalist dogma and prejudice in their struggle with the metropolitan countries. On the other hand, the metropolitan countries did not themselves fulfil the imperial ideal. They formed the empires in national rivalry with each other. They taught nationalism to the overseas peoples not just by the precepts of their European philosophies but by the example of nationalist discrimination against them. Though it is true that some newly independent countries are worse ruled than they were under the empires, still, the old imperial systems were necessarily unjust in that they were nationalist, whereas the new independent systems at least could be just. In these terms, independence was at least a beginning.

In some particular cases of imperial disputes after 1945, the imperial spirit was still at its height, in others waning. In Angola and other Portuguese territories, independence movements have developed but are at present weak. Whether or not they grow further, they exemplify a clear conflict between the imperial and independent systems of government. At the other extreme were the disputes within the British empire where the idea of independence was accepted by both sides and the strife turned largely on different views of timing and practicalities. Somewhere in between lay some of the disputes in the French and Dutch empires. These illustrate a situation very common in other areas of life. Those who control the old system are more or less willing to make changes but are determined to control these changes and to have the strongest voice in shaping the new system. Against them they have the root and branch revolutionaries who will tolerate no delay.

There were large elements of this in the Indo-China disputes which began with the return of the French in 1945. Most Frenchmen whether in Indo-China or in France would not have asserted that the empire could be run in the postwar world and indefinitely into the future exactly as it had always been run in the past. But most were in one degree or another determined that France should re-establish control and should have charge of any future development. They could not accept that their empire should be torn from them in large part by the aggression of the Axis powers. It was France's due, particularly in honour, that the old position should first be restored. They had no confidence in their nationalist opponents, particularly those who were Communist like Ho Chi Minh, and did not believe that they were truly representative of the people. They were determined that any new system should do justice to their interests as well as to those of the people.

In the Netherlands, the authorities were often in deep difficulties with public opinion, and yet they and their representatives in Indonesia appreciated for the most part very clearly that the old imperial system would have to be greatly changed. They recognized the inevitability of striking a new balance between interests and were often indeed convinced that this was just. But the new system must do justice to all; to them, with their settlers and their great economic stake in Indonesia, and to the Indonesians themselves for whom they felt responsible. The gap between their proposals and those of the leaders of the Republic was often wide; perhaps it could never ultimately have been bridged. Yet there was at least no absolute conflict of principle; and it is safe to say that a great and perhaps over-riding part in the failure to reach enduring agreements was played by factors of confidence and power.

The Republicans did not in the last resort trust the Dutch to the necessary extent. The legacy of suspicion and hatred was too great. The Dutch, for their part, resented the Republic as something instituted under the auspices of the Japanese and, still more important, did not trust the Republican leaders or believe that they were the best representatives of the interests and opinions of the Indonesians.

The Republicans, having declared independence in the last days of Japanese rule, believed that they must make, and in popular and international support, had the power to make the Dutch recognise this before further negotiation on future relations between the two countries took place. The Dutch, for their part, believed that in material resources and in the sentiments of the Indonesians, they had the power to repress the Republic and to construct a new system in co-operation with more moderate nationalists. In this, they were in the grip of feelings which arise time and again in disputes. Those who represent the *status quo* may or may not agree with proposals for reform but above all they cannot stomach the particular men who put them forward. These men, the first revolutionaries who have been willing to bear and have borne the heat of conflict, are often the most extreme and the most embittered. How can such men be trusted to do justice? Is it not essential to find, to build up and to recognize more moderate opponents who may?

The Power Factor in Disputes

With this, we may turn to the second of the two causes of disputes, the factor of power, the ability that is to do greater damage to the interests of another and so to coerce him. Power is not always one of the causes of a dispute but it is so in many and certainly in most of those we have mentioned.

A dispute may be caused simply by a grievance and its denial. For various reasons, the two sides do not even consider their respective power. Only a narrow interest is at stake. All the rest of their interests are closely interlinked. They know without need of reflection that they are in each other's power. Besides, all the rest of their interests may be justly provided for. They may have confidence in the sense of justice of the other side, and themselves be concerned to do what is just. They may be tied by sentiments of long association in one political community. On every count, the use of power, especially of force, is inconceivable. They expect peaceful dispute, argument and perhaps in the end bargaining and compromise, the acceptance of authoritative decision.

At other times and places, the situation is entirely different. Many interests in life are at stake. One side at least has no concern to do what is just or no confidence in the sense of justice of the other. Sentiment has waned or was always lacking. The only question now is which, if either, has a margin of power in such links of interest as there may be between them; and which has the stronger will, organisation and resources for the use of force.

In this kind of situation, individuals or groups do not even voice a demand when they know that they would inevitably lose the ensuing power struggle. A man does not raise a grievance with another when he calculates that if he did this, he would forfeit the other's support in some more important matter. A people living under a tyranny will not express their grievances if this would only invite instant repression. There is no dispute. There is at most a continual situation of friction.

Conversely, when a dispute does break out, it is not merely because the two sides are ambitious or incensed by injustice, but also because they believe they have the power to get or to keep what they want. In the disputes we have mentioned, ambition or grievance is not enough as an explanation of their origins. The two sides were prepared to voice their demand and this, at least, in principle, requires a calculation. An ambition or grievance is all very well but how will other interests be affected? Even where all interests are at stake as under a national constitution or a federal or imperial system, still there is the matter of degree. The maintenance or change of the structure might ideally be best for the pursuit of interests and yet these interests will be greatly hazarded in a struggle. Is the struggle worth the hazards, will the gains outweigh the losses, what is the comparative ability of the two sides to damage the interests of the other and to coerce the other successfully without intolerable loss? In the disputes we have noticed, the two sides failed to make these calculations, whether through passion or disorganisation or some other cause, or they calculated and came to a favourable conclusion, and so the dispute began.

For the most part, more detailed points on the factor of power are best made in the context of the dynamic aspect of disputes to which we shall shortly turn. We should, however, mention here one of the disputes we have cited, in Hungary in 1956, because in it the Communist Party leaders and the Soviet Union behind them, so obviously fell foul of one of the traditional maxims of statecraft, that a system is in greatest danger of overthrow at the moment when it begins to reform itself. The rulers show the weakness of the old and thus encourage demand for the new. After the death of Stalin in 1953, the leaders of the Soviet Union were divided and vacillating on future relationships within the eastern European bloc and so in consequence was the Party in Hungary. Both were on the horns of the old dilemma, and control of policy fluctuated disastrously between those who advocated appeasement to avert explosion and those who urged that concessions would merely invite it. The outcome was that second only to popular repugnance for the regime in Hungary was popular awareness that it was in disarray, so creating the conditions for demonstration and finally insurrection.

There is a close connection between what is wanted and the power to get it, and the connection works both ways. On the one hand, the scale of ambitions is readily expanded by a sense of power. Even those who are concerned for justice can be easily deluded as to what is due to them by awareness of their own power and the weakness of the other side. Sometimes indeed precise ambitions or grievances or ideas of any sort are less important as a cause of dispute than sheer power. The secession of Katanga was perhaps a case in point. A striking feature of the situation in 1960 for the leaders of Katanga was the collapse of order at the centre compared with their ability to preserve ordered government in their province, and the general weakness of the rest of the Congo compared with the resouces of Katanga.

Conversely, ambition and perhaps still more a sense of injustice are important sources of power. The strength and passion behind a cause determine how much will be sacrificed in an effort to win victory. To take further an example already discussed, both the leaders of the Indonesian Republic and the Dutch had a strong sense of justice and yet there was greater clarity in this on the one side than on the other. The Republicans had declared independence even before the Dutch returned; they were committed to it; to that extent, whatever the uncertainties about future relations with the Netherlands, they were certain of where they stood. The Dutch, for their part, were in some confusion. They were not standing straightforwardly on the restoration of the old imperial structure. They were clear in their determination to restore their control but only as a starting-point for change. What this change should be was a matter of deep dissension amongst themselves, and the ambiguity of their aims in the struggle weakened them in pursuing it. It is one thing for a nation to fight strongly for an old order, another thing to fight for more or less of change. The Dutch exemplified, in short, another aspect of the maxim of the weakness of systems at the moment of reform.

Very often, no doubt, in the various disputes which we have mentioned, neither the leaders of the two sides nor the people who supported them paid much attention to calculations of power. They may have been just but they were not prudent. We should, however, pass on to a recognition of the extreme difficulty, even with the best efforts, of calculating comparative power. Even if power consisted exclusively of resources and organisation for the exercise of force, the problem would be great enough. Because it also consists of the strength with which a thing is wanted and of the willingness to sacrifice other things, the problem of assessment is one of the greatest in statecraft. Moreover, the most obvious feature of the circumstances in which this problem is faced is that a dispute is not an instantaneous confrontation with all the facts laid out at one moment of time for assessment, but a growing confrontation. The assessment of ambitions and grievances and power has to be made at each stage in relation to possible future developments about which there can be no certainty.

The Dynamic Aspect

Usually an internal dispute is preceded by a longer or shorter situation of friction. In this, ideas are growing of what is wrong and what is wanted. There is at first only a shapeless, negative discontent; later this crystallises into positive demands. Simultaneously, power also is growing. A group is forming in support of change, the defenders of the existing position are establishing their common view amongst themselves in opposition, and both are developing a general disposition to take action depending on a favourable opportunity.

Sometimes, the conflict remains indefinitely as a situation of friction. The tension between Chinese minorities and other inhabitants in the states of south-east Asia varies in degree and is variously handled by governments, but in Indonesia in past years, it has from time to time reached the pitch of persecution. No one can say whether the Chinese of Indonesia will one day form their grievances into an attack upon the system under which they live, but at least the possibility is clear. Sometimes, in any event, as in the disputes we have mentioned, a sense of grievance and a sense of power come together to cause explosion.

In some states, the power element has to a great extent long been in existence in the shape of self-conscious ethnic or religious groups. Especially when the ordinary process of political conflict has a marked communal or confessional character, nothing more is needed than a dispute issue. In some cases, moreover, even the dispute issue may largely pre-exist. In Lebanon, the two communities had long had a series of understandings between them of which they were always very aware; the terms of association and hence also of dispute were well-known in broad terms and required little formulation.

In most internal disputes, however, both issue and power have to grow in uncertainty and confusion. The notion of independence from an empire, seemingly obvious in retrospect, often required great effort to formulate and still more to spread to a significant group. The land reform question may be well-known in general terms but it comes to a point, as in Guatemala in 1952, with the taking of office by a particular government, which must then thrash out a set of measures in the particular circumstances prevailing. In Hungary, grievances, communication among the people, a sense of possibilities required some years of silent growth before reaching the necessary pitch for dispute in the early summer of 1956. In Yemen, a faction had to gather in awareness of common aims by a process of exchange of ideas, both difficult and dangerous.

In the growth of ideas and power, the rôle of leaders is plainly crucial and yet always hard to assess. Every dispute contains a greater or lesser element of purely personal conflict between leaders. In Guatemala in 1952–54, the two principal protagonists, Colonel Arbenz and his eventual successor, Colonel Castillo Armas, and many of their followers, were all in the same political tradition, that of the revolution of 1944 which had overthrown the old-style dictatorship of Ubico. The conflict was in some degree a matter of personal rivalries and indeed of normal disagreement on the best way of running the affairs of the country. In Lebanon, the leaders of the opposition to Chamoun were incensed by the prospect of indefinite exclusion from office threatened by the President's manoeuvres. Similar comments could be made about Sallal in Yemen, Hatta and Sukarno in Indonesia, Ho Chi Minh in Indo-China, Tshombe in Katanga and all the rest of the leaders and equally of their opponents, established in authority, in all the disputes we have cited.

In assessing the origin of disputes, exaggerated importance is often attached to this element of personal conflict. The opponent is seen as inspired by ambition, and the self-righteous hatred thus aroused prevents penetration to the deeper causes of conflict. In fact, the personal motives of leaders may not be a matter of sheer ambition. They may involve a sense of injustice. The personal conflict between Chamoun and his opponents in the Lebanon, for instance, was not an ordinary personal conflict but a dispute in which a sense of injustice at exclusion from office was involved.

Far more important than this, whatever the character of the personal conflict, it is not enough by itself to create a great public dispute. For this, great public issues are required. By way of illustration, in Oman in 1954 and again in 1957, the Imam and his brother raised the cry of injustice in relation to the suzerain, the Sultan of Muscat and Oman, demanding greater autonomy, even 'independence'. This seems to have roused little echo among the Omanis, and the two would have lacked power but for external sympathy and support. For a public dispute to arise, the leaders must strike a strong chord among the people at large.

The real importance of leaders in a dispute therefore lies first in the intellectual effort involved in the formulation of public ideas, in identifying what is wrong in the existing situation and in shaping the remedy. Usually leaders do not create these ideas but borrow from what they take to be similar situations in earlier times and places; the panacea is the abolition of the monarchy or the attainment of independence or land reform or the dogmas of Marxism or whatever it may be. Still, these broad ideas need, and to some extent receive, refinement to the particular circumstances. Leaders are important, secondly, in seizing the imagination of the people, in emboldening them in calculation, in organising them, and then in using the power thus gathered. It is in these two senses rather than in the element of personal conflict that the role of leaders in disputes is very great and their responsibility also. They may form and propagate ideas which are exciting but delusive. They may make the people reckless of calculation in order to inspire them, and yet fail even to calculate carefully on their behalf.

The fact that demands are shaped gradually over time under the leadership of particular men makes its own contribution to the origins of disputes. No doubt in many disputes, the most important point is that the demands of the opponent are, and always would be, simply unacceptable, and indeed in some disputes, this is the only point which really counts. In Yemen, the demand was for the abolition of the monarchy and here plainly, even if this had not involved the attempted killing of the ruler, surrender while there was any power to resist was not to be expected. The same is true of disputes involving Communist revolutionaries; their ideas are clear enough to all concerned and are simply unacceptable to their opponents.

On the other hand, in many disputes, some part is played by the fact that those who demand change are striving to define to themselves what exactly it is they want and are therefore unable to communicate this precisely to their opponents. In such cases, resistance is based not so much on the character of the demands as on their obscurity. There is deep uncertainty as to their significance and from this springs fear and instinctive resistance. When the ideas first appear, they are necessarily new for that particular society and necessarily to some extent disruptive and therefore suspect. They are half-formed and can easily be dismissed as ignorant and impractical. Their negative and destructive aspect is usually the first formulated and the clearest. They are imprecise in scope, often raising the spectre of demand after demand, concession after concession, without limit. Above all, as we have said, they are often put forward by men in whom there is no confidence or who can be suspected of personal ambition or who, in any case, are easily treated with the contempt which established authority accords to those who seek to teach it its own business. On some or all of these grounds, a group forms in opposition to change or a government commits itself to a stand of resistance, before either side knows with any certainty what is being demanded, and a gulf of bitterness and extremism is opened which cannot later be bridged.

Such factors as these arise in various and sometimes unexpected forms in disputes. We mentioned earlier an obvious case, that of Guatemala in 1952, when the imprecision of the Arbenz programme and the character of the regime led to immediate fears of limitless sequestration and Communist tyranny. Less obviously, in the dispute over the independence of

South Yemen, a significant part was played by what the British considered to be the negativity and impracticality of the views of the leaders of the Colony of Aden.

The independence movement erupted suddenly in Aden in 1958 because many there feared that the British were working towards an amalgamation of the Colony with the federation of sheikhdoms of the hinterland Protectorate which they were then creating. The towns-people feared that this would lead to domination by the sheikhdoms and they demanded independence for the town forthwith. They did so without making any proposals as to what should happen to the hinterland.

The British at that time wished to maintain a base in Aden after independence, and it was partly in order to create security for this base, partly because some arrangement or other had to be made for the hinterland and partly because town and hinterland seemed to them most viable as a unit that they pressed forward the federation scheme and eventually the idea of amalgamation. The British felt little or no sense of right in their aim to keep a base but they did feel this strongly in seeking to create some practicable successor order in the area. They showed insensitivity to the likely attitudes of Adenis in 1958 and yet at the same time, the Adenis exasperated them by refusing to grapple with the question of the hinterland. The Adenis were, in consequence, less able than they might otherwise have been to deter them or even influence them as they pushed forward with their schemes. In this way an extra touch of incomprehension and conflict was added to the relations between the two sides.

Of equal importance to the confused growth of ideas as a cause of disputes is the uncertain growth of power. It is a rationalist absurdity to suppose that disputes could be avoided if only men would scrutinise their interests with sufficient care and calculate in advance the course of a conflict. Very often, no doubt, they simply will not do this, but equally often, they cannot. Diplomacy since the beginning of history has involved the merely verbal enactment of a power struggle, thus avoiding the necessity of actually engaging in it; both sides see or can be brought to see the realities. Frequently, however, the uncertainties of power are so great that the matter has to be tested in action. The dispute is precisely a trial of strength.

A few people within a state put forward an idea for change. A few people protest against a course of policy as unjust. Except where such action invites immediate repression, why should they not do so? If support gathers, they can go forward; if it does not, they have lost little. As to the defenders of the existing position, who can be sure at this point how many will join in the demand or how strongly they will struggle for it? Governments, especially, cannot simply give way to each and every demand. Even where they have some concern for justice, justice cannot be seen instantly but requires controversy, which means in practice, resistance. Their established power makes this resistance all the more certain. Even in the clearest cases, where an opposition group of great potential pre-exists, for instance, an ethnic or religious community, who can tell whether those who first voice demands will succeed in the often gigantic task of mobilising the community for action? So the two sides commit themselves to conflict in deep uncertainty as to power; and if the conflict grows, if to that extent the facts become clearer, still, by that time, the defenders of the existing position have already taken their stand and withdrawal has become harder and defeat more calamitous.

A special aspect of the power calculation in internal disputes is the question of external support. It is impossible for foreign influences literally to create an internal dispute; the necessary motivation is necessarily local. Moreover, in a nationalist world, though foreigners can play a great part in the formulation of ideas as the United States, the Soviet Union, Egypt and others have done, it seems equally impossible for foreigners to provide the leadership when matters come to the point of action.

External support on the other hand, at the very beginning or later, whether by way of material resources or diplomatic action or the like, is frequent and this always presents very complex questions for calculation. Will a Communist party be able to count on the assistance of Communist states and how much of it? Will secession in the Congo or Nigeria receive international recognition?

These calculations may fall now one way, now another in the life of a dispute. The Austrians of the South Tirol always had a certain degree of power because they bordered on Austria; but for this, perhaps as little would have been heard of their grievance as of those of many another ethnic minority. In the immediate postwar years, however, Austria needed all the international friendship it could get and was in no position to give more than subdued sympathy to the South Tirolers' case. The Paris Agreement of 1946, whereby Austria renounced any claim to the territory and the South Tirolers were to receive a measure of local autonomy, was greeted internationally as a statesmanlike solution. Even in 1948 when the Italian government established the joint Trentino–Alto Adige (South Tirol) regional government which left the South Tirolers in a minority, the South Tirolers still only made muted protests even though feeling themselves tricked. Protest and agitation only became serious in the mid-1950s and, though there were many reasons for this, one was the revival of the fortunes of Austria. It was not that the Austrian government encouraged the dissidents or wished to alter its part in the Paris Agreement; merely, that the strengthening of Austria inevitably placed the dissidents on stronger ground.

The Development of Circumstances

To developing power and developing ideas, one final factor needs to be added in explanation of the origins of disputes, the development of circumstances. In all disputes, the general intentions of the two sides only partially explain their actions. Their actions also depend on the particular situation confronting them and this is largely created by their opponents and others. They seize on incidents, issues and opportunities presented by the opponent; or they respond to the actions of third parties in a way which brings them into dispute with the opponent. Some disputes are not so much created by the parties as created for them by the interaction of lines of policy in their society, or perhaps in the world community at large, for which they are not responsible.

One of the most momentous disputes which can be seen in this light is the Palestine dispute. It has many aspects and yet this aspect, the part played by the development of circumstances, is one of the most significant. Looking at the rights and wrongs of the matter in static terms, perhaps the most prominent feature is the conviction of the Palestinian Arabs and the Arab states that they are the rightful successors to the British and that the state of Israel is the substitution of a new imperialist tyranny for an old.

On the other hand, looking at the matter as it developed historically over the years from the 1914–18 War, other features also come into relief. There were, it is true, from the very outset of Jewish immigration, some Zionists who looked to the eventual creation of a Jewish State; but there were others who were intent only on the creation of a national home for the Jews in Palestine under British rule, seeing nothing in this incompatible with the rights of the Arabs already there. No doubt the seeds of ultimate dispute were sown in these early years, especially by the conflicting policies of the British, and yet at that time, when they embarked on their policies, neither the British nor the Jews nor anyone else could clearly foresee the eventual departure of the British or, in so far as they did, that this would mean Jews and Arabs confronting each other in enmity. The state of Israel, and therewith the sense of injustice of the Arabs, was less the outcome of an original, deliberate intention than the outcome of action and interaction over many years, culminating in the mid-1940s in the problem of how to react to the withdrawal of the British and to the threat of war with the Arabs. As always in the origins of disputes, what was done by all the parties was different from what each separately would have liked to do, and original intention was moulded out of all recognition by the development of circumstances.

4. *The Origins of Disputes Between States*

Of the various kinds of disputes between states, the most frequent is that in which two states or groups of states are in direct conflict with one another about a particular piece of territory or some other possession or the government of a state or the like.

Sometimes several disputes of this kind go on at the same time about the same thing. The Austrian question from 1945–55, which can also be called for convenience the Austria dispute, consisted of at least two disputes; between the Western powers and the Soviet Union; and between Austria and the Soviet Union. The former dispute depended for its existence on the latter in some respects and *vice versa* in others. The two disputes were inextricably connected and yet different from the point of view of those involved in them and raising different problems for them.

More than this, even Austria's dispute with the Soviet Union was in fact not one, but manifold. The most serious issue was the continued Soviet occupation of part of the country but there was also the issue of the disposal of German assets and others still more detailed. In general, any dispute, either from the outset or over the life of it, is on a close view a tissue of component disputes, sometimes small, transient episodes conducted by junior officials, sometimes small points but enduring, sometimes great matters in their own right. The German question was not merely a pattern of interconnected disputes between the Western and Eastern powers, the Federal Republic and the Eastern Powers, the Federal Republic and the Democratic Republic, and so on; each of these in turn was a set of disputes about cooperation, reconstitution, elections, reparations and much more; and a series of disputes of which the periodic incidents and crises over Berlin were the most important.

These distinctions are worth noticing as a preliminary for two reasons. First, we have to be ready to accept that the usage of the word "dispute" is a shifting one. Within the general meaning of a conflict in which something is demanded as a matter of right, it can be used now broadly, now narrowly. What in one context can be called one of the issues in a dispute, can in another be called a dispute. Second, the more substantial point, it is plainly important in the practical handling of any dispute to try to decide whether it is part of a broader dispute and in what way, and how it connects with the disputes of other states about the same thing or with quite different disputes, and which of them is the key to the whole.

Before launching out on a discussion of inter-state disputes, it may be helpful to indicate briefly the course we shall take. First, we shall try to illustrate the various reasons why states value the things they dispute for. In the course of this, it will continually be obvious that for at least one of the antagonists, the value of the thing depends entirely on their belief that it is theirs. Accordingly, we shall next try to suggest the reasons why states think things are theirs. Finally, we must discuss the fact that, just as in internal disputes, the outbreak or avoidance of disputes between states depends greatly on whether they think the thing worth the wider cost and on how they judge comparative power.

Interests and Honour

A state may value a thing primarily or even exclusively because it is interested in the thing in itself. In 1958, a dispute broke out between Iceland and Britain because Iceland claimed that its territorial waters should henceforth extend to twelve miles rather than as previously, four. What was at stake was the fishing of these waters, a matter of the deepest importance to Iceland's economy and of some importance to Britain's. More widely, what was at stake for Britain among others was the effect of this move in the current world-wide question of the extent of territorial waters. What was not at stake to any great degree was national honour. Economic success is a source of honour but Iceland was not a competitor with Britain in this; it was simply a competitor in the fisheries. It was plainly not seeking to humiliate Britain; it wanted only the fish.

States may, on the other hand, value a thing not through intrinsic interest but precisely as a matter of honour. First, contrast with Britain's dispute with Iceland, its dispute with Spain over Gibraltar. Britain in 1963 still had some strategic interest in Gibraltar and was also concerned for the well-being of its inhabitants; but the best way to express Britain's attitude is to say that it was concerned for its honour. The British rejected the Spanish demand because to submit to it would be to lose honour before the Spanish nation, the people of Gibraltar, the world at large, and, perhaps above all, before themselves.

The British attitude in the dispute illustrates each of the three aspects of honour. Honour is won and lost by success and failure in activities which men prize; it is won and lost by acting or not acting according to a certain code of conduct; and it is at stake in any dispute in the special form of personal or national dignity. Acceptance of the Spanish claim to Gibraltar would have meant to the British the loss of a vestige and symbol of past imperial success; the abandonment of a community of people who counted on them for protection; and the humiliation to their dignity of suffering the loss of what they believed was rightly theirs.

Spain, for its part, was probably not seeking purposely to humiliate Britain; it had other motives. Sometimes, however, the humiliation of the opponent is indeed the purpose or at least a valued effect. China in 1967 appears to have had no interest in ending British rule in Hong Kong; it seems to have approved disturbances only in order to show that the territory was in its power. Cuba's agrarian reform law of 1959, involving the expropriation of United States companies, was both a matter of intrinsic interest in that it was directed to the control of a source of wealth, and a matter of honour in the sense of Cuban control of the Cuban economy. It gave still further satisfaction as a blow struck at the United States.

Cuban satisfaction sprang ultimately from feelings of revenge for past denial of what was due to their interests and honour. Such feelings were important in many another dispute. The incident of the flags which touched off the Panama Canal dispute in 1964 was a symbolic exchange of vengeful insults and, in the dispute as a whole, the Panamanian people were eager to see the United States atone for past injustices. Egyptians and all Arabs exulted at the nationalisation of the Suez Canal Company in 1956 above all as revenge against Britain and France. Iranians rejoiced at the nationalisation of the Anglo-Iranian Oil Company in 1950 as vengeance, if not exactly against Britain, certainly against the Company. Yugoslavia claimed Trieste in 1945 in part as revenge on Italy for past sufferings. In all these disputes, the worth of the possessions contended for was so great that it is impossible to say definitely whether interest or the passion for revenge was the major motive. It is at least suggestive that if for a moment in imagination we leave out this passion, conflict between the sides instead of cooperation becomes scarcely credible.

Reputation for Power

Whether states value a thing in terms of interest or of honour, they always in addition value it in terms of reputation for power. The seizure of the thing will mean a loss of reputation to the one side and a gain to the other, perhaps with far-reaching implications.

Honour in its various aspects and this factor of reputation for power are frequently nowadays given the single name "prestige". Prestige is properly an extravagant form of honour and reputation, showy rather than solid, optical not real. It is the form sought by the national leader as wonder-worker, dazzling mankind with his brilliance, and sometimes by whole nations, a common enough occurrence, for which we may grudge the loss of its own specific word.

Whatever this factor of reputation for power is called, it enters into all disputes in some degree, even between non-competitor states, still more between competitors or enemies, and most of all if it is clear that the opponent's intention is precisely to ruin the reputation for power. States are deeply concerned as to whether the exposure of weakness will encourage the opponent or other states to make yet further claims. Even in its dispute with Iceland, Britain had to consider the effect of successful defiance by Iceland on its reputation. When the Suez Canal Company was nationalised, a major issue at stake was whether Britain and France any longer had the will or ability to defend their possessions in the old way in the contemporary world. There is as yet no certainty about why China insisted on its territorial claims in Ladakh to the point of invasion of India in 1962; yet we can certainly say that even if a blow at India's reputation for power and hence influence was not part of the intention, and even if Indians themselves were loathe to recognise the implications, this effect was nonetheless at stake.

Simultaneously in the autumn of 1962, reputation for power was the crux of the Cuba missiles crisis. We noticed in an earlier chapter how in 1945–6, the United States, for various reasons including this one, would not tolerate the unpredictable thrusts of the Soviet Union. In exactly similar terms, President Kennedy denounced the Soviet action in Cuba as a deliberately provocative and unjustified change in the *status quo*. In neither the one set of cases nor the other were American interests in the countries in question the basic concern. Nor yet was strategy the heart of the matter whether in the old form of the Dardanelles or the new form of the disposition of nuclear missiles in Cuba, Turkey, and elsewhere. The essential point in American eyes was whether the Soviet Union was to be allowed to act suddenly, secretly and drastically anywhere it liked in the world, even in Latin America, in disregard of United States power.

Security

States sometimes value the things they dispute for, not in themselves, but as a means to other things. For example, it seems clear that the Soviet Union, in maintaining its occupation of part of Austria for ten years, was not much concerned with Austria; it valued its position there in relation to Germany and as a possible piece to play in bargaining over the whole European settlement. Its purpose in Cuba may have been confined to the protection of Cuba; but more likely it wished to collect a bargaining piece in relation to other disputes with the United States or to demonstrate its power with an eye either to these disputes or to controlling its socialist rival, China.[1]

[1] See Adam B. Ulam, *Expansion and Coexistence, The History of Soviet Foreign Policy* 1917–67, London, 1968, Chapter X.

Some might think it an obvious gambit for states to raise a dispute in one section of the world as a means to getting satisfaction in another; and yet at least since 1945, this does not seem to have been approved state practice. Such tactics offend the sense of justice of one of the leaders of world politics, the United States, and are suspect to many others. Similarly, as regards disputes actually in being, the United States and others show a marked distaste so far as enemies are concerned for bargaining away a stand in one dispute for satisfaction in another. These disputes, they think, are matters of human merit and need, and horse-trading, chess playing and general machiavellianism are not allowed.

The most momentous form of valuing a thing as a means rather than as an end in itself is the question of security. A piece of territory, an installation, control of the government of a state or the like give the means, strategically or in terms of resources, to protect interests and honour. On this account, states want things and wish to prevent others getting them.

In practice, it is often difficult to distinguish between the search for security and intrinsic interest in a thing. A state may scarcely know itself which it wants, some arguing one aspect, some another, some both. The dispute between the Western powers and the Soviet Union in 1945 about German reparations was perhaps in broad terms clear enough. It was about intrinsic interest, about the wealth to be taken from Germany. Even so, underlying this, were conflicting views on the economic and general settlement of Europe with important security implications for the future.

The interconnected disputes on the control of Germany and the reconstitution of the Axis satellites and liberated states in eastern Europe were even more ambiguous. The Soviet Union had a strong interest in the economic resources of Germany and of eastern Europe and in many other lines of political and cultural activity there. It probably wished to close these territories to the West because it wished to exclude Western competition in these matters. There was the honour too of the aggrandisement of Russia on a scale undreamt of by the Czars. At the same time, the Russians had just fought the greatest and most terrible war in their history. They wanted control of the defeated Axis states for security against them. They wanted control of Poland as an hereditary enemy; there was a long history of injuries between them of which this was the latest stage. Their desire to have their own way in the region was increased by their disagreement with the Western powers on how best to achieve security and by their suspicions of the Western powers. These suspicions, Marxist-Leninist and more traditional, sprang from real evils and injuries in the past and from the individual reaction of a particular nation to them.

Probably, on balance, security was the dominant motive of the Soviet Union; it was certainly so on the Western side. The Western powers wanted "the open door" in eastern Europe, freedom to pursue political, commercial and cultural activities there. Honour also was involved, both in the sense of a desire to share in the great work of reorganising Europe and in the sense of a feeling of loyalty to the liberated states. But above all, there was the security question. They wanted to settle Germany and eastern Europe on such principles that these countries would never again disrupt the peace of the world. Rapidly, another anxiety overshadowed this. What was the significance for the West of Soviet actions? What inference was to be drawn from their treatment of Poland and other eastern European states? What was the implication of their abandonment of war-time cooperation, their unilateralism, their ruthless disregard for Western interests and honour? Fear of the Soviet Union as a threat to the security of the West began to grow.

The Ideological Factor

We should add here the ideological question. For nearly a generation, the intellectual leaders of Western and Soviet societies had been engaged in an ideological dispute about the right structure of society; and, given the cultural influence of these countries, it was a momentous dispute for the course of politics in all others in the world. On the other hand, it would be an error to describe the conflicts between the Western Powers and the Soviet Union as ideological disputes. The American people did not want their government to embark on an ideological crusade, and there is little to suggest that successive Soviet governments were concerned with this either. Their business was foreign policy, and concern for the justice of the arrangements under which other societies lived was not and never could be the heart of this.

Though the disputes between the Western Powers and the Soviet Union were not about ideology, these states were nonetheless concerned with ideology in important ways. Some people in the West cared about the political arrangements of eastern European countries for one reason or another, and when the Soviet Union ended their independence, were outraged by the enforced introduction of Communism. Many others liked the thought that countries abroad should imitate their national way of life, and whenever Soviet actions put an abrupt stop to this, were angered by the affront to national honour. All this was equally true on the Russian side. They for their part, took pride in the spread of Communism and were outraged and humiliated by its suppression.

Far more important than this, ideology was a matter of security and in consequence, by the usual paradox, a matter of enormous fear. Whenever the Western powers or the Soviet Union took control of another state, for instance, Germany, Japan, and the eastern European countries in 1945, they immediately began an ideological revolution, remaking the society so far as they could in their own image and likeness. This, they thought, was the way to ensure a peace-loving state or a friendly neighbour or a dependent state. This line of thought had fearful implications for relations between them. It was obvious to the Western and Soviet peoples that if their enemy should ever conquer them, they would not simply suffer some national loss and humiliation; their entire way of life would be overthrown. Accordingly, whenever they saw their enemy threatening or crushing the rights of smaller states, they not merely feared for the rights of their own but did so with an intense awareness of these enormous, further stakes. Not merely the standing, possessions, and territorial integrity and sovereignty of their state were in jeopardy but their whole society. In this way, the fear and hatred behind demand and resistance in the East-West disputes was vastly increased; and there was all the time the added dread that fear and hatred might one day tilt the balance of the enemy's calculations in favour of war.

The Sense of Justice

With this, we may turn to the second main aspect of the origins of disputes between states, the sense of justice. In each of the conflicts we have mentioned, it was the very essence of the matter that the states concerned were not simply competing to outdo each other in extending their influence, in setting up new installations around the world, in commercial success, in tonnage of fish landed at their ports, or whatever it might be. They were disputing over who should have a piece of territory held by one of them; over who should control the affairs of a state, the nation itself or foreigners; over who should own an existing installation; over what the boundaries of fisheries should be; over "ours", "yours", "theirs". It is this element, this infusion of the conflict with a sense of legitimacy which gave a special character to these conflicts and which brings to life and makes comprehensible the value that the states attached to the things contended for.

Ordinary competition between states involves honour, but in disputes, this concern is immeasurably sharpened. To be beaten in the competition for allies, influence, trade, the growth of the economy and the rest is a setback for a state; but this is nothing to the humiliation of suffering the seizure of what it considers "ours".

A deliberate blow at the honour of another state may spring, as we have seen, from feelings of revenge for past injuries. An over-riding determination to achieve security at whatever cost to others may spring from fear based on bitter experience. This is as much as to say that the background of bad relations from which many disputes arise is precisely a conviction of past injustice.

A state takes revenge on another or ruins its reputation for power not by ordinary competition but exactly by successfully asserting a claim to what its opponent considers its own. If a state can see some plausible ground for a demand on it by another, it will dispute for it mainly according to its degree of interest in the thing; but if it can see no plausible ground, only enmity or aggrandisement, it will dispute with all the determination that springs from wider fears for its whole security.

It is when a great power can see no justification for some sudden thrust by a rival, affecting its reputation for power, that it demands withdrawal. It is when it sees not simply a conflict of interests between some smaller state and its rival but when it sees a dispute over interests which are rights that it demands to participate. And it is when it sees the rights of the smaller state over-ridden by the rival, without what it considers good cause, that it begins to fear for what is its own.

Finally, it is exactly because these conflicts are about something which is "ours" that they are so serious for the internal politics and structure of the states concerned. If a government as currently formed or a state as currently constituted fails in promoting the interests and honour of the nation in the competition of international life, there may be pressure for change. But if it fails to secure what is "ours", a government is likely to be overthrown and a state to lose the loyalty of its subjects. Legitimacy internally is closely connected with the vindication of legitimacy abroad.

What then are the grounds on which states think that something is theirs or due to them or to other smaller states? In beginning our attempt to answer this question, we should warn that this section of our book will be the crudest and most primitive of all. There is no area of the study of international politics so important and so little developed as the systematic, comparative discussion, case by case, of reason and unreason, justice and injustice in the demands that states make on one another in their disputes.

It may be agreed, however, that the starting-point from which states, like individuals, think on the issue of justice is existing possession, the *status quo*. Whoever has a thing, it is his unless another can show cause why not. Whatever the existing position, that is right until someone can show better. If a state which demands or makes change cannot show this, it is suspect as a force for chaos. Alarm for security in the widest sense is instantly aroused. The *status quo* has a prima facie justification against the revisionist in all eyes, usually even his own. The onus is on the revisionist.

The grounds on which states attack existing possession or affirm it against attack fall into two groups: on the one hand, historical, geographical and ethnic grounds; on the other, various forms of merit or need. The peculiarity of the first group is that they are ancillary to the second and are rarely, if ever, put forward in isolation. Their function in conflict, like international law in one of its facets, is to identify and delimit the claim, not to act as the substantial ground.

When, therefore, Morocco claimed Mauritania as part of its ancient empire or Spain claimed Gibraltar in terms of the Treaty of Utrecht, nothing so absurd was being claimed as that the world should be reorganised simply in fidelity to the past. The historical element was merely the framework within which substantial injustice, past, present or threatened, was alleged. In Spain's claim to Gibraltar from Britain, or in Indonesia's claim to West Irian from the Netherlands, or in the claims to the Suez and Panama Canals and the Anglo-Iranian Oil Company, the sheer facts of geographical location had, it is true, a certain appeal to all minds; but these facts were still not the substantial ground of the claims as though states should say that whoever is nearest to a thing should have it.

Ethnic arguments played a part in feelings that Kashmir should go to Pakistan, Cyprus to Greece, certain border areas of Ethiopia and Kenya to Somalia. Yet the force of the argument did not lie in a flat assertion that because a group of people belonged to the same culture, speech or race, they should therefore form part of the same state. The force of the argument was definitional, identifying a comprehensible group in human affairs as the object of a claim. Substantial grounds had then to be argued why the existing position should be overthrown and they should be incorporated into a state. The historic leaders in the formation of nation-states, having developed the concept of the nation, had also to argue the need for it to have its own state. Even the Nazis, who came nearer than anyone else to urging sheer race as a reason in itself, felt obliged to plead not just that the Sudeten Germans were Germans, but that they, and in them the German nation, were suffering injustice.

The substantial grounds of claim and denial, of the sense of justice and injustice, are, as we say, various forms of merit and need. What is meant by feelings of merit can be exemplified first by recalling the feelings of the British and Americans in their disputes with the Soviet Union over the control and reconstitution of Germany and eastern Europe They believed that their opinions and interests were to be heeded by the Russians as a matter of right, earned by their share in the struggle against the Axis. Their right was not given by the Yalta and Potsdam agreements; it was the right of victory in a just cause.

To take a different form of the feeling of merit, the British felt that the Anglo-Iranian Oil Company and the Suez Canal were "theirs", the Americans felt that the Panama Canal was "theirs", not merely because they were the existing possessors but because it was they who had built and developed them. The Egyptians, the Iranians, the Panamanians on their side also felt merit. They each had some sense that existing possession of territory or resources had been over-ridden in the past at the time of the making of these installations by the British and Americans; the historical element in their claims contained the substance of a sense of past injustice. But, in addition, there was the feeling of revenge for more general injuries in the past to the interests and honour of their nations. To say that a state values a thing for revenge is to say that it is convinced that it merits a thing in just payment for old wrongs.

In the climate of world opinion in those years, there was also a trace of a sense of justice grounded on economic need. The British and Americans were rich, the Egyptians, Iranians and Panamanians were poor. However, at that time, poverty had not as yet been fully elaborated and established as a ground of demand between states, and in talking of need, we must draw our examples from other areas of politics.

Among individuals, there is a right of necessity to do in special circumstances what may not ordinarily be done. Actions may be taken, things may be demanded in a way which is only justified by grave cause. This right of necessity can, at the same time, be seen as part of a wider right, the right given by need. We speak most commonly of the right of necessity when the occasion is urgent as at a moment of crisis and imminent danger, but the needs involved are also wide and long-standing. Certain things are always required by men, not as a matter of individual ambition but of common human need.

All this arises equally in inter-state politics and with it all the problems involved. "Necessity is the tyrant's plea." Individuals in their private affairs, states in all their affairs, act as their own judges, ambitious for their own needs, resistant to those of others. Yet, though this is true and could not be otherwise, it is also true that some states at some times are more ambitious than others, some less resistant than others, and that they handle the problem of judging necessity and weighing need against need better or worse.

There are no rules, and could be no rules, for condoning or condemning such actions as the British willingness to invade Norway in 1940 in anticipation of the Germans, or the Allied invasion of Iran at the height of the War. Equally plainly, there are no rules which could decide on the justice or injustice of the Soviet Union's actions in its search for security in Germany and eastern Europe in 1945. The Soviet Union, the United States, Britain, all believed that they had a right of proven need to re-arrange the affairs of the region. The statesmen of each had to weigh the facts of the problem, guided not by rules, but only by the many relevant partial propositions which they had in their minds about the nature of inter-state politics. The Western powers believed that the Soviet Union weighed wrongly, concluded wrongly and did what was not needed for its security. They believed that the search for security neither required nor justified the character of Soviet actions both in relation to themselves and to the peoples of the region. Because they could see no adequate justification, they began to challenge Soviet actions; they began to think the Soviet Union ambitious and to fear for their security and to shift their policies towards strengthening it; and so "the Cold War" began.

One of the conflicting needs involved in this calculation was the need for national self-determination. This principle, one of the most prominent and complex in the politics of recent generations, may be summarised, in the first place roughly, as the belief that for men to pursue their interests and maintain their dignity to the full they need to be allowed to determine who shall rule them. It was this belief that gave a sense of justice to the Polish government-in-exile in its dealings with the Soviet Union in 1943–45 and to the Austrian government in calling for the ending of the Soviet occupation of the eastern part of the country. The Western Powers also believed in this need and it added to their sense of right regarding eastern Europe. Communist doctrine, on the other hand, held that the nation was an obsolescent concept and that the good of men everywhere lay in rule by the vanguard of the proletariat led by the Soviet Communist Party.

Closer consideration of the Polish and Austrian demands reveals the importance for states, in their attitudes to self-determination, of two further concepts. First, they have regard to the *status quo*. Second, their concern is with precisely the nation.

In the Austria case, for example, the *status quo* was that the eastern Austrians were ruled by Austrians; the Soviet occupation was considered on all sides, even the Soviet, to be abnormal. Accordingly, the Austrian government did not feel called upon to argue on a fundamental level that the eastern Austrians ought to be ruled by Austrians. All accepted this, and the dispute was about Soviet delay in allowing it. When, in contrast, a state wishes to alter the *status quo* so as to take a group of people under its rule, it does feel called upon to argue. If, for example, Austria had claimed the South Tirol after 1946, it would in this instance have argued the case for saying that the South Tirolese ought to be ruled by Austrians.

We could perhaps safely conjecture the grounds on which Austria would have argued. However, let us take an actual dispute in another part of the world, Somalia's claim against Kenya. Somalia argued, in the first place, in terms of the preferences and interests of the people of the disputed area. An enquiry held in the area by the British shortly before Kenya's independence showed that a very high proportion of the people would have preferred on independence to join Somalia. In detail, Somalia could argue that the existing border cut through the economic and social system of the people of the area and was plainly artificial in terms of their interests.

Arguments based on enquiries, plebiscites and elections as showing the interests of the particular group of people in question, have enjoyed increasing cogency in recent generations. No doubt, in this case, they contributed to Somalia's sense of justice in its claim. The weakness of these arguments is that states, even as claimants, do not believe that they are fundamental. States are concerned fundamentally not with the interests of particular groups of people, but with the interests of the nation, a more important and, at the same time, often delusive entity. A claimant state takes up the cause of the particular group mainly on the grounds that they are its nationals and that their severance under another state is an injustice to the nation.

As to why it asserts that they are properly its nationals, the only reason may be ethnic homogeneity, but usually the ethnic argument acts with historical and geographical arguments as a means of defining a substantial wrong done to the nation. For example, the group of people have been torn from the nation by conquest in the past and must be restored to it now.

The opponent, for its part, sees that the interests of the particular group are not the fundamental point, denies that they are to be considered the other's nationals, is confident that they will come to feel part of its nation whatever their ethnic stock, rebuts the suggestion that the *status quo* can be overthrown on grounds of past injustice even if such existed, asserts that the whole affair is sheer national aggrandisement, and, in sum, rejects the claim utterly.

In this way, the self-determination of a particular group of people is greatly complicated, perhaps even frustrated, by their own and others' thoughts on their nationality and by the fact that they are being claimed by another state. When a whole nation seeks self-determination against an empire, these problems do not ordinarily arise. Yet even here there are episodes which remind us that it is always the nation that counts for statesmen and citizens rather than particular groups of people, the nation which must have justice.

For example, the sense of justice which surrounded Indonesia's aim to drive the Dutch from West Irian was based on the need for self-determination. How could this be, given that the Papuans themselves had expressed no views and the direction of their need could scarcely be guessed? The explanation was that self-determination did not relate to the Papuans exactly but to the Indonesian nation and the Afro-Asian nations which supported it. In their original struggle for independence from the Netherlands, the Indonesian leaders had had to define the extent of the nation for which they were struggling and they decided, after some controversy, that it included all the peoples of the Netherlands East Indies. The Papuans of

West Irian were now to be freed as part of the nation. For the Afro-Asian nations generally, it was at least clear that the Netherlands, an imperial power and long the enemy of self-determination, should be driven out of Afro-Asia completely. As to who should succeed the Netherlands as regards West Irian, who else but Indonesia?

On the same grounds, various Afro-Asian states supported Spain in its claim to Gibraltar. Mainly, no doubt, they wished to harass Britain on quite different problems, but partly they were convinced that Britain, as an imperialist enemy of national self-determination, must be driven out of all overseas possessions, whatever the alleged views of the Gibraltarians themselves. Again, India claimed Goa not so much in terms of the wish or need of the inhabitants of Goa in particular, but in terms of completing the self-rule of the Indian nation as defined ethnically, historically and geographically.

We should add that if the Netherlands, Britain and Portugal had been able to grant independence to the people concerned previously, the Indonesian, Spanish and Indian claims would have lost this particular source of strength. Morocco's claim to Mauritania illustrates this. When that territory was ruled by the French, Moroccans felt deep conviction and gained much sympathy in their demands that it be made independent under their historic rule. But later when Mauritania had been made independent separately, Morocco's claim, now no longer against an imperial power but against an independent state, dwindled rapidly both in fervour and support.

Just as a dispute may centre on a part of the nation, so it may centre on an aspect of national life and yet still be grounded on the need for national self-determination. This was so, for example, in the disputes over the Suez and Panama Canals and the Anglo-Iranian Oil Company and, indeed, in most disputes over natural resources and foreign commercial activity. In addition to the elements of redress and revenge for the past in the claims to these installations, they were looked upon as continuing vestiges of imperialism or as quasi-imperial in themselves. They represented foreign domination of the economy and, through the economy, of the whole life of the nation.

There is a final form in which feelings of merit or need create a sense of justice, a negative form, negative and yet nonetheless passionate. This arises when, in the course of international affairs, a possession, so to speak, comes loose or threatens to come loose from ownership. Then the feeling is not so much that the state has a positive right to the thing, as that no other state has a better right to it and that it would be unjust for another state to seize it.

This feeling arose in its bitterest form in the Kashmir dispute and was, indeed, the deepest element in the sense of justice of the two sides. Kashmir, at the time of partition and independence, was left vacillating between India and Pakistan, its status as yet indeterminate. The passion with which the two states believed it should be theirs sprang not from a sense of positive right under the legal agreements on princely decision or under the contrary principle of ethnic self-determination. On these points, the two states contradicted themselves in the two cases of Kashmir and Junagadh. It sprang from the conviction that it would be intolerably unjust that the other should have Kashmir or Junagadh. This was the counterpart of the right of revenge, the conviction that the age-old enemy, the secessionists who had divided India, the oppressors who had made division inevitable, should not be rewarded for their injustice with any inch of territory which could be kept from them.

In a milder form, these same feelings played some part in the Gibraltar and Kuwait disputes. As in the Indian sub-continent, so now in the Mediterranean and the Middle East, Britain was withdrawing one by one from its possessions and protectorates, some of them miniature, valuable, vulnerable, and, most obviously in the case of Kuwait, a possible object of seizure by neighbours. Under these circumstances, it seemed right to make a claim with whatever arguments could be mustered if only as a sign that it would be unjust for anyone else to succeed to the British.

With this, we may end our discussion of the issue of justice. We have avoided comment on the validity of the various grounds on which states say that things are theirs or due to them or to other smaller states. Judgement can only be exercised when these are deployed in detail in a given dispute, argument set against argument. Nonetheless, we have perhaps said enough to indicate that the cries of justice in disputes between states are not all of equal worth; that some have great merit or need behind them, and others, little but ambition and greed; and that states in assessing the legitimacy of another's actions and in deciding in the light of this their response, are indeed engaged in a real, not an illusory, task.

The Factor of Power

The conflict of ambition and justice in and between the claims of states brings us naturally to the final factor in the origins of inter-state disputes, power. Some disputes are to some extent thrust upon the parties by circumstances, and, in that case, the factor of power in explaining their origins is less important. Some disputes, on the other hand, arise from a more or less voluntary and calculated challenge by one state to another. In such cases, part of the calculation is how making this claim will affect the security and promotion of all the other interests of the state and its honour among states. The thing demanded is, after all, only one of a range of things valued. Links of activity with the challenged state, political and commercial and so on, will be jeopardized; links of activity in cooperation with it, for instance, a security alliance, will be threatened also; so will such links with any other states which favour the challenged party. Then too, wealth will be affected, both in commercial activities disrupted and in the resources expended. Is the dispute worth all this? Is the thing sufficiently important, is it vital in terms of interests and honour?

These questions are from another point of view, questions of power. What are the prospects of successfully coercing the other side? Can the network of activities linking the two states with each other and with the world of states, be manipulated by diplomacy so as to put superior pressure on the other side? What of propaganda, economic pressures, armed force, the possibility of war?

As to the state which is challenged, it too is involved in these same calculations. There is, to be sure, the immense difference that only in extreme circumstances can a challenged state choose not to dispute, that is, when the power of the other side is plainly overwhelming; otherwise, it cannot simply give way. Still, its estimate of power makes a great difference to the manner in which it takes up the challenge.

These calculations are the element of prudence in justice and of expediency in ambition. They are subject to the greatest error. Interests are hard to evaluate, honour is hard; a state may take decisions, preferring one interest to another, honour in one direction as opposed to another, which later it bitterly regrets. The sense of power of a state, derived from its national self-awareness, may be quite different from its usable power, even in general, to say nothing of the particular dispute before it. The opponent, his resources, his abilities, the tenacity with which he will struggle for his cause, are all equally difficult to assess correctly. Every aspect of these calculations is handled, not just amid the normal confusion of the conduct of affairs, but under the special pressures of urgency, high emotion and popular clamour engendered by a dispute.

We have been speaking so far in terms of foreign policy calculations. It is worthwhile also to put the matter in terms of the international system. What we are saying is that for the origins of inter-state disputes, the presence or absence of links of interest and honour between states is crucial. Where such links are overwhelmingly strong between two states, for instance, when there is an urgent common threat to their entire national security, they will not dispute at all. When the links of interest are moderately strong, their dispute will be cautious as for instance in the case of Japan and the United States in the matter of Okinawa. When such links develop between two states which perhaps have disputed for generations, their dispute may dwindle and become soluble as, for instance, the Saar dispute between France and Germany.

In these links of interest and honour, the more important, on the whole, are not those which run directly between them but those which relate to disputes with other states. Political, commercial, cultural and other activities in common readily become envenomed by any dispute between them and are more easily sacrificed than activities in cooperation with one another towards outsiders. Moreover, in the contemporary world, the great majority of states, African, Asian, Latin American, have, thanks to their past, very weak direct links with one another. What restrains dispute among the great number of new states in the world is, among other factors, linkage in relation to the great powers.

Links of interest and honour are not the same thing as relations of friendship, indifference, competition and enmity. These arise from ethnic kinship, ideological and cultural similarity, shared experience and the like in the case of friendship; from similarity of scale in the case of competition; past disputes or present ambition in the case of enmity. Relations of enmity contribute, as we saw, to the outbreak of disputes and, equally, relations of friendship contribute to their avoidance. The more friendly two states are, the less likely is the issue of justice to arise.

Still, it remains true that, between states, what is crucial is the links of interest and honour. Even between competitors or states with the deepest of past grievances, disputes do not arise so long as cooperation is to their present mutual advantage. Many of the countries of Europe are competitors, many hate each other cordially, most have many grievances which they could turn into disputes, and yet they hang together in alliances against common threats without much dispute because it is to their greater advantage.

We should illustrate this series of points on the subject of power, at least briefly, from the disputes which we have so often cited. To take the smallest, Britain and Iceland were involved in a considerable network of mutual interests. Each had to balance Iceland's risk, notably to its exports, in a prolonged quarrel with Britain against the pressures on Britain for concession; that is, Iceland's significant but shaky membership of NATO, the drift of international opinion revealed by the maritime conference shortly before the outbreak, the risk to Britain's honour of forceful action against a small state. In contrast, the reasons of Somalia and its neighbours for disputing were comparatively unrestrained by reasons for not disputing. The same was true of India and Portugal over Goa and, to a lesser extent, in many another of the disputes we have mentioned.

In the two disputes concerning Cuba, the one between Cuba and the United States, the other between the United States and the Soviet Union on the nuclear missile base, the calculation of interests centred mainly on the power aspect. Who would prove to have the margin of power? In each case, we see at every turn in the story how power depends not just on material resources and strategic disposition but on factors of the mind, on relative willingness to use force and on the relative importance which each side attaches to the interest at stake. Interests moreover were backed by a sense of justice of varying strength. The United States was less concerned to win than Cuba; it was more concerned to win than the Soviet Union. Therefore it lost; therefore it won.

We see how dwindling links of interest can encourage dispute very clearly in the Suez Canal case. Until 1955, the Egyptian leaders, whatever their aspirations, tensions and conflicts with Britain and France, were always constrained within the traditional pattern of links with them and other Western powers. In 1955, entirely new perspectives of non-alignment and of rapprochement with the Communist states opened to them, and to that extent the path to dispute was cleared.

It is, as we say, these links of interest which count whether in restraining a dispute or in the power to fight it, not the state of relations in the sense of the feelings of two nations about each other. In the Anglo-Iranian Oil Company dispute, Mossadeq appears hardly to have calculated the relative pressures which the two sides might be able to exert on each other. One reason for this was probably that, despite the passion against the Company, relations with Britain were friendly and Britain's current government was a past enemy of imperialism and a present exponent of nationalisation at home. Mossadeq could, perhaps scarcely credit that Britain might face him with anything so drastic as the economic throttling of Iran until it compromised. Equally calamitously, India's bold style of dealing with the border issue with China when this first arose was determined, not in an atmosphere of calculation, but in an atmosphere of the five principles of peaceful coexistence, of Indian and Chinese brotherly love. The Indians were reluctant to accept that friendly words are not friendship and give even less grounds for the expectation of non-violence.

The Dynamic Aspect of Disputes

In these comments on the factor of power, we have spoken continually of calculation and yet we may suspect that in fact many states in many disputes calculate little. This may be through recklessness; but it may also be through the extreme difficulty of the task, given that disputes are not static, as our discussion so far may have seemed to imply, but essentially dynamic in every aspect.

What is important here is the manner in which disputes between states often grow from small original moves. Sometimes, it is true, a dispute begins abruptly with some drastic action; then, the enemy of calculation is the pressure of crisis; decisions are taken, pronouncements are made which cannot afterwards be recalled. More often, a dispute begins with minor indications, minor remarks and minor actions, a tentative, uncertain probing of the ground by one side, hardly noticed by the other. The dispute is already under way before either side is sure that there will, in fact, be a dispute and before it has seriously measured the possible implications.

Whether they grasp the existence of a dispute abruptly or slowly, states still make their initial decisions in deep uncertainty as to relative power. There can be no question of a once-for-all, cut-and-dried calculation. "On s'engage, puis on voit". It is true that states, like military commanders, engage with a greater or lesser understanding of basic possibilities, but to ask for anything in this respect is to ask for much. The ability to see deep from the outset into the realities of a situation, to see far into how it may unfold, is exceptional even among the leaders of nations, to say nothing of the nations clamouring behind them.

There is one further aspect of the dynamic nature of disputes. Disputes arise because circumstances are, in one way or another, favourable, tempting or even compelling. In the origins of some disputes, this factor is very marked. It was, for instance, of the greatest importance that the first postwar disputes between the Western powers and the Soviet Union arose, not so to say directly, but in the course of their conflict with the Axis. They did not set out to dispute with one another; rather they got themselves into a certain position in the context of one set of circumstances and then began to dispute about these in another. The sheer fact that the Soviet Union was already in Germany, Austria and Poland was half, if only half, of the making of the disputes over those countries.

Circumstances can be influential in other ways. Somalia, for instance, on independence inherited the border dispute with Ethiopia from its former rulers. Little decision was required to dispute; rather, a decision would have been required not to dispute. Moreover, at the time of Somalia's independence, Kenya was in the midst of the same process and it was scarcely conceivable that Somalia should not take a hand in the protracted discussions of the arrangements for the new state. Similarly, Morocco raised its claim to Mauritania as part of an external dispute with France and remained saddled with it as an external dispute with Mauritania. The same was true of its claim to a border area against Algeria.

Perhaps the clearest cases of the force of circumstances are those in which, to use our earlier phrase, a possession is coming loose from ownership. In ordinary times, Yugoslavia might well not have claimed Trieste; it saw a compelling opportunity in the turmoil of war, the defeat of Italy, and the approaching settlement. The outstanding example is, however, that of Kashmir. The Indians and Pakistanis certainly had every disposition to quarrel with one another but the fact that the future of this border principality was not settled before the ending of British rule, created a blatant opportunity, a scarcely resistible temptation.

The Influence of Internal Politics

There remains one whole level of explanations of the origins of disputes between states which we have so far scarcely touched on in our discussion: the internal politics of the states concerned. We must mention this briefly now. For it is clear that all the beliefs of states about the value of things, the justice of their cause, and their power to win are the expression of an intricate pattern of debate, judgement and decision within the state. Moreover, not only are external aims weighed against internal costs in the ordinary manner, but structural and sectional concerns may be involved. Governments and citizens may have to consider whether external dispute will be harmful or beneficial with regard to internal tensions threatening the structure of their society. Governments must consider the bearing of a dispute on their retention of office or power, and groups within the community, the effect on their particular interests. More widely, the whole condition and mood of a nation will affect its readiness to plunge into foreign dispute.

If we intend to say little about these factors, it is because generalisations seem at present impossible and perhaps always will be impossible. It is easy to see that a government without the internal problem of Quassim in Iraq or Sukarno in Indonesia might never have taken up the Kuwait and Malaysia disputes; that the political struggle within Morocco had a bearing on the dispute over Mauritania; that the exaltation of great victory influenced Soviet actions in eastern Europe. But it seems that something of the sort, if in a lesser degree, can be said of every state in every dispute, and, furthermore has to be said differently. Proposed generalisations about the disposition of states to dispute based on their form of government, their class structure, their wealth or poverty, their internal unity or discord and the like, have all, so far at least, proved unconvincing. It seems as though the internal factors bearing on the decision to dispute or not to dispute differ in each case and must accordingly be left to the historian.

We will take this line of thought further, though even more tentatively. In the ordinary course of foreign policy, in the ordinary process of competition between states, it may be that internal factors are the key to the explanation of why a state acts as it does. The limits of choice about what the state should do for its prosperity are wide and so accordingly is the room for sectional pressures. The state expresses its individuality very strongly. An observer would have to pay more attention to the particular state, its personalities, politics, interest groups and so on, than to his general understanding of states in order to make a fair guess at what it will do.

In disputes, on the other hand, provided the state has the loyalty of its citizens, the limits of choice and the room for sectional pressures are narrower. Particularly if it is facing a demand rather than making one, it is likely to act much as any state would. It is less of an individual. Its psychology matters less than its membership of society; the question is one of justice. Exactly how it acts will still depend on its individuality but it will tend to act, like any other state, in terms of the value it attaches to the thing, its convictions of justice and injustice and its power, all in relation to its opponent and the society of states generally. It will tend to act, in other words, in terms of external factors, and it seems, accordingly, that in seeking to explain the origins of disputes between states, we can safely place most emphasis on external factors, as we have done in this discussion.

Error and Miscalculation

We have a final comment in a similar spirit to make. It concerns the formulation and conduct of policy by antagonists and, in particular, the part played by error. Here we are obliged first of all to make a distinction between two levels of error: the first, the shallower, on which we may say that all states sometimes make mistakes; the second, the deeper, on which we may think, if we wish, that all states always make mistakes.

As to the first, foreign policy is conducted in the same degree of darkness as the rest of human affairs, and no doubt some disputes are touched off by clumsy handling, misunderstanding, bluntness in the manner and timing of presenting a claim and the like; but it is hard to find cases when this can plausibly be called more than the spark to the powder of conflict. In disputing the inclusion of Sabah and Sarawak in the Malaysian Federation, Sukarno was incensed by a failure to consult Indonesia at an important stage; but even in such a case as this, it would be hard to argue that the mistake in diplomacy was responsible for the dispute.

More frequently, we can argue that a dispute would never have happened if a state had not over-estimated its power, or underestimated the cost, or misjudged the value of a thing and the significance of its loss. It may fail to see the full significance, as Britain did in the remilitarisation of the Rhineland in 1936, or it may exaggerate this, attributing to another state's action an importance which it would not otherwise have had and which thenceforth attaches to it. This was perhaps the case in the Eden government's reaction, with the example of the Rhineland in mind, to Egypt's seizure of control of the Suez Canal, though here there would in any event have been a dispute on some scale or other. This was again perhaps the case in the United States intervention in the Vietnam war in 1950 when it re-interpreted the rebellion against the French in the light of the Communist victory in China and began to see it as part of the onward march of the great Communist powers.

In general, there is no doubt that the correct assessment of the significance of another state's actions sometimes presents a hard problem, one of the hardest in statecraft. At the same time, we should not exaggerate its importance. It usually concerns how vigorously to dispute, not whether to dispute at all. Moreover, in most of the many inter-state disputes of the world, the extent of what is at stake is, at least in broad terms, clear enough. Inter-state disputes are in this respect cruder and blunter affairs than the great domestic disputes of societies.

As to the deeper level of error, it is the current fashion in thinking about foreign policy and inter-state conflict to insist that everything depends on perception. States, it is stressed, do not have interests, competitors, enemies; they perceive their interests, they perceive other states as competitors or enemies. They do not fight for justice against ambition, order against barbarism; they see themselves as fighting for justice, they have an image of themselves as fighting for order.

This insistence that everything depends on perception is in one way harmless. It reminds us that no state knows all the truth, that its sense of justice will always be shot through with ambition, that states do well to avoid arrogance and to temper their convictions with humility. In talking about any aspect of foreign policy, there is no harm in abandoning the Victorian-age phrase that everything depends on "the judgement of statesmen" in favour of the visual-age phrase "the perceptions of policy-makers". In talking of justice, there is no great loss in substituting "See the other side's point of view" for the classical admonition *audi partem alteram* ("Listen to the other side".)

Insistence on perception may, however, spring from currents of contemporary belief that inter-state conflict is all ultimately a delusion. The belief is either that there is nothing to choose between two states in conflict since both are struggling for purely subjective and personal ends; or that inter-state conflict is always a mistake which could be avoided if perceptions of interests and of the opponent could be clarified. We will not attempt to refute such attitudes here, the enervating cynicism of the one and the dangerous optimism of the other. Our whole book is the best we can offer by way of answer. We will only affirm the contrary belief which is that conflict is indeed in the final sense, a tragic error, but an error ingrained in nature and an inevitable one. Interests are real interests, honour is a real sentiment, competitors are really competitors, enemies are really enemies, justice and ambition, order and barbarism, are in real conflict in which it is possible to be nearer and further from them and to be more or less right about them, even if no one may ever claim to see the whole truth and possess it on his side.

In concluding this discussion of the origins of disputes between states, we should recall that we have been considering throughout only the first and most frequent kind of such disputes, that in which two states or groups of states are in direct conflict about a particular piece of territory or some other possession or the government of a state or the like. The next most frequent kind is that in which a state intervenes in a dispute, whether internal or inter-state, and thus itself enters into dispute. This kind, we shall consider in later chapters.

There remains a kind of dispute between states whose shape can be so far only dimly discerned but which may become increasingly prominent in coming years. The disputes which we have been discussing are comparable in their primitive type to disputes within states between particular individuals or groups in which each side claims a particular possession or the right to some particular activity. But the most complex disputes within states are those where the members of the society are struggling over the distribution of possessions and activities, seeking to make or remake a structure of rules which shall do justice to the interests of all.

Something of this sort has also appeared from time to time in the past in inter-state politics and has arisen, once again, since 1945 in matters ranging from the rules of international organisations to the question of the territorial waters of states and the exploitation of the seas. It may already be possible to consider conflicts about the international economic system and especially between economically richer and poorer countries in this light. Territorial disputes may in time become symptoms of a multilateral dispute on the distribution of the resources of the earth. So far the states of the world have felt too little sense of common membership of one society for them to make passionate demands on each other in this form and to become inflamed in this manner with a deep sense of justice and injustice. This may, however, as we say, come about in the future. If it does, all the factors which we have seen at work in the origins of the primitive kind of dispute between states, will be at work again under a different form.

5. *The Prevention of Disputes*

IN discussing the nature and origins of international disputes in the last three chapters, we have in effect already said all that we can about their prevention. To the extent that statesmen and citizens reflect on disputes in general, on what they are and how they begin, they will be better placed to prevent them. For the rest, the prevention of any particular dispute depends on the particular situation and the men involved in it, and this is ground on to which we cannot go. The purpose of the present chapter is thus merely to draw out the implications of what we have already said in as practical a form as possible.

Disputes within states and between states will be considered separately in view of the difference between them, and the nature of this difference should be recalled as a preliminary. The difference most commonly noted is that internal disputes take place in a setting of community, authority and law, and are therefore far more manageable and far less dangerous. However, this refers to private internal disputes whereas those with which we are concerned are great public disputes, those in which precisely community, authority and law are in question and in which the society threatens to break down into a condition resembling inter-state society. For us, the most significant difference between internal and external disputes is that the internal disputes are about the structure of the society while the external disputes are as yet on the whole of the more primitive type where what is at issue is the control of some particular thing.

This does not mean that in discussing external disputes, we can neglect questions of structure. We shall need to consider the contribution which changes of structure in inter-state society might make to the prevention of disputes. However, we should say at the outset that we do not believe that such changes and especially proposals for wholesale, schematic reform, deserve the emphasis that they have often received in this century. In our view, the prevention of disputes between states depends, now and for many years ahead, on the skilful conduct of policy by states in their dealings with one another. It is a matter, not of the reform of international politics, but of wisdom in foreign policy.

Since internal disputes, on the other hand, are about the structure of society, prevention here does indeed turn on issues of structure. Admittedly, these disputes do not arise through some process of spontaneous combustion as the more determinist and impersonalist kind of historian would have us believe; particular individuals must choose particular courses of action; and, in that sense, prevention depends here too on wisdom in the conduct of policy. Nonetheless, it may be granted that a discussion of disputes within societies should focus on their structure, that is, so to say, on the permanent policy of groups within them towards each other, rather than on the particular conduct which touches off the crisis.

Justice and Power

Whether we are discussing internal disputes or external, whether on the level of structure or of policy, the common theme will be that the prevention of disputes depends on two factors, justice and power. A structure of society prevents disputes by being just and by being powerful. Policy prevents disputes by doing justice and by using power.

Justice and power are not alternative methods of preventing disputes; they are inseparable. To be intent on justice while neglecting power is to be vulnerable to injustice. To neglect justice and to rely solely on power is to be vulnerable to justice. In recent generations, democracies have sometimes neglected the first of these propositions to their cost, dictatorships the second.

Part of the reason for this neglect in Western democracies is a traditional belief that justice and power are opposing principles. Justice belongs to the realm of the good; power to the realm of evil. There is no need to discuss this belief at length and besides, it would no doubt be fruitless to do so, for, as Meinecke, the greatest modern exponent of a necessary opposition between morality and power, once wrote: ". . . average English minds cannot fathom the problem of power politics because from practical instinct, they do not wish to".[1] We must be content simply to state that our discussion of the prevention of disputes is based on the belief that, great as are the moral dilemmas of statecraft, an opposition of principle between justice and power is not one of them. Justice should not be elevated to the position of a final good equivalent to love or friendship. Justice has no more place than power in the Christian or Hellenic or Marxist view of heaven. It is a reflection of the realm of the good in the realm of the evil, acting there according to its conditions. Justice acts not merely by doing justice and avoiding injustice but by preventing injustice with power.

As a final, more down-to-earth preliminary to our discussion, we may mention a remark made to the authors by a contemporary statesman. It was that to study the prevention of international disputes is to misconceive the nature of international politics; states do not wish to prevent disputes,

[1] Friedrich Meinecke, *Die Idee der Staatsräson*, ed. W. Hofer, Munich, 3rd ed., 1963, p. 466.

they wish to win them. This remark was no doubt made on the assumption, perhaps later dispelled, that the authors were naive idealists working on yet another project for permanent peace, and in this sense it was pertinent. On any other supposition, however, the remark would be superficial. States do not wish to win disputes; they wish to win things; and usually, they wish to win them without dispute if they can. It is to this conception of the subject, to the question of the avoidance of disputes rather than to their abolition, that this discussion is directed.

1. Disputes within States

In the last fifty years, many have believed that the right road to the ending of disputes within societies is the establishment of democracy, or fascism, or socialism, or capitalism. Yet, these conflicting theories are all concerned with the right structuring of society, that is, in the first place with a conception of justice; and there is much value in constantly referring back to this basic quality in social life which no one can define absolutely but which most can in some measure recognise. What matters about a society, especially from the viewpoint of disputes, is not how it is theoretically labelled but whether it is just.

Whenever this is borne in mind, it is, for example, at least more difficult to be satisfied with a society merely because it is called a democracy and to remain blind to suppressed social and political ills which may grow into a dispute. Or again, most citizens of Western countries believe that representative democracy with its provision for orderly changes of government and peaceful conduct of political disputes is the ideal constitution. They have often been less willing to accept that such a constitution would be unjust in the circumstances of many societies of the world or, from another point of view, impossible for lack of agreement on justice. For the position is not that if the many turbulent states of the world would only adopt democracy, they would be rid of their disputes; it is that because they are deeply divided by disputes, they cannot achieve democracy or any other stable constitution. For a stable constitution, many conditions must be fulfilled but especially a wide measure of agreement on what is just in the organisation of that particular society.

The Requirements of Justice

It would be absurd for us to attempt to state rules for the attainment of justice and thus for the prevention of disputes derived from the score or so cases of internal disputes which we have particularly studied or, indeed, from any conceivable number of cases. Yet the absurdity of any such ambition should not be taken as an excuse, as it has often been by political theorists in the past fifty years, for evading the responsibility to say something of practical value to statesmen and citizens about the achievement of justice in political society. It is at least possible to offer partial propositions which, while having no absolute and exclusive validity in all circumstances, should be considered and weighed against each other in all. If we are serious about the study of the prevention of disputes and willing to tackle the roots of the problem, we must at least make an attempt at doing this.

Many of the cases of internal disputes cited in our earlier chapters illustrate an obvious proposition about the relations between governments and subjects. This is not, as sometimes seems to be supposed, that a government should regulate the activities of its subjects unless the subjects can show why not; quite the reverse; the onus is on a government to show why it should. Most of the comments which we make in this discussion apply best to modern or transitional societies where the idea is at work that the structure of society could be different from what it is; but this comment applies in essentials to traditional societies as well. Men do not like governments and it is an illusion of certain contemporary political ideologies to suppose that they ever will, that a form of government could be constructed that would end the tension between governments and subjects. Regulation of activities without a conviction of need always leads to a sense of injustice. This conviction of need can grow suddenly, as in time of war, or be induced, as by a totalitarian faith; but otherwise the common presumption must be observed if dispute between government and subjects is to be prevented.

Arbitrariness is an equally well-known cause of a sense of injustice and the attempt to structure a society with a framework of rules is a necessary defence against disputes. Perhaps the final way of stating this is that political society is an expression of the human need for order whereas arbitrary action threatens chaos. In an arbitrary society there is a permanent tension which can only be temporarily overcome by a conviction of need arising from crisis or induced by ideological conditioning. Communist theory has shown since its origins an unwise disdain for the supposedly bourgeois concept of rights. It has been unfortunate for the advancement of Communism in the world that the idea of "socialist legality" was not developed at an earlier stage in its history.

A just provision for political participation in the political life of the country is the next aspect of the prevention of disputes clearly raised by the disputes cited earlier. The crux of the problem has long been expressed in terms of the proposition that those who are equal should participate in politics equally and thus of the criterion of equality: birth, wealth, divine guidance, possession of ideological truth, political skill. To these, the criterion of race might be added though perhaps this criterion is to be seen rather as a complete denial of political community with the "inferior" race and, as contemporary African and Asian theorists would argue, as a form of imperialism of one people over another.

In this notoriously complex area, at least one useful distinction is reflected in the studies we have made. It is that in any society, there is a small number who enjoy the activity of politics for its own sake and a great mass who, while perhaps ready for political excitement, are basically concerned with the results of politics in terms of the promotion of the interests of the community and their interests in particular. The problem of the prevention of disputes in this area is thus a twofold one. As to the smaller section of the society, the criterion for participation in political life and in government which in the last resort most agitates them, is that of equality of political skill. They feel their capacity for politics and are incensed by its denial. The problem of the prevention of disputes is that of considering, in the light of this and of the fact that these people provide the leadership of deeper and more dangerous movements, whether they should not best be admitted to the political sphere.

As to the majority, they are less concerned with criteria and more concerned that the government, however chosen, should advance the interests of the whole and maintain the balance that they consider just between the interests of the parts. It is impossible to say generally what criterion will best ensure this but it is easy to see in contemporary states around the world the operation of criteria which plainly do not, and of which the outcome is a ruling class incompetent in the general interest and favourable only to its own. Whether the wealthy, the white, the vanguard of the proletariat or any others rule, dispute cannot in the end be prevented in these conditions.

One prominent aspect of the matter nowadays is the achievement of economic justice between groups within a society. Here we should especially notice one widespread fallacy about the prevention of disputes. In recent years, the United States and other Western countries have discovered an interest in allaying the revolutionary unrest in developing countries if only for fear of being drawn into more costly and more dangerous forms of intervention. With this in mind, they have given economic aid to those countries in order to reduce poverty and promote economic development. But it is not poverty that causes revolutionary unrest; it is injustice. And it is not economic development that prevents dispute; it is the opportunity of all groups to derive their share of benefit from what is going forward. The immediate effect of economic development, far from being sedative, is to create a turmoil of social change, of hopes and fears. As the outlines of who is benefiting most become clearer, a host of new grounds for friction and dispute are created. This is not to be countered by the economic expertise in which the Western countries are so wealthy and by virtue of which they call themselves the developed countries, but by political wisdom concerned with justice.

In our earlier chapter on internal disputes, we included a discussion of disputes which arise out of foreign business investment, often leading to foreign government intervention in one form or another. The problem of prevention here appears to be primarily one for the investing companies, if only because they are the party most free to control its own conduct. The problem seems to centre on their establishment of their own identity: are they enclaves of foreign nationals relying in the last resort on their own nation's power; or are they business organisations, adopting the host country as their own with all its risks and responsibilities for good or ill? In recent years, there has been a clear development in the latter direction, including most recently some tendency on the part of great companies to distance themselves from their own national governments, preferring to solve their troubles for themselves. In time perhaps, genuinely international companies will emerge, owing no allegiance to any particular country; but if this happens, such companies will thereby have a new source of power and new temptations to deal insensitively and as aliens with the countries in which they operate. Whether for the present or the future therefore, international business needs to develop for itself a common code of investment practice.

So far, we have been discussing the prevention of disputes among social groups but the same considerations apply among tribes or communities within a state, or other kinds of federations of nations. As far as constitutional provisions are concerned, it is clear that these must give to the units an equal share in the government of the whole to the extent that they are equal. However, the factors to be taken into account in this are extraordinarily elusive, and there is frequently a discrepancy between the constitutional position and the facts of who predominates. What matters is that the system, whoever predominates, should actually work so as to seem the best possible in the interests of the whole and the most just to the interests of the parts. This is as much as to say that if a unit of people belongs to a federation and needs to do so, it should act towards the others in the spirit of a federation. This proposition, so obvious in the saying, has been brilliantly observed in some contemporary states and recklessly disregarded in others, neglected in some degree by all the old empires and variously neglected and observed in the new international groups of today; and they have suffered or avoided disputes accordingly.

The Contribution of Power

We come now to the second of the qualities needed in the structure of a state if disputes are to be prevented: power. Justice by itself cannot resist ambition and needs the support of power. This proposition, however, works both ways in as much as the most unjust state structure can prevent all challenge so long as it can maintain the power to do so.

The most fundamental element in the power of a state structure is the links of interest which bind the citizens and groups within the citizenry together. In a just society, these links are not usually experienced as power; they are a matter of habit, animated by sentiments of community. Nevertheless, they retain this character as can be seen whenever there is friction. The parties need each other and so have power over each other, preventing dispute or, at any rate, total dispute.

It is on these grounds that a vital aspect of the building of new states throughout much of Asia and Africa today is the creation of a network of interests overcoming the traditional divisions within the community. It is not a question of building monolithic interest groups since these would merely substitute new factions for those of religion, language, tribe or whatever it may be. It is a question of ensuring that the citizens belong to many different interest groups according to the various aspects of their lives and thus at any time of friction need their opponents in other respects as much as they need their allies in this.

It is impossible to generalise about where the main division of interest lies in all the states of the world; and, for whatever generalisations are worth, the Marxist notion that the main division lies between capitalist bourgeoisie and industrial proletariat is probably less significant, especially for the southern part of the world, than the division between town and country, modern industrial economy and rural economy. Wherever the divisions lie in any particular case, we should mention, referring back to an earlier point, that it is in this field that economic aid to developing countries may have a part to play. It is not very likely that economic aid, especially by attaching conditions to it, can do much to promote social justice in developing countries. It is more plausible that it can be used in such a way as to create links of interest between social groups or at least to avoid widening divisions and in this manner make a contribution to the prevention of disputes.

Beyond the power created by a network of common interests is the uniting of the nation by some sense of national purpose. This is a subject of extraordinary importance not merely for the prevention of internal disputes but of external also.

A political community can be seen as one of the kind of human association which has no collective purpose other than the making and maintenance of the structure within which the members live. On this view, the only valid objects of a sense of national purpose are the building of a just framework of the nation and its defence against internal or external attack. The nation is to be united by its leaders towards these goals and only these. To the extent that the leaders are successful, they contribute by the power of a common ideal, a common faith, to the prevention of disputes within their society.

On another view of the nature of a political community, however, the leaders are not content with the mere making of a structure for social life, with seeking justice and the erosion of divisive groupings by this means and by the promotion of common interests. Rather they engulf the whole political process and all the groups which engage in it in an ecstasy of totalitarian unity which knows no reason, only passionate emotion. It is clear enough from all history that unity of this kind can be highly successful in submerging internal disputes and yet equally clear that it is tense, unstable and transitory. The faith is based on dogma or on the personality of one man and is frequently dependent on conflict with the outside world. It does not last even when it is not overthrown from within or defeated by opponents abroad.

This same instability is the weakness of a state structure based on force. Force can prevent disputes but it does so by suppressing the friction, often without removing it; and it provides no stable bond of unity among rulers who rely on it. No doubt there are times and matters in all states where force must be used; the enemy of justice is not force but injustice. Nonetheless, it is plain enough that no state can be based predominantly on force for long. It must face the problem of winning and sustaining predominant consent, the consent whether of faith or interest or, most lastingly, of justice.

We must now finally make some comments, no longer in terms of the structure of societies, but in terms of action.

The widest of them is this. The contribution which any individual at any given time can make to change in the structure of a society and thereby to the prevention of dispute is usually, no doubt, very limited. Nonetheless, it arises from what has been said that a great contribution can be made over time by the sensitivity of many individuals to relations of justice and power in their society. These are indeed, as we have said throughout, the key factors in the prevention of disputes. It follows that it is the deepest concern of those statesmen whose aim in politics is the peace of society that there should be continued vigorous discussion of what justice and power require.

In many countries today, debate on the achievement of constitutional, social and economic justice is at the heart of political life. However, these practical debates are frequently ineffectual, and this for a variety of reasons which include one that is relevant here. They can no longer draw, as they could in previous generations, on a more fundamental philosophical debate on the nature of political society conducted in the great centres of civilisation. In both the leading countries of the world today, the United States and the Soviet Union, such debate is moribund. In the one, discussion of political behaviour is taken as a substitute for discussion of political values; in the other, all discussion is imprisoned within the limits of a dogma now obsolete. On the widest level of politics, the prevention of disputes within the states of the world requires action to end this stagnation of political philosophy and a real fulfilment by these two countries of their claim to precedence in teaching nations how to live.

Let us turn from the widest to the most detailed level of prevention. In the course of practical politics, the crux of the problem for the statesman who is concerned to do what he can by justice to avoid dispute, is not that of determining what justice would be, difficult though this is; it is his dependence on followers who want nothing of the sort. He must therefore know how to argue with these people in terms of the expediency of justice and, still more, of the expediency of understanding the sense of justice of opponents. This same expediency of understanding is equally vital to those statesmen who are not concerned with justice for its own sake at all.

For, in the first place, all such people must make calculations of power, the heart of expediency, and in this they cannot afford to neglect the contribution that a sense of justice makes to the power of their opponents. Second, it is important for any regime to be able to identify a situation of friction before it hardens into a dispute, and it is particularly important for a repressive regime because for them there is no such thing as peaceful dispute; the situation hardens and explodes into violence simultaneously. They therefore need to exercise a particular kind of continual calculation in which an understanding of the sense of justice is essential. They need, that is, to be able to identify discrepancies between how things are and how groups in the population think they ought to be; between the degree of regulation and arbitrary action and the strength of conviction of its necessity; between shifts in the number and power of those demanding change and their own power to resist it.

In liberal regimes, the courage needed to take action in times of apparent quiet against dangers which may never arise is immense. All are preoccupied with current, more urgent issues; action means disruption and cost to the interests of many; the arguments for "leaving well alone" are always formidable. A statesman is most likely to overcome these forces of inertia if he has confidence in his judgement based on sensitivity to issues of justice and how they develop in political life.

For those who seek change under whatever kind of regime, it is expedient not merely to demand justice but to offer it. For, though there are many reasons why people resist change, the main reason is that something will be lost without prospect of countervailing gain. If, therefore, serious dispute is to be avoided and aims attained, it is essential to spend no more time on formulating demands than on considering what picture of the future might be given to the opponent which will reassure him as to his interests on the whole. Though sometimes little can be done in this respect, sometimes much can, and here, too, an understanding of the sense of justice of others is vital.

These concluding comments have been based for practical reasons on the expediency of understanding justice. There is no need to tell some men that they should try to be just; and there is little point in telling others; they can only be attracted by expediency. It is not that expediency is the right defence of justice or that it can ever be conclusive against the sceptic; but it is the most practical. Moreover, in thinking about a world filled with disputes, it is surely unnecessary to dismiss all hope that those who are forced to reflect on justice for expediency's sake, may from time to time catch some glimpse of its value for its own.

2. Disputes between States

We began our discussion of the prevention of internal disputes by calling to mind the struggle to reform the structure of national societies and we may begin our discussion of disputes between states in a similar way. For centuries, many have believed that the key to the prevention of dispute and war is the reform of the present international system of independent sovereign states. The great empires were in their way attempts at the creation of a universal state for the establishment of order and peace. Reformist thinking of other sorts has in recent generations gained increasing respectability among statesmen and citizens. It nowadays seems increasingly absurd to many that humankind should be divided into a hundred and thirty separate states, each charged with sovereign responsibility for the interests of its share of people, and armed for this task with weapons of final destruction. The ingrained idea of "the nation" leads men to dispute for things on grounds of national interest and honour which may have little relation to their interest and honour as individuals. It leads them to nurse resentments and to revenge injuries done to others a generation or more previously as though done to themselves. It leads them to believe that their inherited possessions and wealth generally are merited by them and to repudiate furiously any demand on them by the unmeriting poor.

It is clear, however, that these divisive group loyalties cannot be ended by a mere change of organisation from the nation state to some other form of international system. Presented with most schemes for a world state, we are free to object that the old vices would simply live on, reflected in new sub-groups, and that the world state would simply transform the present inter-state disputes into internal disputes. More to the immediate point, there is no prospect of statesmen and citizens accepting radical change suddenly, except perhaps in the aftermath of a catastrophe which it is the whole object of these schemes to prevent. Paradigms of world or regional states, provided they are human not angelic, are a valuable method of political theory, currently greatly neglected, but they have no value as plans for action.

A new international system with less violence and closer association between states cannot be constructed artificially. It can only grow in the course of international politics. The pace of growth will depend on the degree to which statesmen and citizens are sensitive to the situation in international politics and to certain qualities needed in the conduct of foreign policy.

In the first place, the nations, for all their disputes and in all their disputes, are driven forward to new relationships by the strongest of all dynamics, by power, the power especially which they have over each other of mutual devastation of interests and perhaps of final destruction. Even if this power were to be reduced by measures of disarmament among great states or among small, this would itself involve the making of new relationships. In one way or another, there is hope of curbing the human attitudes which the nation-state expresses through the existence of power and the fear that it engenders.

For this hope to be fulfilled, the first of the qualities needed in the conduct of foreign policy between states is a deepening and widening sensitivity to the realities of power in the contemporary world. Progress towards a new international system depends on the degree to which the theoretical acknowledgement by statesmen and citizens of the dangers of the nation state is actually reflected in their policies towards other states. They must fear not just the nation-state but their nation-state. They must question not just whether power but whether their use of power in this or that particular issue will really solve their ills.

There is, at the same time, another quality needed in the conduct of foreign policy, less often stressed. The nation-state has its vices but it also has its virtues. It is the largest and best unit so far developed for securing justice for its members. It may not be necessary to forwarding their ordinary interests in life or, at any rate, may not nowadays be the best unit for that. The national interest and honour in which it involves them may be a delusion benefiting none of them as individuals. But the nation-state is necessary if they are to secure justice in their dealings with one another and in their dealings with foreigners. It is the best defence that they have against domestic or foreign invasion of what is theirs.

It follows that the other great quality on which progress towards a new international system depends is that states in their foreign policies should show justice to each other. Only to the extent that they try to do this will their citizens cease to cling to their own nation-state. Admittedly, today as always, states can associate purely on the basis of the power which they have to harm or benefit each other. But if the aim is to do everything possible to prevent disputes and especially if the aim is to erode the significance of the nation-state, power in foreign policy must be accompanied by justice.

New International Entities

So far we have been speaking very generally about the qualities needed in the foreign policies of states if a new international system is to develop. In looking at the matter in greater detail, we may first consider the most advanced kind of development, namely, when a particular group of states is seeking to unite in a new international entity.

Here what is involved is an effort to make several nation-states into a new international state and several societies into a single society. Here, accordingly, what is needed is a common view of the right structure of the new entity. The members must be concerned to see that the proposed arrangements between them for making internal and external policies are just; and equally that the structure of the new society, political, social and legal, satisfies the sense of justice of the citizens. Only to the extent that this is achieved and demonstrated in practical experience and that mutual confidence is thereby engendered, will citizens find the new entity a satisfactory substitute for the nation-state and agree to transfer their loyalties to it.

We should stress the phrase "satisfactory substitute", however, for as we said a moment ago, it is quite possible, now as always, for countries to be brought together in an association which neglects justice and which is held together solely by interest and power. In recent years, for example, there has been a widespread belief in western Europe that the best way to make progress towards unity is the promotion of links of interest across frontiers between citizens of the different countries, notably in commercial affairs. This, it is hoped, will eventually erode for them the significance of their nation-states and give rise to a new international state.

We have here at bottom a quasi-Marxist attitude to the way in which the activities of life determine the structures of life. On this view, the inherent needs of national activities give rise to the structure of the nation; and correspondingly, the inherent needs of activities across frontiers will give rise to the structures of a new international entity.

The importance of links of interest between the members of a state in holding it together is undoubted. Nonetheless, it is essential to distinguish. The pursuit of interests can by itself give rise to a structure, but one that consists of nothing but power. A structure which is also just arises not automatically from the pursuit of interests, but from political beliefs. It is only political beliefs and a growing similarity of beliefs that can create a new state satisfactorily replacing the nation-state. Without this, if the new state comes into being and endures at all, it is, in however modern a form, a tyranny.

Sometimes this is granted and yet with the hope that the necessary similarity of beliefs can be produced precisely by growing links of interest. Private cooperation will create political understanding. Yet repeated historical experience suggests that, for example, a businessman can persist indefinitely in holding one attitude to a foreigner as a businessman and quite another as a citizen, as a political being. He cooperates with the foreigner commercially in the greatest amity and yet continues to mistrust him regarding the structure within which such activities go forward. The two levels of life, the one private and individual, the other political and collective, remain different.

When national beliefs on matters of structure have grown comparatively close as in western Europe, when they are shattered and fluid as in western Europe in the post-war years, a satisfactory basis may exist for the aim of unity. What is then needed if the new community is to be not merely powerful in relation to its members but also just, is the setting up of institutions for political debate. These might be inter-governmental political organisations or representative assemblies. What matters is that the growth of the pattern of transnational links of interest should be guided in such a way that justice is done to the separate nation-states and to the different groups within the new society.

Relations within Groups of States

We have been speaking in these last paragraphs of an international association of a very advanced kind. In this case, foreign policy must pay close attention to the development of the structure of the association in terms of both power and of justice. Matters are different when some less ambitious form of association is in question, NATO, OAS, EFTA, COMECON, IMF or whatever it may be. Here where separate states do not aim at unity, their foreign policies need not, and in some respects should not, be deeply concerned with the structure of their association. They need rather to show sensitivity to power and justice in the ordinary process of policy towards their partners.

Admittedly, these associations viewed as power structures, can have great effect in preventing disputes among the members. Links of interest deter conflict. But the members do not form the associations to this end and it would be beside the point to suggest that they should be concerned to structure them to this end. They come together with a view to their national interest and honour. They have a common fear of some external enemy or some other concern such as commerce, or economic development, or monetary affairs. In some cases, the states scarcely shape the structure of their association at all. It is decided for them by the overwhelming preponderance of power and capacity for force of one of their number, as in most Western and Communist associations today, especially in Latin America and eastern Europe.

There is, it is true, one respect in which states today go some way towards deliberately creating associations of interest with a view to the avoidance of disputes. The post-war United States philosophy of arranging maximum freedom of trade and capital movements between states, especially in western Europe, was partly aimed at the removal of a source of friction and at the building of links of commercial activity as a deterrent to disputes. The later preoccupation of the richer states with the flow of resources to the poorer, has so far had a different aim, but this may be changing.

The aim has so far been to achieve military, diplomatic, ideological and commercial benefits for the rich countries and to promote economic growth in the poorer. Both these results are highly elusive and, moreover, threaten to create as much friction as they prevent. The search for direct benefits arouses the mistrust of the poorer countries. Their economic growth builds up their power without regard to what use they may make of it in their foreign policies. However, the flow of resources has had the politically valuable side-effect of forming the basis for numerous associations among all the states concerned, involving them in many links of common activity and thus making a significant contribution to cohesion among them. There are some signs that the richer states may henceforth see the flow of resources in this light and deliberately set out to use it in this manner.

We should notice, paralleling our discussion of the power structure of domestic societies, that one adjunct to the bonds of interest in associations between states has so far developed very little, the bonds of common faith. In their day, the great empires had much success in inspiring the loyalties of their subjects. Contemporary international associations are arid and unloved and to that extent weaker. It is a sign of the optimistic rationalism of the times that only this among all the many aspects of international organisation has received little study.

Perhaps, however, the associations which we are at present discussing are necessarily too utilitarian for ideals. They are, as we have said, involuntary or formed solely out of particular interests. They remain subject to reappraisal at every new turn in the wider pattern of world politics. The structure of interest and power may be highly compelling and long-lasting and yet it cannot prevent a state breaking away, often in bitter dispute, whenever an opportunity arises and it recalculates its position. So far as interest and power are concerned, this can only be avoided by the state and its prospective new associates calculating well.

Something can also be done to prevent rupture by another means. To have the best chance of enduring and of preventing disputes, the associations we are discussing must be just as well as powerful. The hegemony of great states within their spheres of influence will no doubt long make an important contribution to such order as there is in the world. Yet, the more the association rests on power alone and especially on force, the more restless it remains and the more prone to breakaway whenever opportunity arises. When the associates are not so unequal in power, fair dealing will no doubt come more readily to them if only for expediency's sake; but they have still more need of it in that the links that bind them are still more easily burst apart by resentment at injustice.

It is obvious, at the same time, that the quality of justice cannot lie to any great degree in the structure of the association. In associations between states, the members must always remain unequal in many ways. One or some of them are inevitably in a position of superiority with regard to the others. The idea of states as persons and the doctrine of the equality of states have great value but they have also led to great aberrations. It is a frequent absurdity of nationalism to ignore the inequality of states, to resent it and to refuse to accept it as one of the fixed limits within which a statesman must conduct the foreign policy of his country. There is also absurdity in seeking to conceal this inequality with an immense apparatus of democratic organisation and with such devices as equal voting. Much is revealed of good and ill about the nature of American political philosophy that this practice, undreamt of in international economic institutions, was reserved for political institutions such as the United Nations.

Beyond such inescapable relationships, the structure of an inter-state association also consists of the arrangements for mutual military assistance, or commerce, or whatever it may be between the members. Here, certainly, a great state may coerce the others into arrangements which are blatantly unjust. If so, it must expect dispute. Even among partners of less unequal power, coercion and injustice may be plain. The states responsible must expect resentment. But, for the rest, where sovereign states that have no intention of unity are concerned, it would be out of place to be preoccupied with the justice or injustice of military alliances, trade agreements and the like. These are to be seen as freely made bargains even though there may be great disparities of degree of interest and so of bargaining strength. The issue of justice between these states lies less in the structure of their associations than in how they conduct themselves on specific issues that arise between them in the ordinary process of foreign policy.

Relations between Groups of States

So far in our discussion, we have been speaking of the avoidance of disputes among the members of inter-state associations. What of disputes between these associations, between the "power blocs" of the world?

One traditional method for the prevention of such disputes is agreement between the leading states on spheres of influence. However, important though this is, it is not fundamental. Spheres of influence can only be established and will only be observed so long as the leading states, and to a lesser extent their associates, agree that the spheres satisfy justice and, still more no doubt, reflect the balance of power between the sides. It would, for example, be superficial to suppose that the disputes between the United States and the Soviet Union after 1945 could have been avoided if only they had agreed on their respective spheres of influence. They could not agree until satisfied as to justice or until they had arduously established by conflict where the boundary of power lay and, in consequence, the boundary of their spheres.

We must therefore turn to balance of power itself as a method of prevention of disputes. It is first of all obvious that if a state judges that a balance exists, so to say, naturally, it is likely to be deterred from a challenge to another. Here, however, we are speaking of balance of power as a deliberate method. In one sense a balance of power cannot be a method of preventing disputes since it cannot be made in abstract but only in the course of dispute. After each of the three general wars of the past one hundred and fifty years, statesmen have dreamed of preventing future wars by arranging in the peace settlement an ideal balance of power among the states of the system. In 1815, the notions of Castlereagh and Metternich along these lines were dispelled by reminders of reality by Talleyrand. Mechanically contrived balance could not ensure peace; everything would depend on the willingness of the powers to keep it. In 1918 and 1945, similar notions in many minds attended the creation of the League of Nations and United Nations, paradoxically in the name of abolishing the principle of balance of power. In future, any state tempted to embark on aggression would find all the others arrayed against it. In the event, this mechanical conception merely confused the old procedures of forming an *ad hoc* balance once the particular state to be checked had been identified.

Once a balance of power has been established in the course of a dispute, as between the United States and the Soviet Union in the years after 1945, it becomes crucial in preventing the development of the dispute into war. Probably also, it prevents some further disputes between the parties. Having arrived at mutual deterrence in their quarrels over one set of issues, they are cautious about provoking new quarrels over others.

These comments on the principle of balance of power indicate that it, too, points away from preoccupation with structure and towards the ordinary conduct of foreign policy as the key to the prevention of disputes. A balance cannot be made in advance, only in the going. Ideal structures of power relations, "system building", merited the scepticism of classical diplomacy. Even when an *ad hoc* balance has been achieved globally, regionally or locally in the course of foreign policy, the arrangements cannot be left to rigidify into a permanent structure. If disputes are to be prevented, policy must be continually on the watch, seeking to modify balance in one direction in favour of balance in another, to shift and change and adapt as the pattern of relations between states develops.

At the same time, the principle of balance of power in one sense merited the scepticism of reformers. By itself, it is not enough; by itself, it entails a race to outstrip in power, continual tension and the risk of war. A position of balance is never objectively clear to all parties; it is more a matter of judgement based largely on intangibles. What seems adequate deterrent strength overall may not, in fact, deter when some localised opportunity arises or when, against a background of high tension, bitterness gathers over some particular incident. If every effort is to be made to avoid this, power against enemies must be accompanied by continual diplomacy aimed at acting justly towards them.

This is the hardest truth of all for states to accept, genuinely in practice. There is no necessary opposition between power and justice in as much as power can be used well; but there is a spiritual tension in that considerations of power make for blindness to justice. Weak nations are envious of the powerful and prejudiced against them; powerful nations are arrogant and overbear the claims of the weak. "The whole history of the world is summed up in the fact that when nations are strong they are not always just, and when they wish to be just, they are often no longer strong."[2] Where there is conviction that a balance of power will deter or where there is hope that in time crushing power can be mobilised and where there is

[2] Winston Churchill, House of Commons, 26 March 1936.

hatred arising from past injuries, it is the hardest thing in the world for statesmen to look honestly for whatever justice there may be in an opponent's action and to persuade their own nation of it. States, as we suggested in discussing the origins of disputes, can assess justice, like power, better or worse; not all demands are equally coherent, cogent and valid. The difficulty lies in a disposition to do it.

The responsibility, not for the deeper causes, but for the actual outbreak of a dispute, lies mainly with one of the sides. It is the side which makes a demand or which makes so drastic a challenge to the *status quo* that the other cannot fail to demand redress. Conversely, when on any of the numberless issues lying ready in the politics of the various regions of the world, a dispute was avoided, it was because a state did not make a demand or a challenge.

Why this restraint? It is possible in some cases merely to say that while the state had the desire, this was outweighed by other interests; it had not the necessary power. It is never possible to say that a state had the desire but refrained merely through considerations of justice. Such considerations are never found alone; they are always mixed with considerations of power. On the other hand, it would be an error to go to the other extreme and to assert that restraint is always simply a matter of power.

The restraints of power and justice are to be seen primarily as habitual and only secondarily as calculated. The picture is not one of a world of states continually afire with limitless amibition against all the others, only held back by conscious calculation. The citizens of a state normally have a set of basic, undiscussed assumptions about their state's place in the world, about what it can and cannot do, ought and ought not to do. These give limits to its amibitions and are the main explanation of why it avoids dispute on most of the innumerable possible issues.

We have, however, placed the emphasis of this discussion at the point where statesmen and citizens have a degree of calculated control. Though habitual limits are first in importance, the contribution of deliberate restraint at the moment of a particular issue is also very significant. Faced with an occasion for demand or challenge in the course of foreign policy, statesmen and citizens are free to grapple with the problems of power and justice or to turn from them.

The other state, the state which receives a demand or challenge, has, as we have said, little responsibility for the actual outbreak of the dispute. It cannot fail to deny the demand or take up the challenge in some degree, and its freedom lies in the manner, firm or reckless, peaceful or aggressive, in which it does so. In this, it too can grapple with the problems of power and justice or turn from them. This is an essential aspect of the development and limitation of disputes, and we must consider it in our next chapters.

In concluding this chapter, we should add only this. We do not mean to suggest that sensitivity to power and justice are the only qualities of statesmen and citizens necessary if they are to avoid disputes. Many other skills are certainly required. We have said nothing strictly practical about the avoidance of disputes in this discussion. Nothing strictly practical could be said in advance of a particular case. Even when a case has arisen, what counts can scarcely be said, only done by men of practical talent who have learned diplomacy by watching it. All the known skills are needed; the ability to understand the position of the other; to assess what is the whole of the issue and whether it is to be treated as a whole or step by step in parts; to decide how it is to be most persuasively presented to the other side and to the world at large; to know when suavity, protraction and obscurity are called for and when is the moment for a thrust to the very edge of a demand; and so on through the annals of the finest statecraft.

Yet it is to be remembered that the skills of diplomacy can lie in very different hands. The most terrible ambition can wield them as adroitly as the clearest wisdom. That is the reason why we have said that the avoidance of disputes depends in the end on sensitivity to power and justice.

PART TWO: DEVELOPMENT

6. *The Development of Disputes Within States*

In discussing the origins of disputes within states, we took the moment of outbreak, rarely clearcut in practice, as being the moment at which a demand for change in some aspect of the structure of the society is made by some considerable group, whether a reforming government, or an opposition faction, or members of a community in a mixed state, or of a nation in an empire. In discussing the development of these disputes from that moment, our attention will be fixed on the two aspects most relevant to our study as a whole: the use of force and the intervention of other states. Any internal dispute has some repercussions on the outside world, but it is these developments, and especially the second, that transform a dispute into a serious danger to international peace.

The Use of Force

An explanation of why force is used in a dispute is best cast in terms of the culture and circumstances of the particular society in question. Nevertheless, we can say that the heart of the explanation lies in the two factors on which our discussion has centred throughout. A group demanding change may hope that it will eventually get its way by peaceful methods and think force unnecessary; alternatively, though it sees little hope of this, it may consider that the balance of its interests and honour makes force inadvisable. This will be seen on reflection to amount to saying that the exclusion of the use of force depends, first, on a wide measure of agreement within the society on justice; and, second, on organised deterrent force behind peaceful procedures and, more basically, a close interdependence of interests.

It follows, and is indeed obvious, that small disputes, those which interest only a few deeply or which interest many but only partially, are easily contained within peaceful procedures, whereas great disputes, which interest many deeply, are not. However, even great disputes are sometimes contained, as the history of political and social reforms in many countries shows. A great dispute may itself reveal that there is, in fact, a wide measure of agreement on justice, obscured beneath the existing distorted structure, and the dominant group may concede with little worse than lengthy and impassioned debate that the demands for change are, after all, just. Both sides, though deeply divided as to the existing manner of pursuing their interests, may nonetheless believe that the best possible manner requires them to depend on each other and end the division.

When moderation of this sort is shown, it is not to be explained simply in terms of the traditions of the society in question. We cannot say that the opposing groups in one country avoided force merely because of their inherited political and social beliefs whereas the opposing groups in another just as inevitably used it. In any society, there is always some possibility of calculated restraint on the part of the men concerned. There is always some chance – to speak in terms used of Latin America but applying *mutatis mutandis* to any area of the world – that "if we consider Christianity's preference for peace, the enormous problems of civil war, the logic of violence, the appalling evils it produces, the risk of provoking foreign intervention, the difficulties of setting up a rule of justice and liberty on the basis of violence, the value of peaceful methods . . . will appear in its full light".[1]

Let us now illustrate these general comments on force and restraint in disputes by the disputes which are the basis of this study. We can say as a starting-point that in some cases there was no hope of the achievement of aims without force; for example, in Guatemala of removing President Arbenz; in Yemen, of abolishing the monarchy; in Oman, of suppressing the Imam's defiance; in Nigeria, of establishing the kind of federal government the rebels wanted. At the same time, there was clearly nothing predetermined about these aims; they had to be decided upon, not calmly, in extreme tension and confusion, but decided upon nonetheless. We may suppose that in their decisions those concerned gave some thought to the justice of the matter. We can be even more confident that, in expediency of prudence, they were deeply influenced by calculations of power. They aimed for what they thought they had the necessary force to get.

The same is true of the two great imperial disputes which we cited in our earlier chapter, in Indo-China and Indonesia. For many months, it seemed that aims might be reconciled without recourse to force. Whereas in Angola, for example, there was from the first a plain incompatibility between Portuguese policy as it then stood and the demands of the dissidents who eventually attempted armed revolt in 1961, in the two earlier disputes neither side adopted an uncompromising attitude at the outset in 1945 and, indeed, agreements in principle were reached at Hanoi in March 1946 and at Linggadjati in November. Yet, in the end, the moderation shown and the agreements reached proved superficial. It

[1] From a document on violence prepared by a sub-commission of the 2nd General Conference of Latin American Bishops, Medellin, 1968; see *Le Monde*, 5 September 1968.

would be going too far to say that the two sides were in reality merely manoeuvring tactically, seeking to gain time in which to improve their positions; there was, it seems, some uncertainty of aims on both sides and a great confusion of conflicting opinions as they felt their way forward. We can say, however, that throughout these months of negotiation, the French and the Dutch were deeply influenced at every turn by one crucial belief. They believed that in the last resort they could muster the necessary force to subdue their opponents, both in sheer military terms and, still more, because in their view their opponents did not really have the support of the people as a whole. Eventually, this belief led them to take armed action.

Calculations of force are easiest and force is used most lightly in every sense of the word if the bulk of the population can be discounted. In Latin America in the past, the continual *coups d'état* have often been mainly a way of changing the government under the control of a small section of the population. Even in the Dominican Republic, where a dispute began in June 1963 over President Bosch's reform programme, the affair had throughout much of this character. The President did not rouse the country behind his aims, and in September 1963, he was not so much overthrown in the course of a national dispute as dismissed by an elite for intolerable views. In the more turbulent *coup d'état* of April 1965 which led to United States intervention, Colonel Caamano and his associates shared the ideals of Juan Bosch but nonetheless the atmosphere of elitist politics remained. They were determined to forestall a right wing *coup* against the crumbling government and to assert the former President's claim as vigorously as possible in a fluid and uncertain governmental situation.

In Guatemala in 1954, the main explanation of the use of force, such as it was, is the series of miscalculations made by the Arbenz government. When these reached a certain pitch, the rebels needed to do little more than march without opposition on the capital. The Arbenz government took office following the elections of 1951 with the widespread support of the peasantry, the labour unions and the army. They then challenged powerful opponents in the most incautious manner possible and at the same time steadily alienated their various supporters. The government pleaded the restiveness of the peasantry as their grounds for rejecting the modest land reform proposals of the landowners and for proceeding to massive measures, but the real explanation seems to have been an extreme zeal which overrode all prudence. As the quarrel with the landowners grew, as United States pressures intensified, reliance on Communists and the Communist countries deepened and this alienated many in all sections of society. The peasants began to lose interest in the government's programme as its practical benefits proved small, the unions to lose faith in the campaign against the United States companies as the sacrifices mounted without prospective gain. To the army, the final blow was the attempt to raise and equip paramilitary units. The rebels at this point made a display of force against a government which few would support and which had already almost collapsed.

The politics of the military were decisive for the use or avoidance of force in many disputes in other areas of the world. This is clear enough, given that the military are the main element of organised force in any society, but let us illustrate it briefly by comparing the crisis in Yemen in 1962 with that in Jordan four years earlier. There were many differences between the two countries, but the demands which caused dispute were similar: solidarity with Egypt and a new political order in the cause of Arab liberation and social progress. In both countries, the opposition was unlikely to succeed by peaceful means. In Yemen, the friction eventually led to the *coup d'état* of 1962. The leaders of the opposition were a powerful section of the army. In Jordan, on the other hand, the leaders of the opposition were politicians and hesitated to use force or, at least, were forestalled in doing so. The army was loyal to the King. Why the military thought and acted as they did in these two countries and many others is to be explained in terms peculiar to each country and we will not attempt to generalise about it.

In the disputes so far mentioned there was a fair measure of central control over the use of force by the leaders of the factions, by rulers, governments, the military. It was their calculations that mattered. So it was also in Nigeria where the friction between the members of the federation exploded into violent dispute in the *coup d'état* of January 1966. So it was also in Greece in December 1944 where a clear opportunity for the Communists to seize power presented itself and would pass with the disbandment of their partisan forces, the return of the King, and the restoration of stability after the defeat of the Germans.

The calculations of the Communist leaders in Greece were made not only under great personal strain but amidst intense popular excitement, particularly in Athens. Leaving aside deeper and older layers of passion, four years of fighting against the Germans, the emotions of victory, the bitterness against collaborators had led to an atmosphere in which recourse to force is easily understandable. For all that, the crucial decisions were taken centrally among the Communist leaders. In other disputes, central control over recourse to force was weak or entirely lacking. In a turbulent mood throughout the population, individuals or small groups took to violence in a manner that was, at best, roughly coordinated and, at worst, chaotic. In Palestine in 1945 and Aden in 1963, the first use of force was the work of extremists. In Lebanon, the strikes and demonstrations of the winter against President Chamoun swelled through a first incident of violence in May 1958 into the confused fighting of the summer. In the Congo in 1960, the train of violence was touched off by the mutiny of the Force Publique. In these disputes, as in the others, all concerned calculated their actions in their way, but separately and narrowly so that no one could judge where actions would lead or have much control over the course of events.

In Hungary in October 1956, the unorganised popular demonstrations against the government perhaps amounted to a threat of the use of force but the first clear use was the action of the police in firing on a demonstration on the evening of 23 October. Whereas in Poland the ruling section of the Party, faced with popular pressure, transferred office relatively smoothly to a more acceptable leader, in Hungary they attempted repression and so transformed unorganised demonstration into unorganised insurrection.

All this amounts to saying that the lack of control over the popular movement was decisive for the course of events. We recounted in an earlier chapter how the Soviet government and the Communist Party in Hungary had for some years been increasingly divided and vacillating in their rule of the country and how this greatly emboldened the population. However, there was a darker side to the picture. The disaffection and disunity within the Party meant, as in any totalitarian country, that there was no organisation left which could represent and, at the same time, control and limit the demands of the people to what was prudent. In Poland, the Party remained sufficiently united under skilful leaders and was thus able to harness the popular movement. In Hungary, the Party was not able to do this, and the outcome was sweeping popular demands for independence of the Soviet Union. The disarray of the Communist Party was thus both a major cause of the popular movement and a major cause of its extravagance and ultimate failure.

The decision of the ruling section of the Party in Hungary to use force was probably influenced by expectations of support from the Soviet Union. In some of the other disputes we have cited, outside states contributed to the decision in one way or another. The most diffuse and potent way was that of example. A little earlier, for instance, we contrasted the dispute in Angola with those in Indo-China and Indonesia, and by way of further contrast, it seems certain that in Angola recourse to force by the rebels was deeply influenced by the example of many years of successful anti-imperial force in other countries of Asia and Africa.

In other cases, actual intervention contributed. In Guatemala, the United States, beyond other pressures, assisted the rebel forces. In Oman, military understandings with Britain emboldened the Sultan to suppress the Imam's revolt. In Lebanon and Yemen, expectations of Egyptian assistance may have encouraged the rebels to use force, and similarly in Aden where both Egypt and Yemen sympathised with the rebel cause. We suggested in our chapter on Origins that none of these disputes was strictly created from abroad though the Oman dispute came near to this in the role played by Saudi Arabia. Equally, external support could, it seems, in no case be called the crucial factor in the decision to use force, though it may have come near to this in some.

External Intervention

Let us now turn more squarely to the question of external intervention in disputes within states and first by defining roughly what we mean by it, in view of the ever-widening meaning attached to the word in international polemic in recent years. Just as the ordinary process of national politics is different from dispute, so the ordinary involvement of outside states in that process is different from intervention. States are continuously engaged in putting pressures on each other's foreign policies, and in this way and more directly by the influence of their social ideas, deeply affect each other's internal politics. This sometimes extends as far as deliberate interference in the political process of a kind commonly resented, for instance, in the choosing of the members of the government or in the framing of internal policies. What we mean by intervention, however, is an attempt to influence the course of a dispute. A country is undergoing a more or less clearly defined conflict about its political or social structure. An outside state seeks to influence the course of this conflict by word or action.

Outside states can influence a dispute in other ways than by intervention. Neutrality and inaction are negative influences of great importance. Merely continuing past policies can amount to taking sides, for instance, continuing financial and military relations with a government now struggling with a rebel faction. This kind of involuntary influence shades imperceptibly into intervention, is indistinguishable from it at the margin, and provides the justification for the remark ascribed to Talleyrand that "non-intervention is a metaphysical and political phrase meaning about the same as intervention".[2]

As a final preliminary, we should notice that intervention can be mediatory or partisan. It is with the latter that we are concerned at present but it sometimes overlaps with mediation. States sometimes intervene with the primary purpose of excluding an extreme solution to the dispute and then, while maintaining this attitude, stay to mediate. This kind of

[2] See Sir Charles Webster, *The Foreign Policy of Palmerston*, London 1951, p. 99.

mediation, backed as it is by power, has in the past been more often successful than any other kind.

The Aims of Intervention

Our line of approach in this discussion is to seek to give a general explanation of why states sometimes intervene in disputes and sometimes do not; or, to put the question another way, why some disputes lead to intervention and others do not. Our point of departure is the fact that all states are concerned in some degree with the government and society and affairs generally of other states. Sometimes they are averse to abrupt change; sometimes they desire it. This is not a matter of distinct classes of states, but of all states on different occasions. The United States, averse to Communist revolutions, desired rapid if not perhaps revolutionary change in the European empires and desires it still in Communist states. The Soviet Union, while revolutionary with regard to much of the world, is conservative in eastern Europe. Egypt has been a revolutionary state for the last eighteen years, but revolutions once made have to be consolidated and defended.

To speak first of states in a conservative stance, they have developed a whole pattern of national activities which intertwines with that of the state now riven by dispute and they do not wish this disrupted. Their political activities (as a power analyst of international politics would stress) extend perhaps to rule over the other state, or to military protection or alliance. Their commercial activities (as a Marxist analyst would stress) are such that the other state in some degree or other forms part of their economic system. They have (as any realistic study of, for instance, United States attitudes to western Europe in the postwar period would emphasise) a cultural relationship, embracing a more or less wide and deep range of human concerns. These various interests make of the state in dispute in some fashion an extension of their home society, perhaps looked upon primarily as a defensive extension. They value these interests in themselves and for the honour that they bring in the world. A state fears the loss of a piece of its empire or sphere of influence not merely for interests but for shame and humiliation.

Abrupt governmental and even social changes are a common occurrence in the world and usually states endure them without intervention. The familiar pattern is disrupted but perhaps it can be restored in time, or at least sufficiently nearly. An urge to intervene arises in its narrowest form when a faction threatens some specific interest, for instance, the property of United States citizens in Guatemala, Cuba and the Dominican Republic, or when the situation is such that the lives and property of nationals are endangered as Belgium judged to be the case in the Congo in 1960; or when national honour is involved in the fate of kinsmen, Austria's, for example, in South Tirol.

The interest in intervening widens when there is the possibility of a state breaking the whole pattern of common activities permanently. It is at its widest when there is the prospect that the state will form alternative links with a rival state. Then the outcome of the internal dispute affects the wider competition of interests and honour in international politics, whether among small powers regionally or the great powers globally.

This concern took various forms in the disputes we have cited. Britain was interested in intervening in Greece ultimately through fears of the orientation of that country under a Communist regime towards the Soviet Union, and perhaps especially in terms of its traditional policy of barring the Soviet Union from the Mediterranean. The Soviet Union intervened in Hungary not perhaps for fear of a gain to the West but at least of a loss to itself. It seemed clear that Hungary was about to break away from the Soviet political, ideological, cultural, commercial and, perhaps above all, security system in a manner which, whatever Hungary's subsequent status, was intolerable both generally and especially in terms of the rivalry with the West.

Beyond this, states in a conservative stance have always felt a more general concern. A rival state has intervened in an internal dispute in some country or other; they themselves may care little about this country in particular, but at least they care deeply in terms of what they see as the aggression of their rival; they have an urge to counter-intervention to resist unilateralism and aggrandisement with its threat to world security and, with it, their own.

This attitude appears to have been normal to all states throughout history but is particularly marked in the period of the League of Nations and the United Nations and, above all, in United States foreign policy since 1945. Moreover, in these years, the whole matter took a special form, an ideological form.

Some of the internal disputes we have discussed were in part about the right course for the country in international politics, as in Lebanon, Jordan and Yemen; but even where this was not so, even where the dispute was primarily about the internal structure of the society, the outcome often had, or was thought to have, great implications for international politics. For, in the eyes of certain revolutionary groups, their new social philosophy was not just a local ideology for restructuring their own society, but was linked in brotherly solidarity with social philosophies arising in other countries. In the eyes of conservative states, the threatened new regime was not just an unknown and possibly troublesome quantity; it was part of an aggressive international movement. Even if their rivals in world politics had not promoted the attempted revolution as states, they had done so as the organising centre of an ideological movement. Even if they had not done this, even if they had had no significant part in initiating the affair at all, the effect of the victory of the new social philosophy would be that they would have gained an ally or satellite and thus extended their aggressive system.

In the contemporary world, there have been several philosophies or movements appearing simultaneously in many countries: the struggle for independence against the European empires, neutralism and non-alignment, European unity, pan-Africanism. But a crucial aspect of these movements from the point of view of other states was that they did not have any marked appearance of being centrally controlled by any one country to its own advantage. The two movements which did appear to have this character were Communism and Arab nationalism, the one being seen in the West as advancing the interests of the Soviet Union, the other of Egypt. From the viewpoint of the United States, Britain and many other countries, a Communist or Nasserite uprising must be resisted, partly because the country concerned would become troublesome and unpredictable; partly because the victory of the uprising would represent the extension of an alien social philosophy in the world; but mainly because it would represent an expansion of the Soviet Union or Egypt by "indirect aggression".

A state considering intervention with such thoughts in mind is often faced with a dilemma: on the one hand, intervention may itself cause the very effects feared; on the other hand, the effects may come about anyway and forbearance sacrifices any chance of preventing them. In Greece, it is true, it was practically certain that a Communist regime would in any event be closely linked with the Soviet Union and there was little risk that British intervention would ensure this. In Hungary, the Soviet Union, whether through a sense of dilemma or some other form of indecision, held back until the rebels had made their intention to renounce the Warsaw Pact unmistakeable.

In Guatemala, President Arbenz relied from the outset on Communist officials in the bureaucracy for the implementation of his reform programme, but the hostility of the United States certainly reinforced the trend towards the Soviet bloc, leading eventually to recourse to arms supplies from it. The United States was well aware of the dilemma when Fidel Castro came to power in Cuba and sought to show restraint; but Castro was determined to break the links with the United States on such a scale as necessarily to involve, willingly or unwillingly, alternative links with the Soviet Union. Six years later in the Dominican Republic, the United States decided to play safe, brushed the dilemma aside and intervened straightaway on the mere suspicion that the reinstatement of Juan Bosch might lead to Communism and alignment with the Soviet Union.

On the whole, the dilemma was not one with which governments in a conservative stance, still less the populations behind them, had much sympathy in the disputes we have discussed. They tended to take a pessimistic view of the likely effect of a Communist or a Nasserite revolution and to stress the factors making for the alignment of the state in question with their rivals. Their own conservative sympathies had long been clear to all through their dealings with the existing regime and their known attitudes in the international ideological struggle. They would not escape the revolutionary faction's enmity or its tendency on victory to form links with rival states simply by holding back now. This enmity and these links might not endure perpetually but they were likely to last for a considerable time. It was best to assume the worst and, so far as this factor went, to intervene to prevent it.

The dual conviction that violent action by a Communist faction anywhere represents the expansion of the Communist bloc and aggression by it played an important part in the intervention of the United States in the disputes of the Far East. If North and South Korea had been two ordinary states, the United States might not have intervened in June 1950 on behalf of the latter. As it was, North Korea had been reconstituted after the defeat of Japan by the Soviet Union and the United States assumed that the North Korean attack represented aggression by the Communist bloc. If this was allowed to succeed, the whole country would thenceforth be a Soviet satellite and the security of all other countries would have suffered a heavy blow.

The United States Administration had at this time for some months resisted the popular assumption that the new Communist regime in China necessarily made that country a Soviet satellite, but the delay in recognising it and accepting its admission to the United Nations had increased the mutual hostility, and in the June crisis, the Administration was itself ready to assume that China, too, must in some sense be implicated in the North Korean aggression. This appears to have contributed considerably to the decision to protect Taiwan and to the intervention thereby in the dispute between the Kuomintang in Taiwan and China.

The Communist conquest of power in China also transformed United States' attitudes to the dispute in Indo-China. In 1945, many Americans had shown marked favour for Ho Chi Minh. Later, United States policy developed a lukewarm sympathy for France. The Viet Minh was an independence movement and thus in principle to be favoured in the same way as the republican government in Indonesia. On the other hand, it was a Communist movement and thus somewhat suspect. Moreover, the

French, besides being an important ally in the European theatre, were abandoning their resistance to independence and were striving to organise a non-Communist successor regime. So far this was an obscure business in a remote corner of Asia and the United States had more pressing preoccupations elsewhere. Now, however, with the shock of the "fall of China", United States' attention was abruptly focused on the danger that if the Viet Minh were to win, this would represent yet a further aggressive expansion of "the Sino-Soviet bloc". So purposive assistance to France, intervention in Vietnam began.

The Sense of Right in Intervention

We have cast this discussion of intervention so far in terms of states in a conservative stance. The motives of revolutionary states are basically the same, the promotion of their interests and honour in the world, the difference being that they are on the initiative, seeing their cause as best served by supporting radical change in other countries. We may move on then to discuss a further factor in explaining intervention. It is that revolutionary and conservative states alike did not want to intervene in internal disputes as they might want this, that or the other thing in their day-to-day foreign policies; they felt or at any rate claimed that they had a right to intervene. As we noted earlier, states inevitably influence each other's internal affairs in a multitude of ways and most sharply by the pressures they exert on each other's foreign policies. At the same time, it has always been held by states that there are limits to deliberate interference in their internal political process. If these are over-stepped, rights are infringed. These limits have varied from period to period (propaganda is, for instance, an uncertain area today) but nonetheless they have always existed. If they are transgressed a new quality of ill-feeling arises and this reaches its highest intensity if there is intervention in a dispute about internal political structure. Correspondingly, states that intervene in an internal dispute, like states that embark on conquest, always feel called upon to give an explanation for their action in wider terms than their own desire. Often in the past, and universally today, this takes the form of claiming an over-riding legitimacy.

The important aspect of Communism and Arab nationalism in this context was that they provided a legitimation. In intervening in internal disputes, the Soviet Union and Egypt were certainly promoting their interests and honour but, they could claim, on the level of justice. For Communists, not the *status quo* or state sovereignty but world-wide social revolution was the fundamental principle of human affairs, and the progress of this revolution ought to be supported against the forces of reaction. By this creed, Soviet intervention whether on the initiative or in a conservative stance, as in Hungary in 1956 and Czechoslovakia in 1968, was legitimised. For Arab nationalists, the disunity of the Arabs, the complacency of certain Arab governments in face of Western and Zionist imperialism, the old social structure of the Arab countries, were all injustices to be lifted from the back of the Arab nation in conflict with the forces of repression.

We have here sought to imply that even in the theories of Communism and Arab nationalism there was a certain element of defensiveness in the justification of interventions. A more traditional kind of legitimation entered strongly into Soviet state policy and this was entirely defensive in spirit: the Soviet Union ought to intervene if there was a manifest need to do so for the security of the nation; it ought not to do so if this would jeopardise security.

These defensive beliefs, together with considerations of power and the circumstances of the Soviet Union generally, go far towards explaining the pattern of its interventions. The Soviet Union was in practice less ready to intervene to help bring a Communist Party to power than to assist it against the intervention of capitalist states, as in Greece, Guatemala and Vietnam, or against counter-revolution, as in Hungary and Czechoslovakia.

In Cuba and the Congo, the Soviet Union eventually went beyond actions which could readily be understood as defensive assistance to further actions which were more obviously on the offensive. The repudiation of these actions as "adventurism" at the fall of Khrushchev seems to have meant that they were reckless in terms of power but it seems also to imply the absence of a sense of legitimacy behind them whether in terms of Communism or Soviet state security.

As regards revolutionary Egypt, it is still harder to assess the various elements in the emotions of government and people, and yet here too we should at least notice that defensiveness and fear seem to have been greater in some interventions, that is, wherever the struggle against Israel and Western imperialism were closely involved, than in others, for instance the intervention in Yemen.

On the side of the Western states, the feelings of legitimacy behind intervention were entirely defensive in nature. They felt a right to protect the lives and property of their nationals against attack and seizure. Beyond this, they seemed sometimes to claim a right to support any friendly government against internal overthrow or the pressures of another state; and sometimes also, a right to intervene to assist the repression of a social philosophy which they disliked or which in their view would deprive the people of the country in question of their liberties. These last were doubtful principles, however, and do not seem in the end to have been fundamental. Basically, they felt a right to intervene to assist any state whose independence from other states was threatened by the use of force, whether internal or external, and by the imposition of a new social structure which would bind it to a rival power bloc. Their own security at its widest was at stake, and they had a manifest ground of need to intervene. These same feelings inspired the Asian, African and Latin American states in their interventions and counter-interventions. They too were against the crushing of independence by imperialism, whether European, American, Soviet or any other, however brought about.

The Calculation of Power

With this, we should turn to the last of the factors explaining intervention and non-intervention, the calculus of all interests and the margin of power. Here, we may risk the opinion that this factor normally makes for restraint in intervention, for conservative and revolutionary states alike. States can intervene in innumerable ways in innumerable degrees, rhetorically, diplomatically, economically, with material supplies and direct force. Any of these represents some cost to interests to be set against gains. Resources will be expended, risks of counter-intervention or even counter-attack will be incurred, the goodwill of some states will be alienated. The goodwill of others will be won but only provided that the intervention can plausibly be seen as defensive and not as an act of aggrandisement.

Sometimes a swift intervention can be made with overwhelming force in a neighbouring country. In other cases, however, a state is committing itself to a possibly protracted chain of events which it controls even less than in any other type of international action and which is highly unpredictable. Once committed, withdrawal will have its costs to interests. The pressures to increase the commitment will grow if it is known that further power is available. The ultimate benefit, especially in the case of revolutionary states, is, as we shall notice, very uncertain. All states usually count these possible costs at the outset before committing themselves. Sometimes, whether through intensity of feeling or a beguiling sense of national power, they do not.

States which avoid an open, general commitment to intervention are in the best position to act flexibly and cautiously. The Soviet Union and Egypt on the whole made only the vaguest undertakings in advance of particular disputes. Exceptions to this were the Warsaw Pact and the broad proclamations of Egypt, and in general, the more a revolutionary state succeeds in the world, the more it begins to face the problem of automatic commitment to assist allies and satellites. In the postwar decades, however, the Soviet Union and Egypt were in a fair position to choose whether to intervene in a dispute or not.

The Soviet Union, for its part, made full use of this position. It had the further advantage that its regime was of a type that left its leaders free from popular clamour for action. The only strong pressures were those from within the Soviet Party and from Communist parties abroad whose faith in the Soviet Union and allegiance to it had to be preserved. However, at least until the quarrel with China, these pressures appear to have been exerted as often in the direction of caution as of adventurousness. Finally, and no doubt most important of all, the Soviet Union was confronted with another even stronger power, the United States, and was deeply concerned to avoid the incalculable danger to its interests of a drastic clash.

We should notice here a further characteristic of intervention which makes it a dubious gamble, though how far it entered into the calculations of the Soviet Union is a matter of speculation. However great the interest of a state in revolution abroad and however intense its sense of right, still the obvious but crucial fact is that in a nationalist world it has no power to create a revolutionary movement in a foreign state, only to support and make use of it. This means first and equally obviously that the opportunities for a state to intervene in the internal disputes of others are rare. There must first be some local group which welcomes intervention. It means, second, that the ultimate benefits from intervention are insecure.

These benefits are supposedly that the new regime will thenceforth have a similar ideology to that of the intervener and will be an ally gained to the general enhancement of its interests. To some extent, as we said earlier, the history of the dispute will tend to make for this result; the new regime will cling to its erstwhile supporter in view of the past and probably continued hostility of its enemies. In general, both the United States and the Soviet Union did much by their pressures in the postwar years to reinforce the solidarity of the opposing bloc. Yet, despite these considerations, just as conservative states have some grounds for pessimism from their viewpoint, so too have revolutionary states from theirs. The history of international politics, confirmed by the experience of intervention in recent years, suggests that a new regime after victory strives to follow its own national interest and tends to shake off dependence on its former supporter if it can. Unless the intervening state has the power to make a permanent set of links to hold what it has gained (and even this is often costly enough) its gains from its intervention are likely to be temporary.

These considerations are perhaps a further explanation of why the Soviet Union's interventions in any depth were rare and for the most part confined to neighbouring states where its power was greatest. One of its principal interventions was made at arm's length, that is, in Greece where the initiative was taken by Yugoslavia, Bulgaria and Albania. In Greece, Guatemala, Vietnam and Cuba, its intervention took the form of countering the intervention of other states. There was apparently no commitment to ensuring the victory of the faction supported. After the death of Stalin, some Soviet interventions were at longer range but otherwise retained these characteristics. In the Khrushchev period, as already noted, there were some extravagances, but the results were not encouraging. Most states were sensitive to the fact that Soviet actions in Cuba and the Congo went beyond defensive support and were more alienated than impressed.

Revolutionary Egypt intervened with considerably less caution. The internal nature of the regime and its claim to leadership of the Arab world required continual boldness. There was, moreover, no other regional state capable of deterring Egypt by the threat of massive counter-intervention and, of the world powers, one, the Soviet Union, was Egypt's ally and the other, the United States, was a decidedly pliable counter-force. But while these factors encouraged Egypt to follow an adventurous course, the benefits from its interventions in Lebanon, Jordan, Yemen, South Yemen and Oman were sparse. Resistance to Egypt was far from massive but it operated nonetheless even among Arab nationalists. Egypt's prestige was perpetuated but at great cost, and it is likely that this and other gains in influence in the region could have been won, and won more solidly, by less dramatic means.

The leading conservative state, the United States, far from avoiding an open general commitment to intervention in the disputes of the world, voluntarily incurred this by two sets of measures: first, its various undertakings to resist aggression, beginning with the United Nations Charter; second, its proclamations, first explicit in the Truman Doctrine of 1947, that rebellion by armed Communist minorities amounted to aggression. The basic idea behind this, deeply influenced by inter-War experience, was that all recourse to armed force in international politics, anyway where great states were concerned, must be immediately checked. It was a conscious effort to avoid the dangerous vagueness of the old diplomacy and indeed there can be little doubt that it has done much to deter the use of force. On the other hand, the idea had the defects of these virtues. The open general commitment and the institutionalisation of it in alliances meant the sacrifice of discrimination and flexibility. If the deterrent failed to work, the principle had to be put into effect automatically with little regard to the circumstances of the particular case.

Whereas the Soviet Union could on the whole pick and choose its commitments, the United States could not fail to support any kind of government assailed by any kind of movement which could plausibly be regarded as benefiting another great power without loss of credibility of its whole grand principle of security. Whereas the Soviet Union could afford merely to match the intervention of others and gave no undertaking to ensure the victory of its side and could withdraw and accept defeat in a particular case in the wider interests of its cause, the United States was committed to outbidding the intervention of others and to ensuring victory for the side it supported. Its wider cause was precisely to win in any particular case. It had to go on and on until it won.

The United States originally entered very readily into this far-flung commitment to intervene through a strong conviction that this was the best way to secure its interests but equally through a strong sense of overwhelming national resources. Changing circumstances and its experience over the past twenty years culminating in the Vietnam War have made for progressively greater caution.

The first great postwar intervention by the United States in internal disputes was the Marshall Aid programme, followed in later years by its policy of military and economic assistance to governments threatened by Communists. Among the disputes we have cited, however, its first intervention was in the Greek civil war. The British in 1944 had been drawn into intervening not simply by interest but by their ability to do so. Being in position in Athens, it was unthinkable that they should stand idly by. They believed that they could control the situation by a mixture of force and of undertakings on the constitution which would rally the majority of the population. They did not expect outside support for the rebels and, indeed, in view of their agreement on the Balkans with the Soviet Union, had reason to believe that it would not occur. In the first round, the winter of 1944–45, the rebels had to call off the rebellion and make terms, but when fighting began again in the spring of 1946 and the East–West conflict had taken such a turn that the rebels now received the assistance of Communist countries, Britain could no longer bear the cost in resources and the United States was drawn in.

In this and in the interventions in the Far East in 1950, in Korea, Taiwan, Vietnam, the sense of power of the United States played a compelling role. It had the necessary material resources and strategic dispositions and, in the background, it still had an effective monopoly of nuclear weapons. Why not therefore act boldly, resist the Greek Communists, defend South Korea and even conquer North Korea, protect Taiwan and help France resist the Viet Minh? In those cases where it did not intervene, in Tibet and Hungary, power factors in one form or another were again probably decisive.

The intervention in Lebanon in 1958 was in some respects the most hazardous of all in that the United States might have involved itself for years in a morass of Middle East conflict. It went forward boldly, perhaps through shrewd appraisal of the nature and circumstances of the Lebanon dispute, but perhaps through its prior commitment to use its power in just such a situation. Following the upheavals of 1956, the United States had taken a general policy decision that the position must be stabilised and that Egypt's revolutionary expansion, linked as it was with the Communist powers, must be checked. It made a proclamation for this region also, the Eisenhower Doctrine of 1957, and made military dispositions in the Mediterranean accordingly. It was thus already committed in advance to intervention when the *coup d'état* occurred in Iraq in 1958 and the crisis in Lebanon and Jordan reached boiling point. It is unlikely that in such affairs the general proclamation had or ever could have had much deterrent effect but now, in any case, the blank cheque was cashed. In the result, the United States and Britain were fortunate in their intervention. The nature of the dispute in the Lebanon (described in our chapter on Origins) and the situation in Jordan (described earlier in this) were such that the two powers could carry out a brief stabilising role and, that done, extricate themselves swiftly.

Nonetheless, the success inevitably carried a certain price. The Soviet Union was provoked into developing over the following years its capacity to check such unilateral action by the Western powers in the Middle East. More generally, while these and other United States interventions in disputes around the world were from its point of view defensive actions, they could not be immune from suspicions of national aggrandisement. The role which the United States adopted in 1945 of preventing violent change was from the point of view of its enemies a reaffirmation of capitalism and western imperialism and an aggressive attack on the forces of change. Even from a more sympathetic point of view, the United States role necessarily meant a great exercise of its power in the world and an enhancement of its standing. It was for this reason that the United States usually sought to ensure that its action should take place in the context of collective action with other states, first in the United Nations organisation and later in other collective arrangements, OAS, NATO, SEATO, CENTO and other less formal groupings. Wherever possible, as in the Congo in 1960, the United States kept in the background as far as possible. Despite this, some suspicion from many states could not be avoided. The security pacts were mistrusted and their leader especially so. Even for a conservative state, eagerness to intervene, extravagance in intervention, and above all unilateralism means that, however good the cause, as many states are alienated as favourably impressed.

To conclude and summarise this part of our discussion, let us revert to the questions with which we began. Why do states intervene in some disputes and not others? Or, why do some disputes lead to intervention while others do not? It is clear that the answer does not lie primarily in the nature of the disputes themselves. It lies in the motives of the intervening states, their interests and sense of justice, sincere or pretended, and calculations of power. We cannot classify disputes according to their phenomena, least of all according to the amount of death and destruction which the two sides are inflicting on each other, and search in this for the explanation of intervention or indifference. What is still today decisive is the conviction of outside states that they are justified in intervening for the promotion of interests sufficiently valuable to outweigh the foreseeable costs.

One addition should be made to this way of summarising the matter in a similar vein to the ending of our chapter on Origins. Our approach throughout this discussion has been static and analytical. This is perhaps inevitable in a general discussion and yet when we consider any particular intervention, what strikes us most is its dynamic quality and the close interconnection of the factors involved. We cannot explain why the United States in the 1960s was fighting a war on the mainland of Asia or why the Soviet Union was so deeply involved in the Arab–Israel dispute without recognising the manner in which great commitments grow from small steps whose outcome is unforeseeable. We find the motives for intervention which we have discussed at work at every stage and yet as part of a continuous movement of world politics. Actions begun long ago in some quite different area of foreign policy demand intervention in some dispute that arises now. Events in one part of the world influence intervention in a dispute in another. To understand as fully as possible why the Soviet Union countered Belgian intervention in the Congo in 1960, or why it intervened in Hungary in 1956, it is necessary to consider the wider setting of international politics that preceded and accompanied and followed the outbreak of the dispute. We have not been seeking here to give a history of post-War intervention and counter-intervention. We have sought to isolate and discuss the general factors that explain any intervention: interests and honour, justice and power. We must leave to historians the work of showing how each intervention in its unique circumstances and setting came about.

The Consequences of Intervention

Let us now turn to the final aspect of intervention in internal disputes. We have considered why states intervened; we must now consider what happened when they did so, what were the consequences for the dispute and for world affairs as a whole. It is impossible to make complete generalisations about this which are not obvious to the point of truism. We can at most hope to make partial generalisations showing the tendency of politics in this field.

The effect of intervention in four of the disputes that we have cited was to put an end to the affair; but very differently in each case. In Hungary, the Soviet Union suppressed the popular insurrection by force. In Lebanon and the Dominican Republic, the United States landed troops with a similar determination to prevent one form of outcome to the dispute; but it then discovered that its main role lay in stabilising the situation so that the factions could negotiate. In the Indonesian independence dispute, the United States eventually exerted strong pressure on the Netherlands, notably by threatening to suspend Marshall Aid, and this intervention was an element in the Dutch decision to abandon the struggle. An obvious feature of all four cases is that only one great power intervened heavily, but, truisms apart, it would be dangerous to draw general conclusions from that. Even when a great power has the field to itself, it might not necessarily be able to end a dispute quickly.

More usually, a great power will not have the field to itself. As we have seen, intervention always tends to lead to counter-intervention of some sort, if there is time and opportunity for it. When this happens, the effect of intervening is often that the intervening state wins nothing; that both intervener and counter-intervener incur great costs; that the dispute itself is simply protracted and raised to a higher level of violence. This would probably be an apt comment whether on a minor episode, such as the Oman dispute where the Imam had the backing of Egypt and Saudi Arabia, and the Sultan, that of Britain; or on a larger affair such as the dispute in Yemen where Egyptian intervention was countered by Saudi Arabian; or on a great affair such as the wars in Vietnam.

These were all cases of partisan intervention but the outcome may be little better where a state has pacificatory aims. Unless, by exception, it is able to secure the cooperation or acquiescence of rival states, they are likely to denounce its action as unilateralism and its aims as disguised partisanship, and to intervene with an alternative pacificatory formula of their own. The effect of such developments, for example in the Congo, may be to shorten the dispute or at least reduce the level of violence, but even with the best intentions, this cannot be counted on.

Though intervention tended to lead to counter-intervention in the cases we have cited, there is a well-known qualification to be made. If a state went so far as to intervene with its own forces, rival states were unlikely to do the same. The danger of war outweighed their interest. What the intervening state had most to fear was that its rivals would respond with arm's-length assistance to the other side; and, whether they did or not, that force would prove a weaker instrument than it had hoped. For in interventions in internal disputes, still more than in other areas of affairs, military force cannot be isolated from politics. The efficacy of force in ending a dispute depends on the extent to which it is supported by other factors of power and by justice.

An intervening state may have such overwhelming military force, available and suitable, that it can crush armed resistance swiftly. Thereafter, it may be able to maintain the settlement by repression. It may, that is, be itself a repressive society and it may achieve the blend of military deterrence and the other factors of power necessary to control a population. These were the methods used by the Soviet Union in Hungary.

Where an intervening state does not have overwhelming military force or is not the kind of society to rely mainly on repression, it can still end a dispute by force and sometimes end it swiftly. But to do so, it must at the same time satisfy the sense of justice and injustice of sufficient of the people of the country concerned and of its own citizens at home.

In the Congo dispute, Britain and others argued throughout 1961–2 against a United Nations offensive against Katanga on the grounds that it was pointless to deal with a political problem by force. They proved wrong. For when, eventually, the United States, fearing the growth of Soviet influence if inaction continued, promoted an offensive in January 1963, Katanga offered no resistance. The explanation of this was not that the United Nations force was in any sense overwhelming. It was that Katanga's secession was not based on a deep sense of justice and accordingly the ending of it by United Nations forces did not arouse a deep sense of injustice. The background to the secession, as we said in our chapter on Origins, was not of the same tragic intensity as, for example, that of the Ibo in Nigeria.

Outsiders intervened in the Nigeria dispute, not by direct force but by arms supply; and Britain, for its part, did not intervene voluntarily; it maintained its relations with the Federal Government and its customary position as supplier of arms. But the interesting point of comparison is that the British government took the opposite view to its predecessor in the case of Katanga and believed that the Federal Government could swiftly end the Ibo secession by force. In this it proved equally wrong. There were, no doubt, several reasons why Britain took the view it did in the two cases, but one reason seems to have been that it miscalculated the sense of justice in the disputes and, in consequence, the efficacy of force.

The Lebanon and Dominican Republic disputes, very different from the Katanga dispute in many ways, were similar to it in this crucial respect. The United States was not seeking to force a large section of the population to abandon deeply-rooted demands for justice. Rather, it was seeking to prevent the conflict from leading to a result which, in truth, few in the countries concerned desired anyway. After the initial use of force, the United States went far to satisfying the rebels by actually presiding over the resignation of President Chamoun in the one country and the return of former President Bosch to stand for election in the other.

The war in Greece in the late 1940s and the second war in Vietnam in the late 1950s and 1960s presented far greater problems. Here, the opponents received arm's-length support from the endless resources of neighbouring countries which Britain and the United States dared not attack. However, this was not the heart of the matter. It would be superficial simply to say that the crucial contrast between the Lebanon and Dominican Republic interventions and those in Greece and Vietnam was that in the former cases the United States had overwhelming military force whereas in the latter, thanks to massive counter-intervention, it did not. For it is possible to imagine disputes in Caribbean or Middle Eastern countries of such a nature that all the military force of the United States, even without counter-intervention, could not have imposed a solution.

The heart of the matter was once again the factor of justice. In Greece and Vietnam, the enemy was struggling for demands which lay on the deepest level of politics. In these circumstances, force could still be used by the intervening states and was indeed indispensable. But the resistance encountered was inevitably far more tenacious and the accompanying political problem was far greater. The intervening states could not hope to satisfy the sense of justice of convinced Communists; they had to satisfy that of the population at large. They could not simply negotiate with their opponents; they had to take wider and more complex political action among the population and so erode their opponent's support.

In Greece, Britain and the United States had much success. The constitutional concessions made internally and the development of the East–West conflict externally and Western policy in it, confirmed the majority of Greeks in the conviction that their rights as individuals and as a nation would be worse served by a Communist victory than by the existing regime. These things also confirmed British and United States public opinion behind the war. Fighting might have continued indefinitely but for the dispute between Yugoslavia and the Soviet Union which put an end to large-scale outside support for the rebels; but it was already plain that the Greek government and its allies had contained the rebellion and were winning.

In the Far East, the problems for the United States were still greater. For the sake of comparison, let us first recall the varied fortunes of the imperial powers. Unlike France and the Netherlands, Britain had been successful in the use of force in Malaya. This was partly for military reasons; Britain did not suffer heavy outside intervention as did the French; its military position was better in several ways than that of the Dutch. More fundamentally, the reason for Britain's success was that it maintained the confidence of the majority of the population, of its own citizens at home and of the states of the world. It convinced them that it stood for good government and for independence in Malaya.

The United States had the same aims in Vietnam and this was greatly in its favour; but it also had serious disadvantages compared with Britain. On the military side, the enemy was heavily supported from abroad. On the political side, it was not the ruling power but an intervening power. It was not therefore in authority in South Vietnam. It concentrated on its military role. In so far as it had political control, it was acting without long experience of Vietnamese culture. The result was that it found the greatest difficulty in establishing what must be done to confirm the faith of the population and secure their cooperation and by what methods. Lack of progress in consolidating South Vietnam behind the war and, externally, the development of the East–West conflict into a new pattern, slowly weakened the interest of the United States in intervening and the sense of legitimacy of the American people in doing so.

What, finally, was the effect of these various interventions on world affairs generally? It is already clear that it led to a great network of secondary disputes between intervener and protagonist or between rival intervening states. The United States intervention in the Chinese civil war in the shape of its decision to protect Taiwan raised a virulent dispute with China. The United States and the Soviet Union in their interventions and counter-interventions each demanded that the other withdraw or change its policy. The clashes between Egypt and the Western powers in the disputes of the Middle East states deepened their mistrust of each other. Surrounding these principal rivals were scores of other states expressing often vehement opposition to one side or the other. Any intervention set up some degree of strain even among allies and raised such disputes between rivals as often to overshadow the whole course of world politics, hardening existing antagonisms and complicating quite other problems.

On the other hand, the most obvious and vital aspect of the matter was that none of the disputes between rival intervening powers developed into war between them; states that intervened in internal disputes were luckier than states that suffered intervention. To some extent, the preservation of world peace can be explained by a fortunate chance. The countries most important to the great powers, those where they had the strongest interest in intervening, were on the whole in these years the countries closest to them. These were not the same countries for both; the great powers were geographically far apart; the likelihood that both would intervene with their own forces or strike directly at each other was therefore less.

This, however, is not a full explanation. The United States, after all, took a world-wide view of its security and intervened well outside its immediate sphere as in Greece and Lebanon. In one area, the Far East, the traditional spheres of the great powers touched at the margins. Here indeed the most dangerous of these secondary disputes arose, between the Soviet Union and China and the United States over Korea and Taiwan and Vietnam, but still war between them was avoided. Here, as elsewhere, the explanation lay in the last resort not in fortunate geographical chance but in calculated restraint. Whatever mistakes the great powers may have made in assessing their ability to intervene successfully in internal disputes, they made the judgement that they had no interest in these disputes commensurate with the threat or use of nuclear weapons. In the days of the United States nuclear monopoly, this was not an obvious judgement nor one that every state in history would have made.

7. *The Development of Disputes Between States*

In the course of our book, we have mentioned various kinds of disputes between states. There were disputes about truth. There were disputes about the structure of international society and its organisations. There were disputes arising out of rival interventions in civil wars. But most of all, and the origins of these we discussed at length in our fourth chapter, there were disputes in which two states or groups of states were in direct conflict with one another over a piece of territory or some other possession, or control of the government of a state, or the like. We must now consider the development of these disputes through their various stages up to the ultimate disaster of war.

In this century, to go no further back, there have been various fashions in explaining the causes of war, alternating between optimism and pessimism about human nature. Wars are caused by evil rulers or selfish interest groups, misleading the people. They are caused by the nationalist passion of whole populations. Nations drift into war, they misunderstand each other, they perceive a threat where there is no threat, their decision-makers fail to see the objective harmony of interests underlying conflict. Men fight through innate instincts that lead them to aggression.

This last theory is currently enjoying a revival in the shape of studies of the behaviour of animals. As commentators on human affairs, the writers are at best following in the footsteps of Aesop and La Fontaine but without knowing it and not so well. Each of the remaining theories contributes to the understanding of some war or other but not of all wars. For an explanation relevant to all, we must go to a higher level of generality about human politics. In the picture we are seeking to give, wars develop out of a particular kind of human situation, whose origins we have seen, out of disputes.

When we last spoke of disputes between states, we spoke of the state that was making a demand or challenge, its ambitions, sense of justice and feelings of power; its passions and calculations in these matters, its human ability to reason and its human inability to see far, to agree on what is seen, to achieve the effects that it intends.

Beginning now with the state that is confronted with a demand or challenge, we must first recall that it is always obliged to respond in some measure or another. In certain circumstances, its response may be heavily subdued; in others, its response may be totally ineffective; but it must do something. This is one of the great practical differences between a dispute and a normal problem of foreign policy. A state will dislike many an action of other states without necessarily reacting. It can choose. It must react on an issue of rights. It cannot choose. There may sometimes, it is true, be a subjective element in its decision that an issue is one of rights; but usually where territory, possessions or control of government are concerned, neither antagonists nor onlookers are in any doubt about this; and the state must respond urgently, whether the infringement be large or small.

The reasons for this vary from case to case but in the last resort two always remain valid. First, the question is one of interests and honour but on the level of "ours" and "theirs", of justice; and justice cannot be found unilaterally. It requires that opinion be set against opinion in argument. States are most apt to stress this when they are the weaker party; but even the most powerful and ruthless state concedes the point implicitly in that it is prepared to offer a justification for its actions. Second, the question is one of power. So long as the states of the world live under the threat of power, they must fear for their reputation for power. On this account, if on no other, even the greatest state cannot simply ignore a challenge or concede another state's demand out of hand.

So the dispute is joined. The first stage in all the disputes we have studied, after the action or demand which causes it, is the stage of argument, and common observation suggests that this is the general rule in all disputes. The states concerned put their case to each other by diplomatic means, making use of international law where they can, appealing simply to justice when they cannot. Eventually, implicitly or explicitly, they indicate to each other the possible costs of an unyielding stand and of a protracted conflict.

After this stage, disputes vary greatly in the way they develop. Some are settled swiftly; some drift on in a desultory fashion for many years; some rapidly reach and remain on the heights of bitterness. Even among our group of disputes, on the whole the most intractable and bitter of postwar disputes, there were remarkable variations. Why was there sometimes some disposition in diplomacy to listen to the other side and sometimes none? Why was the public stand taken sometimes conciliatory and sometimes harsh and unyielding? Why did some of our cases remain on the level of argument, denunciation and propaganda; why did some involve a breach of diplomatic and commercial dealings; why did some develop to the extreme of war?

We can go some way to answering these questions simply by recalling the origins of the disputes. They arose because a state, leaders and citizens, wished to increase its activities or possessions and its honour. In doing so, it reduced those of another. The other state could see no overriding justification, whether because there was none or because the two states were involved in an inevitable kind of human situation, a conflict of justice, each side convinced of the superiority of its own case. Moreover, this conviction, plausible enough in itself, was sometimes reinforced by existing bad relations between the parties. A state hardened its attitude in a dispute because, from other disputes, it had concluded that its opponent was an enemy.

Recalling these facts, there is in general no great mystery about why disputes should be marked by intransigence, bitterness and violence. We can also see why the intensity of this should vary. We would expect a dispute where the interest was small, where honour was not involved, where reputation for power was little affected and where the parties were neither competitors nor enemies to develop in a low key. Conversely, we would expect a dispute where the interest was great, where national humiliation threatened, where national power might be proved hollow, and where the opponent was a competitor or an enemy, to rise to the greatest heights of vituperation, pressure and war.

Generally speaking, we do indeed find this in our group of disputes. Yet, within this general framework, there are a host of variations which remain to be explained. Austria suffered for ten years the occupation of a third of its territory by the Soviet Union and yet the dispute was conducted in a restrained manner. In claiming Mauritania, the stake for Morocco was a vast tract of its ancient territory and yet it did little beyond a few efforts to enlist the support of some of the inhabitants. Morocco and Algeria, competitors in the region but nonetheless friendly, came to blows over a strip of borderland; Yugoslavia and Italy, with the deepest of old enmities between them, did not fight over Trieste. India and Pakistan, for all their bitterness, were not involved in continual subversion, border incidents and armed clashes. India restrained itself for more than a decade before seizing Goa.

It is plain, in short, that the origins of disputes cannot by themselves fully explain why some develop in one way, some in another, why some are carried on mildly and others reach the heights of coercion and war. Further factors have to be brought into the reckoning. In part, these lie beyond the limits of a general study such as this. Much will depend on the character of particular leaders and the temperament of particular peoples. We can only expect to understand fully why a given dispute developed as it did by studying its own unique history, the interplay of many actions by many people, some intended, some unintentional in their effects.

Of all disputes, however, we can say that what was true of their origins remains true of their development and indeed of their eventual resolution. They are never isolated episodes. They take place as part of the internal and external affairs of the states concerned as a whole, their other problems at home and abroad, their other disputes. The value that the antagonists attach to the particular stake and the lengths to which they will go in struggling for it depend on what they may gain or lose in other areas of policy. They depend from another point of view on the power that the antagonists think they have and can risk using to enforce their demands. This is the main determinant of why some disputes develop one way, some another. The calculations of states in this matter, especially of the mass of their citizens, are often crude and always passionate. Yet it is doubtful whether a state so loses control, as an individual might, that it will sacrifice all its other interests to wound its enemy. On the contrary, what is impressive is how readily the citizens and leaders of a state will choke back their anger if interests and power suggest they must; and how easily their anger seethes over when there is little reason why it should not.

Interests

In setting out to illustrate this, let us turn for a moment to the ordinary course of politics between states. Here it often happens that a state wants something from another by way of voluntary cooperation to their mutual advantage. The two states are in conflict of a sort, the one seeking some benefit, the other denying it until terms are offered that seem a good bargain. In such cases, the very nature of the objective limits the degree of conflict. It would be a contradiction for a state to seek to coerce another to voluntary cooperation. It would be absurd, for example, for Britain to seek to damage the interests of West Germany in order to exact cooperation on the financing of its troops there; or to try to coerce the members of the European Community into admitting it to membership. A state can, it is true, exact money or trade opportunities by coercion, but this is as much as to say that its aim is not a relationship of voluntary cooperation.

Similar situations sometimes arise in disputes and limit them in the same way. The broadest example at the present time is the situation between the economically poorer and richer countries of the world. When in the early 1960s, in preparation for the first United Nations Conference on Trade and Development, the poorer countries studied the relationship for the first time in world terms, their anger was intense and seemed fit to lead to the most violently pursued demands. In the event, their dealings with the richer countries scarcely amounted to demand and to dispute at all, leave alone to efforts at coercion. Even in rhetoric, the word "justice" was rare. The reason for this is not fully expressed simply by saying that the poorer countries were too weak and disunited to coerce. It is more comprehensive to say that they accepted that the flow of trade and finance and technical knowledge was inherently a matter of sovereign decision and of voluntary international cooperation and that on this account attempts at coercion would be self-defeating.

Commercial disputes in general usually have this inherent limitation on their development and are thus usually settled with good temper on both sides. This applies also in some degree to any dispute in which the thing claimed requires the cooperation of the state from which it is claimed. States can, however, easily make mistakes in this field, not least because their statesmen are dealing with commercial and technical considerations which they are least well equipped to judge for themselves. Mossadeq of Iran proved to have miscalculated seriously in simply seizing the country's oil industry, for its value depended entirely on the cooperation of the international oil distributors and this was not forthcoming. In the case of the Suez Canal Company, it was Britain's turn to miscalculate in that an important element in the development of its policy in the summer of 1956 was too great readiness to accept the Company's argument that Egypt could not by itself operate the Canal and that consequently an effective boycott of it could be organised. Each case is, in short, a matter of difficult judgement in its own terms. Yet, we can at least say generally that seizure of a foreign commercial enterprise, or indeed any pressure on its policies is liable to be defeated by the fact that the enterprise is part of an international network and is useless in isolation from it.

Similar inherent limitations arose in those of our disputes which involved the control of the government of a state, though they were perhaps exceptional cases in exceptional circumstances. The Polish government-in-exile was in dispute with the Soviet Union for high stakes, the postwar government of the country and its borders, and yet, measured on the scale of international conflict, the dispute remained at a low pitch. The point was not that the Poles had no power to coerce the Soviet Union; this was so obvious as to be negligible. The true terms of the problem were rather that the Poles required the cooperation of the Soviet Union and that this set necessary limits to their demands and to their tactics in pursuing them, limits which in the view of their British and American allies they overstepped.

The Western allies themselves were obliged for some time to work under similar constraints in their disputes with the Soviet Union over Germany and over the European settlement generally. Their belief in a single government for Germany entailed, as did much else, the cooperation of the Soviet Union, and this necessarily imposed patience and good temper in urging their demands. They were more fortunate than the Poles in one respect, however. Their aim of a single government for

Germany was not so indispensable to them as was the Polish aim to the Poles. When they despaired of Soviet cooperation, when their demands in eastern Europe were overtopped by fears for the security of western Europe, they were in a position to change their approach entirely.

In most of our group of postwar disputes, such inherent restraints were much weaker. The thing in dispute was a piece of territory and this on the whole is less likely than a commercial enterprise or control of a government, to set limits by its very nature to the methods used in acquiring it. The claimant would, no doubt, prefer to have the cooperation of the opponent after the territory has been ceded, but this is usually not inherently indispensable to the enjoyment of it. What may sometimes set limits to coercion is the attitude of the population of the territory. Where they do not wish to be joined to the claimant state, measures of coercion which affect them will rouse their hostility and increase the difficulties of eventually ruling over them. Indians, if they were successful, must rule over Muslims in Kashmir, Yugoslavs over Italians in Trieste, Arabs over Jews in Israel, Spain over Gibraltar, Morocco over Mauritania, Iraq over Kuwait. Morocco did, in fact, pursue its claim mildly and this consideration may have had some influence. If it had less influence in the other cases, this would be understandable in most. A population once ceded, whatever its feelings, has strong grounds for making the best of the position.

The next kind of restraint on the development of a dispute is the links of interest that bind the antagonists together in the ordinary process of their national life, for instance, in commerce. Spain for some time moved cautiously in the Gibraltar dispute, but when in the mid-1960s the new British government showed commercial coldness, Spain could to this extent proceed with less restraint.

In most of the disputes that we are considering, however, it was precisely because these links were weak that the parties saw their way clear to beginning their dispute in the first place; and in the same way, there was little here to restrain them in pursuing their dispute. Because we have discussed the matter in the context of Origins, we need say little about it here. In brief, looking back over our disputes, we see that many of them were between former members of empires and these often had few dealings with each other in trade. Even India and Pakistan had so ruptured relations in the course of independence that there was little to restrain them in the matter of Kashmir. In other disputes, the antagonists belonged to separate economic blocs in the world or were in process of joining them, or in some other way had alternatives to relying on each other.

Another kind of link of interest which we also discussed earlier and which is far more powerful in restraining the level of disputes, namely links of common dispute with third parties, was equally weak in most of our cases. Generally speaking, the northern countries of the world at this time were linked by common fear in the East–West conflict; and the southern countries had a strong common interest in solidarity in the face of the former imperial powers and the Soviet Union. However, when we look at our group of disputes in detail, we see that the pressure of common danger was rarely acute. When it was, the dispute was restrained. When it was not, the states concerned were free to vent their anger upon each other.[1]

Honour

To an onlooker, a tragic aspect of many a dispute was how little the antagonists were restrained by the prospective gain to their interests of ending their quarrel and cooperating with one another. They might have few interests in common at present but they could have many. India and Pakistan, the Arab states and Israel, to mention only the most obvious cases, could benefit greatly from each other in many directions. Outsiders constantly deplored what they saw as the reckless sacrifice by the disputants of potential common interests. Many a well-meaning peace plan was based on the material concessions which one side could make to the other or the material gains which they could make in common. Plainly, India and Pakistan could cooperate if they had a mind to, as in the Indus Waters Agreement. How irrational that they should continue at such cost their conflict over Kashmir; and that the Arab states should impoverish themselves year after year by their endless feud!

Yet the outsider has to recall as though himself involved that disputes concern not merely wants denied, but a sense of intolerable wrong; and that the wrong done and the enmity evoked and the redress demanded lie not just in interests, but in honour. The unjust seizure of territory or another possession means a loss of the honour that springs from it. Above all, it is an outrage to the dignity of the nation.

The concepts we have used in all our discussion of disputes, justice,

[1] The works of Lewis Carroll have long been admired for their political insight, and we draw attention to the second verse of one of his famous rhymes:

Tweedledum and Tweedledee
Agreed to have a battle,
For Tweedledum said Tweedledee
Had spoiled his nice new rattle.

Just then flew down a monstrous crow,
As black as a tar-barrel;
Which frightened both the heroes so,
They quite forgot their quarrel.

("Through the Looking-Glass", Chapter 4)

interests, honour, and the distinctions we have sought to make, are painfully artificial for the task. The single concept of honour is inadequate to describe all the emotions of humiliation and all the ways of stating them even in one chosen dispute. It is still more inadequate to describe all the forms of feeling arising in the different cultures and circumstances of fifty disputes. Yet the word can at least recall and stand for these feelings that lie at the heart of every dispute and may be crucial for its development and ending.

The anger of outraged honour can drive a dispute forward even at high cost to existing interests, leave alone to promised interests, until somehow it is appeased. Honour is no more and no less rational than material interests. Material needs usually take precedence over honour; material enrichment, only sometimes. Every state surely has its price but much may turn on how the price is paid. A material concession is often not enough in itself; it must also be made to signify redress to honour.

The weight given to honour against interest when they are in tension depends on the particular people involved in the dispute. The "confrontation" between Indonesia and Malaysia over the Borneo territories was exceptional among the disputes between southern countries in that the two states had strong links of commercial interest. President Sukarno swept these aside, not merely because of his assessment of his internal problems, not merely because he was confident that he could win as he had just won against the Dutch in West Irian, but because he attached high importance to an insult to national honour.

Honour and dishonour for a state may depend on its own beliefs or on those of a wider culture, on the attitudes of the circle of nations whose regard it values. When the moment of crisis came for the Netherlands over West Irian and for Portugal over Goa in 1961, interest was greatly outweighed by prospective cost. Honour, on the other hand, was of great importance. Neither of them fought but for different reasons. Portugal, in some respects one of the most traditional and isolated of western European states, might have fought such a war but this contest was too plainly hopeless. It made only token resistance. The Netherlands had the power to fight but recognised that it would on the whole lose honour if it did so. It was not in the position of Britain which intervened to support one Afro-Asian state, Malaysia, against another, Indonesia. It was not even in quite the same position as Britain had been in Malaya in the 1950s; for its plan for "decolonisation" of West Irian left much room for argument and doubt. The Netherlands would, in short, have the greatest difficulty in avoiding the appearance of an imperial power fighting for a vestige of Asian empire. In its own eyes by that date and those of the countries most important to it, its European associates and the United

States, it would gain no respect by holding West Irian. The United States, in particular, exerted its influence in this sense. Empire was no longer for modern Europe, as it may have been for the Javanese, a source of honour.

Honour in its other aspect, that is, as a code of conduct, placed some restraint on the lengths to which states were prepared to go in pursuing disputes. No state, to be sure, believed that there was any action that was absolutely prohibited morally, except perhaps such extremes as nuclear, chemical and biological warfare. On the other hand, no state believed that even in disputes any action was always permissible against any state in any circumstances. There was some variation among states as to the circumstances and degree of necessity which justified a given action; and, conversely as to when an action amounted to lying, treachery, murder or excessive use of force. Nonetheless, for all of them, there were always moral limits at some point.

In practice, however, this kind of restraint had only a narrow significance in most disputes. Morality affected the details of methods but not the broad methods themselves, propaganda, commercial pressures, force. For the power that most states had of these various kinds to harm each other fell well within the limits of what they considered morally permissible. The practical restraint was smallness of power, not moral code. It was, on the whole, only states in dispute with a smaller state that experienced a tension between what they could do and what they ought to do. The United States experienced this frequently as in the proposal to bomb Cuba during the missile crisis or in the Vietnam war; the Soviet Union possibly also in Hungary and Czechoslovakia; Britain in the case of Egypt in 1956; India in the case of Goa. In most disputes, however, the antagonists had the easy conscience of equal power and equal impotence.

At this point in our discussion, let us look back for a moment over it. We have seen that, in some of our disputes, various considerations of interest and honour placed restraints on their development. There remain many, however, in which this was not so. The stake was high; there was little to be lost in common interests in pursuing it; there was little moral inhibition. So far as these factors went, the disposition to strike at the opponent was unchecked by reasons for not doing so and the disputes in question were set to develop to the most extreme lengths.

In practice, this rarely happened. There was often extreme passion, intransigence and denunciation. There was rarely extreme action. The disputes that we discussed earlier within states and empires or that began as such sometimes led to great coercion and bloodshed, notably the wars in Greece, Yemen, Congo, Nigeria, Indonesia and Vietnam. To these we would add the Palestine or Arab–Israel dispute, the second Vietnam war after the 1954 agreements and the Korean war.

In contrast, the disputes between states were much less marked by violence. To judge this, let us recapitulate them by loose titles: the German question; Austria 1945–55; Poland 1944–45; the United States and Cuba; the Cuba missiles dispute; Mauritania and Morocco; Kuwait and Iraq; Indonesia and Malaysia; the Somalia borders; Trieste; Kashmir; Goa; West Irian; Anglo-Icelandic Fisheries; Sino-Indian Border; Algeria and Morocco; the Anglo-Iranian Oil Company; the Suez Canal; the Panama Canal.

Two of these disputes, the German question and the Cuba missiles dispute, raised grave danger to the world in that the great powers were directly involved. Some in which they were indirectly involved raised considerable danger. Many included some form of breach of relations. Some led to fighting. But, on the whole, the remarkable feature of these disputes, for all the drama, bitterness, disruption and waste that they caused, was how little bloodshed was suffered and how little physical damage the antagonists did to each other or even sought to do.

The explanation of the lower degree of violence in the disputes between states lies in part in the character of the antagonists. States are not one community but two separate communities. They are better placed by the nature of their relationship and of the issues between them to avoid extremes. They are usually also better organised for calculation and control. Beyond this, the explanation lies in the inter-state system and its condition in the twenty-five years after 1945.

Power

To consider this, we may best change the terms of our discussion and look at interest and honour in another aspect. We have so far left largely out of account one major restraint on states: the cost to their interests of coercion and of the disapproval of third states. These are somewhat different from the other restraints of interest we have so far considered and it is best to discuss them in terms of power. The final great determinant of the development of disputes is the power of states to pursue them. We shall say in what follows that even among otherwise uninhibited disputes, most remained at a low level because neither side had the power to raise it. The disputes simply dragged on because neither side had the power to enforce an end. The disposition to strike at the opponent may have been high but the capacity to do so was low.

The importance that we are here attaching to the factor of power in the development of disputes is reminiscent of the frequently-held belief that international politics are above all else a matter of power. We must therefore recall the ambiguities of this idea in order to make ourselves plain.

We have pictured international politics throughout this book as competition, sometimes dispute, for the security and increase of activities, possessions and honour. We may, if we wish, summarise this as a struggle for power, though in our view the phrase covers at best part of the reality, the counterpart being the demand for justice.

Again, we may be struck by the fact that leading groups in the smaller states of the world are deeply influenced in their values by the great states, in their ideas of what their country's interests are and of how to pursue them. Moreover, smaller states are to some degree necessarily obliged to turn to great states for the satisfaction of many interests and to accept the policies of the great states as a fixed point in deciding their own. This also can perhaps be called power, though it can be misleading to do so. For a hierarchy of states is inevitable so long as the world has a system of separate states. To describe it as a power relationship may suggest that it is a deliberately imposed relationship and worthy of resentment by smaller states.

We may, on the other hand, as in our discussion here, speak of power, not as a goal or effect or state of affairs, but rather as a method of attaining goals, that is, of securing or advancing interests and honour. In these terms, it is important to notice that the great majority of international transactions are not conducted by the use of power. The ordinary process of international politics consists of a complex round of influence, argument and bargaining whether in making commercial arrangements, forming alliances, framing joint policies, or whatever it may be. Power, in contrast, is associated with disputes. It is used in disputes, or, to put the matter another way, if it is felt to have been used in the ordinary process of dealings, it is liable to give rise to a dispute. For power is essentially oppressive and coercive. It is the ability to get something without making a return. It is the ability to make a demand.

Because states have disputes, or at any rate live in the continual possibility of them, they are constantly preoccupied with power. They are always in danger of the use of power against them. They remain within the limits of the ordinary process of politics in part through fear of power. Much of this ordinary process is concerned with bargaining to get and retain the protective power of others whether in alliances or some looser relationship. States that rely on protection, or even those that give it, must often suffer power to be exercised over them, with resentment but without risking serious dispute, because they value the relationship too highly. In these and other ways, the whole of international politics is overshadowed by power.

At the same time, though in this sense, power bulks large in the inter-state system, though the absolute power of states is vast and the prospect of its use fearful, in another sense, power is very limited. For the margin of power that most states have or can safely use relative to others is small. At any period in the inter-state system, many states are roughly equal to many others. In the twenty-five years after 1945, they were often in a better position than ever before to know that this was so. Above all, there was a part constructed, part fortuitous balance of power between rivals, great and small, world-wide and regionally. Most states, in sum, did not have much ability to pursue their disputes to great lengths or to impose their demands on each other.

The manner of exerting power, difficult to define comprehensively, is to do damage to the interests and honour of the opponent by withdrawing some benefit to his interests or by verbal or physical attack. Some states, as we have seen, have great links of interest but in that case their power is often evenly matched; neither has power relative to the other, for neither can withdraw benefits much more than the other can. Even where this is not so, as for instance between a great and a small state, either a dispute does not start at all, or if it does, it is often because the small state can have recourse to a rival great state and so balance its opponent.

Some states, on the other hand (and these it will be remembered are of particular concern to us at this point in our discussion), have few links of interest; they are to that extent uninhibited in disputing; but equally they have little power over each other because they have little to withdraw. There is the possibility of enlisting the aid of other states that seem to have power of this sort, especially great states; but this once again is often balanced by the ability of the opponent to do the same and to bring in a rival great state as its supporter.

In this way, states are caught in a net of power relationships which make it exceedingly difficult, even for the greatest, to move decisively in their disputes. What remains is the principal form of power throughout history, verbal and physical force. Words are used, not merely to influence the ideas of states, but to attack the honour of the opponent and of any that support him or fail to use against him such power as they have. This is, in fact, as is well known, the most prominent method of pursuing disputes in the contemporary world. For as to physical force, most states have too little at their disposal for effective action. The customs of war and politics having changed with democracy, a campaign is rarely decisive and a total war, even where there is the capacity to organise it, is equally unpromising. The great states with vast capacity for physical force, for their part, dare not use it.

In such general terms as these, we can readily understand why, even in those disputes in which the antagonists had not much to lose from each other by bitter conflict, most remained at a low level. For lack of a margin of power, little could be done. There is, at the same time, one further general consideration to be mentioned before we return in conclusion to the detailed stages through which a dispute may develop. If, as we have emphasised, states generally had little power to win their disputes, why nonetheless did they so often strike at each other at least in some measure, by denunciation, by proclaiming commercial boycotts, even by physical force? Occasionally it was because they really did have the power to win, as for instance in India's invasion of Goa. Occasionally, it was because they were mistaken about this, as in the attack on Cuba supported by the United States in 1961. Usually, however, or so it seems from the little evidence available, the states concerned did not take hostile action in the belief that this would win the dispute, at any rate outright, but for some other reason. We shall seek to illustrate this, necessarily rather speculatively, in what follows.

The Stages of Development

At the beginning of this discussion, we mentioned the usual first stage of disputes, diplomatic and legal argument. If, in view of all the considerations we have mentioned, the antagonists pushed their dispute to a higher pitch at all, the next usual stage was denunciation and propaganda.

One reason behind this is a reason that applies in some degree to all other kinds of hostile action. A state which believes that it is suffering an injustice has a strong desire to do at least something in response. The feelings of its people demand some expression of anger, censure and abhorrence. Injustice cannot be allowed simply to pass in silence. So the state does all that modern media and such forums as the United Nations allow it to do, to publicise its wrongs.

The public castigation probably also has some influence on the conduct of the opponent though how much is difficult to guess in any given case. At least it means that a government is not left entirely free to choose the version of the dispute that it will give to its own press and public. It is obliged to argue the justice of the matter in front of them with the voices of the outside world. Even totalitarian states are not entirely insulated from this pressure. Moreover, most states value the honour of a certain circle of allies and friends and seek to avoid their disapproval.

In some cases, however, the publicity surrounding an international dispute can have no other effect but to complicate and protract it. This is a matter for careful decision. Publicity may arouse and unite public opinion behind the national cause, but this is sometimes no gain in that the state even with this strength can do little against its opponent; and it may be a loss in that publicity embarrasses diplomacy and that a stand once taken publicly is harder to modify later. It would, for example, probably have been pointless for the Austrians to have raised a continuous raging polemic around their dispute with the Soviet Union. Their one major effort at the United Nations in 1952 aimed only to keep the issue alive. Internationally, the sympathy enlisted by a state in the publicity battle may encourage the delusion that sympathy necessarily portends practical assistance and so lead it to struggle on unyieldingly and fruitlessly.

The next stage of hostility, a refusal to recognise a government or a breach of diplomatic relations, is usually to be interpreted as a gesture of condemnation rather than as an attempt to exert pressure, though it may of course be accompanied or followed by pressure. The motives behind a breach of commercial relations are more varied and may include an attempt to exert pressure; but this rarely amounts to an expectation that such measures by themselves will win the dispute.

We should mention first, in passing, three cases of commercial sanctions in internal disputes. The Nigerian Federal Government may have hoped that its economic measures would make Biafra more amenable but the measures eventually became an adjunct to military hostilities. In the case of South Africa and Angola, the boycott by various African and Asian states seems to have been intended primarily as an expression of standing condemnation of South African and Portuguese policy.

We find similar characteristics in disputes between states. Sanctions always contained an element of condemnation and perhaps of retaliation. Outraged feelings demanded that at least something should be done, that the transgressor should be in some way punished. Beyond such feelings, the United States embargo against Cuba was intended to show up the weaknesses of Castroism as a policy for Latin American states; India's restrictions in the case of Goa signified that the dispute would not be dropped; the Arab boycott of Israel was an adjunct to warfare. Only in the case of the Anglo-Iranian Oil Company, the Berlin Blockade, the Rhodesia dispute, and, we may add, the Soviet–Yugoslav dispute, was there a strong element of expectation that economic action would force the opponent to submit.[2]

Only in the case of the Anglo-Iranian Oil Company was this belief vindicated. The Berlin Blockade seems to have been shrewdly calculated and but for the unforeseeable expedient of the airlift, might well have been sufficient to force the Western powers to modify their new policy for western Germany. The other two cases raised to the full all the difficulties inherent in commercial sanctions. The best known difficulty is that of universality. The state subjected to coercion can usually turn to the other

[2] cf. Peter Wallensteen, Characteristics of Economic Sanctions, *Journal of Peace Research*, 1968, No. 3, pp. 248–67. We are indebted to this article while not sharing some of its conclusions.

trade partners. Stalin may have believed that the Yugoslavs would rather overthrow Tito than turn away from the Soviet Union to the West or even that the West would not respond. More commonly, the essence of the problem is that most states see little benefit to anyone from intervening in most disputes and are not prepared to join in vigorous economic sanctions. In the case of Iran, one single product, itself the very subject of the dispute, was decisive and a strangle-hold was comparatively easy to organise; but this is rare.

There is a less well-observed but equally great difficulty about commercial sanctions. Professedly idealist as well as professedly materialist states in the contemporary world often hold a crude view of the place of the economy in the life of nations. Hit the opponent in his economy and he will soon see reason! But what is hit is the existing process of economic activity of the opponent; whereas what is usually at issue in the dispute is the whole structure of his society and its place in the world, a passionate political vision of how the nation must achieve its economic prosperity and many other kinds of prosperity as well. Such states, moreover, are usually strongly united with no faction waiting to overthrow the government and ready to seize on the economic difficulties of the country as a weapon with which to do so. In short, in the course of world affairs in the past two generations, commercial sanctions have usually been proposed against exactly the kind of state least likely to submit to such pressure.

Intervention

The attempt to organise commercial sanctions is one form of seeking to enlist the power of outside states in pursuit of a dispute. Let us look at this stage of disputes more generally. We shall find in our group of inter-state disputes just as in the internal disputes, that the intervention of outsiders was mainly characterised by defensiveness and caution. If states intervened at all, it was rarely to help one side to make a positive gain; it was usually simply to prevent one side from losing. The actions of interveners tended only in the direction of making a dispute into a stalemate.

Some intervening states were involved in disputes by the development of circumstances: Britain in the dispute between the Polish government-in-exile and the Soviet Union; the Western allies in the Austria and Trieste disputes. Sometimes they became involved by reason of defence commitments entered into before the dispute, as Britain was committed to assisting Kuwait when challenged by Iraq and Malaysia when challenged by Indonesia. Sometimes they became involved in the course of the dispute, the greatest example being the formation by many states of NATO with its commitment to the defence of West Germany and the

Western part of Berlin. But in all these cases, however they came about, the intervening states did nothing more than undertake to give greater or less assistance to maintain the *status quo.*

In most of the other disputes we have cited, outside states had greater choice and showed still greater caution. No state intervened with powerful partisan action over Mauritania, the Algeria–Morocco border, the Somalia borders, Trieste, Panama, Kashmir, Goa, Gibraltar, the Iceland fisheries. In this last case, there was much third-party interest; in others, there was much third-party sympathy and rhetoric; but in no case was there action designed to help either side to enforce victory.

The involvement of outside states in the great disputes of the Middle East was vast, complex and often dramatic, but here too there was no interest in intervening to enable the victory of either side. In the Anglo-Iranian Oil Company dispute, the United States refrained from giving Iran the financial aid necessary to make good its challenge to Britain, and for the rest, sought only to mediate. The other oil-producing states also found that the balance of their interests lay in maintaining existing arrangements with the major oil companies and these supported the boycott of Iranian oil. The Soviet Union appears to have found no means of profitable intervention at all.

In the Arab–Israel dispute, the leading Western powers implicitly undertook to prevent the destruction of Israel but did not try to enforce an end to the Arab state of war. The Soviet Union sought favour with the Arab countries by enabling them to match the power of Israel but has not so far provided the kind of military help that experience has shown to be necessary for victory.

Many states might have been prepared to take some degree of action to prevent so abrupt a change in the *status quo* as Egypt's nationalisation of the Suez Canal Company. But equally, when confronted with a *fait accompli* most states were basically disposed to tolerate this as the new order of things. They would do little to assist Britain and France to win a victory over Egypt, and in September 1956, the likely course of events was that the dispute would drift on indecisively until Egyptian possession was accepted by default. In the event, Britain and France and Israel sought to use force, whereupon many states coalesced to check this action and to prevent Egypt being defeated.

These attitudes on the part of outside states to inter-state disputes are in general terms easily understandable. Mostly, they had no great stake in any particular outcome; they would not sacrifice much to ensure it. Sometimes they had a great stake to be secured; in that case, they defended the *status quo.* Sometimes they saw the possibility of advancing their interests and honour by assisting a state seeking to alter the *status quo* as the Soviet Union did increasingly in the disputes of the Middle East; but there was no great advantage in helping a state actually to win and least of all when the possible costs and dangers of this were taken into the reckoning. A serious thrust from the Soviet Union would merely provoke a balancing counter-intervention by the United States at a risk not commensurate with the possible gains.

Whenever outsiders intervened in inter-state disputes, the result was a series of secondary disputes between intervener and protagonist and between interveners themselves. However, these rarely developed beyond ill-feeling and denunciation because those concerned saw little gain and much risk in pushing them further. Even in a serious case such as the Malaysia–Indonesia dispute, Britain's intervention was restricted to fighting off Indonesian attacks. In the Arab–Israel and Suez Canal Company disputes, the United States and the Soviet Union were more concerned to avoid a clash between themselves than to forward the cause of their clients. The placing of missiles by the Soviet Union in Cuba was, it is true, a case of extreme adventurousness; but it was probably not fundamentally an intervention on behalf of Cuba.

The Use of Force

In sum, the net tendency of the interests and power of outsiders was, as we have said, towards caution in intervention and towards stalemate in the dispute. This was in some ways greatly reinforced by the beliefs of outside states on the issue of justice. States saw no legitimacy in interfering to judge the rights and wrongs of the quarrels of others and crusading at cost to their own nation for the victory of one side. They considered that they had a right to take up or maintain relations with a state involved in a dispute; they had a right actually to intervene in a dispute to defend whatever was theirs; but as to the dispute itself, the issue that preoccupied them was not the merits of the quarrel but the methods. The leading member of international society, the United States, and many other signatories of the United Nations Charter believed that whatever might be the rights and wrongs of a dispute, it must not be settled by force. It was legitimate for them to intervene to prevent this.

This belief placed a further considerable restraint on the development of disputes. It had several aspects. One was the traditional conviction of states, especially the great powers, that they were entitled to stop aggrandisement. Another was the more modern aspiration to make a general rule outlawing war. Another was the fact that the disputes between the Western powers and the Soviet Union and China required them, in their view, to restrain the smaller disputes of other states.

Difficult to define and practise consistently, the belief in the illegitimacy of force did much to immobilise many a dispute. In the twenty-five years after 1945, not merely did the strongest state in the world take action to establish a broad balance of power deterring aggrandisement; it continually took detailed action to restrain any antagonists from any use of force at all. If despite this warfare began, the United States did whatever it could to curtail the fighting as in the Suez Canal dispute, the Arab–Israel conflict, the Chinese invasion of India in 1962 and the fighting between India and Pakistan in 1965. Other states worked in a similar fashion regionally, for example, in the border fighting between Algeria and Morocco in 1963 and Somalia and Ethiopia in 1964.

The methods of restraint used by the United States and others consisted in part of power. The United States had great power over the countries of Latin America. It had considerable power over the countries of Western Europe because they needed its military protection and economic co-operation, though this was balanced by the fact that it needed to protect them. It had comparatively little power on the other hand over the states of Asia and Africa. In its military and economic aid diplomacy, it suffered great frustrations. The withdrawal of all aid from Indonesia could not induce it to end the confrontation with Malaysia. Aid on the contrary frequently increased the capacity for violence. Ethiopia fought with United States weapons, Somalia with Soviet. In Asia and Africa much turned on whether the United States and the Soviet Union had similar interests, as they had, by exception, over the fighting between Pakistan and India.

Where the United States, Western states generally, India and many others had remarkable success at this time was not in power but in influence. They influenced the ideas of world society away from recourse to force. The Soviet Union retained older principles according to which the initiation of force was sometimes justified, but it too nonetheless contributed strongly to the general movement of ideas. Warfare was no longer to be considered as such an honourable activity; and it was rarely to be seen as an honourable method of achieving ends. A climate of opinion was created in which a state that took to force had a greater onus of justification to discharge than ever before. As a gesture to the times, even when force was used, a declaration of war was usually avoided.

This general disapproval of force in the world community sprang from a changing moral sense reflecting on interests. War, anyway as a general conception, was now too costly in things too highly valued: life, activities, possessions. To this must be added the last of the various kinds of restraint on force, the calculations of the antagonists involved in a given dispute. What was to be gained in return for the cost? What was the likelihood that the use of force would win victory in the dispute? Whatever the general disapproval of war, many states might still have seen an adequate justification in their own case. Whatever their condemnation of others, their own use of force might still have seemed legitimate and honourable. What they lacked was the capacity for force, the strength to fight successfully. We said in our earlier comments on the moral limitations on all forms of power that for most states the practical limitation was inadequacy of power. This was especially true of the use of force. Many states might have fought but few had the ability to win at acceptable cost.

Despite this restraint and all the others we have discussed, a few disputes did reach the final stage, and force was in fact used. Why was this? In some cases, the reason may have been that the stake was considered to outweigh the various costs to interest and honour, the cause was considered just, the method legitimate and honourable. Even the United States, Britain and India could not always sustain their general opposition to the use of force as the invasions of Cuba, Egypt and Goa showed.

Beyond this, in seeking to understand any given case, we must always take into account that a state that uses force is not necessarily aiming to win the dispute by force. The outbreak of violence may have some other explanation. When we consider our own group of cases, it seems in many of them as though the state that initiated force did not intend to use much force, did not plan to incur much cost, showed no great reluctance to abandon its attack under the persuasions of outsiders. Force seems to have had some lesser purpose than outright victory.

In 1948, the Arab states may have believed that they could "drive the Zionists into the sea". It is very doubtful whether they, or at any rate their leaders, believed this at any time thereafter or that this was their aim. Their continuous pressure and raiding activity and armaments development signified rather that they were not reconciled to what had happened and would not abandon the dispute on Israel's terms.

When in 1956, Britain and France invaded Egypt this does not seem to have been in the expectation that they could win the Suez Canal dispute by a simple exercise of force. Rather, it seems, they hoped to transform a drifting situation into one which presented the United States, in particular, with the makings of a solution more favourable to the Western states. Israel in 1956 and 1967 was not seeking to win its dispute by force but to punish and to deter and to show that force would make no progress.

Somalia perhaps believed that border skirmishes would keep its dispute with Ethiopia open, preventing it from drifting into oblivion. Morocco perhaps aimed to give a sharp demonstration to Algeria that it must negotiate on the border issue. In 1947, India and Pakistan may have hoped actually to win Kashmir, but when in 1965 Pakistan attacked India, this signified exasperation and protest at India's new measures for the territory. Out of all the disputes we have discussed, only four seem to show a high degree of belief that the dispute could be settled outright by force: Goa, the Sino-Indian border, the Indonesia–Malaysia confrontation, the Bay of Pigs invasion of Cuba. In the first two of these cases, the belief was correct; in the other two, it was not.

The Persistence of Disputes

In place of a direct summary of all that we have said in this discussion about the development of disputes between states, let us end by seeking to answer a simple, obvious question: why do so many disputes trouble the world for so long? The great disputes of Europe, the Middle East and Asia after 1945 lasted for ten, fifteen or twenty years. The disputes that dominate world politics today were the dominant disputes twenty-five years ago. Sometimes they began with crisis; intermittently they have erupted into crisis over Berlin, war over Palestine and Kashmir, threat to Taiwan; but basically they drag on with much discussion, some danger, deep bitterness, year after year unsettled.

Our first answer is that disputes drag on because neither side has the power to win them. Partly by necessity, partly by virtue, the world of states has had much success in outlawing war; but for this gain, it has inevitably paid a price. It has removed the oldest method of ending disputes rapidly. It has not yet found another.

Yet why, if neither side has the power to win, are the disputes not settled by bargaining? To the world generally it often seems clear that a challenge has been beaten off and cannot succeed or that a *fait accompli* is indeed accomplished and cannot be reversed. Settlement on the basis of the *status quo* seems inevitable. The Western sector of Trieste grows together with Italy; the Yugoslav controlled sector with Yugoslavia. Half of Kashmir becomes part of the Indian system; half, part of Pakistan's. North Korea becomes one society; South Korea another. The Western position on Germany is embodied in the Federal Republic; the Eastern, in the Democratic Republic. Why then do the antagonists not accept this? They may have ceased to demand their own way and now be disposed to bargain; or they may maintain the most peremptory demands; but in either case, they go on and on with the affair interminably, to the neglect of the more crying problems of the world.

One source of explanation lies in the internal politics of the antagonist states. In the last years of the Trieste dispute, Italian governments feared overthrow if they abandoned the claim to the whole of the territory. The revolutionary regime in Egypt had been called into existence partly in the context of the struggle with Israel. Kashmir was a symbol in relations between Hindu and Muslim in India. The dispute over Germany was crucial to the success of the Western allies in ruling postwar western Germany and to maintaining the internal unity of some eastern European countries and of the Soviet empire as a whole.

Yet, in the last resort, these internal factors derived their strength from the external situation. Domestic attitudes depended on the fact that progress in the dispute was not entirely excluded. Whatever the world generally might think, a nation that wanted to hope could still see hope. In the last years of the Trieste dispute, the diplomatic situation in Europe was so complex that Italy still had some chance of winning concessions. Egypt and its allies could still see in the support of the Soviet Union and in their own potential for economic growth some reason not to accept as final the terms offered by Israel in their days of weakness. The affairs of Kashmir and Pakistan and India continued in a turbulence from which one day victory might be plucked. As to the German question, the Soviet empire in eastern Europe was so unstable that it was difficult to speak of simply accepting the existing position and erecting a settlement upon it.

Once a continued challenge is plainly futile, once a *fait accompli* is plainly unalterable, once the *status quo* is manifestly stable and secure, a dispute will begin to lapse. A challenge, at first vigorous because possible, becomes wearisome through lack of progress. Resistance to a *fait accompli* dies harder because a loss always wounds deeper than a gain denied; but it too dies at last. Blows struck in the dispute compound and perpetuate it but are at length forgotten. Time, in a word, can bring an end; so also can some shift in those factors that explain the origins and development of the dispute; the phase of solution opens. Until then, the antagonists answer our question with another: why should they abandon their dispute? They have interests at stake and no greater interest forcing them to settle; honour is involved, requiring satisfaction; their cause is just and must be vindicated; and even if they have no power to enforce their demands, there may still be in the situation, some possibility of hope.

8. The Limitation of Disputes

THE problem of limiting the disputes of the world is not that of creating a new world government but of making the existing world government work well. This government is made up of a hundred and more separate state governments. They are unequal in spiritual and material power and so some have primacy. All of them argue and bargain as to how the affairs of the world are to be conducted. They make agreements, laws, with one another under which they and the population of the world go about their business. They each have some force at their command and seek to restrain each other and keep the peace. They dispute and plunge into civil war, like factions within the separate states, when they are ambitious and unchecked and when they think that the laws or superior norms are being broken.

Perhaps in time the development of world society will be such that this diffuse form of government will change into one analogous with the governments of some of the separate states today, with force more centralized and institutions for peaceful change regularised. But if this happens at all, it will not be through attempts to draw up and implement general schemes of reform. A new constitution for the world will grow bit by bit through the actions of governments in response to problems as they arise. Whether in these long range, evolutionary terms or in simple more immediate terms, the answer to the problem of the limitation of disputes lies in good statecraft by those who are responsible for the government of the world.

Good statecraft requires the imagination to grasp the problems that arise and the courage to grapple with them. It also requires an understanding of what will and will not work in human politics, of what action is likely to lead to what response. Much practical experience is needed and much knowledge of the contemporary world and reflection on it.

In all this, our study is confined to one aspect only. We have tried in the last two chapters to illustrate how and why disputes develop, in the belief that an understanding of this assists those who must seek to limit them. The responsibility for peace lying nowhere else than in the actions of statesmen and citizens, much is gained by ever wider understanding of how these actions can lead to war. To put this more broadly, much is gained by a growing self-consciousness on the part of states in disputes. They are not simply engaged in a struggle with such and such another.

They and the other are both involved together in a certain type of situation, common since the beginning of history, which has its own special characteristics affecting them both.

Having made our contribution to the understanding of this as well as we are able, we have done all that we are able. Perhaps someone can go further, can elaborate a set of techniques which will be of use to a statesman in limiting the next dispute that confronts his country. We do not pretend to this. In this chapter, we shall simply seek to draw together the threads of our discussion, transforming generalities on the development of disputes into the corresponding generalities on their limitation.

1. Disputes within States

In our use of the word, the development of a dispute meant essentially two things: the increase of the pressures of the two sides upon each other, ending at worst in the use of force; and the widening of the dispute by the intervention of outsiders. Correspondingly, limitation also has these two aspects.

The Policies of the Factions

If we look first at disputes within states, it is clear that responsibility for limitation lies primarily with the internal factions. Possibly each among the leaders and followers in these factions cares only for his own personal advancement and safety and not at all for the well-being of the society in which he lives. Possibly, however, they have some concern for this and, if so, limitation depends upon the extent to which they understand the nature of force. They need to reflect that there is sometimes injustice so terrible and unyielding that only force will serve. They need also to consider that anyone who seeks or resists change has always two causes whether he recognises this or not: the justice that he demands and the preservation of a society in which to establish it.

In more detailed terms, the limitation of disputes depends on good judgment of the efficacy of force in given circumstances. In Nigeria in January 1966, for example, a group of soldiers came to the conclusion that they could carry out a *coup d'état* and, presumably, that they could successfully rule the country afterwards. In the event, having for the first time in Nigeria made control of the government a matter of force, they could not sustain their victory, the position was reversed six months later by superior force, and the factions set out on a course which led to civil war. The decision reached in Janaury 1966 may or may not have been reasonable in all the circumstances. The point is only that this decision, together with those of others later, is the right focus of practical interest in considering the experience of Nigeria; that on these decisions depended the development or limitation of the dispute; and that the decisions could have been different.

The limitation of internal disputes next depends upon the degree of understanding by the factions of the nature and consequences of external intervention. Our discussion in the preceding chapters will certainly not allow us to offer any general rule on this matter. We can only point out how frequently it happens that a faction succumbs to the very powerful temptation to accept external support; and now frequently, sooner or later, in one manner or another, this leads to counter-intervention so that the only result is to raise the level of force profitlessly.

The temptation is naturally at its most powerful in disputes where the great powers and indeed all significant powers are united in favouring the same faction. Here, it seems, that this faction can safely accept external support without fear of counter-intervention. In practice, however, it has to be borne in mind that the unity of outside states readily crumbles so soon as one of their number actually goes so far as to intervene. States are always troubled at the sight of intervention by another and, however much they may share its opinions, are always disposed to counter it.

If the factions do not invite intervention, they may nonetheless have it thrust upon them; and here the basic requirement for the limitation of disputes is an understanding by factions in states that they must carry on their disputes within the limits laid down by the attitudes of outside states. If it is absurd to enthrone justice on the ruins of society made by the factions themselves, it is equally absurd to establish it amid ruins made by the intervention and counter-intervention of outsiders. The factions must either restrain their demands on each other and their method of pursuing them with an eye to this danger or be ready to pay a high price in destruction worked from abroad.

The danger of demanding too much and losing all is naturally greatest in the case of small states dominated by a great power capable of crushing unopposed intervention. It is a reality which it is futile to overlook that a revolutionary cause must be advanced within the limits of tolerance of the dominant power. These limits must be considered first at every stage, tactics settled afterwards.

The difficulties of manoeuvring successfully within these limits are so formidable and the skill and luck required so great that we prefer not to try to give examples of recklessness and failure from among the relevant disputes we have considered. Let the reader decide for himself what he thinks in the four relevant cases: Greece, Hungary, Guatemala and the Dominican Republic. Did the revolutionary faction judge well with regard to the likely reactions of the dominant great power? We prefer to give a commonly agreed example of considerable skill and caution which nonetheless ended in failure. Nine days after the Soviet invasion of Czechoslovakia on 20 August 1968, the President of the National Assembly said in a broadcast: "This situation is, alas, not new in our history nor is it unusual. Here lies the tragedy of the quest for new socialist achievements, the tragedy of those seeking to lead the way, the tragedy of the attempts by people pursuing great and noble aims. Such an effort is never easy and is twice as difficult for small nations, involving twice the risk of failure, frustration and misunderstanding. I think we were aware of this risk. I think we anticipated that we would have to pay for all this. However, and I should like to stress this, we did not expect a force such as that which the night of 20–21 August brought upon us."[3]

The politics of the faction demanding change in Czechoslovakia appear to exemplify uncommon realism about the limits within which the internal conflicts of small states must be fought or not at all; but, calculate as they might, consider how they might the situation in Soviet terms, they could not in the end be certain of Soviet judgements and misjudgements. It is common enough for men to be revolutionaries; it is less common for such men to understand prudence; and it is least common of all for the confusions, misunderstandings and blunders which they inevitably unleash when they precipitate a crisis to fall out in such a way that they have in addition, luck.

The Policies of Outside States

Next to the factions involved, the limitation of internal disputes depends upon the policies of outside states, and this in various ways. In the first place, they have dealings with the existing regime and cooperate with the existing social order. They may do this because they want to or simply because they have to for the conduct of their own national affairs. Whichever is the case, the effect is the same; they are making the *status quo* workable and to that extent supporting it against the forces of change. In this way, their policies in some measure or another enter into the explanation of recourse to force by factions demanding change.

Many a statesman, while perhaps conceding this, would argue that it is inevitable in the nature of things and has no practical implications. The conduct of world affairs would soon become impossible if states continually passed judgement on the regimes of those with which they had dealings and modified or ended their dealings accordingly. This is true. Yet some contribution is made to this difficult matter by bearing in mind the distinction between the ordinary process of politics and dispute. When a state judges that another is moving into a situation of friction in its internal

[3] *The Times*, 30 August 1968.

affairs with all the signs of coming dispute, it is well-advised not to drift along but to make a definite moment for a reappraisal of relations. For if a dispute does eventually break out, its dealings with the existing regime may have serious implications and pose acute dilemmas; whereas if it foresees these at an early enough stage and pays attention to them at a high enough level, it may be able to avoid them.

The result of the reappraisal may be to reduce relations or present their significance differently or modify them in some other way. Alternatively, the result may be a decision to strengthen cooperation with the existing regime in the hope of averting unwelcome change. Whatever is done, the state should understand clearly that in dealing with another which is in a growing state of friction, it is incurring a degree of moral responsibility and taking a practical stand which may eventually have repercussions on its interests for good or ill.

It is not usual to call the mere continuation of relations "intervention" and plainly the word can hardly be made to cover this without intolerable strain. Nonetheless, the situation in its moral and practical effects is the same as intervention. The character of politics within the state has changed from normal conflict, peaceful or turbulent, into a conflict of justice; and so accordingly the character of dealings with the state has changed from what is normal to what amounts to intervention. Often this will not matter very much; many outside states will carry on dealings with a government in dispute and so, in a strict sense, be quasi-interveners; and no one will blame them or resent an injury. But sometimes in the case of those outside states whose dealings are significant for the outcome of the disputes, it will matter greatly.

Let us now look at intervention proper, that is, support for a faction that is demanding change, or assistance to a government of a sort designed to help it to crush that faction. Here, the limitation of disputes depends on good judgement by the intervening states. They may, it is true, judge the situation very exactly and decide with their eyes open on actions which will lead to a great increase in the scale of the struggle. The practical possibilities for limitation lie in the margin of cases when they judge badly and believe that their intervention will have effects that it will not have and so intensify the struggle to a degree that they would never have wished.

Once again, our discussion in the two preceding chapters will certainly not allow us to offer a general rule in this matter. What it does suggest is that the costs of intervention usually prove higher than could ever have been imagined at the outset and the benefits lower. For, to summarise that discussion, there is first of all the danger of counter-intervention arising from the ingrained disposition on the part of states to resist intervention by one of them in another. They will seek ways of countering it in a manner which may at first sight seem improbable and will take action if circumstances are at all propitious and if the intervention is not managed rapidly and presented as a *fait accompli.*

If, however, there is no counter-intervention, so far so good; the intervening state can give the regime or the rebels the margin of power necessary to victory. But the problem does not end there. Often enough, the intervening state must now either give its victorious ally a continuous and costly flow of support necessary to hold the position; or persuade it to take the necessary measures to appease dissident opinion. The costs and difficulties of this are all the greater in that the intervening state is now committed to its ally, cannot lightly threaten to abandon it and the ally and all the world know this. Sometimes, on the other hand, the victorious ally no longer needs the intervening state; it is firmly in control of the country; but in that case, there is no certainty that its policies will continue to accord with the interests of the intervener. In short, an intervening state is liable to win for its pains either a troublesome ally or no ally at all.

Looking now at counter-intervention, the next stage in the development of disputes, we have already implied that this is frequently a tragic necessity. It involves the same risks and costs as intervention, it increases the sufferings of the country concerned, it is undesired by the states undertaking it, and yet it is necessary. States will inevitably seek to counter-intervene to safeguard their interests in the country concerned; and indeed, on a wider view, they must seek to counter-intervene to prevent the element of unilateralism, if not of purposive aggrandisement, always present in any intervention. The possibilities of limitation are thus here once again confined to those cases where a state considering counter-intervention makes a misjudgement. One variety of misjudgement is worth particular attention in as much as the experience of the past twenty-five years gives a plain reminder that states sometimes think that others have intervened and that they are engaged in counter-intervention when in fact this is not so.

We saw in our discussion of the development of disputes how each of the principal intervening states, the United States, the Soviet Union and Egypt, believed in some degree that its interference in the internal affairs of other countries was defensive or counter-interventionary in nature. The United States believed this utterly; the Soviet Union and Egypt seem to have believed it to a lesser, but still significant, degree. Sometimes they were correct in this belief; their opponents really had intervened first; but sometimes they were deluded by presuppositions.

Communist ideology, and indeed much other thinking in the contemporary world in imitation of it, was unable to accept a distinction between the ordinary, often turbulent process of politics in a state and a condition of dispute. In the Communist view, every non-socialist state in the world was always in a condition of dispute, that is, of class struggle, even though everyone in that state, except an exiguous Communist Party, might not think so. Accordingly, the dealings of the leading capitalist countries with any of them amounted to taking sides in the class struggle. The United States was never simply seen as a country going about its business with a multitude of states, good, bad and indifferent; it was always seen as the headquarters of the capitalist camp, supporting the crumbling forces of reaction everywhere; it was, so to say, a continual interventionist. Correspondingly, Soviet attitudes to world events seem to have included all the emotions and impulses usually associated with counter-intervention.

Such mistaken feelings could have serious consequences if a state is not restrained, as the Soviet Union usually was, by lack of power. They are not, moreover, confined to people and states so exceptional as Communists. Egyptian foreign policy in the late 1950s, for example, also contains this element. In its subversive activities in relation to Lebanon, Jordan and Iraq, Egypt did not believe that it was committing aggression; it did not even merely believe that it was attacking governments that were enemies of the Arab cause; it also believed that the relations between these governments and the Western powers represented continued imperialist intervention in the Middle East against which it was counter-intervening. In this way, a state can feel impelled to attack, not just with the emotions of attack, but with the still more powerful emotions of defence as well.

Presuppositions affected United States policy in a rather different manner. Its opponent, the Soviet Union, was indeed sympathetic to Communist parties abroad and often actively assisted them; United States dealings with governments abroad, in so far as they were a move in this game at all, were indeed truly counter-moves. At the same time, because it believed so strongly in an united world-wide Communist movement centred on the Soviet Union, the United States rated more highly than it might otherwise have done the part played in internal upheavals by the Soviet Union and the significance for international alignments of Communist victories. In consequence, its counter activity in states abroad had a focus that was somewhat misplaced and a scale and haste and bluntness that were excessive.

Intervention and counter-intervention are often so disastrous for the country concerned and so unprofitable and dangerous for the interveners, that the thought naturally arises of seeking to arrange some general international rule of non-intervention. It seems unlikely, however, that this is the best way to make progress. Great powers will always remain sensitive to events in smaller neighbouring states and will always keep in reserve what the hostile critic calls a doctrine of "the limited sovereignty" of these states. The same is in fact true among smaller states themselves. At the present time, the conception of rigidly separate sovereign states does not fit easily with feelings of pan-Africanism and pan-Arabism and European unity and international socialist solidarity and the like. Some or all of these movements may be temporary phenomena; but in any case at all times, it seems impossible that states should not be often deeply concerned with the internal conflicts of others, and this may widen and deepen in coming decades. Such areas as Europe and eventually the world generally may regain the close social and economic unity of nineteenth century Europe and, if so, the impulse to intervene will be as strong as it was then. No general law of non-intervention is likely to be proof against it. The most that can be hoped for is that states will grow in understanding of the formidable nature of intervention, and judge well in the circumstances.

Even such partial measures as a general ban on arms supplies to countries torn by civil violence, though perhaps feasible for smaller states, are unrealistic for the larger. Their decision on arms supplies can be wise or reckless; minimalist with regard to force in human politics or maximalist; reached solely politically or influenced by commercial greed; but they cannot evade responsibility for their interests or for the course of world affairs generally by adopting a rule of complete abstention.

This brings us to the question whether at any rate intervention and counter-intervention of a partisan sort could not be avoided by organising a kind of intervention, perhaps under United Nations auspices, designed solely to limit the internal dispute and end the bloodshed of civil war. We shall comment on United Nations operations generally towards the end of this chapter. For the present, the first and clearest point is that states are reluctant to intervene in the quarrels of others unless they are sure that their own people have an interest at stake. If, however, we assume the existence of some states having a humanitarian concern or any kind of interest in a particular quarrel the point now is that in taking responsibility for stopping violence, they are also taking responsibility for a solution to the dispute. "Police actions" are always followed by judicial actions of some sort; in domestic affairs, legal; in international affairs, political. Simply stopping the fighting may, in itself, represent a decision against one of the parties; alternatively, the interveners are the controlling force in a settlement that makes decisions between the parties.

This being so, such intervention will not necessarily be for the good. Even if the outside states are drastic enough and sufficiently united in their interests to enforce peace rather than increase or prolong war, they still have to prove themselves superior in finding a just settlement to the factions themselves. "Hundreds of thousands can die in Indonesia and nobody worries. The Tibetans are swallowed up in China and forgotten. Nigeria is more in the category of Indonesia and Tibet than of Cuba and Czechoslovakia. Is it better so? Supposing all the peoples and governments who have expressed their deep concern about developments in Nigeria had insisted on taking a hand in events, would anyone have benefited? Would fewer Biafrans have starved? Would a formula bridging Nigerian unity and Biafran separatism have been found?"[4]

Depressing though the answers to such questions may be, it would be wrong to swing back to the opposite extreme, a doctrine of non-intervention. A great state or a concert of states can act powerfully and justly in taking charge for the time being of the affairs of a country. Such intervention can never be a mere neutral and negative ending of bloodshed; it will always involve a process of political conflict, political debate and political decision; but this is no argument of principle against it. Possibly over the coming years, the frequency with which outside states combine to suppress civil wars will increase and rightly so. They may well judge that the disruption and suffering are more unjust than any conceivable settlement could be and act determinedly to end the violence. The problem of the coming years is at least as likely to be indecisiveness and scrupulosity as arrogance and precipitation. All that can be said is that there should be no doctrine of intervention either, a climate of world opinion according to which it is always best for outside states to exert pressure on the factions immediately and to do so with preconceived methods. Whatever domestic analogies may suggest, the matter in inter-state politics must long remain one of judgement in the circumstances.

Throughout this discussion of the limitation of disputes within states, we have assumed one particular condition in the world, and it deserves final stress. It is the present degree of balance of power, especially between the great states. The true end of power is to create the conditions for justice. A balance of power means a situation in which no state can impose a demand, whether a demand of its own or of some state or faction that it supports. Many elements contribute to this situation, resources, organisation, strategic dispositions and the like; but what is above all indispenable is a vigorous determination on the part of each great state not to allow the others sole control of the course of world affairs.

Whenever a balance of this sort exists globally and wherever it exists regionally, unilateral intervention is deterred by the prospect of counter-intervention, by cost, danger and sterility. Peacekeeping intervention becomes possible by the great states in concert or by groups of lesser states.

[4] *The Times*, leading article, 21 August 1968.

Conversely, if the degree of balance that has been achieved in the past twenty-five years should crumble, the most rapacious intervention would become possible and all prospect of peace-keeping intervention would be at an end. The internal disputes of states might still be limited but not in the conditions of power that are favourable to justice; rather, in a tyrannical manner which few would welcome.

2. Disputes between States

If we now turn to the limitation of disputes that arise directly between states, the same theme of balance of power must again be prominent; but before discussing this, we must set the scene with some more general remarks.

Compared with the twenty years after 1918, the world since 1945 has been well ruled by the governments jointly responsible. Whether as regards understanding of the realities of power in international politics or the observance of expedient limits in the pursuit of ambition, or the condemnation of inter-state war as an institution, or the spread of organisations for international cooperation, the statesmen of the leading countries have as a whole been wiser and more successful than those of the previous generation. If we grasp the vast changes in the map of the world since 1945, the scale of the achievement in avoiding major war must strike us as very great. In the great disputes of the world, the stakes have been as large as any in history and the hatreds and fears as intense, and yet restraint has been evident at every turn. We tried in the previous chapters to show the reason of the development of disputes. In so far as it was a tale of foolishness, this was only the ineradicable foolishness of the whole of human life, the continual passionate pursuit of interests and honour. Much evil was done; but at least, if our concern is with the limitation of disputes, the most striking feature is how well the broad measures necessary to this end were recognised and, on the more detailed level of particular disputes, how rarely we can point to gross misjudgement of the likely consequences of actions.

It follows from this that our discussion here is not based on the supposition that the statesmen who today handle the disputes of the world have overlooked some great body of general wisdom or of detailed techniques which we, as outside observers, can point out to them. At all times, the theorist follows the practitioner and cannot precede him; his function is to assemble, analyse and display the good practice of some for the benefit of others, and as we say, at the present time, good practice has not been lacking. Accordingly, our comments will consist for the most part of noticing lines of effort towards the limitation of disputes already in hand;

and how necessary these are; and how fragile; and how dependent on continued statesmanship. We shall try to avoid casting our every comment in the tedious form; "statesmen and those others who are responsible for making public opinion should do thus and so". Any who are not already doing it and should chance to read this, can translate comment into admonition without help from us.

In these years, several traditional lines of effort towards the limitation of disputes have dropped into the background: the banning of war, universal disarmament, judicial procedures. Probably, it is true that in the past twenty-five years, there has been no inter-state issue worth the initiation of war and that the presumption against war has been well-founded. There was value in having this presumption established in the United Nations charter. Yet, at the same time, there has been growing awareness that general norms and declarations have only a restricted influence on the thinking of states. What matters is that they should each judge their own particular dispute well and conclude that it, in particular, is not worth violence.

Similarly, there has been growing recognition that universal disarmament of the nations is too general an approach, and that the better line is that particular states in dispute with one another should seek to control their armaments. It is also nowadays clearer that the nature of inter-state disputes is not such that they can often reasonably be submitted to judicial process. Even less promising is the notion that the international community should define aggression, should establish in some agreed objective way the occurrence of an aggression and should then enforce recourse to peaceful procedures of some sort.

What all these various developments in international thought amount to is that, after some generations of schemes for the reform of international society, the older idea is now returning to favour that the solution to the problem of peaceful change lies in the quality of the diplomacy of states. States, not by banning war or by disarmament, but in their diplomacy, must handle their power in such a way as to limit their disputes. States in their diplomacy, not a judicial tribunal, must be concerned with justice in such a way as to limit their disputes.

Limitation by Power

What this way is, we must now consider. In doing so, we shall have to alternate continually between two different perspectives: the contribution that the states engaged in a dispute make to its limitation; and the contribution that all states generally make to the limitation of all disputes.

To begin with a state that initiates a dispute, we should recall that the first and most obvious way in which disputes are limited is by an immediate, overwhelming *fait accompli*. About this we need only make two kinds of comments briefly. In the first place, most states are confronted with serious power difficulties, especially in present-day circumstances. The greatest among them can act in this way towards those in which their rivals are little interested but not towards others and least of all towards each other. The smaller among them may have the power to seize the thing at stake, a piece of territory or a commercial enterprise or whatever it may be, and may be very tempted to do so. But looking further ahead, the question is whether they have sufficient power thereby to end the dispute. They may well merely reverse the roles in the conflict and the conflict itself may well go on with all its costs and dangers.

Current power circumstances may, however, change or in some particular case not be inhibiting. The other difficulties of presenting the opponent and the world with a *fait accompli* are those of justice and prudence. Few would be prepared to say that a unilateral *fait accompli* by a state can never be just. We would only note that there may be some importance for a state in seeing that it is so. For there is a connection between the character of a state's foreign policy and the character of its public life generally. Moreover, if the circle of states significant to the state concerned do not agree that the action is just, it will pay a high price in suspicion created. Then again, the prize will sometimes be valueless unless the political or commercial world is prepared to cooperate afterwards. Finally, states have to bear in mind that an attempt at a sudden *fait accompli* that fails, causes by its unexpectedness one of the most dangerous and unpredictable and uncontrollable kinds of situation in international politics. We shall return to this point again later in this discussion.

If the first way of limiting disputes is that of overwhelming power, the second is that which we have already stressed, balance of power, the inability of states to impose a demand. A condition of general balance in the international system among the great states is the basic means of limiting the disputes between them; it also prevents their domination of the world; and it also helps to limit the disputes of smaller states by helping to maintain local balance between them. It creates in short the essential framework within which the affairs of the world can go forward peacefully. Without it, all other efforts towards the peaceful handling of inter-state disputes are vain.

The great powers themselves have most responsibility for the maintenance of this situation and for the continual development which is necessary to maintain and improve it over time. This is not to say that the basic approach of the great powers to foreign policy is, or ever could be, the maintenance of an abstract system of balance of power and therewith the limitation of disputes. Their basic approach is the pursuit of their interests and honour. However, they can show understanding of the nature of international politics in deciding what to do in pursuit of these and vigour in doing it; and this will make towards balance between them. The future of the limitation of inter-state disputes depends, in other words, primarily on the continuation of the present position in which the great powers have a comparable degree of involvement in world politics.

The smaller states, to an extent and in ways that are well known, can contribute something to the maintenance of balance between the great states and to the prevention of the two undesirable extremes: on the one hand, collusion and condominium over the world by the great states; on the other, war. As to the local balances between these smaller states in the various regions, the point is also clear enough that these are maintained partly by the skill of the states themselves, and partly by the actuality or, at any rate, the possibility of equal great power patronage of competitors.

One aspect of this requires particular mention, however, the supply of armaments by the great states. The military effect of these is often enough that the local balance is simply lifted to a higher level of power or that indecisive fighting is raised to a higher level of destruction. As we noted in an earlier context, a general self-denying ordinance by the great powers is improbable though an informal understanding may sometimes be worth working for. This is a field for diplomacy to foresee the likelihood of an arms race in a given situation; to seek to demonstrate to the great power opponent the fruitlessness of it militarily and perhaps also in terms of the advancement of influence; and to try to persuade the local states of the various risks incurred for no gain to them as states. Whatever the benefit to groups within the state, they, as states, are merely raising the level of their balance or of their mutual damage to no purpose.

In sum, the supply of arms with the aim of balance is often clearly necessary and the problem is to achieve the minimum level. The supply of arms with the aim of gaining influence or of preventing a rival from gaining it is a much more dubious matter. Though there can be no certainty on this, there is much in the history of the past twenty-five years, particularly in the Middle East and North Africa, to suggest that these hopes and fears are often based on a shallow and short-sighted analysis. The argument all turns on the immediate gain to be made or the immediate loss that is threatened, not on wider or longer considerations. Moreover, at least among the Western states, armaments supply has been allowed to become an important item in national economic rivalry. Considerations of balance of power and of influence are pleaded publicly but this too counts covertly. It is referred to in such phrases as "a contribution to the national balance of payments problem" but it is really to be called greed.

Though there has been a fair degree of balance in the crucial military sphere in the years since 1945, in another important sphere of international politics, the economic, there has been marked imbalance. We have noted from time to time in this study that disputes arising in this sphere, that is, multilateral disputes over the distribution of the world's resources, may become increasingly prominent; and also that any kind of economic dispute, whether distributive or over some particular commercial matter, tends to have stronger inherent limitations than, for example, a territorial dispute. At the same time, there has been another factor making for limitation, the overwhelming dominance of two great states; but this is not a satisfactory form of limitation.

In the past twenty-five years, that is to say, there has been not one world economic system in which the great states balance each other, but broadly speaking two systems, each dominated by a great state, the United States and the Soviet Union. The results of this imbalance within each system have been very different in each. Few in the lesser states in the United States system, whether in developed or developing countries, would claim that they have been as unjustly treated as have the lesser states in the Soviet system; relationships are not determined solely by power but also by the beliefs of the state that wields it. Nonetheless, it remains true that United States ideas and activities dominate its system's industrial, trading and monetary affairs; and that these inevitably tend to give priority to the advancement of United States interests. If an amicable counter-balance of various Western and Southern groupings is not worked for and achieved in the present relatively harmonious times, and if the domination continues, it is to be feared that resentments will grow, that recrimination and revulsion, not cooperation, will be the keynote in times of economic difficulty, and perhaps that a counter-balance of an antagonistic sort will eventually emerge.

Closely related to the power aspect of limiting disputes is that of links of interest and honour between states. We have already discussed this matter in relation to the prevention of disputes and need not labour it again here. In brief, our review of Development confirmed how the presence of these links makes for restraint in disputes and their absence, for lack of restraint. The most important of these links are those of common dispute with another state. Disputes in Africa, for example, have frequently been restrained in large part by invoking the common cause against South Africa. Links having to do with the ordinary process of the life of states, for example, in industry, trade and finance, are less important but still significant. In consequence, all policies, whether by the great powers or anyone else, which aim at promoting security cooperation or economic cooperation or whatever it may be, have two results: the particular result aimed at and the general result of limiting disputes.

The remaining aspect of the limitation of disputes which has a certain relationship to power is that of influence on ideas. The great powers are not simply great powers but also great cultures, and the ideas that they propagate about international politics have a deep influence on the conduct of the world of states as a whole. In contrast to the inter-war period when some of the leading states not merely accepted war as an institution but exalted it, the leading states today are united in condemning inter-state warfare. Indeed, they have ideologies which shift the emphasis of human affairs from inter-state or international competition entirely.

The Communist ideology of revolutionary struggle is plainly a serious source of conflict; but, in as much as its focus lies within states where power is much smaller, it is at least less dangerous to peace than an ideology of unlimited inter-state rivalry. American ideology also has always been more concerned with peoples and their constitutions than with states and inter-state politics; and in so far as it does attend to the inter-state aspect of human affairs, the relationship that it exalts is co-operation.

All these ideas, which have their own historic roots and are no mere reflection of the increasing costs and dangers of war, have their own most potent influence in discrediting and dishonouring war. They thus contribute profoundly to the limitation of disputes between states. For the future, the preservation of world peace will depend heavily on the vigour and depth of the debate on political ideas in the leading states of the world and the determination with which they stand against new ideologies of conflict, violence and war.

Influence on ideas is, then, the third of a trinity of forces that make for the limitation of disputes: power, links of interest and honour, influence. Yet, it is certain that these are not the only forces at work in international politics and that to appeal to them is not a complete answer to the question of how inter-state disputes are, and must be, limited. The inadequacy of these forces by themselves is well known, even if what is to supplement them is controversial.

For, as to power, if the international system is unbalanced, disputes are limited in the worst way; that is, one side is simply crushed. If the system is balanced, the *status quo* is favoured against change. In more detailed terms, a balance between opponents may result in a dispute soon dying away for lack of progress; but this is not necessarily the best solution nor a lasting one. In great disputes, where there is deep concern and unshakeable hope, the dispute does not soon die away and the balance may be one of high tension, perhaps at an ever higher level of organised alliance and counter-alliance and capacity for mutual destruction. Each side knows that the other would strike if it could and is manoeuvring to tilt the balance in its favour. So far as balance of power by itself goes, an incident or an accident or a limited action misunderstood may, at any time, cause an explosion. Balance of power may be the essential framework within which the affairs of the world can go forward peacefully. But, by itself, it is not enough.

As to links of interest and honour, the crux of the matter throughout the course of a dispute is whether these are valued more highly than the thing at stake. The worst case is that in which it proves that neither side values them more highly; the links are simply snapped. Alternatively, one side values them more highly; it is then at last obliged to make concessions in whole or in part; it may, in time, forgive and forget these under the influence of greater events; equally likely, it may store them as a national humiliation against the day of revenge. The best case is where both sides value the links between them more highly. Here the dispute drags on in a low key and may become obsolete eventually. But there is always the possibility that some change in the wider international situation of the states concerned will lead to one or other of the first two outcomes, unrestrained conflict or resentful surrender.

As to the third of the trinity of power, influence on ideas, the particular ideas to which we referred, condemnation of war and of nationalism and the exaltation of cooperation, are still plainly not fundamental. The idea that war is, in general, damnable is only persuasive to an individual state when it is not faced with what it considers to be an intolerable wrong. The strong, the rich and the satisfied can easily deplore nationalism and inter-state rivalry and racialism; but the weak, the poor and the discontented must first be offered some alternative conception of how they are to better their condition. As to international cooperation, the greatest of the new guiding ideas added to international relations in the past quarter century, it means in itself nothing, however great its appeal in rhetoric and propaganda. Cooperation, working together, is as much what the slave does with the slave-driver as what one free man does with another.

This is to say, in other words, that denunciation of nationalism and war and eulogies of international cooperation are the merest cant unless they are backed by concern on the part of those who utter them, for justice. The same is true of the other members of this trinity of forces. The most perfect balance of power imaginable and the strongest conceivable links of interest and honour between states still leave relations between them tense, restless and explosive unless they are animated by a spirit of justice.

Translating this into terms of diplomatic action in the course of a dispute, a state surely does well to look to its power position, to consider how it stands relative to its opponent in the calculus of interests, and to try to exert influence upon it and on the world of states by appealing persuasively to every last derivative of the ideology of peaceful relations between states; but it goes still further towards the limitation of the dispute if its statesmen and citizens have such a character that they will listen to the other side and will try to do what is just.

Limitation by Concession

With this we come to the second main aspect of the limitation of disputes. We have discussed what may be called collectively power: overwhelming power, balance of power, links of interest and honour, influence on ideas. We are now to discuss concession. A state involved in a dispute may take an unyielding stand because it is satisfied with its power. Alternatively, it may be willing to enter into genuine negotiations, and this, too, may have the effect of limiting the dispute. It may be ready to do this on one of the three grounds: justice, which we have already mentioned; prudence; and expediency.

The opinion that states in a dispute sometimes limit it because they seek to do what is just cannot be proved. Considerations of power and any concern that there may be for justice are so fused in the natures of men and statesmen as to defy any certain and precise analysis. Nonetheless, the opinion has a grounding. For, to speak in the first place roughly, when we reflect on past generations and centuries of the history of diplomacy, one contrast strikes us again and again. We see occasions when a statesman took on behalf of his country everything he could get. We see other occasions when a statesman was content to take less than he might have done for the sake of good relations.

This concern for continued good relations with an opponent may have various roots: on the one hand, a range of attitudes from the most calculating machiavellianism to a plain, mercantile shrewdness that forbears to ruin a potential customer; on the other, an attitude which seeks a certain quality in human life. If we try to put the matter more exactly, we may best do so in terms of two kinds of states.

The one holds what it has and takes what it can get to the limits of power. It considers the interests of both sides in a dispute but only on a shallow level, that of what each wants, how much it wants it, and the power that they have to get or keep it. If the outcome of this calculation is favourable, it holds to its course; if unfavourable, it concedes as a matter of expediency.

The other kind of state holds what it has and takes what it can get to the limits of justice and power. It considers the interests of both sides on the deeper level of what they merit and need in relation to each other. It, too, makes the calculation of costs and of power, and, if the outcome is favourable, it holds to what it thinks just; if unfavourable, it concedes as a matter of prudence.

We must say that we are not following here the same line of contrast as in the controversies of twenty or thirty years ago, realism against idealism, morality against power, selfishness against altruism, and the like, controversies still echoing today for lack of any substitute discussion that matters to practical men. Whatever their value in their time, these contrasts do not seem today to reflect the permanent alternatives of statecraft.

Again, the line of contrast is frequently drawn between states that consider only their own interests and those that also take into account the interests of others; but it may be possible, even with little help in the present condition of Western moral philosophy, to go one step further than this, as we have done. For both the best and the worst states consider the interests of others, and the line of contrast seems rather to lie in the level on which they do so, the sense of the word "interest" in which they do so.

The one state is concerned with the interests of its opponent solely as desire, in order to gauge the strength of comparative desire and thus to make the calculation of power. It is well advised in this, as we have said before, to try to look beyond desire to the sense of justice of its opponent because this affects power; but, whether it does so or not, in the end it is only concerned with power and with how much it can safely hold or seize. The state, on the other hand, that takes account of the interests of its opponent in any deeper sense than this necessarily takes a view, not just of the desires of its opponent but of the merits of these; it is concerned with justifiable interests. In that case, it is making a judgement of the justice of the dispute. If it acts on its judgement, it is seeking to do justice.

In describing the two different kinds of states, we plainly do not mean that any actual state or statesman has ever perfectly exemplified them. It is a question of degree, of nearer and further, from occasion to occasion. Nor are we suggesting that the one kind of state is more successful than the other. No amount of analysis of the fortunes of states would allow a conclusion on this. It is a matter of different conceptions of success in human life and which of them a state admires and holds. To argue for the one conception over the other would take us further than ever beyond our ability. Accordingly, we do not mean to recommend that states should try to do justice to one another. The most that we can say, and do mean to say, is that when one or both the states in a dispute are in some measure concerned with justice, this is a force making for the limitation of the dispute.

When we come to the other two grounds for a conciliatory stand in disputes, prudence and expediency, we are allowed by all the best minds of the age to make recommendations. For it is agreed by all that any state, whatever its vision of success, must weigh what is desirable against what is possible. To speak only in terms of prudence (since the considerations arising for expediency are the same in their effects), the question that always confronts a state involved in a dispute is: granted that we want, and should in justice have or deny such and such a thing, how far is it prudent to try to enforce this?

Sometimes, it must be admitted, prudence will forbid concession because of its effect on reputation for power. It has always been a maxim of statecraft that concessions from weakness are dangerous and that a state should lean towards mobilising and demonstrating sufficient power to avoid this impression. This may be the prudent course even when the state is inclined to admit that there is justice in the opponent's demand. For the circumstances of the demand remain important, that is, the preponderance of the opponent, and still more on occasions, the manner of the demand, that is, threats or unilateral actions. The most widely known episode to which this applies is the Rhineland crisis of 1936. We should add that, on the other hand, it is common to invoke prudent regard for reputation for power as a reason for intransigence too hastily without real support from the facts of the given situation; or to invoke it as a form of expression of quite different emotions.

If the decision is taken to mobilise countervailing power before any talk of concession, this necessarily involves in a sense expanding the conflict; but only in the sense of achieving or proclaiming balance, not of aggressive actions. The ideal is to remain conciliatory towards the opponent. In practice, to come anywhere near this ideal is one of the hardest feats of statecraft. In mobilising power, popular passions become inflamed against the opponent; his fears become acute; and even if explosion is avoided, the confrontation becomes so embittered and entrenched that the original thought of ultimate negotiation is quite forgotten. The rearmament of the Western states in their disputes with the Soviet Union probably showed a clear margin of good statecraft over bad as regards these points. But, in saying this, it is hard to know how much to allow for the fact that the Western alliance was throughout calmed and sobered by superiority in the most powerful weapons; or again how much to allow for the quality of Soviet statecraft.

Sometimes, on the other hand, prudence requires, not the mobilisation of power, but willingness from the outset to negotiate concessions. The details of this, the calculations involved, need no further emphasis at this stage in our study. What does need emphasis at least for Anglo-Saxon consciences is the more general point that prudent concessions are not merely necessary but right. Prudence is not the same as "mere expediency"; it is a virtue as much in statesmen as in anyone else. Power, we said earlier, makes for a tense, restless and explosive world; but so also in practice does justice; and so above all do power and justice combined. The saying "*fiat justitia et pereat mundus*" is the greatest example in politics of how a theoretical truth can be a practical lie. No virtue is complete without the others. Unqualified, justice has a terrible self-righteousness. States go to war not for what they merely want but for what they consider just; but it is a commonplace of the whole history of human affairs that neither side is ever wholly right. One may well be more nearly right than the other; but equally this margin may well not be worth the cost of conflict. Not only the man of expediency, but the prudent statesman also, will insist that the point of justice is the protection of interests and honour and will struggle against the sacrifice of these to a figment called justice for its own sake.

Intractable Disputes

These considerations lead us directly to the third main aspect of the limitation of disputes. For what about those disputes where no concession is judged possible? Or where the stage for concession has not yet been reached and where for one reason or another, the two sides are determined to struggle on unyieldingly? We include here some of the greatest of the disputes that we have cited in this book. They continue today virulent and intractable. We should recall at this point once again that such disputes make in their way a great contribution to world peace. Their existence limits many another, lesser dispute between states. But what about the limitation of these disputes themselves?

The states engaged in them need more than ever the virtue we have just been discussing; not now in the sense of counselling concession but in the sense of restraint in the manner of conducting a dispute where no concession is judged possible. The word "prudence" is out of fashion today; other, more complex words and phrases please us better, "limited war", "controlled escalation", "crisis management" and many more; but they all signify prudence. In whatever detailed form, this virtue in statesmen and citizens is the reason why the great intractable disputes of the world are limited to the extent that they are.

Looking back over the history of past generations, it sometimes seems to us that there was a fatal dynamic in the very nature of disputes driving the protagonists irresistibly onwards towards war. But the only dynamic lay in their minds; and the crux of the matter was that they did not think that war was fatal. They still believed that war was a normal and even glorious contingency of human life and were willing to accept it if it came.

In the disputes themselves, there was and is no daemonic force, no necessary spiralling of pressure and counter-pressure. Some disputes go to extreme lengths but others do not. Interests and honour do not inevitably demand that one step in hostility must be followed by another; nor does reputation for power. If a demand is rebuffed, if the first measures to implement it do not succeed, a state still has the choice of resting its side of the quarrel where it stands. It need suffer no harm to its reputation for power by its failure to go on if it presents its decision to the world in a certain way. As to a state faced with a demand, nothing obliges it to respond with hostile actions or to do more than counter those that are done to it. It is not necessity but prudence or the lack of it, that governs the ascent of action and reaction in disputes.

So soon as a dispute begins, the leaders of the state proclaim to their people and the world the justice of their cause. They do this in order to arouse the determination of the people and to mobilise the power of the state. This is, in itself, inevitable and what matters is how it is done. It is, above all, not inevitable that the opposing state should be depicted as evil and the threat that it poses be inflated. This arouses a quality of emotion which may well not be necessary to national strength; which may well, on the contrary, prove the enemy of such strength as years succeed months of struggle; and which certainly adds the most dangerous elements to the development of relations with the opposing state.

Again, so soon as a dispute begins, calculations of power may suggest some form of hostile act against the opponent, from rhetorical denunciation to armed force; but in prudence, power is always the worst way of winning, whether as regards the dispute itself or the wider future that will follow victory. It is better to try by all possible means to remove from the demand such elements as may not be indispensable and which stiffen the resistance of the opponent: the humiliation to honour; fears that this demand will be a prelude to others; anxieties as to reputation for power. It cannot be said that a state should always proclaim in advance that it will never have recourse to power pressures in the dispute; but sometimes if it does so, the gains in terms of the attitudes of its opponent may outweigh the losses.

If the decision is taken to resort to power pressures, prudence demands calculation and recalculation at every stage. The stages that we discussed in the preceding chapters were rhetorical denunciation, the withholding or breach of diplomatic relations, the breach of commercial and other relations, the use of force. The question throughout, obvious but extremely difficult, is whether the possible benefit outweighs the possible cost. About this, one general remark can be made. States need to be clear about what kind of benefit they are seeking. Is the intention to coerce the opponent into doing or ceasing to do something? If so, is this clear to the opponent? Is it something that he could do? Is the pressure or the extra pressure exerted commensurate with the scale and nature of the demand so that there is some chance that he will comply? If these and the similar questions elaborated for particular cases cannot be answered in the affirmative, then the action will have no other effect but to intensify the dispute pointlessly.

Alternatively, is the hostile action intended to mark an injustice done, to express emotions of disapproval or abhorrence? Is it intended as punishment, whether retributive or as a deterrent to others? Or is the aim to keep the dispute alive and to prevent an unsatisfactory position from becoming accepted by the quiet passage of time? Any of these motives for a hostile action may be reasonable in given circumstances; and yet it remains true that the costs are usually heavy, for the opponent is driven still further from compliance and the dispute is deepened. Statesmen would plead that it is often public clamour that forces them to strike some blow at the enemy; but the clamour may sometimes depend on confusion in the public mind between an expression of anger and a measure intended to have some effect; and the question is how far the statesman has tried to clarify the public mind.

At every stage in the attack and counter-attack of a dispute, the main maxim of prudence is minimum response. This is especially relevant in crisis. A state that begins a dispute with an attempted *fait accompli* or that provokes a crisis sometime in the course of a dispute usually has plenty of time in which to calculate at least the first step; for example, the nationalisation of the Anglo-Iranian Oil Company and the Suez Canal Company; the decision to establish a missile base in Cuba; the various actions that precipitated the Berlin crises of 1948, 1958 and 1961; China's bombardment of Quemoy and Matsu in 1958; Egypt's closure of the Straits of Tiran in 1967, the prelude to the Arab–Israeli fighting of that year. The respondent, on the other hand, has comparatively little time to calculate his reaction, and it is this that creates acute danger.

What is first of all necessary is that the state that initiates the crisis should understand this, should realise the risks as well as the gains of surprise. Statesmen, like men generally, surely have a highly idealised picture of their opponents and find it hard to imagine the reality. They need to understand that in provoking a crisis, they are plunging their opponent from the first, and both sides eventually, into a situation of extreme confusion and highest tension and perhaps, at last, of deep weariness in which good and predictable judgement is almost impossible.

As to the respondent, he has more need for a maxim to guide action under this strain than at any other time in politics and it is that of minimum response. In the initial shock and uproar, the necessary question is: what is the true degree of urgency of reaction, of commitment to a course, and above all, of strong reaction? As the crisis develops, both sides need in prudence to minimise the scale of the issue to the level consonant with mobilising their power and demonstrating their determination; to seek at every turn of action and reaction, for whatever is the least step that will hold them on course; and they need to reduce in every possible way the difficulties of the opponent in breaking off the crisis. They need to believe that the bold thrust, the brilliant coup, the dazzling victory are no longer an admirable style in statecraft.

There has been a growing conviction at least in the United States and the Soviet Union in recent years that prudence suggests not merely self-restraint in crisis, but the making of standing joint arrangements to facilitate this. However deep their disputes, both of them wish to avoid error and catastrophe. An "incident" can never cause a war; that depends on what the states concerned wish to make of it against the background of their general feelings about war. The most spectacular incident in the past twenty-five years of American–Soviet relations, the U2 incident in 1960, remained fully within Soviet control. Accidental war between the United States and the Soviet Union is, at least at present, very difficult to imagine; their strategic dispositions give them time to establish the facts. Nonetheless, it is obvious that the great powers need now, as always in the past, the best possible arrangements for communicating their intentions. They need, that is, both the technical means and, above all, the general understanding of each other's minds on which communication in a crisis depends. They are, moreover, dependent on each other for the general regulation of armaments, both economically and strategically, in cost and danger.

Valuable as such joint efforts are, we are still obliged to admit that in the end what counts most is the more basic forms of prudence. For understandings on limitation are most needed at times of high tension between states; and at such times, they are almost impossible to make, maintain or trust. The United States and the Soviet Union began to collaborate on their common nuclear danger only when tension between them was already slackening. In 1970, joint arrangements for limitation were less necessary between these two than between the Soviet Union and China, where they were also less possible.

On the whole, and certainly as regards most states of the world in disputes with one another, we can as yet scarcely hope that they will establish lines of collaboration limiting the extent of enmity. Even the maintenance of diplomatic relations between opponents is still often considered unthinkable. States are still very far from the ideal of an international society in which there is understanding of disputes as a common situation and a framework of cooperation over-arching the area of conflict. The most that we can realistically expect for the moment is that states will exercise prudence in their disputes, each for itself and on its own account.

The Role of Outside States

We must now look in conclusion at the role of outsiders and of the world community in general in the limitation of disputes. As regards partisan intervention, we need say little. Many of the considerations governing it are much the same as those governing intervention in internal disputes. Perhaps the most difficult issue concerns advance commitments to intervene, security guarantees, covenants and the like.

These limit disputes by deterrence but expand the dispute if the deterrent fails. There is great value in a clear indication to an opponent of where the security line is, geographically or in some other respect, that he must not over-step. This requires not mere generalities and papers signed but an intelligible, conscious, visible and demonstrated involvement of the guarantor's security in that of the guaranteed states. But this, in turn, means that the threat aimed at in the guarantee must be correctly identified and evaluated and must genuinely be a threat to the guarantor's security. If this is not so, the line drawn may fail to deter, and the guarantor may either betray his commitment or be involved in expanding the dispute dangerously and profitlessly.

We must next make some comments on "peace-keeping intervention", or to put it more broadly, the limitation of disputes by the world community. As in our discussion of internal disputes, the first comment must be that states only intervene when they believe that they themselves have some interest at stake. To take an example from the disputes we have cited, in 1948 the United Nations Palestine Commission appealed to the world for action to prevent the outbreak of fighting between Arabs and Jews plainly impending. There was no response.

With this basic point on states' attitudes in mind, let us look at the United Nations. There is a constant tendency in discussing world politics to think of the United Nations as an autonomous entity possessing power and to criticise and abuse it and seek to reform it as though it were a world government that culpably fails to solve international disputes. In reality, if we wish to think of a world government, there is only one and that is the one composed of the governments of the separate states of the world. The United Nations is to be seen primarily as one of the places and means which they can use to limit their disputes and the disputes of others if they wish to do so. As often as not, the practical possiblity is limitation rather than solution, the holding down of an affair until changes in the world cause it to die away; and when this is done, it is done not by the United Nations, but by states using the United Nations procedure.

This situation is changing continually with the development of international society and the point may eventually be reached where, although certain states take the initiative and are the moving force behind a "peace-keeping" action, they can nonetheless be seen as acting in the name of the whole world community in accordance with the outcome of its political debate. But for the moment at least, the better focus is on states using the United Nations as an instrument rather than on the United Nations as a collective entity.

States use the United Nations first and most generally as a forum for voicing their opinions. Here the organisation comes nearest for the present to being an entity greater than the sum of its members, that is, not an instrument of any of them in particular. The debates of the United Nations reveal and express a certain degree of common international concern. Most particularly, certain common norms are continually invoked or counter-invoked in terms of which any given state must seek to explain and justify its actions. This is a clear gain for the limitation of disputes. For most states are in some degree desirous that their action should look well in the eyes of the world; and there is reason to suppose that the obligation to justify themselves in terms of common norms presses them a little nearer to those norms in practice.

The price paid for this gain is well known, however. The debates at the United Nations are necessarily political debates and vigorously partisan; and the enormous labour and energy expended on them and the bitter public stand into which they force protagonists is the enemy of "quiet diplomacy" aimed at the reconciliation of the parties. We may say generally that the gains from the institution of United Nations debates outweigh the losses; but in any given case, the decision to submit a dispute to this debate is a matter for careful judgement by states.

As regards stronger action for the limitation of disputes, it seemed in 1945 that the great powers might use the Security Council as their joint organisation for controlling the disputes of the world. As it turned out, this or any other approach was impossible for several years. Recently, however, the United States and the Soviet Union have used the United Nations as a means of avoiding separate competitive intervention. The United States has taken the initiative in promoting the intervention of the Secretary-General and, after fighting, of military forces supplied by smaller powers. Such actions are a sign made by the great powers to each other and the world that their policy in the dispute is non-partisan or is limited at this particular point in its partisanship. The Secretary-General and the military forces are also subordinate agents in pacifying the situation. They are, finally, a symbol in it, in a way which may have some influence on the minds of the disputants, of the idea of a common international concern.

We should notice that regional organisations are also effective in a similar way. For example, in the fighting between Somalia and Ethiopia and Morocco and Algeria, the two sides might have called on the support of the United States and the Soviet Union and these might have felt obliged to intervene, but for the existence of the Organisation of African Unity. The Organisation allowed the great powers to remain relatively inactive and enabled the African states themselves to intervene in the name of a body that symbolised the very potent idea of an African common concern greater than the dispute.

So far, this method of limiting disputes by the great powers and others has depended on the consent of the parties to the dispute. It is possible for the future that, when a dispute is dangerously inflamed and the outside states can reach close accord, they will impose intervention on the parties. However, for the present, the parties have their own reasons for accepting intervention with no more than perhaps some degree of pressure upon them. They may, for example, anyway wish to go no further with their hostilities or think it prudent not to. On these grounds, Britain and Egypt accepted military intervention under United Nations auspices in 1956; and Algeria and Morocco and Somalia and Ethiopia accepted conciliatory intervention through the Organisation of African Unity in 1963 and 1964. Similarly, one of the parties may accept United Nations intervention as an honourable way of extricating itself from a dispute which it does not wish to fight, as, for example, the Netherlands in the case of West Irian.

Sometimes, the parties to the dispute do not merely accept, but actually invite, the intervention. It is here the disputants themselves who are using the United Nations method of limiting the dispute. Until 1948, the convention was that only one of the disputants need make the invitation, as, for example, in the case of the observer group on the Greek borders in 1947; but later there needed to be at least the consent of both, as in the case of the Lebanon borders observer group in 1958. Sometimes both the disputants wish to make joint use of the United Nations as when Egypt and Saudi Arabia had recourse to an observer mission as a way of ending their arm's-length fighting in Yemen in 1963.

In picturing the United Nations as an instrument of states we do not mean to reduce the status of the Secretary-General to that of a cypher. He is usually a subordinate actor but still an actor; and sometimes at certain junctures in a dispute he may take the initiative in a way no one else could. So, for example, Hammarskjöld reduced for a while the mounting tension between Israel and Egypt in April 1956. U Thant's intervention eased the problem of the Soviet Union at a critical point in the Cuban missile crisis. Nonetheless, the point remains that, creative as the Secretariat and Secretary-General may be, they must be creative within the pattern of politics of the states concerned with a dispute and cannot seek to impose their own policies on a situation.

Sometimes, the states themselves forget this and confront the Secretary-General with an impossible task. In the Congo, the United Nations intervention was both an African counter-intervention against Belgium and a substitute for intervention by the great powers; but the Secretary-General was continually left to act without the consent of one of the factions in the Congo and in a totally confused relationship to the other. After the fighting between India and Pakistan in 1965, an observer mission was called for by some states while strenuously objected to by others, notably the Soviet Union. Frequently, the Secretary-General, or some official group, is ordered to proceed instantly to some inflamed dispute and to produce forthwith comments and recommendations, even though this may be the last thing that is useful at that moment. Here, the states assembled at the United Nations, or some of them, are using the Secretary-General to create a mere show of activity, evading the fact that it is their comments, recommendations and, above all, their actions, rightly timed, that are decisive in limiting disputes.

The United Nations, in sum, can neither limit disputes nor solve them. It cannot impose its will for it has none. Its agents cannot act without the consent of states. It is an instrument of states. All the procedures of the United Nations which are often thought of as intended for the solution of disputes, diplomacy, mediation, military forces, are useful, often more so, for limiting disputes, for temporising, for spinning out a dispute with talk until it is soluble or obsolete. But these procedures are not, and never can be, set in motion by some *deus ex machina* in human affairs, whatever the temptation to talk so, whatever the longing for deliverance by a world authority, whatever the simple desire to push responsibility on to someone else, anyone else, for controlling the disputes of the world. They are set in motion only by states, by their statesmen and their citizens.

Wherever, then, we turn in discussing the limitation of disputes, whether it is to the actions of protagonists or interveners or the organisations of the international community, the problem remains the quality of statecraft of states. It is on this that the limitation of disputes ultimately depends. The problem is not simply one for diplomatists. Anything that they can do or that can be done by international cooperation to improve the quality of the diplomacy of the many states of the world and their methods of making foreign policy is valuable. But diplomatists count most in the normal process of politics between states and least in disputes. In disputes, more than at any other time, it is the politicians and the public who are in control and whose attitudes and conduct are decisive.

We shall surely be asked here once again at the end of our discussion what new techniques for the limitation of disputes we have suggested, what proposals we have made for the improvement of international organisation? Once again, we answer that such questions confuse the roles of the observer and the practitioner of international politics and the contributions which each can make. It is for practitioners, who are actually handling disputes, to create the ways of doing so in the very course of doing so. The alleged practical suggestions of outside observers are time and again either irrelevant abstract schemes or the oldest tricks of the diplomatic trade dressed up in novel jargon.

Our contribution to the matter has been an elaboration of the truth that whenever a dispute has been limited, it was because the statesmen and citizens of the countries concerned understood the use of power, tried to do justice, acted with prudence. Very well, then; but what is the value of saying that? For is it not already obvious enough to everyone in every state of the world, governments, legislators, journalists, the man in the street and in the crowd, and all who form his attitudes on the disputes of the day?

Perhaps it is. Perhaps we must face a further question. How are these so obviously desirable qualities to be strengthened? We answer that there are several ways in which this happens, one of which lies within our sphere. It is the way of reflection, not on current events or on history, but on politics; of growing more aware, not of this or that dispute, but of disputes as a kind of human situation; of thinking about power and weakness, justice and injustice, prudence and recklessness, and how these develop or limit a dispute. Such reflection has its effect on the minds of men where, it is rightly said, wars begin. Few minds are directly affected but they are the ones who, in turn, influence the whole mass of nations. This, at all events, is the thought that encourages those who conduct the kind of discussion we have attempted here.

PART THREE: SOLUTIONS

9. *The Solution of International Disputes*

IN the present Part of this book we propose to consider what is meant by the solution of international disputes, meaning by that expression the termination of disputes with the mutual agreement of the parties concerned. It is clear, however, that this is not the only way in which a dispute may end; an outcome may be imposed by force or threat of force on one or other of the parties, and although this may for all practical purposes terminate the dispute either permanently or for the foreseeable future, it is an assumption of this study that this is not the kind of termination which is considered desirable; we are concerned here essentially with the *pacific* solution of international disputes. It is therefore proposed in this chapter to discuss the solution, in the sense of the termination of international disputes as active subjects of debate between the parties, whether that termination is achieved peacefully or forcefully, and hence we propose to distinguish between the "peaceful solution" of international disputes, in which the element of mutual consent predominates, and the "coercive solution" of such disputes, in which the element of force or threat of force predominates.

As will be seen, however, there remains a third possibility, and this a very frequent one, even if a dispute is neither peacefully nor coercively solved; namely, that it should become quiescent, dormant or obsolete, or in other words no longer actively pursued by either or both of the parties concerned. We must accordingly take into account the conditions under which this particular outcome occurs.

In later chapters of this Part we shall consider the efficacy of the various well-established means for the peaceful solution of disputes which the international community has developed: in particular the United Nations and regional agencies, negotiation, mediation and the use of good offices by third states, international organisations and individuals, arbitration and adjudication. It is worth pointing out at this stage, however, that so far in this book we have distinguished between, and treated separately, disputes *within* states and disputes *between* them. While it is indispensable to do so when studying the origins and development of disputes, this sharp distinction seems less necessary to pursue when we are considering the resolving of international disputes. It may be that international and intra-national disputes are similar in that neither can be regarded as peacefully solved, unless some formula representing a common frame of mind is arrived at between the parties. It is true, too, that we may have much to learn from the process of resolving disputes within countries which has its application to the resolution of disputes between them. Nevertheless, it would carry us far beyond our terms of reference to consider how all social and political differences, internal and international, are concluded. Where the solution of an international dispute depends upon the prior solution of an internal dispute (as may have been the case in the Lebanon crisis of 1958) we can do little more in this study than draw attention to that fact. But in general in the present Part of this book we shall be concerned with internal disputes only in so far as their continuance is a source of international friction and the termination of that friction depends upon action at the international level. The subject of our study, in other words, is the peaceful solution of *international* disputes. We can hardly take within our embrace the whole field of human conflict.

We propose therefore to regard a dispute as "peacefully solved" when an agreement has been reached between the parties such that they regard the matter as closed, at least for the sort of future which lies within the scope of practical politics. The agreement may take the form of a written understanding in appropriate legal style, such as a treaty, or there may be something more in the nature of a tacit agreement that a *modus vivendi* has been reached. This consensus, however, should be somewhat more than a mere agreement to differ, or simply representative of a readiness to let the matter drop for the time being. The agreement should in some way spell out a mutual and considered arrangement which is regarded by both sides as reflecting their interests. When, on the other hand, the two or more sides have gone no further than to agree that their differences should merely be laid aside as causing more trouble by their continuance than any conceivable agreed solution would be worth, we are disposed to describe the dispute as "quiescent". Without having been solved in the sense already stated, the dispute no longer figures on the agenda of diplomacy for the states concerned, though hostile exchanges about it may continue on the verbal level.

In addition, as we have already stated, there are solutions of disputes, as for instance that of the Goa question in 1961 or the Hungarian crisis in 1956, in which the 'agreement' has been little less than an act of *force majeure* on one side or the other. It should be recalled, of course, that in the world of international relations the reasons which induce states to enter into agreements between themselves always lie on a spectrum ranging from the pole of pure consent at one extreme to the pole of pure coercion at the other; nor can it be a realistic expectation that any high proportion of international disputes will be ended with the consent freely given of all the parties concerned. Nevertheless, it is contended here that there is a qualitative difference between a situation in which one party to a dispute submits to the other's will at the point of the pistol, so to speak, and that in which there is something in the nature of "give and take" on both sides, even though force or the threat of it may even in that situation loom in the background. It is an object of the present study to consider ways in which the former type of situation becomes less frequent and the latter more frequent.

Thus we propose to identify four categories of dispute, viewed from the point of view of their outcome: the quiescent, the unsolved, the coercively solved and the peacefully solved. If we take the 50 disputes which we have studied for the purpose of this book we find ourselves able to divide them into the previously mentioned categories in the following manner: (1) quiescent – 11 disputes; (2) unsolved – 9 disputes; (3) coercively solved – 14 disputes; (4) peacefully solved – 16 disputes. The following tables set out the manner in which the 50 disputes are individually placed within the four categories.

TABLE 1

Quiescent Disputes

South Tirol, 1945 to present
Cyprus, 1954–59 and 1963 to present[1]
Muscat and Oman, 1957–59
Quemoy–Matsu, 1958
Berlin, 1958–61
United States–Cuba, 1959–61
Sino-Indian Border, 1959–65
Laos, 1957–65
Algeria–Morocco, 1958–63
Yemen, 1962–67
Hong Kong, 1967
Total: 11 disputes

TABLE 2

Unsolved Disputes

Kashmir, 1947 to present
South Africa, 1948 to present (including the two issues of *apartheid* and South-West Africa)

[1] See p. 235, *infra*.

China: Taiwan, the UN, 1949 to present
Vietnam, 1954 to present[2]
Angola, 1961 to present
Gibraltar, 1963 to present
Chinese minority in Indonesia, 1965 to present
Rhodesia, 1965 to present
Arab–Israeli conflict, 1967 to present[3]
Total: 9 disputes

TABLE 3

Coercively Solved Disputes

Poland, 1944–45
Greece, 1944–49
Palestine, 1945–49
Indo-China, 1945–54[4]
Korea, 1947–53
Berlin, 1948–49
Tibet, 1950–59
Hungary, 1956
Congo, 1960–63
Kuwait–Iraq, 1961–63
Goa, 1950–61
Cuba missile crisis, 1962
Nigeria, 1966–70
Czechoslovakia, 1968
Total: 14 disputes

TABLE 4

Peacefully Solved Disputes

Austria, 1945–55
Indonesian independence, 1945–49
Trieste, 1945–54
Indonesia and West Irian, 1950–62
The Anglo-Iranian Oil Company, 1950–53
Guatemala, 1952–54

[2] This could be regarded as the "second phase" of the Indo-China dispute listed in Table 3.
[3] A development of the Palestine, 1945–49, dispute listed in Table 3.
[4] The "first phase" of the dispute listed in Table 2 as "Vietnam, 1954 to present"; see n. 2 above.

Suez, 1956
Anglo-Icelandic Fisheries, 1958–61
Lebanon and Jordan, 1958
U2, 1960
Somalia, 1960–65
Aden (South Yemen), 1963–67
Mauritania–Morocco, 1958–69
Indonesia–Malaysia, 1963–66
Panama Canal, 1964
The Dominican Republic, 1965
Total: 16 disputes[5]

We must, of course, hasten to concede that, as with all attempts to distinguish between types of phenomena as fluid and diverse as human action, the process of classifying international disputes from the point of view of their eventual outcome must in some cases be or seem to be somewhat arbitrary. In the above tables, for example, we have described the 1945–49 Palestine problem and the Indo-China dispute which culminated in the defeat of French forces at Dien Bien Phu in 1954 as "coercively solved", which may seem ironical considering the situation at the time of writing (summer, 1970) in the Middle East and Vietnam respectively. Nevertheless, it is not improper to regard the Palestine problem as having had a definite outcome, though achieved primarily through superior military force, in the sense of the ending of hostilities and the formation, if only *de facto* in Arab eyes, of the state of Israel in 1948. Similarly, the Geneva accords of 1954 did represent the conclusion, again with force playing the predominating role, of a certain phase of the conflict in Vietnam in so far as that conflict lay between the French and associated groups of Vietnamese nationalists, after which a new phase of the dispute, this time with the United States as one of the principal actors, seems to have opened.

In the same way, there might be some question as to whether the disputes over *apartheid* in South Africa, Angola and Kashmir should fall into the "quiescent" or the "unsolved" category. It is proposed to group all three under the latter of these two headings since none of them can

[5] It will be noted that in previous chapters of this book we have described the Quemoy-Matsu dispute as a "crisis" in the course of the China problem, the U2 affair as an "incident", and the Chinese minority in Indonesia question as a "situation of friction" (see Introduction, p. 4). These are appropriate terms in dealing with the origins and development of differences between states. We now propose to use the conventional term "dispute" to describe all these types of situation in so far as they may be classed together for the purpose of considering their settlement or solution.

be considered at the time of writing in mid-1970 as no longer on the agenda of diplomacy. They are still to a greater or less extent active problems for the states directly concerned and, in some of these cases, for the world as a whole, though the critical level of tension arising from them fluctuates from time to time.

A proposed categorisation of international disputes, it is suggested, cannot be invalidated merely on the ground that each and every example cannot be fitted neatly into one or other of the categories proposed without there being any question whether it might not fit equally well into some other category. There are bound to be ambiguities and obscure lines of demarcation in drawing distinctions between different forms of human situation. A system of classification would be invalid only if the placing of a *majority*, or at least a high proportion, of the disputes considered were to be uncertain, and this is patently not the case in the above tables. Moreover, the categories proposed correspond to the divisions which are normally used in everyday discussion about the outcome of disputes in the real world, and this in itself is some evidence of their accordance with the facts. It should none the less be emphasised that the above tables represent the position approximately at the time of writing (summer 1970); an "unsolved" dispute today may be peacefully or coercively solved tomorrow, a "quiescent" dispute may later flare up and be solved pacifically or forcefully or left "unsolved"; and so on.

Before examining our four categories in somewhat more detail the relative numbers of disputes which we have placed in each group merit some comment. It will be noted in the first place that a high proportion of international disputes since the Second World War have in fact been "solved" in that they no longer seem to constitute irritants in the relations between the states concerned, and that some sort of *modus vivendi* has been worked out resulting in a tacit or explicit agreement to respect the new *status quo*. Combining our tables 3 and 4, as many as 60 per cent of the disputes in our complete list fall into this group. It is true that almost a half of these experienced an outcome in which force played the predominating role, that is, in our terminology they were "coercively" rather than "peacefully" solved and force played by no means a minor role in the others, too. The object of endeavour of any civilised society must be to enlarge the "peacefully solved" and diminish the "coercively solved" categories. Nevertheless, that so many disputes get disposed of at all is some reason for self-congratulation.

If we add to the 30 disputes out of the total of 50 which we regard as "solved" the 11 instances which we have defined as "quiescent", it is evident that over four-fifths of the major international disputes since 1945 are no longer active sources of difference between the states among which they originally arose; and even if we combine merely the "quiescent" disputes (11) with the "peacefully solved" (16) – reminding ourselves that in the latter force or the threat of force played a relatively minor role – we find that well over 50 per cent of international disputes since the war either petered out without seriously affecting the subsequent relations between the parties or were settled by more or less peaceful means. This is a higher proportion of disputes which were pacifically resolved than might be expected from the commonplace descriptions of international relations as a condition of unmitigated anarchy. It testifies at least to a considerable capability in the existing structure of international relations to "de-fuse" or render harmless a high proportion of the disputes which arise within it. But it also implies a distinct potentiality in the international system for continually manufacturing new sources of friction, to deal with which states must either solve or temporarily shelve some at least of the existing disputes in which they may be engaged. It cannot be repeated too often that the death of many international disputes lies in the birth of new disputes. Some at least of the latter may in their turn be expected to fade from the diplomatic agenda as and when new occasions of quarrel enter into the international system.

The Quiescent Disputes

Taking in the first instance, then, the 11 disputes which we propose to regard as quiescent or obsolete at the time of writing, the Berlin question is naturally by far the most important. All four occupying Powers, Britain, France, the Soviet Union and the United States, tried in the two years following Germany's military collapse in May 1945 to agree on arrangements for German unity in which Berlin would once more resume its place as the capital city. This effort finally failed at the Moscow and London Foreign Ministers' conferences in March and December 1947 respectively, and on two occasions, in 1948 and from 1958 until 1961, the Soviet Union seemed bent on driving the three Western occupying Powers from the western sectors of the city. On both occasions the Western Powers refused to be driven out, partly because of conviction of the validity of their legal title to remain there under the Potsdam agreement of 1945, partly because they considered it vital, if they were to retain Western Germany as an ally, to give no indication of wavering over West Berlin. The stakes for the Western Powers therefore, lying as they did in the whole balance of power in Europe, were far too high to surrender and those Powers seemed ready to fight to the utmost of their strength to retain their rights in Berlin. This the Russians and their East European allies appeared on both occasions ultimately to recognise and their pressure against West Berlin declined, especially after the building of the Berlin Wall in August 1961.

Since then there has been intermittent interference by the East German authorities with access from Federal Germany to West Berlin, as for instance in February 1969, when East Germany and the Soviet Union protested against the holding in West Berlin of elections for a new Federal German President. The strict limitation evidently placed by the Communist authorities on the extension of such pressures, however, is some indication that for all practical purposes they are at present content to leave the Berlin situation substantially as it is.

The South Tirol, Muscat–Oman, Quemoy–Matsu and Algeria–Morocco disputes may be considered quiescent within our definition of the term for not dissimilar reasons, although the implications of these issues are far less considerable than those of Berlin. Austria continues to press the case for more effective self-government for the Austrians incorporated in Italian territory at the end of the First World War, but is clearly in no position to do much more about it, having no powerful states to support her in her cause.[6] Similarly, in the other three cases the sides wishing to change the *status quo* – the Omani dissidents (as alleged by the UN Special Committee on Colonialism), the Communist Chinese and Morocco respectively – have simply been unable to have their way and have settled down to a more or less grudging acquiescence in the existing situation, though the Special Committee of the United Nations General Assembly has continued to describe the Omani situation as a "serious problem". This was one of the strongest reasons why Morocco achieved no territorial change to its advantage, even though the actual fighting in 1963 had been in its own favour. To which may be added the fact that Algeria gained some profit in its dispute with Morocco from being identified by many people in the Arab world with the rising cause of "progressive socialism" as compared with the alleged "reactionary monarchism" of King Mohammed I and King Hassan of Morocco. Thus, both of these factors, the mental resistance among the African states to frontier changes in general and the allegedly "superior" political complexion of Algeria, were in accord with the "climate of the times" and hence operated as restraints against revisionist claims.

The Sino-Indian border dispute of 1959–65, which reached a critical stage in October 1962, falls into the same group since the Chinese seem to have achieved their object of demonstrating their military superiority over Indian forces in the areas concerned and had no wish to press the matter further. On neither side was there any inclination towards war *à l'outrance* and the affair had already served China's purpose by the

[6] Officially the Austrian claim is for a different interpretation of the Gruber-de Gasperi agreement concerning the inhabitants of South Tirol. The agreement, sometimes known as the Paris Agreement, was concluded on 5 September 1946.

time the pressure was taken off. There may moreover be a sense of mutual advantage in a situation which is otherwise disagreeable to one or other of the parties, and this allows the situation to remain without strong pressures to change it. A good example is Hong Kong, which we have included in our list of quiescent disputes, though there is some case for regarding it as a situation of friction, or a potential dispute. Here there is on the British side a realisation of the difficulty of holding on to the colony should the Communist Chinese resolve to undertake its seizure with substantial military forces and without regard for casualties; on the Chinese side, it would seem that their present thinking is that Hong Kong possesses more value for them as a source of foreign exchange than if it were incorporated into the official Chinese domain. The Peking Government therefore seem ready enough to discharge their anti-imperialist tirades against Hong Kong while being averse to attempting its immediate annexation.

So far we have spoken of two forces which help render a dispute quiescent: superior strength on one side and the relative unimportance of the object at stake as compared with the hazards of pressing on with the attempt to secure it. There are, however, two further circumstances to be taken account of. In one there may be a change in external factors which causes a change in the balance of forces in the immediate area of conflict: the Greco-Turkish conflict in Cyprus and the Yemeni situation are cases in point. The accession to office of the regime of the colonels in April 1967 appeared to change the attitudes, both of the Greek Government toward the prospect of war with Turkey on behalf of the Greek Cypriots, and of many of the Greek Cypriots towards the new rulers in Athens; in this new context peaceful co-existence between Greeks and Turks in the island, with the help of a United Nations force, became a more feasible proposition; and when violence was sparked off again in May 1970 it was a case of Greek, in the form of the National Front, which still sought *enosis* with the Motherland, against Greek, in the form of President Makarios and his followers, who had renounced it. Similarly, the changed position of Egypt resulting from the catastrophic six-day war with Israel in 1967 facilitated a public revision by President Nasser of an attitude towards the civil war in Yemen which he seemed to have privately changed some time before; henceforward, with the withdrawal of Egyptian forces from their role of supporting the Republican side in the Yemeni civil war, that conflict continued at a desultory level but faded as an international form of friction.

In the other set of circumstances the imponderable consequences of pressing the argument, on one side, and the unlikelihood of any settlement which would meet the need of the aggrieved party, on the other, combine to lower the tension level. In this group we would place the Cuba–United

States controversy arising from Dr. Fidel Castro's alleged campaign of subversion in the Americas and the problem of Laos. In the former, the failure of the Bay of Pigs invasion of April 1961, which could only have succeeded had it been backed by United States military strength on a national scale of operations, closed the forcible phase of United States pressure to topple the Castro regime since President Kennedy evidently concluded that full-scale military operations against Cuba would place the United States in an intolerable position with respect to world opinion, as well as run the risk of nuclear conflict with the Soviet Union. In Laos, on the other hand, the lines of conflict were never as clear-cut as they later became in Vietnam, and hence the incentive for the United States to commit forces to prevent a take-over of the country by the Pathet Lao was less. It is doubtful, considering the nature of the terrain on the frontiers between Laos and China, on one side, and Laos and North Vietnam, on the other, whether the country will ever be free from guerrilla movements supported from outside. But the United States appeared to decide, as it also later did in Cambodia and Vietnam, that its power to contain such movements was limited. The internal conflict seems no longer to be a subject of international strife, though there were some indications in the summer of 1970 that the argument between Laos and North Vietnam could be resumed.

Eight of the above-mentioned quiescent disputes (Cyprus, Algeria–Morocco, Muscat–Oman, Quemoy–Matsu, United States–Cuba, the Sino-Indian border, Laos and Yemen) involved hostilities on a limited scale. One, the Berlin dispute of 1958–61, though no blood was shed, contained the risk of world war on the widest possible scale of destruction. Nevertheless, since these disputes have passed, for the present at least, into a phase of quiescence, there seems to be little further that should or could be done at the international level to accelerate still more their withdrawal from the headlines of the world's press. In the case of the Berlin dispute, strenuous efforts were made – though with a substantial element of "public relations" about them – at the four-Power Foreign Ministers' meeting in Geneva in the summer of 1959 to agree at least on an interim arrangement concerning Berlin pending further consideration of the larger question of all-German unity. These efforts failed and the situation remained critical until the Berlin Wall was built in August 1961, largely, it seems, to prevent a collapse of the East German economy and to maintain the frontiers of Communism. Since then the Berlin problem has created no serious trouble, though access routes from the city to the West still have a certain nuisance value for the Communist authorities. If any attempt were made now, by one side or the other, to re-open this, or any other of the 11 problems in this category, with a view to bringing it into the class of "peacefully solved" disputes, it could be that the effect would merely be to resuscitate the old tension; it may be for this reason that suggestions in the second half of 1969 and the first half of 1970 that new quadripartite talks might be held over Berlin seemingly made little advance.[7] These are all assuredly cases in which there is wisdom in the old principle *quieta non movere*.

Unsolved Disputes

As we have explained, our second category of disputes, those which are still "unsolved", differs from the "quiescent" group in that there is no tacit or formal agreement between the parties to consider them as no longer forming items on the agenda of diplomacy. The unsolved dispute is one in which an active search for a solution continues; neither side has yet given up the hope that progress might be made with the dispute in such a way as to yield more benefit to itself than by leaving it unsolved. The dispute, in short, remains under purposive, if perhaps only intermittent, consideration. It will be seen from our Table 2 on page 189 that we have placed 9, or almost one-fifth, of our selection of 50 disputes in the class of "unsolved" questions. It is clear that these further fall into three types, if one considers what may be called the predominating factor in keeping them unsolved; these types, when examined, shed a certain amount of light on the question why some disputes remain in the "unsolved" category.

The first group comprises those disputes in which the prevailing state of public opinion or, to use a term implying a lower degree of articulation, public mood in one or other of both of the states concerned does not accept as admissible the only kind of solution which the governing authorities believe they can reasonably expect under existing conditions. We must place three of our 9 disputes in this group: the China problem, or rather the issue of Communist Chinese representation at the United Nations; Gibraltar; and the Arab–Israeli dispute, or complex of disputes. While in each of these cases other factors than public opinion may exercise a powerful influence, it is contended that one or other of the governments directly concerned might be willing to make concessions which would facilitate progress were it not for the fact that the state of public opinion to which that government is answerable prevents, whether justly or unjustly, progress being made. Yet in each case the side seeking a change in the *status quo* has too much force and persistence behind it to allow the issue to become quiescent.

In the first of the three issues mentioned in the preceding paragraph, that of Chinese representation at the United Nations, the dispute is not so

[7] See p. 279, *infra*.

much between the ostensible focus of the controversy, the Chinese People's Republic, and the state hitherto chiefly obstructing that regime's admission into the world organisation, namely the United States, but between the latter and a heterogeneous group of UN Members, including Britain, which have been pressing for Peking's recognition. Considered strictly from the standpoint of national interest, the United States would have little to lose and perhaps something to gain from reversing its stand on this issue, which is already criticised by a very high proportion of informed American opinion. It is common knowledge, however, that following the United States' experience of Communist China during the Korean war, together with the survival of many old paternalistic attitudes of Americans towards the Chinese people, no American politician can expect to win votes by calling for the recognition of Communist China at the United Nations. The greater likelihood is that he would lose them. In much the same way, any British Government would find it exceedingly difficult to transfer Gibraltar to Spanish sovereignty after the referendum in Gibraltar in September 1967 which almost unanimously opposed that course of action, even though Britain today has no great economic, military or other material interest to serve by retaining the Rock. Nor would Parliamentary opinion at Westminster allow much freedom of negotiation to any British Government if it became known that a transfer of sovereignty to Spain was actually in contemplation.[8]

The Arab–Israeli Conflict

The third case in this group, the Arab–Israeli conflict, illustrates that, for public opinion to be effective in denying to its government the margins of manoeuvre necessary to make agreement possible, it is by no means essential that the state concerned should be a representative democracy in the Western sense of the term. Hardly any of the Arab states are liberal democracies as the British or Americans understand that concept. Nevertheless, it is clear that at the time of writing one of the strongest obstacles to an Arab–Israeli agreement is the refusal of the Arab states to recognise the state of Israel and to negotiate face to face with it, enhanced as this obstacle may be by the reluctance of the Israeli authorities to make clear what their terms for an agreement might be if the Arab states steeled themselves to this revolutionary *volte face*. We cannot be confident that, even if such a face-to-face exchange were held, all the difficulties in the way of an enduring solution would be overcome; nevertheless, the opening

[8] A similar case of public and Parliamentary opposition to any governmental disposition to transfer the sovereignty of dependent territories, though it is not included in our fifty case studies, is that of the Falkland Islands and South Georgia. Here again the absence of any "material" interest in retaining the territories in question is notable.

up of direct lines of communication between the disputing states would naturally seem to be the first step, or one of the first steps; a mediator, like Dr Gunnar Jarring, can do something to stimulate such direct negotiations, but unless he is able to effect them in the end his powers are limited. We cannot know, either, whether the leaders of the Arab states, if the decision were wholly theirs to make, would take the momentous step of recognising the state of Israel; but the incentives leading Egypt, Jordan and Syria, the states which lost territory to Israel as a result of the six-day war in 1967, to do precisely that must be strong indeed. But it is equally well known that for President Nasser, for instance, to have offered diplomatic recognition of Israel's existence would at once have stripped him of what remained of his title to speak as leader of the Arab peoples, and that for other Arab leaders, and perhaps also for President Nasser himself, any such action might have been equivalent to signing their own death warrant at the hands of the many violently anti-Israeli guerrilla movements which populate the Arab world. Indeed it is no exaggeration to say that an indispensable condition of acting the role of a leader of Arab opinion in the mid-twentieth century is to do nothing which would make a negotiated settlement with Israel easier. Similarly, though possibly to a less degree, there may be presupposed on the Israeli side, too, the existence of a public opinion which, reasonably or unreasonably, would make life difficult for any politician who had the temerity to propose a solution of the conflict which seemed to abandon, except for a very high price, the gains of the 1967 war.

Vietnam

Our second sub-group of "unsolved" disputes also includes two representative cases: the Vietnam conflict since 1954, and especially since the Tonkin Gulf incident of 1964, and the Angola question. Varied as these conflicts may be in almost all other respects, they share the important common feature that in each of them very substantial interests on both sides are engaged and yet any conceivable resolution of the conflict which would not represent an instant and total defeat for one side might well represent, or seem to represent, such a defeat for the other. When such examples of international confrontation occur we are almost bound regretfully to conclude that violence must play an important role in determining the outcome (as in fact it is doing so in these cases) since violence is capable of increasing the benefits of an agreement for the side getting the worst of it and force down the price which both sides demand for an end to the conflict. This must be said, however, with the proviso that one of the tragedies of violence as a means of settling international disputes is that once a community has suffered casualties on any considerable scale in the violent phase of a conflict with another community it is not unusual for it to expect that its rival should pay an even higher price for a settlement than was demanded by itself at the outset, since to settle for less would represent an act of dishonour to its own dead. It seems that this has been one factor influencing the more "hawkish" sectors of United States opinion during the Vietnam war: the more the casualties mount, the less their readiness to write off this investment in the conflict and "call it a day". At the same time, of course, increasing casualties in Vietnam were a factor in, say, the change of President Johnson's attitude towards continuation of the war.

In Vietnam, to take the earlier in point of time of these disputes, the stakes are and always have been high for both sides; complete military victory so far has eluded the two sides, though for different reasons, and yet almost any conceivable negotiated solution must involve the abandonment by one side or the other of interests so far claimed intermittently to be vital. What appears to be at stake for North Vietnam and the Vietcong is the unity of all Vietnam, preferably under Communist auspices, with all elements of foreign control eliminated and foreign armies driven back to the countries whence they came. What is at stake for South Vietnam is its survival as an independent, non-Communist regime, and perhaps the very lives and material assets of its present leaders in Saigon and the South Vietnamese who have associated themselves with them. What is at stake for the United States is its good name and dependability as a staunch friend of allies throughout the world, totalling more than 40 in number, who feel themselves threatened by some of the chief opponents of the United States. The administration in Washington, as former Secretary of State Dean Rusk has often said, has had to ponder how its pledges to allies throughout the world would read if it were known that the United States withdrew its support from South Vietnam.

Hardly any solution, it seems, could be acceptable to the United States and South Vietnam which did not involve a clear separation of the two parts of the country, at least as long as North Vietnam remained under Communist control. At the same time, it is difficult to believe that the North Vietnamese, after twenty or more years of fighting against foreign control, would accept a solution which implied the legitimisation of a foreign-backed regime in the south; once again, the scale of existing investment in the war inhibits a quick solution. Throughout the Vietnam conflict it has commonly been said by "moderate" opinion in the United States and by sympathetic critics of America's Vietnam policy in the world outside that a "political", and not a military, end of the conflict must be sought; or, in our terminology, that the conflict must be peacefully and not coercively solved. Some advance in this direction was made when talks opened in Paris in May 1968 between United States and North Vietnamese delegations and when South Vietnamese and National Liberation Front representatives, after protracted negotiations, were admitted into the talks in December. Nevertheless, the slow progress made at these discussions and the increase in military operations in the months following these first quadripartite exchanges suggested that the fighting would have to continue until one or other side, or both, agreed to a lowering of political sights.

Angola

Turning now to the Angola question, the second in our sub-group in the "unsolved" category, the same principle seems to apply, namely that the objects of each side appear to represent, if accepted, the total, unmitigated defeat of the other. The independent African states which support the native African guerrilla movements in Angola look as though they will be satisfied with nothing short of the wholesale defeat of Portugal; or in other words the achievement in Africa of what was done to the Portuguese enclaves in India in 1961. Yet, considering that Portugal's military situation in Angola seems by no means desperate, there appears to be no good reason why that country should not continue to hold on to Angola, especially since, if the conflict is to be resolved along the lines desired by the African nationalists, Angola must slip entirely out of Portugal's control. On the other hand, for the independent African states to accept Portuguese rule in Angola is to repudiate the very principle of anti-colonialism on which most of these states are based.

The Nigerian War

The Nigeria–Biafra problem, until its settlement through the victory of the Federal Government's forces early in 1970, was another instance of the same kind. The Federal Government seemed to be content with nothing less than the total abandonment of the Biafran claim to the right to secede from the Federation; the Ibo people, on their side, were evidently convinced that this would mean their root-and-branch extermination, though it may be that their ambitious leaders cajoled them into this belief, and it seemed that as long as they possessed the means to fight they would do so. As things stood until the Federal Government's victory, a resolution of the conflict could hardly be conceived which did not represent a total defeat for one side or the other, though a defeat for the Federal Government would have been primarily a moral defeat, whereas an Ibo defeat, at least as the Ibos saw it, would be tantamount to genocide with themselves as the victims. Accordingly, the two sides were prepared to continue fighting, with the assistance of arms supplied by more powerful states outside, until one or the other either won the conflict outright or was compelled to settle for less than it originally intended. To this may be added that, after the civil war in the Congo in 1960–63, there was a natural reluctance on the part of other states and the United Nations to become deeply involved in political efforts to resolve the conflict.

The Nigeria–Biafra conflict, until its forceful settlement in early 1970, lay on the borderline between the second and third (and final) of our sub-groups of "unsolved" disputes, and there may be some doubt whether, at least as seen from the Biafran side, it did not more properly fall into the third sub-group. The latter comprises disputes which call into question the entire "way of life", political or social or both, of the parties concerned. In this category we would include the question of the Chinese minority in Indonesia (and perhaps in South-East Asia more generally), the dispute concerning the regime of *apartheid* in South Africa in so far as this has been raised to the level of international debate, and the Rhodesia and Kashmir questions. For the parties, or one of them, to give ground in these disputes is, or seems to them to be, to sacrifice in effect all the values which make them distinct national communities. It is, or has the appearance of being, a matter of all or nothing, either "fighting on the beaches" or yielding up all that it means to be a distinct nation with a distinct way of life.

Clearly in the first of these issues, the Chinese minorities question, the state of the dispute has varied in accordance with the state of relations between China itself and the South-East Asian countries in which the "overseas" Chinese live. Whenever Indonesian foreign policy, for example, has been following a pro-China line, the Chinese minority in that country has enjoyed a relatively trouble-free existence. Whenever conflict has been intense between political factions in Indonesia itself, however, as for instance during the *coup* against Dr Sukarno in 1965, Chinese settlers have been as much at the mercy of the host country as the Jews have been in Europe during times when economic stresses and strains or political tensions not necessarily directly connected with the Jewish question have placed the existing order in jeopardy. For the Chinese, as for the Jews during such critical periods, their whole way of life, and indeed their sheer bodily survival, have been called into question.

Kashmir

But it is the Kashmir dispute, with its wider effect on Indo-Pakistan relations, and the dispute over South Africa's racial policies, to which may be added the dispute between the United Nations and the Smith regime in Rhodesia, which best illustrate the point under discussion. The conflict over Kashmir is only very superficially a conflict about title to sovereignty over a certain country; only superficially, too, is it a conflict over title to govern a country with a certain sort of nationality or religion – if it were, the present situation in Kashmir would seem to support the Pakistani side of the argument. In reality and considered at the fundamental level, the Kashmir dispute is partly a conflict about power, but also a symbol of the entire conflict between India and Pakistan which can be traced back to the original partition of the Indian sub-continent in 1947. For Pakistan to concede that the predominantly Muslim population of Kashmir can be rightfully ruled by a secular and Hindu state, India, is to strike a blow at the whole hitherto theocratic character of the Republic of Pakistan. For India, on the other hand, to agree that, simply because the Kashmiris are predominantly Muslims, the country should be ceded to Pakistan, or even allowed its fate by referendum, would be to endorse the rightfulness of Pakistan's existence as part of the Indian sub-continent which seceded and formed a state of its own; it would also go far to concede that the 40 million Muslims now living in India also have a right to self-government or to secession in order to join Pakistan. To admit either of these claims would contribute towards undermining at least the moral or ideological solidarity of the Republic of India.

South Africa: Rhodesia

The point is made even more conclusive when we consider what are the issues at stake in the conflict between South Africa and the illegal Smith regime in Rhodesia, on one side, and the majority of United Nations Member-states who have supported sanctions against both, on the other. For an independent African state, or a liberal-minded Englishman, to substitute majority African rule for the system of white supremacy now prevailing in South Africa and Rhodesia – the situation in both countries is by no means the same, but for external critics for all practical purposes it is – is merely to carry to its logical conclusion the decolonisation process which has taken its course in the rest of Africa and the basic principles of national self-determination and fundamental freedoms without regard to race, sex, language, or religion which signatories of the United Nations Charter are obliged to respect. For white South Africans and Rhodesians, on the other hand, it would mean the virtual extinction of their present way of life and a total surrender to people they regard, at best, as little more than children of the highly complex economic system and assets which their own skill and labour have built up over the years.

In all cases which we have placed in this third sub-group of "unsolved" disputes, and especially the last two examples, what is at stake is enormous indeed; it is nothing less than the whole way of life and possibly the sheer existence too, of the organised community which is defending the *status quo*. For that community there can hardly be said to exist a half-way house between total victory, mitigated perhaps by certain symbolic concessions to world opinion, and total defeat. They must either give in and bow the knee or fight to the death. It may be presumed that national communities, as distinct perhaps from individual persons, will fight to the death, or at least maintain a sustained semblance of doing so, rather than give way on a matter on which their whole survival seems so nakedly to depend.

Finally, it is worth reminding ourselves, before completing this section on "unsolved" disputes, both of the time factor involved in placing disputes in any such category and of a certain inevitable arbitrariness of any attempt to sub-divide such categories further, as we have attempted to do. On the former point, we have emphasised from time to time that we are speaking of the state of international disputes at the time of writing; in a matter of months or years some of these "unsolved" questions may have entered the "peacefully solved" or "coercively solved" categories, which we shall be dealing with next; or they may become "quiescent", while new disputes will have arisen and remained "unsolved". The most we can do is to indicate the kind of forces which tend to keep a dispute on the "unsolved" list. On the second point, that of the absence of neatness of definition of the sub-categories, it is true, for instance, that the Arab–Israeli dispute, in which we have singled out the state of public feeling on both sides as a powerful factor making resolution of the conflict difficult, could also be considered within our third sub-group, in which the whole "way of life" of a community seems to be at stake; we have also mentioned the Nigeria–Biafra conflict as possibly falling into this third sub-group, though in fact we have placed it in the second. We would repeat once more, however, that our intention is to single out what seems the *predominating* influence at work causing resistance to the resolution of disputes. Only the most elementary student of international relations would suppose that a complex phenomenon like a dispute between nations could be summed up in one phrase.

Coercive and Peaceful Solutions

It now remains for us to examine our third and fourth categories of disputes, those in other words which we describe as having been "coercively solved", in that force or the threat of force played a primary role in deciding the outcome, and those we describe as having been "peacefully solved", or in other words where there was a distinct and dominant element of mutual consent in the resolution of the conflict, even though this consent may have been itself influenced by considerations of force. Before we consider what common features these two groups of dispute possess, however, it is as well to summarise certain conclusions we have reached from considering the "unsolved" group since inferences may be drawn from these which have a bearing on the positive conditions on which "peaceful solutions", or the *pacific* determination of disputes, may be reached. Since we have seen, in considering the "unsolved" group, that an intransigent public opinion may stand in the way of a negotiated solution and that such solutions are hard to reach where any conceivable compromise must be regarded as a total defeat for one side or the other, or where the whole way of life of the party or parties concerned is, or seems to be, at stake, it follows that a dispute is possibly more likely to end in a negotiated solution in the following circumstances: (*a*) where public opinion or powerful sectors of it are open to being persuaded that the outcome proposed does not involve an intolerable sacrifice of vital interests, honour or principle; (*b*) where the bargaining position of the two sides are so close together that it does not seem an intolerable sacrifice of interest, "face" or principle for one or other of the two sides to offer concessions which make a final solution possible; (*c*) where the issue at stake does not involve what we have called the whole way of life or indeed the sheer physical survival of one or other or both of the parties. To these very general conditions of solutions being arrived at must be added certain further conditions which we believe will become apparent when we examine our fourth and final category of disputes, namely those which we claim to have been "solved".

Coercively Solved Disputes

We must, however, first dispose of the cases which we have called "coercive solutions", namely those in which naked force or the threat of it played a predominating role, and these we have listed in Table 3 on page 190. In some cases force was actually used and blood shed, whether on a minor or major scale; such cases were Greece, where, with British and American military assistance, the Communist forces were finally beaten, Palestine in 1945–49, Indo-China in 1950–54, the Korean war of 1950–53, Tibet in 1959, Hungary in 1956, the Congo in 1963, where the Katangese secessionist movement was crushed by United Nations forces with powerful American backing, Goa and the other Portuguese enclaves in India in 1961, and Czechoslovakia in 1968, though in the latter two instances practically no physical resistance to overwhelming force was offered. In the other cases in this list force was present in the background and might well have been used had the other side not succumbed to the demands of the party threatening force. As examples of this, we would cite the Polish crisis of 1944–45, in which local Soviet military predominance secured the establishment of a Communist-dominated regime not obviously acceptable to the mass of the population, and certainly not to the other Great Powers involved; the Berlin crisis of 1948–49, in which the

Western Powers seemed willing to use the utmost of their military strength to avoid being driven from West Berlin; the preservation of Kuwait's independence in 1961–63 owing to the military support afforded first by Britain and later by an Arab defence force; and the Cuba missile crisis of 1962, where United States military force was concentrated at the single point of preventing further Soviet vessels carrying missiles and their accompanying equipment to Cuba.

The fact that a sizable proportion of the 50 disputes considered, that is, over one quarter, were ended as a result of military force applied or threatened, is a salutary reminder that such force must always be taken into account in the consideration of international disputes; and many even of the disputes in our fourth, or "peacefully solved", category were not disposed of without a show of force in the background. There is a natural disposition on the part of students of this subject to believe that, given a reasonable degree of "goodwill", all international disputes are capable of being resolved quietly and rationally. This our study does not bear out. The relationship of military forces is, we may be sure, always present in the minds of governments when conducting their disputes with other countries, except perhaps where, as in the case of Britain and the United States, there exists such a long tradition of cooperation and mutual sympathy as to render the whole idea of force being used on either side quite unthinkable. But this is by no means the normal condition of international disputes. We have seen, too, when considering the nature of "unsolved" disputes, how inevitable it is that military pressures should constantly be resorted to – and counter-pressures, too – when states are seeking to resolve their differences; this is particularly true of international disputes. If the issue is a sufficiently important one and if, after prolonged argument, no bridging of the gap between the two sides comes into view the temptation to put the matter to the test of force is irresistibly strong, sometimes, it may be, against the better judgement of the responsible Ministers.

But this leads to the question of what factors cause disputes to fall under the heading of "coercive" rather than "peaceful" solutions at all. Why does force predominate in one case rather than the other? One obvious answer is that one side may possess superior military strength and can gain its object without significant resistance; such was the case in Poland 1944–45, in Tibet in 1959, Hungary in 1956, the Congo in 1963, Goa in 1961 and Czechoslovakia in 1968. It will be seen that in some of these cases (Poland, Hungary, Czechoslovakia) effective resistance was not offered because it could only have been offered by the rival super-Power and the latter was not willing to run the risk of outright war in defending the country under pressure. Also the force applied could not always be described as "aggressive"; for example, in the Soviet Union's deployment of force against Poland, Hungary, Czechoslovakia, during the periods mentioned, a distinct principle of national security and the maintenance of an established sphere of influence were involved for the Power using force. In other instances, negotiations had failed and yet the issues at stake for both sides were too vast for the dispute simply to drag on or be allowed to lapse; such was the case in Greece in 1944–49, Palestine in 1947–48, Indo-China in 1945–54 and Korea when the north invaded the south in June 1950. In the Kuwait example the annexation of that country and its oil resources no doubt seemed at first easy game for the Quassim regime in Iraq; it later became clear that this was not so and General Quassim was unwilling to take on virtually the whole of the rest of the Arab world even for such high stakes. This leaves the Berlin crisis of 1948–49 and the Cuba missile crisis of 1962 as examples where there existed a rough parity of military strength and a clear intention on one side or the other to use this strength. In view of the nuclear aspect of the military situation, the imponderable consequences of a full-scale military exchange appear to have been far in excess of the advantages to be gained by pressing on with the enterprise. The Russians discontinued their blockade of Berlin in 1949 and withdrew their missiles from Cuba in 1962 because a certain parity of military power, or enough of a parity to make a full-scale engagement disastrous for both sides, especially when the military power included nuclear weapons of the greatest destructive power on either or both sides made the attempt to overwhelm the opponent by brute force inadvisable.

In all, or most of these questions, then, the issue proved to be non-negotiable either because the interest at stake, as for example national security, was too great, or force could succeed without fear of retaliation, or, in the case of the nuclear Powers, the implications of military struggle had to be brought out into the open before one side would submit. The inference from all this would seem to be, first, that, in a world where national security is not provided for otherwise than by the state itself, the state, where it is able to do so, will use every means, including force, to assure its security requirements, and secondly that any provision of procedures for peaceful settlement of disputes cannot ignore the need to construct the kind of balance of military forces, globally or regionally, which inhibits the unilateral use of sheer strength in the interests of the stronger.

Peacefully Solved Disputes

If we now consider Table 4 on page 190, consisting of disputes which were "peacefully solved", or made subject of some final agreement even in circumstances in which some element of force or threat of force entered into the ultimate outcome, we may first segregate the cases in which the principal factor making for the solution was a change in the pattern of international alignments or a change in the balance of internal forces in one or other of the contending parties which paved the way to agreement. There are three cases in our Table 4 which illustrate these phenomena: the question of an Austrian State Treaty, discussed between the four occupying Powers between 1945 and 1955, the Trieste dispute and the Malaysia–Indonesia confrontation. In all these instances alterations in the structure of international or, in the last case, internal alignments resulted from causes which lay outside the nature of the dispute itself and made possible a revision in the structure of interests of the states concerned and hence of their attitudes. Whereas, before this change in the pattern of alignments occurred, it seemed profitable to pursue the dispute, after the change the balance of interests favoured an agreement.

The Austrian and Trieste disputes illustrate the importance of a change in the pattern of international alignment. The Austrian problem, after ten years of deadlock between the four occupying Powers, was quite suddenly resolved in bilateral talks between the Soviet Union and Austria in April 1955, when the Soviet Union evidently reversed its former position and accepted at a four-power Foreign Ministers' meeting in Vienna in May the draft State Treaty which committed Austria to neutralisation. The general cause of this appeared to be a decision of the Soviet Government in that year to try to stabilize the Central European situation and devote themselves to winning diplomatic support for the Communist cause among the Afro-Asian states. The particular cause of the Soviet *volte face* seems to have been the admission of the Federal German Republic into Western European Union and the Atlantic Pact in 1954–55. This event led to the formation of the Warsaw Pact in 1955 – it is no coincidence that the Warsaw Pact treaty was signed on 14 May 1955 and the Austrian State Treaty on the 15th – and this in its turn made possible the stationing of Soviet forces in Bulgaria, Hungary and Rumania under the terms of that treaty, and hence reduced the need for Russia to retain her occupation rights in Austria. At the same time, these events permitted the Soviet Union to use her change of policy towards Austria as a means of justifying still further the presence of her troops in those three allied countries. Equally, it now became important for the Soviet Union to make a bid for West German public opinion on the basis of the new Soviet attitude towards neutralisation; for this purpose a neutralised Austria could be, and was, presented to German public opinion by the Soviet Union as an example of the kind of neutralisation of Germany which Russia at that time desired.

It is equally clear, to take the case of the Trieste dispute, that once

Yugoslavia had broken with the rest of the Soviet bloc in 1948 a corridor was opened to an accommodation between Belgrade and Rome by which the previously disputed Trieste peninsula was simply divided between them, though this agreement was not achieved until 1954 after long and arduous negotiations. When the Trieste situation again became critical in 1953, a year before the agreement was concluded, Yugoslavia no longer had Soviet support behind her and at the same time the Western Powers were anxious to have President Tito's goodwill. The presence of Yugoslav forces in the Trieste peninsula was intolerable so long as Italy belonged unequivocally to the Western group of Powers and Yugoslavia belonged unequivocally to the Soviet bloc. When Yugoslavia became neutral, a target for Soviet abuse and threats and from 1951 a recipient of Western economic aid, such a presence even carried with it certain advantages for Italy and for the NATO pact of which Italy was an original member.

In the case of the Malaysia–Indonesia confrontation, however, it was not so much a change in international alignments as a change in internal political alignments within Indonesia which caused a peaceful termination of the dispute. With the fall from power of President Sukarno in the *coup* of 1965, the "crush Malaysia" campaign which had been so peculiarly his personal enterprise fell to the ground and it was not long before Malaysians and Indonesians were embracing one another at Bankgok in 1966 as brothers under the skin. As with Dr Mossadeq in Iran in the early 1950s, the fall of leaders committed to certain international disputes facilitates their resolution.

Proceeding to the next group of significant factors in the peaceful resolution of international disputes, it is evident that states may recognise the mounting economic costs of a dispute and thus come to admit that "the game is not worth the candle". As time elapses, they accept the fact that they will not attain what they intended and hence that it is wiser to cut their losses and reach an agreement. Such economic pressures may be deliberately applied by some third state or they may arise spontaneously from financial weaknesses of one or other party to the argument. As examples of the former selected from Table 4, it is evident that the United States' decision partially to suspend Marshall Aid to the Netherlands in January 1949 played an important role in inducing that country to end its "police action" against the new Indonesian Republic and to agree to its independence in that year. In much the same way, the United States refusal to support the pound in 1956 seems to have been one of the decisive factors causing Britain to bring a speedy end to its armed action against Egypt during the Suez crisis and thus opened the way to a resolution of that particular phase of the Middle East conflict in the following year, though we must not, in this case, underestimate the realisation by members of the British Cabinet of the impact of their Suez policy on political as well as economic relations with the United States. It seems certain, too, that the Iranian Government's failure to market its oil after the nationalisation of the Anglo-Iranian Oil Company in May 1951 played a part in that Government's acceptance in 1954 of a settlement of the ensuing dispute with Britain which was more unfavourable to itself than it had anticipated.

On the other hand, economic measures can operate in a more positive sense to facilitate the resolution of a dispute. On the whole, the United States succeeded in securing in Guatemala in 1954 a regime more suited to its interests as a result of armed support of that regime; the successor government to the Arbenz regime which was installed with the approval of the United States Ambassador to Guatemala affirmed on more than one occasion the condemnation of Communism which Washington had sought. But the pill was sweetened for Guatemalan critics of the new regime by the cooperation of United States companies in Guatemala in agrarian reform, the investment of new United States capital in petroleum production in that country and the improvement of transportation facilities with United States aid. Again, though this dispute is not included in our list of 50 case studies, the termination of the Indus Waters conflict between India and Pakistan in 1961 was made possible by the offer of economic assistance to both countries by the World Bank. Similarly, though political factors, such as the need to keep Iceland loyal to the NATO alliance, encouraged Britain to accept the "six-plus-six" formula in its dispute with Iceland over territorial waters in 1961, it was also well understood in Britain that if it persisted with its refusal to accept the Icelandic territorial waters legislation, the economic losses might in the long run be far greater than those sustained under the eventual agreed formula.

As for the other type of economic method which acts as an inducement to terminate a dispute, namely where one or other party is simply not economically robust enough to carry the quarrel further, there can be little doubt that the general and familiar economic difficulties confronting Britain in the mid-1960s hastened the total British withdrawal from Aden and South Arabia in November 1967. This was a pre-condition both of the formation of the independent Republic of South Yemen and the opening of quite a different phase of conflict within the new republic itself and between it and Yemen.

A third group of circumstances which may operate to draw a dispute to a close without one or other or both of the parties having achieved all or even a substantial part of the original claim are those where world or regional opinion is ranged against the state or states concerned; there is a sense in one or other of the parties that it is "struggling against the tide of history", or against the "climate of the times" and hence that it cannot win a wide enough diplomatic or moral support to end the struggle on its own terms. This seems to have happened with the Netherlands in its dispute with Indonesia over West Irian between 1950 and 1962. The United Nations Temporary Executive Authority for West Irian which the Netherlands and Indonesia agreed to accept on 15 August 1962 was an intervention which the former could not stand out against, the temper of United Nations opinion being what it was; on the other hand, President Kennedy was able to bring pressure to bear on Indonesia to abandon its claim to the immediate annexation of the disputed territory, not only because of the world strength of the United States, but because that country had traditionally aided and abetted the struggles of ex-colonial countries against the "old order" and hence was in a position to make Indonesia's argument somewhat easier to present at the United Nations and elsewhere. The transfer of sovereignty over West Irian to Indonesia in May 1963, after six months' UN administration and with provision for a plebiscite before the end of 1969, was to all intents a cession of the territory to Indonesia; but this could hardly strike the majority of Member-states at the United Nations as "imperialism" in the old-fashioned sense of the term. The "climate of the times", in other words, was on Indonesia's side. Similarly, the United States itself reached an agreement with Panama on 24 September 1965 which ended the dispute between the two countries over the canal, partly because the US Government accepted the justice of the Panamanian claim to sovereignty over the canal zone and a fairer share of the profits from the canal, but mainly because it recognised that to deal roughly with a tiny Central American state could do its standing no good in the eyes of world opinion. These were no longer the days of "walking softly and carrying a big stick"; and even if they were, the fact should not be too blatantly trumpeted when the major charge against one's world antagonist (in this case, the Communist camp) was that it did not respect the rights of small countries.

The "climate of the times" may be that of a particular region rather than that of the world as a whole, and this appears to have been a factor in the easing of tension in Somalia's disputes with Ethiopia, French Somaliland and Kenya, and in Morocco's dispute with Mauritania over the independence of that country. In neither dispute has there been a definitive solution in the sense of a formal or informal agreement between the parties, though for all practical purposes the Sultan of Morocco's official pronouncement of 26 September 1969 and the final Treaty of Solidarity of 8 June 1970 provided a kind of formal termination to the conflict. But there has been in both cases more or less of a tacit acceptance of the *status quo*. In both cases, too, the reluctance of the new African states as a whole to countenance changes of frontiers, for obvious and natural reasons, created a general lack of confidence in the continent as a whole towards the Somalian and Moroccan claims respectively.

We are left then, out of our list of 16 "peacefully solved" disputes, with three, the Lebanon–Jordan crisis of 1958, the U2 affair of 1960 and the Dominican Republic dispute of 1965, which require to be treated separately, though the reasons for the peaceful resolution of both are of general interest. Taking the last case first, since it is the easier to dispose of, it is hard not to conclude that the United States simply miscalculated the situation in the Dominican Republic when it landed its marines on the island on 28 April 1965 on the apparent assumption that the *coup* against the Cabral regime three days before represented a Communist attempt to seize power. It was not long before the authorities in Washington recognised that the parties in the civil war which it was backing, leaders such as Wessin y Wessin and Imbert, were not the national heroes they had imagined and that their fears of Communism had been exaggerated. Such miscalculations are not surprising considering the treatment the United States had experienced at the hands of the Castro regime in Cuba and its world-wide role as the defender of liberal democracy against Communism; it is nevertheless a peculiarly clear instance of what contemporary international relations theorists call "misperception of the nature of threats to national security".

The Lebanon–Jordan crisis of 1958 is in its international aspect more difficult to analyse. Certainly there seem to have been real threats to the independence of these countries from the radical wing of Arab nationalism, at that time centred in the UAR. Certainly, too, the landing of United States and British forces in Lebanon and Jordan respectively gave pause to the forces allegedly practising subversion against those countries. At the same time, the Anglo-American armed intervention seems to have injected into the Arab states as a whole the recognition that, unless they were able to settle their own quarrels peacefully, they would themselves encourage the very threats to their independence from external Great Powers of which they were always complaining. It was this recognition, it appears, which led to the resolution moved by ten Arab states at the emergency session of the UN General Assembly on 7 August 1958 which committed them not to interfere in each other's internal affairs. The crisis was resolved, in other words, because it had been escalated by Britain and the United States to a point where it had to be peacefully resolved by the Arab states themselves if they were to avert the total conversion of the Middle East into a cockpit for warring external Powers.

There was a somewhat similar recognition of the dangers of proceeding further with a dispute which was not important enough to run the risks of escalation in the U2 affair in 1960. The United States could have retaliated against the shooting down of its aircraft by some forceful measure which might have had imponderable consequences, and in any case the development of espionage through artificial earth satellites and other means was already rendering U2 methods obsolete. The Soviet Union, on its side, seemed to seize upon the U2 incident rather as a pretext for calling off the "summit" conference arranged for May 1960 than as important in itself. This was never a big enough issue for conflict between the super-Powers.

Conclusion

We may conclude then by saying that the military, political and economic factors which help determine whether a dispute becomes quiescent or remains unsolved or is peacefully or coercively solved, within the meaning of these terms as previously stated, are not unnaturally complex. Inevitably we have in this chapter oversimplified the role of each of these factors by implying that every single dispute is dominated, so to speak, by one or other circumstance which determines what the outcome of the dispute shall be. In reality, of course, the normal situation is that an entire family of such factors is at work. Nevertheless, it is useful in understanding the problems of helping to resolve international disputes to try to isolate those forces which happen to be salient. Perhaps we can best sum up by saying that by far the majority of international disputes, including some of the most dangerous ones, are either solved or settled in that some kind of formal or, it may be, tacit agreement is reached defining the new *status quo*, or become quiescent or obsolete in the sense that they no longer figure on the agenda of diplomacy for the states concerned. We have pointed out, however, that of the disputes in the former of these two groups, at least a half were settled predominantly by the use of force or threat of force, and that even in those disputes which were peacefully resolved there often existed substantial elements of force in the background.

If we are asked what kinds of dispute best lend themselves to peaceful solutions, using as a basis for judgement international experience since 1945, we might usefully rehearse the conditions we have already stressed. They are:

(*a*) Public opinion must allow the governments concerned to establish mutual communications with a view to reaching an agreement.

(*b*) There must be no risk of the demands of one side appearing in the eyes of the contrary party as though they represented its total defeat.

(*c*) The issue itself must not involve, or must not be presented in such a way as to seem to involve, the whole "way of life" of the peoples concerned.

(*d*) It is possible that a change in the international or the internal political alignments of one or both of the parties concerned may occur which leads to a reassessment of its or their general interests and hence its or their interests in the matter in dispute.

(*e*) A peaceful solution is also possible to a dispute where there is either some definite economic gain to be anticipated from an agreement or at least the avoidance of some determinate economic loss; or where one or other of the parties comes to recognise that it is battling against the "climate of the times" or the general trends of world opinion; or where it becomes obvious to one or other of the parties that it has miscalculated the threat to its interests implicit in a particular situation and that the threat was not as great as was thought; or where, in a regional dispute, local states realise the importance of a peaceful settlement in order to avoid conflict-causing intervention by external Great Powers.

10. The Role of the United Nations

UN Procedures and Machinery for Peaceful Settlement

The primary purpose of the United Nations Organisation, as defined in its Charter, is the maintenance of international peace and security; the latter phrase occurs no less than 31 times in the Charter and the first words of its Article 1, laying down the Purposes and Principles of the Organisation, are "to maintain international peace and security". As to how this object is to be attained, Article 1 (1) places primary emphasis upon the taking of "effective collective measures for the prevention and removal of threats to the peace, and for the suppression of acts of aggression or other breaches of the peace", and only secondary emphasis upon the bringing about by peaceful means and "in conformity with the principles of justice and international law" the "adjustment or settlement of international disputes or situations which might lead to a breach of the peace". The implication of this last phrase would seem to be that disputes or situations which are *not* likely to lead to a breach of the peace are not of primary concern to the United Nations.

This phraseology, though understandable in the light of the overwhelming need in 1945 to prevent further armed hostilities such as had torn the world apart for six years or more, is unfortunate in that it suggests that a state must establish that a dispute or situation is likely to lead to a breach of the peace before it can be placed before the Organisation; and it is evident that the most effective way of doing so is to act in such a manner as to make a breach of the peace likely. The Charter itself, in other words, may be said by its very wording to serve as an encouragement to the aggravation of international disputes. Moreover, this reacts upon the attitudes of other Member-states which may not be parties to a given international dispute. The more dangerous a dispute is, or can be made to appear, to international peace, the greater the incentive for the general mass of Member-states to use their influence to resolve it even though they may want the issue ventilated whatever the pretext. But this in itself may in its turn act as an inducement to the parties, or one of them, to adopt a more menacing attitude merely as a stimulus to other UN Members to take an active interest in the affair. It is true, of course, that by Article 34 of the Charter the Security Council "may investigate any dispute, or any situation which might lead to international friction or give rise to a dispute" and by Article 35 (1) any UN Member "may bring any dispute, or any situation of the nature referred to in Article 34, to the attention of the Security Council or of the General Assembly", both of which may lead to UN intervention at any stage of a dispute or situation. Nevertheless, read as a whole, and taking into account the tendency of governments to deal with practical rather than potential problems, the Charter does appear to place a premium upon deferring the consideration of disputes until they have reached a critical phase.

This primacy of emphasis in the Charter on peace rather than the resolution of disputes is reflected in certain other of its provisions. Article 2 (3), for example, obliges Member-states to settle their disputes by peaceful means "in such a manner that international peace and security" and – as though as an afterthought – "justice, are not endangered". This is followed by paragraph 4 of the same Article which enjoins Members "to refrain in their international relations from the threat or use of force against the territorial integrity or political independence of any state, or in any other manner inconsistent with the Purposes of the United Nations". Further, Chapter VI of the Charter, which is headed "Pacific Settlement of Disputes", leaves it to the parties concerned, by Article 33 (1), "to seek a solution by negotiation, inquiry, mediation, conciliation, arbitration, judicial settlement, resort to regional agencies or arrangements, or other peaceful means of their own choice", before bringing their differences before UN organs, and, once more, the disputes referred to in this Article are those "the continuance of which is likely to endanger the maintenance of international peace and security". Again, Article 99 gives the Secretary-General powers of personal initiative developed by Dag Hammarskjöld until he came up against the interest of a major Power in the Congo, but even this discretion is legally limited to questions "which in his opinion may threaten the maintenance of international peace and security". Above all, the United Nations, as is well-known, is authorised to take enforcement action for the settlement of an international dispute only after the Security Council, operating under Article 39, has "determined the existence of any threat to the peace, breach of the peace or act of aggression". Similarly, by Article 11 (2) any question relating to the maintenance of international peace and security "on which action is necessary" must be referred to the Security Council by the General Assembly either before or after discussion. This is merely to underline the point that all resolutions of UN organs on the resolution of disputes have recommendatory force only, unless the Security Council, using its stipulated voting procedures, is acting under Article 39 and the following Articles of Chapter VII of the Charter.

This is not to say, however, that, with the limitation referred to above and with two more reservations to be mentioned later, the UN lacks any procedures, agencies or other resources for the peaceful settlement of disputes if the disposition to use them and to comply with their findings exists in the parties. Full accounts of these procedures and agencies are to be found elsewhere;[1] it is intended here merely to provide a summary outline of them. In the first place, the General Assembly, representing all Member-states, may by Article 10 discuss "any questions or matters within the scope of the present Charter" and may make recommendations to Member-states or the Security Council or both, except that, by Article 12, no such recommendations may be made while the Security Council is exercising "in respect of any dispute or situation the functions assigned to it in the present Charter". The General Assembly may also, by Article 11 (2), discuss any questions, again "relating to the maintenance of international peace and security", brought before it by a Member-state, the Security Council or a non-Member provided the latter accepts for the purpose of the dispute the obligations of pacific settlement provided by the Charter. There is no limitation on what the General Assembly may discuss or recommend under this head, though, in theory at least, matters "essentially within the domestic jurisdiction" of Member-states are not within its competence by the terms of Article 2 (7).

Secondly, by Article 35 (1) any Member or, by Article 35 (2), any non-Member may bring a dispute or situation "which might lead to international friction or give rise to a dispute" to the attention of the Security Council or the General Assembly. It is, of course, for these bodies acting under their ordinary rules of procedure to decide whether they will place such matters on their agenda.

Thirdly, the Security Council is authorised by Article 33 (2) to "call upon" parties to a dispute to settle it by peaceful means when the Council "deems necessary". Moreover, at any stage of a dispute "likely to endanger the maintenance of peace and security" the Security Council may "recommend appropriate procedures or methods of adjustment". The Security Council further has the right by Article 37 (1) to take charge of a dispute dangerous to peace if the parties fail to settle it by peaceful means and, by Article 38, may make recommendations with a view to the pacific settlement of a dispute if the parties request it to do so. There then follows Chapter VII of the Charter, by which the Security Council is authorised to take whatever enforcement action, military or economic, it deems necessary, subject to the normal voting procedures being complied with, when it has defined any situation (which may include disputes and even

[1] See especially "The United Nations and Peaceful Settlement" by D. W. Bowett, which forms Annex III of the *Report of a Study Group on the Peaceful Settlement of International Disputes*, published by the David Davies Memorial Institute of International Studies in 1966.

internal or domestic situations) as constituting a "threat to the peace, breach of the peace or act of aggression". All Member-states are obliged by Article 25 of the Charter to comply with the Security Council's decision when it is acting under this heading.

Fourthly, by Article 52 the Charter makes provision for regional arrangements and agencies, and encourages Members to make use of such arrangements for the settlement of local disputes before referring them to the Security Council. The Security Council is further authorised under this Article to encourage the peaceful settlement of local disputes by means of regional agencies "either on the initiative of the states concerned or by reference from the Security Council".

Fifthly, there are the latent powers residing with the Secretary-General by Article 99 to use his initiative in settling disputes either, as expressly stated in this Article, by bringing them before the Security Council when they seem to him to threaten international peace and security, or, in accordance with the practice which has developed with successive Secretaries-General, by using his good offices or those of his representatives in helping to settle disputes either at the request of UN organs or the parties concerned or, in suitable circumstances, on his own initiative. Clearly, many factors, including the personality of the Secretary-General, his conception of his office, his standing with the states chiefly concerned and the prevailing local situation in the area of the dispute, will play their part in determining to what extent and with what effectiveness this discretion will be used.

Sixthly, and finally, there are the resources of the International Court of Justice, to the Statute of which, annexed to the Charter, all Members of the world organisation are adherents. The role of the ICJ, and other judicial tribunals, in the settlement of disputes, is dealt with in more detail in a separate chapter of this book.[2] By Article 36 (3) of the Charter the Security Council is enjoined, when making recommendations to the parties for the settlement of a dispute, to take into consideration "that legal disputes should as a general rule be referred by the parties to the International Court of Justice". The words "as a general rule" were no doubt intended not to exclude reference to other judicial or arbitral bodies to which the parties may previously have agreed to refer disputes arising between them. It should be remembered, however, that under the existing Statute of the ICJ, no state is legally obliged to refer a legal issue in any dispute to the Court unless it has previously agreed to do so by the so-called "Optional Clause" (Article 36 of the Court's Statute); less than half the Members of the United Nations have done so and almost all have in-

[2] Chapter XIV, *infra*.

corporated reservations, sometimes very far-reaching, in their declarations under the Optional Clause.[3]

It will be seen then that the UN does have abundant facilities at its disposal, including informal opportunities for private meetings between delegates of disputing states, for the resolution of international disputes if the will is there. Nor have the two major reservations to this statement had much material effect in practice. As for the first, Article 2 (7) excludes from the Organisation the right to intervene in matters which are "essentially within the domestic jurisdiction" of any state except when the Security Council is exercising its powers under Chapter VII of the Charter. States involved in disputes have frequently successfully invoked this Article in order to prevent discussion of a question at the UN; but, to take merely one example out of many, this has not prevented race relations and policies in South Africa being debated and forming the subject-matter of countless resolutions of UN organs, despite the fact that the Security Council has never agreed to take action in this issue under Chapter VII.

The second reservation concerns Articles 53 and 107 of the Charter, which make permissive actions in relation to a state which during the Second World War has been an enemy of any signatory to the present Charter "taken or authorised as a result of that war by the Governments having responsibility for such action." As with the states pleading domestic jurisdiction, the Soviet Union has often urged Articles as excluding these certain matters – in the Soviet Government's case, German questions – from the UN's purview. But this did not prevent the Berlin dispute of 1948–49 from being considered by the Security Council, although without much immediate result. Moreover, in 1969 the British, French and United States governments issued a statement to the effect that Articles 53 and 107 would not justify any unilateral action.

The Reference of Disputes to the United Nations

Although there is thus a wide variety of means by which international disputes may be brought before UN organs, by far the most common method is for one or other party, or a friendly state acting on its behalf, to move for the inscription of the item on the agenda of the appropriate body. In highly critical situations affecting world peace, however, as in the Berlin dispute of 1958–61, and in the somewhat less serious instance of the question of the Austrian State Treaty negotiations between 1945 and 1955, groups of states in the General Assembly have, seemingly of their own accord, moved to secure a resolution recommending the four Great Powers to negotiate a peaceful settlement. It has also been not uncommon

[3] See "The International Court of Justice", by P. J. Allott, which forms Annexe II.E of the David Davies Memorial Institute report previously referred to.

for resolutions concerning international disputes to originate either in the Trusteeship Committee or the Special Committee on Colonialism (the Committee of Twenty-Four) of the General Assembly. The Special Committee on Colonialism, for example, with its substantial representation of anti-colonialist states, originated the debates on Aden in the teeth of British resistance; only after this resistance had been followed by a British agreement to admit an investigatory mission into the colony could this be created and sent on its way. In much the same way the Special Committee on Colonialism took up of its own accord the Gibraltar dispute and passed resolutions urging Britain and Spain to resume their negotiations with a view to the decolonisation of the Rock. Although the Committee's intervention was undoubtedly favourable to the Spanish side of the argument and Spain seems to have lost no opportunity to do her own lobbying with, for instance, the Latin American and Arab states, the initiative, as far as is known, does not appear to have originated in Madrid: the decolonisation of Gibraltar was simply in accordance with what a majority of the Special Committee on Colonialism considered to be their *raison d'être*.

Another instance where the chief pressure for UN action appears to have come from the Special Committee on Colonialism is Rhodesia; here the Committee of 24, as early as 22 April 1965, called on Britain to take urgent steps to cancel the forthcoming Rhodesian elections, to suspend the constitution and to call a conference attended by all parties to make new constitutional arrangements on the basis of universal adult suffrage. On 6 May the Security Council, at the request of 35 African states, adopted a resolution, on which Britain, along with France, the Soviet Union and the United States abstained, requesting Britain to take all necessary steps to prevent a unilateral declaration of independence by a minority Rhodesian government. After UDI on 11 November, the General Assembly called on Britain to take all necessary action to end "this rebellion by the illegal authorities in Salisbury". On the following day the British delegate, Mr Michael Stewart, asked UN Members to refrain from action to assist the Smith regime.[4] It was only after the failure of the HMS *Tiger* talks between Mr Harold Wilson and Mr Ian Smith in September 1966, and again largely as a result of pressure from the African members of the Commonwealth, that Britain took the initiative of bringing the question before the UN Security Council in December 1966 with a plea, which proved successful, for mandatory sanctions against Rhodesia.

Normally, however, United Nations action in international disputes is set in train by reference of the issue to a UN organ by one or other or both of the states concerned. It is also on the whole rare for both states to agree to refer the issue between them to a UN organ (we are excluding for the

[4] *The Annual Register of World Events in* 1965, London, 1966, pp. 155–6.

present the reference of legal issues to the ICJ, which is dealt with in a separate chapter). The general pattern is for one party to move to invoke the intervention of a UN organ and for the other to resist the reference, claiming either that the matter is one of domestic jurisdiction, or that the United Nations lacks competence, or that the dispute is not one which affects international peace and security; the latter is often a readily available argument in view of the heavy emphasis laid by the Charter, as indicated in the previous section, on peace and security as considerations affecting the appropriateness of the UN for peaceful settlements. The Greek civil conflict of 1946–49 is the only instance among the 50 case studies on which the present inquiry is based in which both sides, or their respective external sponsoring Powers, joined together in making their reference to the UN. The following, on the other hand, are typical examples, selected at random, of a complaint being made to the UN by one side and the other denying the UN's competence or only grudgingly acquiescing in the UN's intervention: the Soviet Union referred the Netherlands–Indonesia dispute of 1945–49 to the Security Council while the Netherlands Government contended that it was a matter of domestic jurisdiction; in the case of the South Tirol dispute, Austria wanted UN intervention while Italy was opposed to it; in the first Berlin crisis of 1948–49 the three Western Powers brought the Soviet-imposed blockade of West Berlin to the Security Council's attention, contrary to the Soviet argument that the matter lay outside the UN's competence as a consequence of Article 107 of the UN Charter; in the instance of the conflict between the Chinese People's Republic and the Nationalist authorities on Formosa concerning the title to represent China at the UN, the Soviet Union first referred the matter to the Security Council on 10 January 1950, only to encounter resistance by the United States.

Why States Refer Disputes to the UN

The motives which induce a Member-state to bring a dispute before the UN, and a particular organ of the UN, and which lead the opposing side to resist the reference or the taking of any action by the Organisation may be presumed to vary. In some instances, more particularly perhaps in "Cold War" issues, it is not necessary to assume that any action will be taken or is indeed considered desirable by the state bringing the matter forward; the debate is initiated 'for the record', or in order that, in the world-wide struggle for the minds of men, the most fair-sounding arguments can be publicly deployed on one's own side while the real process of resolving the dispute may be going on elsewhere. Thus, it is very doubtful whether, when the three Western Powers referred the matter of the Berlin blockade to the Security Council in 1948, they imagined that the Council could take any action of itself, in view of the Soviet veto, to resolve the issue. The same may be said for the case made out by the Western Powers at the United Nations against the Soviet suppression of the Hungarian revolution of 1956 and against the Warsaw Pact invasion of Czechoslovakia in 1968; indeed, in these two instances UN discussions, in so far as the NATO Powers took a leading part in them, could be regarded as substitutes for positive efforts to resolve these disputes rather than as elements in a determinate process of peaceful resolution, which was in any case not available.

In other instances a state may refer an issue to a UN organ because it knows either that the general principle it is defending can clearly be related to some express rule of the Charter itself, or that the political complexion or policies of Member-states represented in that organ will probably dispose them to take a friendly view of the case presented. Thus, with reference to the former of these motives, the Communist states were active in pressing the case for Indonesian independence against the Dutch in 1945–49, against the French in Indo-China in 1945–54 and against United States' policy in Vietnam since 1964; Austria urged her case in South Tirol at the UN; Guatemala appealed to the Security Council in her dispute with the United States in 1954; Greece demanded *enosis* for Cyprus in 1954–59; Morocco brought her case against Mauritania before the Political Committee of the General Assembly; Somalia sought to redress her claims against Ethiopia and Kenya with UN assistance; Mr Patrice Lumumba summoned UN help against the Belgians in July 1960; President Chiari of Panama asked the Security Council to consider his dispute with the United States in 1964; presumably all on the ground that the action complained of was in each case allegedly an infraction of the Charter principle of respect for national self-determination or the Charter's ban on the use of force or threat of force against the territorial integrity or political independence of Member-states.

On the other hand, to take the second of the two motives referred to above, it is clear that reference by a state of a dispute to the UN has often been influenced by the foreknowledge that it would receive a friendly hearing by the Organisation or one of its organs. In the first few years of the UN's life the existence in the Security Council and especially the General Assembly of majorities of Members which could be expected to sympathise with Western arguments in the Cold War disposed the Western Powers, especially the United States, to make the fullest use of the UN to score points off the Communist world and its policies. Hence the American-sponsored and still-born "Little Assembly", created in 1947, and the "Uniting for Peace" resolution of November 1950, both designed to keep the General Assembly in active operation as a peace-keeping and dispute-resolving organ even after the stultification of the Security Council by the Soviet veto. But this American effort to shift responsibility towards the General Assembly was predicated on the assumption that the "town meeting of the world", as Mr John Foster Dulles described that body, would generally echo the Western view of international disputes.

That this was so is shown by the dilemmas created for United States policies with the admission of increasing numbers of decolonised Afro-Asian states into the Organisation in the late 1950s and early 1960s. On the one hand, the United States, both by traditional ideological conviction and through fear of driving alienated Afro-Asian states into the arms of Communist Russia and China, could not but sympathise with Indonesia's struggle against the Dutch, with Egypt's resistance to British and French armed action during the Suez crisis in 1956, and with the Central Congolese Government's struggle against secessionist Katanga in 1960–63. On the other hand, the United States could not follow this anti-colonialist course without inflicting some damage on the interests of her NATO allies which still had dependent territories, especially Belgium, Britain, France, the Netherlands and Portugal. Moreover, as the United States took upon itself responsibilities and commitments not entirely different from those of the old colonial Powers, especially in Guatemala in 1954, against Cuba from 1959 to 1961, in Vietnam since 1964 and in the Dominican Republic in 1965, she has found herself exposed to criticism from the numerically dominant Afro-Asian states in the UN. Perhaps the seeming decline in the enthusiasm shown by American political circles in the last few years towards the UN has had something to do with the diminishing effective activity of the world organisation during this period.

We might add here, as a further example of the tendency of states to refer disputes to the UN because they believe they are likely to obtain a friendly hearing there, the continuous efforts by the Afro-Asian states to secure the condemnation by UN organs of South Africa's racial policies, Portugal's administration of territories in Southern Africa and the Smith regime in Rhodesia. No matter how inconsiderable the effectiveness of the UN in securing the redress of these grievances, suitable verbal condemnations are likely to be forthcoming – perhaps adding to the Organisation's image as a body long on words but short on action – so long as the General Assembly and its voting procedures remain weighted as they are. On the other hand, it is clear that in the Morocco–Mauritania, Somalia, Morocco–Algeria and Nigeria–Biafra disputes most African states have preferred to keep the issue outside the UN as far as possible, perhaps through fear that if the Charter principle of respect for national self-determination were to be strictly applied to the boundaries of the new African states, the territorial integrity of very many of them would be in jeopardy. Moreover, in the Nigeria–Biafra conflict most African Member-states of the UN regarded it as essentially an African, or indeed as an internal Nigerian, problem.

There is one final motive which might be mentioned as disposing states to refer their disputes to the UN and that occurs when all other means of resolving the dispute have been exhausted and the possibility of using force as a final resort is either under active consideration or has actually been decided. It seems likely, for instance, that this formed one of the primary reasons for the British and French reference of the Suez Canal dispute to the Security Council in September 1956 and the United States reference of the Cuba missile crisis to the Council in October 1962. While these may be regarded as attempts, cynical or otherwise, to secure some shred of legality for acts of force prior to their application, they can also be construed as evidence that Great Powers today, and this especially applies to non-Communist Powers, consider that there is something illegitimate about using force without first securing, or at least attempting to secure, the endorsement of the international community in so far as this is represented by the United Nations.

The Extent of UN Involvement in International Disputes since 1945

The first striking fact is that, of our case studies of international disputes since 1945, a very high proportion – some four-fifths, or 39 cases of out 50 – came before UN organs in one form or another. Strictly speaking, the figures should be 39 out of 49 since one of our 50 case studies, the Polish dispute of 1944–45, was dealt with before the Organisation came into existence; the same applies to the first stage (1944–45) of the Greek civil war. This compares very favourably with the record of the pre-war League of Nations, which was for all practical purposes moribund after the fiasco of collective economic sanctions against Italy in her war with Ethiopia in 1935–36; none of the great European disputes which paved the way to the Second World War, such as the Austro-German Anschluss, the Czechoslovak crisis of 1938 and the Polish dispute of 1939, were referred to the League, one of the most important reasons for this being that the revisionist Powers of that time, who took the initiative in these disputes, had already quitted the League. The League was only fitfully revived thereafter in order to deal with the Soviet–Finnish conflict of 1939–40.

It is significant that almost all the post-1945 disputes which have not come before one or other UN organ have been those in which one or other of the parties, or its effective government, was not represented in the Organisation. Thus, disputes affecting Communist China, such as the question of Hong Kong and the Chinese minority in Indonesia, have never come before the UN in main part because of the non-representation of

Communist China in the Organisation. The absence of Communist China and the two Vietnams from the United Nations has also acted as an inhibiting factor in the treatment of the Vietnam conflict by the Organisation, though the determination of the United States to regard the conflict as falling within its own sphere of interest has also played a very important part. On one occasion, in 1950, the Communist Chinese authorities did send a representative to the UN when the Korean problem was under discussion. They refused to do so, however, in 1958 when the suggestion that they should be represented was made by President Eisenhower during the Quemoy–Matsu crisis. The implication would seem to be that if and when Communist Chinese representation at the UN is agreed to, the range of questions dealt with by the Organisation is likely to become even more global. In other words, Communist China in all probability will have the same incentive to refer its disputes with other states to the UN, if its representation is accepted, as other countries have shown as soon as they have been admitted to membership.

The second principal factor which accounts for the non-participation of the UN in the resolution of international disputes since 1945 has been the existence of regional organisations which appeared to be more suitable agencies, and the agreement of their members to use these rather than the UN to try to reach an acceptable adjustment or resolution of the dispute. The two regional organisations which have been most conspicuous in this respect are the Organisation of African Unity (OAU) and, to an even greater extent, the Organisation of American States (OAS), both of which possess developed procedures and machinery for the peaceful resolution of disputes of their own.[5] It was mainly pressures from the OAU which caused the Algeria–Morocco and the Nigeria–Biafra disputes to be dealt with by that organisation rather than through the United Nations. On the other hand, the very powerful influence exercised within the OAS, as well as the UN, by the United States caused the Panama Canal dispute (1964), the Dominican Republic question (1965) and the United States–Cuba conflict (1959–61) to be handled through the OAS rather than through the UN.[6] As already stated, this is fully in accord with the principle embodied in Article 52 of the UN Charter. It may also have the effect of economising on the financial and other resources of the world organisation. It should be remembered, too, that any formal reference of an international dispute to a regional

[5] The role of regional agencies in the settlement of international disputes is dealt with more fully in the following chapter.

[6] Guatemala in 1954, Hungary in 1956 and Czechoslovakia in 1968 appealed to the UN when involved in disputes with the super-Powers dominating the regional agencies to which they respectively belonged. Guatemala and Hungary withdrew their appeals, however, owing to changes in their governments and Czechoslovakia did the same, presumably for fear of making matters worse.

organisation by no means rules out the continuing discussion of the matter in an informal way by representatives of the states concerned at UN headquarters in New York.

Hence it may be presumed that as a general rule all significant international disputes, and most of the insignificant ones, too, will tend to find their way sooner or later on to the agenda of one or other organ of the United Nations, while the two limiting factors we have referred to – the non-representation within the Organisation of certain states, parts of states or governments and the tendency to devolve certain types of disputes on to regional organs – are themselves subject to qualification. How far the UN, when actually considering a dispute, can make any effective contribution towards its resolution, and under what conditions, are questions to be discussed in the following sections of this Chapter. But it is appropriate here to draw three conclusions from this marked tendency of the UN to remain, for twenty-five years, a central channel through which most disputes affecting the international system are processed.

The Uses of the UN

The first conclusion is that this tendency does seem to indicate the need of the various states for an organ such as the UN, if for no other purpose than the ventilation of their international disputes and the recruitment of the widest possible moral support for their own side of the argument. Whether we are to regard the Organisation principally as little beyond a means for "letting off steam" when nothing more effective can be done; or as a delaying mechanism through which speech-making can be carried on while meaningful negotiations are proceeding elsewhere; or as a substantive organ for hammering out compromise solutions; or in any other capacity – these are questions to be examined later. Nevertheless, the frequent recourse of states involved in disputes to UN organs would seem to show that the Organisation does perform a valuable function, and that if it did not exist, it, or something like it, would have to be invented.

The second conclusion is that the internationalisation of disputes through the UN has the effect of continuously bringing to the attention of the states of the world (and most of them are UN Members) the conflicts which agitate the international system, and of reminding them of the interconnectedness of international problems and the common interests of all countries in the resolution of international disputes with the minimum of friction and waste and with the least possible danger to international order as a whole. There exists for the first time in the UN a means by which the now global international community can bring its influence to bear, for good or ill, on international problems, or at least to inform itself as to what those problems are, how they arise and what the arguments of the two or more disputing states are.

This leads to the third of our conclusions, namely that through the airing of international disputes in UN organs public opinion in the different countries is enabled to educate itself in the facts of contemporary international life. It may be that, in certain international conflicts, "too many cooks spoil the broth", and that greater progress is made by quiet conversations between representatives of the communities concerned; but there is nothing inherent in the UN structure or practice to prevent such conversations if the parties prefer them to public debate in the UN's various forums. It may be questioned, too, whether the determined policies of states, especially of Great Powers, can be substantially influenced today, or could be at any time in past history, by anything so amorphous as "world public opinion". Nevertheless, the means exist in the UN for the ordinary person and the organs which shape world opinion, such as the press, to inform themselves about the pros and cons when nations differ. Any such education cannot but have some effect, and there is no reason why as a general rule it should not be a wholesome one, on the rational handling of the sources of international friction.

The UN's Contribution to the Resolution of International Disputes

Once we begin to examine in a more practical sense the role of the UN in the handling of international disputes since the Second World War, however, we at once, and necessarily, enter the realm of subjective assessment. Two primary questions confront us at the outset and the answer to both involves the passing of personal judgements, with a wide scope for disagreement and conflicting interpretations. The first question is how *actively* the UN has been engaged through its various organs in the treatment of this or that contentious question; and clearly that which may seem like fussy and unnecessary interference by one observer may be regarded as masterly inactivity in the eyes of another. The second question is whether UN intervention – or the reverse, the disinclination to intervene – has made any measurable contribution to the "peaceful" or "coercive" solution of a given dispute, as we have defined those terms in the first Chapter of the present Part of this book. Here again, subjectivity is inherent in the question, and that for two reasons. First, there can be room for debate as to what is meant by "measurable", and, secondly, where a given dispute has been resolved, there may well be differences of opinion, not least between the parties concerned themselves, as to whether the dispute could not have been more effectively disposed of, or disposed of in a manner more favourable to one side or the other, if the UN had intervened more actively than it did or, contrariwise, if its contribution had been less significant. For these reasons, in what follows by way of examination of the UN's record to date we needs must tread with the utmost caution.

We propose to begin with the first of our two questions: how active has the Organisation been in the resolution of the international disputes we have chosen to examine for the purpose of this study? The second question, concerning the UN's effectiveness, we shall deal with in the following section. As to the extent or level of the UN's activity, we believe it desirable to distinguish between three types of cases: where the UN's role has been "extensive", where it has been "minimal" and where it has been "nil".[7] The third case is self-explanatory; by it we mean simply disputes which have either not been referred to the UN or which, having been referred, gave rise to a discussion within UN organs which, in any formal sense, was so perfunctory that for all practical purposes we can afford to ignore it. The distinction between an "extensive" and "minimal" role, on the other hand, is much harder to draw.

The UN's treatment of an international dispute may be described as "extensive" when the question has been more or less continuously before a UN organ or organs for a period of time extending into months or years; or when one or more definitive resolutions has been adopted with a view to the peaceful solution or adjustment of the dispute; or when something in the nature of a UN "presence", in the form of a peace-keeping force, an observer group, fact-finding or mediatory mission has been despatched to the site of the dispute; or when UN organs or representatives, as for instance agents of the Secretariat, have been more or less actively engaged in exchanges between the parties with a view to a peaceful solution being arrived at. A "minimal" UN intervention, on the other hand, may be described as one in which an issue was referred to a UN organ without being discussed or without any substantive action being taken, or where an inadequate consensus existed among Member-states for anything in the nature of a UN "position" on the particular issue to be formed, however influential or otherwise such a position might have been for the parties concerned had it in fact been reached. It must be emphasised here again, however, that in distinguishing between "extensive", "minimal" and "nil" roles of the Organisation in the resolution of international disputes, we are referring not so much to success or lack of it in effecting a peaceful outcome, as to the mere extent of the UN's participation in the process of resolution. The question of the UN's success or effectiveness is one to be considered in the following section.

[7] These three categories, with a somewhat different name for the first, were suggested by Miss M. J. Grieve in a paper on the UN's role in the settlement of disputes on which the present section of this chapter has been based.

We propose to divide our 50 instances of international disputes since 1945 into three groups in the following manner:

(1) Where the UN's role as an organ of multilateral diplomacy could be described as "extensive" in the sense defined above: 17 cases.

(2) Where the UN's role could be described as "minimal" in the sense defined above: 25 cases.

(3) Where the UN's role was "nil": 8 cases. This group includes, however, the Polish dispute of 1944–45, which occurred before the Organisation began to function.

In tabular form and in chronological order the three categories of disputes dealt with in the UN forum since its foundation may be set forth as follows:

TABLE 1

UN's Role Extensive

Indonesian independence, 1945–49
Palestine, 1945–49
Kashmir, 1947 to present (including the Indo-Pakistan war in 1965)
Korea, 1947–53
South Africa, 1948 to present (including the two issues of *apartheid* and South-West Africa)
China: Taiwan, the UN, 1950 to present
Indonesia and West Irian, 1950–62
Cyprus, 1954–59 and 1963 to present
Suez, 1956
Lebanon and Jordan, 1958
Congo, 1960–63
Morocco–Mauritania, 1958–69
Yemen, 1962–67
Gibraltar, 1963 to present
Indonesia–Malaysia, 1963–66
Rhodesia, 1965 to present
Arab–Israeli conflict, 1967 to present
Total: 17 disputes

TABLE 2

UN's Role Minimal

Greece, 1944–49
Austria, 1945–55
South Tirol, 1945 to present

Trieste, 1945–54
Berlin, 1948–49
The Anglo-Iranian Oil Company, 1950–53
Tibet, 1950–59
Guatemala, 1952–54
Vietnam, 1954 to present
Hungary, 1956
Muscat and Oman, 1957–59
Anglo-Icelandic Fisheries, 1958–61
Laos, 1957–65
United States and Cuba, 1959–61
Sino-Indian Border, 1959–65
Somalia, 1960–65
U2, 1960
Angola, 1961 to present
Kuwait–Iraq, 1961–63
Goa, 1961
Cuba missile crisis, 1962
Aden (South Yemen), 1963–67
Panama Canal, 1964
The Dominican Republic, 1965
Czechoslovakia, 1968

Total: 25 disputes

TABLE 3

UN's Role Nil

Poland, 1944–45
Indo-China, 1945–54
Quemoy–Matsu, 1958
Berlin, 1958–61
Algeria–Morocco, 1959–63
Chinese minority in Indonesia, 1965 to the present
Nigeria, 1966–70
Hong Kong, 1967[8]

Total: 8 disputes

[8] As stated above, perhaps this is better regarded as a situation of friction (see p. 195, *supra*). The Chinese do not appear to have formulated a distinct claim to the island although incidents intermittently recur, such as the detaining of a group of British citizens in China as hostages for the Chinese imprisoned in Hong Kong after the riots in 1967 during the 'cultural revolution'.

UN's Nil and Minimal Roles

It is convenient to begin our examination of the distribution of the case studies through these three categories with the last and least numerous group: that consisting of disputes in which the UN's role was "nil". In each of these instances, except that of Poland, informal and unrecorded discussions in the corridors, lounges and bars at UN headquarters in New York need not necessarily be ruled out; in one, the Berlin dispute originating with Mr Khrushchev's note to the three Western Powers of 27 November 1958 proposing the demilitarisation of West Berlin, a *voeu* was expressed by the General Assembly in favour of negotiations between the four parties to the dispute. Nevertheless, in all these cases, the United Nations for all practical purposes need hardly have existed.

There are three possible reasons why this should have been so. First, as in the case of the Indo-China conflict of 1945–54, the Quemoy–Matsu dispute of 1958, the Chinese minority in Indonesia question and the Hong Kong issue, the non-representation of one of the leading parties – in all four cases, the Chinese People's Republic – or its refusal to attend UN debates as a non-Member within the terms of Article 35 (2) of the Charter, excluded UN intervention. Secondly, as in the instances of the two African disputes, the Algeria–Morocco and Nigeria–Biafra conflicts, the existence of very strong pressures exerted by a large number of states intimately concerned with these questions against the holding of a public hearing at the UN militated against any role of the Organisation; in the Nigeria–Biafra conflict, too, these pressures based themselves on Article 2 (7) of the Charter which excludes UN intervention in matters of domestic jurisdiction. Thirdly, as in the second Berlin dispute of 1958–61, the general inability of the UN to intervene in any significant manner in a straightforward confrontation between the super-Powers and the respective alliances they lead, no matter how dangerous these confrontations may be for the peace of the world, incapacitated the Organisation as far as attempting any mediatory role was concerned. It is noteworthy in this connection that during the first acute Berlin crisis of 1948–49, when the United States still retained its monopoly of nuclear weapons and for that reason super-Power conflict was less heavy with implications for world peace and survival, six members of the Security Council were able to undertake, though without success, a mediatory role between the four Powers.

As for the factors which account for the division of positive UN intervention in international disputes into "extensive" and "minimal" groups respectively, these are naturally much more difficult to isolate. It is clear, however, as in the case of the "nil-role" disputes, that the non-representation of one or other of the parties concerned weighs heavily against any active UN intervention. The Tibet problem, the Vietnam conflict and the Sino-Indian border disputes are examples of this; the strong global interest, of a moral as well as of a political nature, aroused by the first and second of these questions and the fear excited in India, which enjoyed for many years the status of being a highly respected UN Member, by China's pressures against her northern borders, may be said in each case to have offset to some extent the absence of Chinese Communist representation at the UN in bringing these questions to the Organisation's attention at all. Again, as in the case of the "nil-role" disputes, the super-Power type of conflict is by its very nature not amenable to effective treatment by the General Assembly, while the existence of the Great-Power veto on the Security Council means that any discussion of super-Power differences in that organ must be largely restricted to propaganda functions only. Thus, in our Table 2, the Greek civil war, the Austrian question, possibly Trieste, certainly the first Berlin crisis (1948–49), the U2 incident of 1960, and the Cuba missile crisis of 1962, were necessarily beyond any significant UN intervention since the ultimate decisions lay in the hands of the super-Powers. Some qualification must be added, however, in the case of the Greek civil war at the end of the Second World War; in the first place, as explained elsewhere in this book, Yugoslavia's defection from the Soviet bloc, rather than any decisions on the part of the super-Powers *inter se*, played a decisive role in settling the problem, and, secondly, the Greek civil war was frequently the subject of debate at the UN and hence there is a case for describing the UN role as somewhat more than minimal, though it would be wrong in our opinion to regard it as extensive.

Somewhat similar considerations arise in the case of disputes, usually between super-Powers and lesser states, which develop within the geographical sphere of influence of the former. Included in this group in Table 2 are the Guatemala (1952–54), Hungary, Cuba–United States, Panama Canal (1964), Dominican Republic (1965) and Czechoslovak (1968) crises. In such situations each of the rival super-Powers may seek to make political capital, at the UN among other places, out of such uses of force or other forms of pressure by the other against weak client states, although often, as in the cases of the Hungarian and Czechoslovakian crises of 1956 and 1968 respectively, these efforts were, on the American side, at most somewhat half-hearted. But, as the United Nations has grown in membership with the creation of newly decolonised states, such efforts are bound to be made in the knowledge that they are likely to be regarded as examples of the pot trying to call the kettle black. In any event, the super-Powers, sometimes with each other's tacit agreement, have made it abundantly evident that they intend to remain paramount within their own spheres of influence and that there is nothing the UN or any other international organisation can do to change the situation.

The tendency of less powerful states than the super-Powers in situations where their local position is a strong one to resist UN intervention in their efforts to control conflicts in which they are involved is also illustrated in Table 2 by Britain's success in rebutting the Arab states' efforts to invoke the Security Council against alleged aggression by the Sultan of Muscat against the Omani dissidents and the unavailing efforts of the Trusteeship Committee of the General Assembly to prevail upon Britain to give up her support of the Sultan of Muscat in his dispute over Oman. The same may be said of British resistance to UN intervention in the conflict in Aden in the mid-1960s.

Furthermore, it is clear that the UN's role is bound to be limited where an ex-Imperial Western Power seeks, without resort to force, to secure redress at the hands of UN organs against a weak non-European state, as Britain tried to do in the Anglo-Iranian oil dispute in 1950–51, or where states are bent on using force to settle their disputes and the permanent members of the Security Council are too divided in their attitudes to effect any combination to prevent them. Thus India was able to annex Goa and other Portuguese enclaves in Indian territory in 1961 owing to the Indian Government's determination under no circumstances to be deterred by the UN or its Charter and the existence of enough sympathy on that Government's side among the Afro-Asian and Communist states to make any UN condemnation of its action out of the question.

Two other circumstances may finally be mentioned from the historical record since 1945 which appear to militate against active intervention by the United Nations. One, as in the Anglo-Icelandic fisheries dispute, appears to arise where relations between the parties are otherwise sufficiently intimate that a long drawn-out wrangle at the UN is felt on both sides to be undesirable. Moreover, in the case of the dispute between Britain and Iceland, there existed another forum, NATO, in which they could wash their linen more privately; it seems that a purely informal suggestion by the British Foreign Secretary of the day, Lord Home, to the Icelandic Foreign Minister, Mr Gudmunsson, at a NATO meeting in December 1960 that they should clear this issue out of the way opened the door to what proved eventually successful negotiations. It may be felt, secondly, among the numerically powerful group of new Member-states at the UN that issues which divide them should as far as possible be kept out of the UN limelight, that organ being more suitably reserved for the struggle against colonialism. No doubt this explains the lack of enthusiasm among the African states for the Somali reference of her border dispute with Kenya and Ethiopia to the UN. To this may be added, as we have previously noted, the unreadiness of African states as a whole to see their common frontiers thrust into uncertainty through any attempt strictly to apply the principle of national self-determination to the African continent.

An Extensive Role for UN

We may now examine, by considering Table 1, the conditions which may be regarded as having disposed the United Nations towards playing an "extensive" role in the settlement of international disputes since its foundation. The most striking fact about Table 1 is that only one of the disputes there listed, namely that concerning Gibraltar, is located in Europe and, strictly speaking, this is somewhat more than merely a dispute between two European Powers, Britain and Spain; it is the fact that the Spanish Government has powerful backers among the extra-European countries, notably in Latin America, which has caused the Gibraltar issue to figure so prominently on the UN's agenda, though it has done so primarily in terms of verbal warfare rather than action. Nor do the cases enumerated in Table 1 include issues arising within the spheres of influence of the super-Powers; Eastern Europe has so far provided no opportunity for "extensive" UN intervention, nor have the Americas, north or south. In fact, apart from the Chile–Argentina border dispute referred to Britain for arbitration in 1965, the Latin American states have been singularly free on the whole from disputes between themselves, a fact which reflects upon a very common assumption that a definite relation exists between internal political instability in a state and its proclivity towards engaging in disputes with its neighbours. The most notable areas for extensive UN intervention, to judge from Table 1, are: South-East Asia (three cases); the Middle East (five cases); Africa (four cases) and Asia (three cases – the Kashmir, Korea and the "two Chinas" questions). These are the geographical areas in which it would seem that the Organisation has been most active in its efforts to resolve international disputes.

Closely linked with this observation is the fact that of the 17 cases of extensive UN intervention, 13 are directly or indirectly associated with the decolonisation process. Either, as in the cases of the Indonesian independence issue, the Palestine question (1945–49), the West Irian dispute, the 1954–59 phase of the Cyprus problem and the Congo crisis, the dispute has arisen out of the struggle of a former colony for independence. Or, as in the South African *apartheid* and Rhodesian independence problems, the dispute has lain between already decolonised states and a country which, in the opinion of the former, still remains to be decolonised from white-minority rule. Or, as in the case of the Suez crisis of 1956 and the Malaysia–Indonesia confrontation, a recently decolonised country

(Egypt and Indonesia respectively) has campaigned against what it considers to be relics of colonialism existing in its territory or adjacent territories. Or, as in the case of the Korean, Morocco–Mauritania and Kashmir questions, the dispute has arisen over the disposition of territory newly emerging from conditions of colonial rule. Even the "two Chinas" question can be construed as having decolonisation overtones about it since the Chinese Communist regime on the mainland seems to regard itself as dedicated to the expulsion of so-called Western imperialism from its own territory and especially from Formosa, which it looks upon as the seat of a puppet of Western imperialism.

This leaves, out of our 17 instances of "extensive" UN intervention in international disputes, the Lebanon–Jordan crisis of 1958, the Yemeni civil war, and the second phase of the Cyprus problem extending from 1963 to the present. Here again decolonisation overtones were by no means wholly absent. In so far as the Lebanon–Jordan situation arose out of pressure from the United Arab Republic against those states, that pressure was ostensibly exerted in furtherance of President Nasser's struggle to unite the Arab world against alleged Western imperialism; the same may be said for the UAR's intervention in the Yemen. Again, the struggle against "imperialism" has been a vital factor in the Arab fight against Israel which culminated in the six-day war of 1967, the aftermath of which is still, at the time of writing, unsettled. Although there was insufficient consensus among the only UN Member-states able to muster enough force to prevent the six-day war or, so far, to impose a settlement after the war's conclusion, the UN's involvement in the crisis both in 1967, as shown by the unanimous Security Council resolution of 22 November of that year, and in the three years following has been extensive within our meaning of that term. Although, to take a further example, the Greco-Turkish conflict which sprang into violence in 1963 and led to the formation of the United Nations force for Cyprus (UNFICYP) by the Security Council in March 1964 was a conflict of antagonistic national communities within a single independent state, much of the trouble sprang from the manner in which Cyprus itself was decolonised by the London and Zürich agreements of 1959.

That decolonisation has provided the main part of active UN intervention in international disputes since 1945 is not surprising. Apart from the Cold War, in which UN intervention has been limited for the reasons given earlier, decolonisation has in fact been by far the most significant international development since the Second World War. It is still hard for us to grasp the full magnitude of this immense revolution in human affairs; almost a half of the world's population has seen its international legal status altered within the last two decades and the state-members of the international system have more than doubled in numbers. That this process could not have been accomplished without a certain amount of violence and conflict; that the decolonised states should continue to harbour suspicions and grievances against their former rulers, from which actual disputes easily spring; that some of the new states should be prey to internal instabilities and economic problems which may take the form of antagonism towards, or quarrelling with, their neighbours; all this is to be expected. The extraordinary thing is not that this vast transformation in the whole character of the international system should have bred conflict; the remarkable thing is that it took place as smoothly and peacefully as it did.

Nor is it surprising that the United Nations should have been deeply involved in decolonisation disputes. Its Charter commits Member-states with responsibilities for dependent territories to facilitate their progress towards self-government and also to economic and social advance which inevitably stimulates the demand, not only for self-government, but for full independence. As the Organisation's numbers grew with the admission of newly decolonised states, it was bound to take on more and more the form of a machinery for accelerating the decolonisation process, culminating in the formation of the Committee on Colonialism in 1960. Moreover, the states of the Soviet bloc were bound to throw their weight in the Organisation on the side of decolonisation, as a tactic for currying favour with the new Afro-Asian states and hence for reducing their own minority position in the Organisation in its earliest years, as a means of pressing their case against the Western Powers during the Cold War, and perhaps also as an expedient for diverting attention from the Soviet Union's own semi-colonialist position both with respect to the non-Russian peoples within the USSR and with regard to the Soviet Union's allies in Eastern Europe.

At the same time, the United States, with its dominating position in the UN, at least in its early years, was bound to use its influence on behalf of decolonisation, if only to prevent the Afro-Asian states siding with the Communist bloc in the Cold War, even though, as during the Suez crisis of 1956, this could only be done in a manner discomfiting to the prestige at least of some of the United State's closest allies. To this may be added the fact that, before the first signs appeared of a possible Soviet–American détente, which seems to have begun with the signature of a bilateral agreement on outer space which was jointly presented to the UN General Assembly in 1961, one of the principal functions of the United Nations, in the eyes of leaders of opinion like Secretary-General Dag Hammarskjöld, was "preventive diplomacy", that is, the attempt to prevent areas of conflict like the Middle East and the Congo from becoming caught up in the Cold War, or in other words to use the UN as a means of "holding the ring" against intervention by rival super-Powers. This could best be done, it seemed in the days of Dag Hammarskjöld, by creating a UN "presence" in a dispute situation to which the weaker, non-aligned states would make the greatest contribution, or by the Secretary-General using his good offices to effect a resolution or at least a containment of the situation in order to ward off all risk of super-Power involvement on opposing sides of the argument.

This latter function of the United Nations has been rendered somewhat less credible, first, by the sheer scale of the Congo operation of 1960–63, which almost financially ruined the UN, and which in any case could not be completed without the Kennedy administration's determination to throw the weight of the United States behind the UN's effort to crush the Katangese secessionist movement in 1961; secondly, by the inability of the UN to prevent the renewal of the Arab–Israeli armed conflict in June 1967 and thereafter to contribute effectively to any Middle East peace settlement unless the Great Powers were able to agree upon one and impose it themselves; and thirdly, by the East–West détente and diminution of the Cold War which have given both the super-Powers less of an incentive to take an active role of leadership as rival giants in the UN and more of an inducement to try to settle their mutual problems by bilateral negotiations, reporting back the results of these, if any, to the Organisation. Nevertheless, it would still be true to say that, taking the historical record since 1945 as a whole, the UN has as a general rule played an "extensive" role in decolonisation disputes, especially when its interventions have had the sympathy and support of the United States, and a less "extensive" role where disputes have involved the super-Powers alone or their respective alliances, or have arisen within the super-Powers' spheres of influence, or where pressures have been exerted to have the issue settled through regional agencies.

The UN's Effectiveness in Resolving International Disputes

We must now turn from consideration of the degree or extent of the UN's participation in the handling of international disputes, and the factors which appear to govern that participation, to the far more complex and perhaps even more subjective question of how effective UN intervention has been in the actual resolution of international disputes since the Second World War. As we have emphasised, the fact that the UN has "extensively" participated in the management of disputes between states by no means implies that it has always done so to good effect; nor, on the other hand, does the fact that its participation has been "minimal" or "nil", as we have defined these terms, mean that it has either hindered or facilitated the resolution of a given dispute by playing such a minor role.

One method of examining the question we have posed is to compare the three tables given in the previous chapter (pages 189–191) on the resolution of disputes with the tables set out earlier in the present chapter (pages 229-230) which analyse the extent of UN participation in the handling of international disputes. It will be recalled that in the previous chapter we described 11 of our 50 case studies as being those of now "quiescent" disputes, 10 as "unsolved", 14 as "coercively solved" and 15 as "peacefully solved" within the meanings of these terms as previously stated. Bearing in mind that earlier in the present chapter we have identified 17 interventions by the UN in these disputes as "extensive", 25 as "minimal" and eight as "nil", it will be seen by comparing the two sets of tables that the UN's role was "extensive" in only eight cases out of the 27 disputes which were either peacefully solved or became quiescent and hence no longer of serious implications for the international community. At the same time, of the eight cases of "nil" interventions by UN organs, no less than four fell in the two groups of peacefully solved or quiescent issues, which is some indication that where the UN does not intervene the outlook for a peaceful ending of the dispute is by no means thereby rendered remote. Among the 27 cases in these two groups taken together, the UN's role could be described as "minimal" in 15, whereas in our 10 cases of "unsolved" disputes, the UN seems to have played an "extensive" role in four – which might be taken as implying, uncharitably, that active UN intervention does not necessarily bring wholesome results – a "minimal" role in one and a "nil" role in two.

We do not wish to read too much importance into the statistical character of these conclusions. The case studies themselves, as we have repeatedly stressed in this study, are by no means exhaustive of all international disputes since the Second World War. Their numbers are in any case too small for any fully valid statistical conclusions to be drawn from them; moreover, the classification of disputes employed for the purpose of compiling the two sets of tables is bound to have a good deal of arbitrariness and subjectivity about it. Nevertheless, there are certain general conclusions to be inferred from the data given above concerning the UN's effectivness as a dispute-settling agency, and the fact that there exists some degree of accord between these conclusions and more general observations which are often made about the UN's work in this field demonstrates that there is a certain plausibility about them.

The Limitations of the UN

The first point which emerges from a comparison of the two sets of tables is that the UN's record both in resolving international disputes by agreement and in helping them become quiescent is by no means impressive. There is no very close correlation between the extent of the UN's participation in dispute resolution and the actual resolution of international disputes; at the same time, the Organisation seems to have been as actively engaged in the handling of disputes which have remained unsolved as it has in those which have been solved, if not more so. And, as we have seen, half of the disputes which have encountered no UN intervention whatever have in fact been resolved in one way or another.

There are, however, some very important considerations to be set on the other side of the balance sheet. For one thing, many disputes are referred to the Organisation or, having been so referred, remain on its agenda, simply because under existing conditions there is no way in which they can be resolved. The Organisation has to a large extent become the depository of the world's lost causes; what other means of peaceful resolution cannot achieve tends to be relegated to the UN as a place of last resort. There is also the point that the mere ventilation of a dispute before a UN organ and the existence of the Organisation as a meeting-place for the world's diplomats provide an opportunity for other means of peaceful resolution, especially bilateral and multilateral diplomacy, to work themselves out while the public argument at the UN proceeds, and it may be that it is those other means which reap the credit for any successful termination of the dispute which may be reached. The most widely known example of this, though many more could be cited, is the way in which United States and Soviet representatives could meet at the UN to discuss the resolution of the Berlin crisis of 1948–49 after Stalin's famous interview with a journalist which suggested to the United States authorities the possibility of a change in the Soviet position.

The second point which emerges from a comparison of the two sets of tables is that the UN, by interposing delay through public debates and the "letting off of steam" in a crisis, by clarifying the essential facts of a dispute through its missions of inquiry, by its calls for a ceasefire when hostilities have actually broken out and the provision of teams to supervise an agreed ceasefire, and by the organisation and despatch of peace-keeping forces, can render a useful service by "de-fusing" a tense situation or "keeping it on ice". But the Organisation's record is far less impressive when it comes to actually working out the terms for an agreed solution. Negotiation in the traditional manner, with or without the assistance of UN mediators, with or without the more or less quiet pressure of other interested UN Member-states, still remains the most effective method for resolving international disputes. Indeed, it has been argued in some quarters that the public form of debate at the UN is a hindrance rather than a help in the peaceful process of effecting diplomatic compromises in that it may serve to make the parties more intransigent than conciliatory. It has been argued, too, that the UN, by keeping international disputes "on ice" rather than making an effective contribution towards resolving them, tends to conceal the real nature of these problems. This is a stricture which could be passed on the UN emergency force in the Middle East at the time when its withdrawal was demanded by President Nasser just before the outbreak of the six-day Arab–Israeli war in June 1967; the world seemed up to that moment to have forgotten about the Middle East powder keg, and this no doubt partly owing to the appearance of quiescence stimulated by the presence in the area of UNEF for the preceding ten years. Secretary-General U Thant, surveying this incident, wrote that the "tendency for peacekeeping operations originally set up as temporary expedients to assume a semi-permanent character because no progress is made in settling the basic causes of the conflict is a serious reflection on the capacity of the UN to settle disputes".[9]

As against this, it must surely be said that to keep a dispute in a stable condition and prevent it meeting with a forceful outcome is to be counted an achievement of sorts. One of the most important requirements in any international conflict at the present day is to buy time: time to reflect calmly on where events are leading, time for emotions to cool, time for mental adjustments to be made which permit the parties to learn how to live with the situation if they are unable positively to resolve it. That time, in suitable circumstances, the United Nations allows its Member-states to buy.

Conclusion

It is beyond our scope here to review the wider reasons why the United Nations has not proved as effective an instrument for maintaining world order as was hoped in 1945. Clearly, the sudden onset of the breach between the Western Powers and the Soviet Union almost before the Second World War ended enfeebled an organisation the Charter of which gave such primary emphasis to cooperation between the great powers. Subsequently, with the rapid expansion of the Organisation's membership resulting from decolonisation, resolutions of UN organs tended to lose much of their force, based as they were on the equality of the voting power of the greatest with that of the smallest states, many of the latter having

[9] Introduction to the Annual Report of the Secretary-General on the work of the Organisation, 16 June 1966–15 June 1967 (Document A/6701/Add.1). It has been argued that the total withdrawal of UNEF, from Gaza and Sharm al Shaikh, as well as from the Israeli-Egyptian border, was more than President Nasser asked for and hence that the six-day war of June 1967 was partly touched off by UN action.

understandable, though sometimes irrational, biases against their former colonial rulers. Our concern must be to take the UN as it stands today, emasculated as it may have been by such historical developments, and to judge its efficiency as a forum for the settlement of disputes.[10]

Considered as such, we have seen that the Organisation does not lack machinery or procedures for the peaceful solution of disputes if the parties (who need not even be UN Members) are disposed to make use of them. No doubt there is room for improvement here and there in this provision of machinery and procedures, but almost all proposals for such improvements as for example the advance formation of permanent "stand-by" forces, ready to be rushed at a moment's notice to the site of a dispute during its critical phases, encounter a fatal stumbling block in the form of an inadequate consensus among Member-states to implement them. A further improvement sometimes suggested is that the Organisation should discard what some describe as its "inferiority complex" and employ leading public figures, such as former Prime or Foreign Ministers of major countries, as its mediators, thereby gaining greater leverage for its pacificatory work. We were more impressed, however, by the reminder given to us in an interview with Secretary-General U Thant (who incidentally described the mediatory resources at his disposal as "adequate") that a mediator, besides having personal knowledge of the dispute in question, must be personally acceptable to the parties; it by no means follows that an eminent public figure, especially from an important country, necessarily would be.

But if changes in the UN Charter were feasible so as to enhance the Organisation's effectiveness as an agency for peaceful solutions of dispute, it might be wise to consider shifting the emphasis somewhat from that on "peace and security" to that on "settlement". It is unfortunate, as we have urged in the first section of the present chapter, and leads to a certain artificiality of argument, if a state has to plead that a dispute is a threat to international peace and security in order that it may be inscribed in the agenda of a UN organ. But there are admittedly strong arguments on the other side.

It would also be desirable in our opinion to compile, as we have attempted to do, though in a very superficial manner, in this chapter, a case-book of UN practice in the settlement of international disputes. It was

[10] It need hardly be said that in using the term "United Nations" in this chapter we refer, not to an agency which is in some way more than the sum of its Member-states, but a contrivance by which states may do collectively and universally what otherwise they would do bilaterally or regionally. The League of Nations, H. A. L. Fisher used to say, represents the maximum of world government which the states are ready for at any one time. The same may be said of the UN.

proposed in Part I of the study by the David Davies Institute of the Pacific settlement of international disputes that consideration might be given to the issue of a United Nations Handbook of Peaceful Settlement Procedures.[11] The usefulness of such a Handbook would be as great today as when the original proposal was made. Nevertheless, such a work could usefully be carried much further in the form of an attempt to codify and classify the methods so far employed in the Organisation's history for the resolution of disputes and to examine the conditions under which these methods have proved more or less successful.

The authors of the present study, in their conversations with senior officials of the UN Secretariat in New York, were impressed with their zeal, energy and devotion to the task of "saving succeeding generations from the scourge of war". However, there was notable in the Secretariat a certain lack of recorded experience of how the UN had fared in grappling with international problems since its foundation, and in particular of an attempt to generalise from this now lengthy experience about what kinds of disputes, between what kinds of countries and under what conditions, the Organisation is best and least suited to deal with.

It is, in the opinion of the authors, a remarkable fact that there seems nowhere to exist an authoritative and comprehensive study analysing in detail the case histories of disputes which the UN has handled and drawing reasoned conclusions as to how the Organisation can best go about its work. We have tried superficially in the present chapter to provide an example of the kind of analysis which seems called for of the distilled experience of the United Nations in this field. Plainly to execute any such work with the thoroughness required would exceed our present resources and would almost certainly need the cooperation of many hands. But this would be amply compensated by the value to Member-states and the Organisation's officials themselves of knowledge of what the United Nations, on the basis of its past experience, is best fitted to attempt and what tasks it would be well advised, in its own interest, to leave to other agencies.

[11] *Op. cit.*, p. 45.

11. *The Work of Regional Organisations*

The Nature of Regional Organisations

Alongside the development of the world agency for international co-operation, the United Nations Organisation, has gone the formation and elaboration of regional international organisations now covering every part of the globe.[1] It is natural that these agencies should have developed means and methods for resolving disputes between their members as well as providing support of such of the latter as are involved in disputes with non-member states.[2] It is to the activities of such regional organisations in the field of the resolution of international disputes that we now turn. Here, as in dealing with the United Nations in the previous chapter, we shall be mainly concerned with the conditions which appear to facilitate or, as the case may be, militate against the use and effectiveness of these organisations for such purposes.

The Origins of Regional Organisations

But we first must consider some of the general factors which cause such organisations to be formed in the first place. Regional agencies created by treaty among states situated within a recognisable geographical area of the world may be described as the product of two mutually inconsistent factors: the growing interdependence of nations which has resulted in the general proliferation of permanent international institutions in the twentieth century and the fact that this interdependence has even now not progressed so far that every state has an equal interest in, and continuous contact with, every other state in the international system; Ghana, for example, has obvious common interests with, and somewhat similar problems to face as, Nigeria or Sudan which it does not have with Ecuador

[1] The terms "regional agency" and "regional organisation" are used in the present chapter interchangeably. According to Hans Kelsen, *The Law of the United Nations*, London, 1950, p. 319, "regional agencies are international agencies established by regional arrangements" and "regional arrangements are treaties concluded by states which are in a relation of geographical propinquity". As Kelsen explains (*ibid.*) the expressions "regional agencies" and "regional arrangements" are confused in Article 52 of the United Nations Charter.

[2] For a legal account of some present-day regional organisations see *Settlement of Disputes in Special Fields*, by J. F. McMahon, which forms Annexe IV of the David Davies Memorial Institute report already quoted.

or Thailand. There is also a third factor at work which has an important bearing on the work of regional organisations in the resolution of international disputes, namely that power is not equally divided throughout the international system, and it is natural that the greatest Powers should make an exceptional impact upon other states in their immediate geographical vicinity and should wish to organise them within a regional forum in which, as far as possible, a local or regional consensus on common problems can be shaped.

Hence it is not surprising that the first mention of a "regional understanding" in a world-wide multilateral treaty should have referred to the Monroe Doctrine, a pronouncement by the United States on the common interests of countries of the Western hemisphere, from which common interests the Organisation of American States (OAS) was eventually to emerge. This was in Article 21 of the Covenant of the League of Nations, which stated that "nothing in this Covenant shall be deemed to affect the validity of international engagements, such as treaties of arbitration or regional understandings like the Monroe Doctrine, for securing the maintenance of peace". It is significant, too, that, with one notable exception, the regional organisations which have sprung up with such profusion since 1945 and with which we shall be concerned in the present chapter have been founded on the basis of the predominance in the area concerned of one Great Power, or at most two. That exception, the Organisation of African Unity (OAU), may well have failed to fulfil the hopes of some of its founders because it lacked the consolidating force of a paramount Great Power within it. The Great Power which might have played this role, the Republic of South Africa, was naturally disqualified from doing so by reason of its racial policies.

Two Types of Regional Organisation

We must, however, distinguish, by referring to the UN Charter, between two kinds of regional organisation. The one is the collective defence organisation, such as NATO or the Warsaw treaty system, which has been explicitly formed under the aegis of Article 51 of the UN Charter. This article allows for individual and collective self-defence against armed attack as an exception to the overall ban on the use or threat of force contained in Article 2, paragraph 4, of the Charter. The second type is the "regional arrangement" or "regional agency" proper as referred to in Chapter VIII of the Charter. Article 51 does not appear to anticipate the formation of elaborate international organisations for collective defence, such as NATO or SEATO, which have been found necessary in an age in which the economic burden of defence has proved so heavy, the collective sharing of defence costs so essential, and the need for some measure of co-ordination of foreign policies for states within a single system of collective defence so pressing. Nevertheless, in practice collective defence systems have developed organisational structures as complex as the "regional agencies" referred to in Chapter VIII of the UN Charter and have associated member-states in as many fields of mutual cooperation as those agencies. It should be remembered, however, that regional organisations have also been apt to move into the fields of economic, social and cultural co-operation when their defence functions failed to develop, as in the case of the South-East Asia Treaty Organisation (SEATO) or were no longer an urgent requirement of their members, as in the case of the Central Treaty Organisation (CENTO).

There is nevertheless one immediate and striking difference, in form at least, between the two types of regional organisation, namely that collective defence systems may apply enforcement measures against armed attack without the Security Council's authorisation, though by the terms of Article 51 this freedom is permitted only so long as the Council has not taken "measures necessary to maintain international peace and security". The "authority and responsibility" of the Security Council to maintain international peace and security is, moreover, left unaffected. Article 53 in Chapter VIII, on the other hand, prohibits the use of force by "regional arrangements or agencies" without the Security Council's authorisation, the sole exception being enforcement measures taken by such arrangements or agencies against states which during the Second World War were enemies of UN members, that is, the former Axis Powers and their allies. But this is perhaps a distinction without a difference when it comes to questions of self-defence. There seems to be nothing in the Charter to prevent "regional arrangements or agencies" as defined in Chapter VIII applying enforcement measures without the authorisation of the Security Council and defending them by reference to Article 51. But in this eventuality the enforcement action would need to be "defensive" only and in response to "armed attack". Thus the League of Arab States, a regional agency within the meaning of Chapter VIII, might have used force legitimately without the Security Council's authorisation in defence of Kuwait, had an armed attack taken place against that country in 1961 and had the League force taken up an effective position. The question, however, was never put to the test.

The Value and Drawbacks of Regional Organisations

At first sight there is an overwhelming case for devolution in the process of resolving international disputes by recourse to regional organisations; and in fact this was the view of the San Francisco conference on international organisation which drew up the Charter in 1945. The Charter states in

Article 52, paragraph 2, that members of the UN entering such regional arrangements or constituting such agencies "shall make every effort to achieve pacific settlement of local disputes through such regional arrangements or by such regional agencies before referring them to the Security Council" and, in paragraph 3 of the same article, that the Security Council "shall encourage the development of pacific settlement through such regional arrangements or by such regional agencies either on the initiative of the states concerned or by reference from the Security Council". The word "shall" in each of the foregoing paragraphs could be construed as having a mandatory force. It is noteworthy that the second of these paragraphs seems to ascribe to the Security Council the duty to encourage, not merely the pacific resolution of particular disputes through these agencies, but the elaboration and refinement of techniques for resolving disputes by these means, though it does not appear that so far the Security Council has gone out of its way to shoulder such a task. Finally, Article 33, paragraph 1, of the Charter, which obliges Member-states to resolve their disputes peacefully, includes "resort to regional agencies or arrangements" among the means by which this obligation should be discharged.

The advantages of such arrangements or agencies in the peaceful settlement of international disputes are clear enough. States situated in a particular geographical region are naturally better acquainted with the problems and characteristics of that region than states situated elsewhere; in consequence, they are more likely than states outside the region to be able to understand the motives and pressures which impel disputing parties situated within the region, to know the kind of settlements which stand a chance of being viable in that part of the world, and to be able, if necessary, to make a contribution towards a settlement by adjustments in their own policies and relations with the disputing states so as to increase the attractiveness of a proposed *modus vivendi* to the parties. The localisation of disputes, too, may serve the purpose of isolating them from the wider, and possibly global, international conflicts into which they might otherwise be drawn. It was to avert the danger of all international differences being caught up in the major Cold War tension that the late Dag Hammarskjöld invented his famous technique of "preventive diplomacy". Hammarskjöld seemed to have realised that he could act most effectively before the dispute became "set" by ventilation in the UN Security Council. In so far as the regionalisation of the process of solving international disputes has the effect of placing a screen between them and the dominating conflict of East versus West, or Communism versus liberal democracy, it may be said to serve the ends of preventive diplomacy. In the world of international affairs everything is linked with everything else to form a seamless web of relationships. Nevertheless, the fragmentation of disputes into small parts, either by isolating the different issues involved in them or by limiting the number of parties involved in them or in any other way, and by dealing with these smaller units *seriatim*, may offer some corrective to intransigent stands assumed by large coalitions of states on issues of major principle.

Finally, and as a logical corollary of the above, the devolution of the management of international disputes to regional agencies may have an economising effect on the resources, time and strength at the disposal of the world-wide international agency, the United Nations. As the number of UN member-states increases and the problems referred to the world organisation mount, so does the risk of its breakdown through sheer excess of work. It is moreover a striking feature of the UN, as compared with its predecessor, the League of Nations, that its proceedings, especially if those of its Specialised Agencies are included, are far too numerous and complex for any single individual to follow in any detail. It would surely contribute to the greater intelligibility of the world organisation's work, on which its public support depends, if as much of its undertakings as possible were devolved on to subordinate agencies. This is indeed the policy which succeeding Secretaries-General have pursued.

But there is also something to be said on the other side. If within any regional organisation there exists no well-established means of resolving disputes between member-states, or if it has never been recognised in that organisation that disputes should be resolved by some such techniques as the international community itself has developed over the years, a member-state may find itself shut off from the larger pacificatory resources of the UN and other such global bodies as a result of the interposition of the regional agency to which it belongs. Thus the apparent lack of established procedures for the resolution of disputes between the Warsaw treaty states of Eastern Europe, a lack resulting from the Soviet Union's refusal to allow intra-Communist disputes to be settled outside Communist circles, has robbed those states of access to organs not controlled by Communist forces, which might be expected to be moved by other principles of justice and fair-dealing than those inspiring the official Communist movement. This fact must have militated against Czechoslovakia and Rumania when they pressed for greater personal and national freedom within the Warsaw treaty system. The only way, it seems, in which a Communist state can adequately assert itself against the Soviet Union is by acting in such a way as to enforce its own expulsion from the Communist society of states as Yugoslavia did in 1948. But this is evidently only possible if the state concerned is sufficiently beyond the Soviet Union's military reach as not to fear overmuch the consequences of defiance.

But this brings us to what is perhaps the greatest drawback of the regionalisation of international disputes, especially when considered from the viewpoint of a small or weak member of a regional agency. We have had occasion to notice earlier how present-day regional organisations tend to be clusters of smaller states round some dominant focus of power, such as NATO, SEATO, CENTO or the Warsaw treaty system, or round some cluster of power, as the smaller states of western Europe round France, Federal Germany and Italy in the communities of the Six. The focus of power, as in the CENTO and SEATO examples, need not even be situated within the region in question. It may be that regional agencies formed on such a pattern are more viable than those which are not: the dominant Power gives drive and thrust to the regional organisation, provides the direction behind its policies and supplies the resources by means of which it discharges its tasks. At the same time, this situation is almost bound to produce a tension between the wish of the greater Power to have its quarrels with lesser states within the region settled "in the family" and the desire of the weaker countries to appeal to a wide international forum in which they are not exposed to the ubiquitous influence of their giant fellow-member and neighbour. In the Charter of the Organisation of American States drawn up at Bogotà in 1948 it was laid down in Article 20 that disputes arising between American states "shall be submitted to the peaceful procedures set forth in this Charter before being referred to the Security Council of the United Nations". This tension arising from a conflict of jurisdiction has characterised the OAS throughout its history, as the experience of the Panama Canal dispute in 1964 shows; President Chiari of Panama had a strong incentive to bring his conflict with his great northern neighbour out into the open at the United Nations, whereas President Johnson, on his side, had every inducement to hush the matter up within the context of the OAS. In other words, the regional agency is not always a means for ensuring that justice is done to the weaker state, or at least that it is seen to be done.

A third weakness of the regional agency as a means for peacefully resolving disputes is that a situation may arise in which states face one another in a particular geographical area in an apparently sterile confrontation for years on end, although they may benefit from having fresh light and a better perspective thrown on the issues at stake as a result of the amicable intervention of outsiders. The non-committed or non-partisan external state or, it may be, individual person brings to the dispute less in the way of preconceived ideas, less of a feeling that it must watch its step in proposing solutions for fear that it may complicate its relations with one or other of the parties to the dispute alongside which it must continue to exist in the same geographical region. Sometimes it may be that a fresh mind can discern precisely the difficulty which needs to be resolved before the road to a definitive solution is opened up and which, through sheer force of habit, has eluded those who have had to live with the problem, perhaps for many years on end. Moreover, a solution which has worked well in one part of the world may work equally well in another, and yet the states grouped together within a regional organisation may perhaps be unaware of this without the intervention of some external state or organisation. Again, an external state or agency, such as the United Nations, may be able to provide the face-saving expedient which states seem often to need in order to legitimise a settlement which at the outset looks unfavourable to their own interests. "Acting in deference to the UN's wishes" has more than once in history served to sweeten the pill of an unwelcome settlement, which may have been arrived at in the first instance by means of a regional agency. To take a current example, a UN plebiscite might be a way of enabling Iran to drop its claim to Bahrein.

In short, while the regionalisation of international disputes has become fashionable in world affairs since the Second World War, it is as well not to compartmentalise the international community too much; access to universal bodies such as the United Nations must be left open, partly to avoid a situation in which a small country feels that it is being unjustly done by within the regional organisation to which it belongs, partly to deter a state from acting all the more intransigently in a given dispute in the knowledge that, however well or ill it behaves, it is not likely to receive an impartial hearing within the local forum of which it is a member.

There is a further difficulty about the search for solutions to international disputes through regional organisations. This lies in the fact that, although so far we have been dealing with disputes arising between member-states of a regional agency, the possibility exists of disputes between a regional agency, or one or more of its members, and an external state or organisation. In such a case we cannot say, as a general rule, whether the existence of the regional agency will make it harder or easier to reach a pacific settlement. It may be easier in so far as the existence of the regional agency is able to give its member-state or states support and encouragement, and hence persuade the external state or organisation to come to terms. Thus there can be little doubt that the existence of NATO was an important contributory factor in the emergence of a peaceful outcome to the otherwise menacing Berlin crisis of 1958–61; the practical unanimity of the NATO Powers on standing firm on the rights of the three Western Powers in Berlin seems to have brought to the Soviet Union and its allies an awareness of the perils implicit in their policies.

On the other hand, regional organisations may make solutions of international disputes harder to achieve if they give the kind of support to a member-state which leads it to believe that it can resolve a dispute with an external state entirely on its own terms, or if the very existence of regional organisations as coherent entities is dependent on the continuance of a dispute with external bodies. It is interesting to see, as an example of the former, how the Federal German Republic seemed to have little disposition to settle its border dispute with Poland so long as NATO was firmly united behind it during the most intense years of the Cold War and was undivided about the justice of the Federal German cause. However, as NATO tended to lose some of its cohesion with the advent of the so-called East–West détente and France expressed its satisfaction with the present Polish–German border, a satisfaction which more than one of the other NATO states may be presumed to share, the Federal German negotiating position on the border question has become rather more flexible. As an example of the latter, that is, the dependence of a regional organisation on the continuance of a dispute with some external state or states or organisation, it is well known how unity within the League of Arab States has varied with the intensity of the conflict with Israel. Remove Israel and the cohesion of the Arab League would be in jeopardy; so would that of the OAU if the present regimes in Angola, Mozambique, Rhodesia or South Africa were removed. An international dispute, in other words, may be necessary to the continued existence of a regional agency, while the temporary recession of disputes between members of a regional agency may have the effect of intensifying disputes between the regional agency, or its members, and external states or organisations.

We may conclude this section by saying that while the development of long-term regional organisations since the Second World War has been natural, perhaps inevitable, and while these organisations now form part of the world structure of international institutions crowned by the UN itself, their value as means for pacific settlement of international disputes is by no means unqualified. Their merits and drawbacks may in fact be regarded as fairly evenly balanced. We shall be in a better position to consider the truth of this when we have reviewed, as we propose in the next sections of this chapter, the more important regional arrangements and agencies which now exist. It is worth pointing out, however, that it is the functioning of these bodies, rather than their institutional structure and legal powers, which we wish to emphasise.

Regional Organisations in Europe

The proliferation of European regional organisations since 1945 bears witness to both the divisive and the integrative consequences of the Cold War. While the unification of Europe has been an aspiration of the European mind since the fall of the Roman Empire, it required the restoration of Russian hegemony in Eastern Europe as a result of the Second World

War to make that aspiration at least a partial reality. The weakness of Western Europe in 1945 and after, combined with the fact of Eastern Europe being under Soviet military control, was a principal impetus behind the Council of Europe, formed in 1949, the European communities of the Six, beginning with the Coal and Steel Community, the treaty of which was signed in 1952, and continuing with the European Economic Community (EEC) based on the Rome treaty of 1957 and Euratom, created in the same year, to which the European Free Trade Association, formed in 1959, was a reaction. On the military side, the Western European Union was created in 1954, when Federal Germany and Italy were added to the Brussels treaty states, Britain, France, and the Benelux countries, which had formed their collective defence system in March 1948. It is significant that the solitary European regional organisation to cut across Cold War lines, the UN Economic Commission for Europe, has remained a weak and purely consultative local branch of the UN Economic and Social Council. *Pari passu* with these integrative movements in Western Europe, the Communist states joined together in Cominform in 1947 and, more effectively, in the Warsaw Treaty Organisation, dating from 1955 and formed by the Soviet Union and several other Communist states, to which the economic counterpart is Comecon, the Council for Mutual Economic Assistance, established by the Soviet Union in 1949.

The West European regional organisations are of two kinds, the supranational and the international, or traditional. The agencies of the Six, such as the ECSC and the EEC, are supranational in that, when fully formed, the unanimity rule of traditional international organisations will disappear and, in theory at least, a member-state will be liable to be bound by decisions against which it may have voted; and also in that their decisions are directly binding upon individuals and organisations, such as business enterprises, within the member-states. Little progress has yet been made, however, even among the Six towards the formation of a single political executive or common defence force. The international or traditional agencies, on the other hand, are those which include states, like Britain, other than the Six; these organisations, such as the Council of Europe and Western European Union, still require unanimous voting before binding decisions can be reached.

It cannot be said, however, that any essentially new techniques for the peaceful solution of international disputes have been discovered or are practised within either type of regional organisation. The same process of argument, debate, negotiation and conciliation is found within the Committee of Ministers of the Council of Europe and the Commission or Council of Ministers of the EEC as are found in non-European or world-wide international organisations. It is true that the European Commission established by Article 19 of the European Convention for the Protection of Human Rights and Fundamental Freedoms, signed at Rome in 1950, breaks new ground among international organisations in that it permits petitions from individuals or groups of individuals and non-state organisations, although the European Court of Human Rights created by the same Convention is still without compulsory jurisdiction.[3] It is true, too, that the Court of Justice of the European Communities which was established in October 1958 as a successor to the Court of the European Coal and Steel Community possesses both compulsory jurisdiction and sanctions to enforce its judgements and draws upon many sources of law outside traditional public international law.[4] Nevertheless, the sense of belonging to a European community has evidently not prevented disputes arising between member-states in which the same kind of considerations of national interest operate as in other areas of international relations, as the dispute between France and the rest of the Six over farm prices which almost brought the EEC to a standstill in 1965 or the dispute between Greece, or rather the military government of Greece established by the *coup d'état* of April 1967, and other members of the Council of Europe which marked the twentieth anniversary of the formation of the Council in 1969. Nor has the sense of constituting a European community prevented member-states prosecuting their disputes *inter se* with the firmness exerted by other member-states of the international system, as the argument between Britain and Federal Germany over support costs for the British Army of the Rhine shows.

Perhaps the most we can say is that during the most optimistic periods in the process of Western European integration there has been a sense of movement, of the more or less orderly putting into operation of a preconceived programme of unification, and this may well have bestowed on disputing states of the European communities a certain perspective and sense of proportion. At best it has been possible among the Six, and to a less extent among the rest of the Western European states, to conceive disputes as holding up a certain dynamic process of integration extending over several years, and hence to desire to bring pressure to bear to resolve them; from this source, it seems, stemmed some of the unpopularity among the Six other than France of President de Gaulle when he was the French President, since he was liable to be charged with obstructing a movement of affairs which had a certain significance outside the narrow interests of individual member-states of the European communities. Generally speaking, this consciousness of a larger, premeditated design,

[3] *European Unity: A Survey of the European Organisations*, PEP, London, 1968, pp. 149–52.
[4] *Ibid.*, pp. 187–9.

which disputes between states may retard or injure, is not a normal feature of international affairs.

The Warsaw Pact

Turning now to the Warsaw treaty system in Eastern Europe, we know very little as to how disputes are settled in practice among these states. In Marxist-Leninist theory it is hardly possible, if at all, for conflicts to arise between Communist states since that theory regards international conflict as the consequence of rivalry between capitalist organisations for foreign markets and opportunities for investment. If conflict does arise between Communist countries, this can only occur for one or other of two reasons: either allegedly "counter-revolutionary" forces have penetrated a Communist state and divided it off from other members of the Communist family (the explanation given by the Warsaw Pact states in their dispute with Czechoslovakia which ended in the invasion of that country in August 1968), or the Communist rulers of a country have departed from the paths of ideological rectitude (the charges and counter-charges employed in the Soviet–Yugoslav dispute in 1948 and the Sino-Soviet dispute in the 1960s). Accordingly, the Warsaw Pact Organisation appears to have no special machinery for the pacific settlement of disputes arising within the Organisation's framework; and no doubt this has the further merit of being convenient for the overwhelmingly dominant state in that system, the Soviet Union.

In practice, however, it is clear that conflicts of interest and viewpoint do arise between the Eastern European states as, for instance, the border dispute between Hungary and Rumania and, on larger issues, between Rumania and the Soviet Union as to how far the former should accept the role accorded to it within the Comecon scheme of things. We must suppose that such conflicts are managed with due respect to the relative political and economic weight of the parties concerned, and to the inconvenience which either side can cause the other if it does not have its way, just as generally occurs in the handling of disputes within the international system as a whole. The interests of Communist states may be somewhat different from those of non-Communist states, but there is no reason for thinking that they are any more mutually compatible, or defended with less zeal when they are incompatible than is the case in non-Communist states.

There are, however, certain special political factors at work in Eastern Europe which no doubt play their part in the resolution of such disputes which occur in that region. First, the fact that the Soviet Union, the predominating power in that area, has been engaged in a peculiar relationship, first of extreme hostility, then of growing like-mindedness with the other super-power, the United States, and that it has also been involved in a continuing rivalry for supremacy in the Communist world with the People's Republic of China, seems to have affected its capacity for bringing pressure to bear on other Warsaw Treaty states when disagreements have arisen within that system. The Soviet Union has witnessed so many challenges to its international position in recent years that it cannot afford to put its foot down too harshly on its allies; when it does so, as in Czechoslovakia in 1968, this appears to have been largely due to its awareness that it must draw the line somewhere in a situation in which it runs the risk of losing control of its alliance or where it fears a threat to its security.

Secondly, and acting as an influence in a contrary direction, the Eastern European Communist governments realise their dependence on the Soviet Union for their survival; the probability, for most of them, is that their power in their own countries would disappear if Soviet support were withdrawn. This situation gives the leaders of the Soviet Union a certain leverage when they are in any dispute with these regimes. Thirdly, we are entitled to assume that in any international sub-system as tightly integrated as the Warsaw Treaty Organisation the incentive for the paramount Great Power to keep disputes "within the family", so to speak, must be very strong, and hence the opportunities for bringing a dispute arising within the sub-system before, say, the United Nations will be few, if they exist at all. This means that the "forensic" characteristics of world-wide organisations such as the UN are far less prominent in the Warsaw Treaty Organisation. Such genuine negotiation or bargaining as proceeds between the Organisation's members seems to be carried on behind the closed doors of traditional diplomacy. Diplomacy – between Ministers, party leaders, civil servants, planners – is the standard form among the Warsaw Pact states to a far greater extent than mediation, adjudication or arbitration. It is ironical that the so-called "progressive" states of the world are perhaps the most traditional as far as the pacific settlement of international disputes is concerned.

The NATO System

The North Atlantic treaty was signed on 4 April 1949 with the object of associating the United States and Canada with the states of Western Europe, including Britain, in the defence of the North Atlantic area against an assumed threat of Soviet aggression. Greece and Turkey adhered to the treaty in 1951, giving an Eastern Mediterranean flank to the alliance, and in the following year a definite structure was given to the pact with the formation of the North Atlantic Treaty Organisation (NATO), headed by a Council representing member-states. The Council remained, however, purely consultative and without power to make binding decisions except on the basis of unanimous voting. The NATO Council provides a forum for regular debate and consultation and has enabled joint, and therefore perhaps more convincing, replies to be made to Soviet pressures and communications. In December 1958, for example, a common attitude towards the Berlin crisis was adopted by the Council; Western views have also been harmonised through the NATO machinery before important negotiations with the Soviet Union, as in preparation for the four-Power "summit" and Foreign Ministers' conferences in 1955, the four-Power Foreign Ministers' conference in Geneva in June 1959 and the abortive four-Power "summit" conference in Paris in May 1960. Consultations have also been effected through these means during the Congo (1960–63), Cuba (1962) and Cyprus (1963–67) crises. While NATO has had little, if anything, to do with the origins of the 50 international disputes chosen for consideration in this study, it has had considerable effects on their development and often their resolution.

During the Berlin blockade of 1948–49 (an event, incidentally, which was materially contributory to bringing the North Atlantic treaty into being), the Soviet Union seemed to realise that the crisis was uniting the Western powers as nothing previously had done and that the counter-measures collectively applied by those Powers were thwarting its own efforts to extinguish the freedom of West Berlin. Admittedly, the treaty arrangements of April 1949 did not in themselves constitute a factor in the resolution of the Berlin dispute, but the unity behind their original formation undoubtedly did.

Similarly, the origins of the four-Power dispute over Austria (1954–55) had nothing to do with the North Atlantic treaty, but the Soviet attitude towards the negotiations over Austria was decisively affected by Federal Germany's attitude towards NATO. Until early 1949 the Soviet Union seemed to desire a negotiated solution of the Austrian problem, but tended to dig in its heels after Yugoslavia's defection from the Soviet bloc, the failure of the Berlin blockade and the consolidation of the West with the signature of the North Atlantic treaty. However, with Stalin's death in March 1953 and the failure of the European Defence Community (EDC) in August 1954, the situation changed. Agreement was then reached between the Western Powers at their conference in London in October 1954 for bringing the Federal German Republic into NATO and using Western European Union to control its rearmament. This appears to have stirred the Soviet Union to initiate talks with the Austrian authorities in February 1955; the idea evidently was to convince the West Germans that if they wanted reunification and an end to the occupation in both East and West Germany they would have to pay the price paid by Austria, namely neutrality. This bid came too late, however; the quickly arranged Austrian

State Treaty of May 1955 did nothing to entice Federal Germany towards a similar status. That country's simultaneous integration into NATO was at once a major blow to Soviet policy in Europe and one of the reasons for the second Berlin crisis of 1958–61. NATO can therefore be described as having played its part in the solution of the Austrian dispute, though not in a way which the Soviet authorities wished.

The 1958–61 phase of the Berlin crisis seems to have had its roots in the integration of the Federal German Republic into NATO and possibly also in the United States' decision to entrust nuclear weapons, though still under the American President's control, to the Bundeswehr. This strengthening of NATO seems to have hardened Mr Khrushchev's attitude towards the alleged "anomaly" of West Berlin and he determined to try to compel the Western Powers to recognise the German Democratic Republic (DDR) in the Soviet-occupied zone of Germany by threatening to expel Western forces from their legal position in the Western sectors of the city. A month after Mr Khrushchev's note of 27 November 1958 on making West Berlin a demilitarised free city, the NATO Council issued statements firmly supporting the three Western occupying Powers and throughout the crisis NATO remained united, fully endorsing, for instance, the stand taken by Britain, France and the United States at the quadripartite meeting of Foreign Ministers in Geneva in the summer of 1959. Ultimately the Soviet Prime Minister's position seems to have been undermined by evidence that the crisis was only helping to integrate Federal Germany into NATO and that the NATO Powers seriously considered West Berlin to be worth a war, both being opposite effects to those at which Mr Khrushchev was aiming. However, NATO's unity had little apparent effect on the practical handling of the dispute and in so far as it was solved, this seems to have been due partly to the effectiveness of the Berlin Wall, erected in August 1961, in stopping the flow of refugees from East Germany to the West, partly to the informal talks held by representatives of the four Powers at UN General Assembly meetings and at the Geneva disarmament conference in 1962.

As far as disputes between NATO members are concerned, it will be recalled that Article 1 of the North Atlantic treaty imposes on signatories the obligation to settle these peacefully. This obligation was further spelled out in 1956 when the Council approved the report of a committee of three, Chapter II of which reaffirmed the obligation to settle peacefully disputes between member-states; recommended that members submit such of their disputes as had not proved capable of settlement to good offices procedures within the NATO framework before resorting to any other international agency; recognised the "right and duty" of member-governments and of NATO's Secretary-General to "bring to the attention of the Council matters which in their opinion may threaten the solidarity or effectiveness of the alliance"; and proposed that the Secretary-General be authorised, with the assistance of three permanent representatives, to "offer his good offices informally at any time to the parties in dispute, and with their consent to initiate or facilitate procedures of inquiry, mediation, conciliation or arbitration".

Both the NATO Council and the Secretary-General figured prominently in two of the most important disputes which have arisen between signatories of the North Atlantic Treaty. In the Anglo-Icelandic fisheries dispute (1958–61) the fact that both of the parties were NATO members was instrumental in the peaceful resolution of the dispute. Since 1956 Communist and neutralist elements in Iceland had repeatedly called for the removal of the NATO base at Reykjavik and it was frequently pointed out by the Icelandic government that Britain's allegedly negative attitude towards Iceland's new legislation on territorial waters provided those elements with some of their most effective ammunition. Moreover, NATO provided the venue for the talks between the two governments on a solution to the dispute; these took place at the meeting of the NATO Council in Copenhagen in July–September 1958, in Paris in December 1959 and in Paris and London in December 1960, where a basis for negotiation was finally agreed upon between Lord Home and Mr Gudmunsson as their countries' respective Foreign Ministers. It is significant that the reasons given by the British government for their final acceptance of the "six-plus-six" formula as a solution to the dispute was the recognition of the "immense importance of the fishing industry to Iceland" and the fact that that country, as an "ally in NATO", was a "country with whom we wish to resume friendly relations". NATO, once again, could not properly be described as a positive agent in the settlement of this dispute, but the circumstances that the two states concerned were members of the same regional organisation, that it was considered vital for Iceland to remain within that organisation and that NATO provided a convenient meeting place for the negotiators were an important contribution towards finding an answer to the problem. To which may be added the fact that the Icelandic government found that the controversy in Iceland about NATO was helpful in pressing its case, while Britain, on its side, could legitimise its acceptance of the "six-plus-six" formula by attributing it to respect for the status of Iceland as an ally.

As for the second of these disputes, the unrest in Cyprus, the internal tensions which had gripped the island since 1955 have been essentially outside the scope of NATO; nevertheless, from the outset the organisation has exerted considerable pressure on Greece and Turkey, whose influence on the island's affairs was all important. As early as 1955 NATO's Secretary-

General attempted, though vainly, to persuade the three countries chiefly concerned, Britain, Greece and Turkey, to seek a solution through the organisation, of which they are all members. Britain and Turkey were agreeable, but Greece was not, on the ground that it would be a situation in which two NATO allies (or three, if the United States, which was lending its weight to Britain and Turkey, were added) confronted one; moreover, the Greek authorities feared that a NATO solution would be more likely to be worked out along the lines of strategic principles than of national self-determination, which seemed to favour *enosis*. Hence the suggestion that Cyprus should become a NATO trust territory came to nothing, while the proposal of Archbishop Makarios that the dispute be referred to the United Nations was resisted by Britain. When terrorism disrupted the peace of the island towards the end of 1958, M. Spaak again offered his good offices at the NATO Council meeting in December and succeeded in inducing the three allies to resume informal discussions. From the latter sprang the London and Zürich agreements, which established the island's independence in the following year; among the factors which led to this settlement were Greece's unwillingness to make herself any more unpopular among her NATO allies and Turkey's wish for the organisation's protection and also for United States aid.

When friction grew between the two communities on the island after independence, culminating in serious clashes in December 1963 and rumours of, first a Turkish, then a Greek, invasion, an emergency meeting of the NATO Council urged restraint on both sides. Then, following the failure of long negotiations between Britain, Greece and Turkey in London in January 1964, Britain, with United States support, proposed the immediate dispatch of a NATO force to Cyprus, together with neutral mediation and an administrative committee to rule the island temporarily, to be formed from ambassadors to NATO.

This plan, however, fell to the ground when Archbishop Makarios, though not the Greek or Turkish government, refused to accept it on the ground that he would get a fairer hearing at the United Nations. Moreover, the Soviet Union contended that peace would be threatened if NATO were involved, and it became apparent in NATO itself that the plan by no means commanded universal support. The British government, now realising that the UN was the only practical expedient, took the matter to the Security Council and from the debate there sprang the UN force for Cyprus (UNFICYP), created on 24 March 1964, after Turkey had once more threatened armed intervention, only to be dissuaded by its NATO allies. Thus, although the ultimate reduction of tension on the island was effected by means of a UN presence, NATO acted throughout the crisis as the venue, perhaps the only venue, where the parties could meet; a form of pressure deterring Greece and Turkey from a serious armed clash; a common interest for the Greek and Turkish governments, deterring them from going too far in estranging themselves from their other NATO allies; and a source of continuous good offices.

In conclusion, one may say that NATO, by symbolising and helping to preserve the solidarity of the Western Powers, has played a vital role in maintaining peace, as well as providing a channel of communication between member-states, a venue for negotiation, and strong inducements to bringing disputes "within the family" under control lest they jeopardise the larger purposes of the alliance. The mere fact that Foreign Ministers, and not infrequently Prime Ministers, are bound to meet together in the ordinary course of affairs at the NATO Council creates opportunities for talking over common problems and opens the way to agreements in the spirit of allies in a broader cause.

The Organisation of American States (OAS)

When we consider the important disputes which the OAS has dealt with in recent years – the Guatemala crisis of 1954, the United States dispute with Cuba since 1959, the dispute between Cuba and Venezuela of 1963, the Panama Canal dispute of 1964 and the Dominican Republic crisis of 1965 – it is clear that in all except the third of these the United States has played a dominant role, and that, except for the Panama Canal question, the instance in which the OAS made perhaps its most notable contribution to a pacific settlement, the dispute arose from allegations of Communist or Castroite subversion and infiltration. The issue of Communism in the Western hemisphere has been a divisive rather than a unifying factor in relations within the OAS, and yet its disturbing implications for the *status quo* were not envisaged when the Rio Pact on inter-American cooperation and the OAS Charter were signed in 1947 and 1948 respectively, although Article 6 of the Rio Pact does refer obliquely to its dangers.[5]

Articles 20–23 of the OAS Charter lay down the basic rules for the peaceful settlement of disputes within the organisation while Chapters IX–XII create the machinery for implementing these rules.[6] The OAS now lacks none of the institutions or authority to make it effective; the OAS Council, representing all member-states, the Organ of Consultation, consisting generally of Foreign Ministers, and that peculiar invention of inter-American cooperation, the Inter-American Peace Committee, made up of five members appointed by the Council, stand ready to move into action immediately in order to pacify a conflict at the request of the parties.

[5] For the text of the Rio Pact, see A. V. W. and A. J. Thomas, *The Organisation of American States*, Dallas, 1963, Appendix B.

[6] *Ibid.*, Appendix A.

Moreover, Article 8 of the Rio Pact allows for the breaking off of diplomatic relations, economic sanctions and finally the application of armed force, to restore peaceful relations should negotiation, mediation or arbitration fail. It is evident, however, that these provisions have been seriously weakened, on the one hand, by the sheer disparity of power between the United States and its fellow-members of the inter-American system and, on the other, by the suspicion of many of the latter that the United States is apt to use the system as a rubber-stamp for intervention in their affairs in the service of its own national purposes. Hence the tendency for many disputes which the OAS was potentially capable of dealing with to find their way to the United Nations agenda owing to resentment against United States dominance in the inter-American system; as examples there could be cited the Guatemala, Cuba, Dominican Republic and Cuba vs. Venezuela questions which will be discussed later in the present section. We have referred earlier in this chapter to the coherence which the presence of a Great Power in a regional organisation can confer on that agency. In the case of the OAS, however, and the same may be said of the Warsaw Pact system, there is another side to the coin in that the Great Power's predominance and policies can sometimes lessen the regional body's effectiveness.

To take first the Guatemala problem, it was in the midst of mounting apprehension in the United States concerning the radical social reforms of Colonel Arbenz in Guatemala that Secretary of State John Foster Dulles, at the Tenth Inter-American conference in Caracas in March 1954, pressed for a resolution declaring Communism a threat to the peace and calling for "appropriate action in accordance with existing treaties". The delegate of Guatemala denounced this move as a pretext for intervening in a State's internal affairs and warned that any Latin American state embarking on a national programme which "affects the interests of foreign companies" would, under the Dulles resolution, be dubbed Communist and therefore be liable to intervention. The resolution was nevertheless carried by the necessary two-thirds majority, only Mexico and Argentina abstaining, although the Latin American states which voted for the resolution evidently did so "without enthusiasm, without optimism, without joy and without the feeling that (they) were contributing to the adoption of a constructive measure".[7] Most of them concentrated their attention more on the latter part of the resolution which stated that it was designed "to protect and not to impair the inalienable right of each American state freely to choose its own form of government and economic system and to live its own social and cultural life".

The United States then signed bilateral security treaties with Nicaragua

[7] Hisp. Am. Report, VII/3 54.

and Honduras and the Central Intelligence Agency (CIA) secretly gave assistance to Colonel Castillo Armas, who, having rallied a body of Guatemalan dissidents, invaded Guatemala on 19 June. Guatemala at once appealed both to the United Nations Security Council and to the Inter-American Peace Committee (IAPC) to convene in order to discuss the "open aggression perpetrated by the governments of Nicaragua and Honduras"; but before the IAPC could appoint a sub-committee for this purpose, Guatemala asked the OAS to suspend all consideration of the matter. The Arbenz regime in Guatemala, it seems, became reluctant to entrust its problems to the OAS since, according to Inis Claude, it realised that "under United States leadership that regional body was more inclined to promote than to prevent its overthrow". The UN Security Council, however, proved to be deadlocked by the veto, only an ineffective resolution calling for a cessation of hostilities being passed. The invasion continued, the Security Council tried again but with no more success, and it was agreed that the United Nations should await until a report from the IAPC was received. Hence it came about that, by default, the IAPC was once more allowed to take up its work and the Arbenz regime had no alternative but to acquiesce. On 26 June ten members of the OAS called for a meeting of consultation "in view of the communist threat", but by 28 June Arbenz was virtually overthrown; the proposed meeting of the Organ of Consultation was postponed *sine die* and the IAPC's sub-committee dispersed from Mexico, where it had been in session. Several members of the OAS were alarmed at the course events had taken in the Guatemala affair and at the UN General Assembly in the autumn of 1954 made clear that, in their opinion, their membership of the OAS did not restrict their "right of immediate recourse" to the UN. We may sum up this episode by quoting from Inis Claude, who writes (*International Conciliation*, March 1964, p. 30):

> It appears that the transfer of the case from the Security Council to the OAS was not simply a matter of having the latter substituted for the former as a peace-settlement mechanism, but a device for reversing the terms of the case. The OAS was prepared to treat Guatemala as the defendant, not as the plaintiff; whereas the Security Council had appealed for the cessation of the attack, the OAS declared its intent to consider means for expediting the demise of the government of Guatemala. In insisting that the government of Guatemala should resort to the OAS, the United States was recommending what it hoped and intended would prove a suicidal act.

Turning to the conflict between the United States and Cuba from the successful Castro revolution in 1959 to the missile crisis in October 1962, this dispute may be said to have originated in the difficulties experienced by the United States in co-existing with a Communist regime in the Western hemisphere. Dr Castro's emergence as a radical leader in the Caribbean and his determination to achieve a revolution in Cuba which could not but be harmful to United States' interests were bound to incur the displeasure of Washington, and the authorities there sought OAS support in an attempt to squeeze him out of power. Many OAS members, on the other hand, were initially not unsympathetic towards Castro, considering that Trujillo of the Dominican Republic was a much more dangerous force. It was the United States which instigated all the moves in the OAS to counteract Dr Castro's Communism, succeeding generally in organising the necessary two-thirds majority without, however, always winning the hearts and minds of the Latin American states.

The unrest in the Caribbean during the first half of 1959 and Washington's increasing alarm over Dr Castro's leftist tendencies led to an OAS meeting in Santiago, Chile, in August 1959. The meeting was "to review all the information available to the OAS on tensions existing in the area, to examine the causes thereof and to suggest courses of action that would revitalise the basic principles of the OAS". The IAPC was formally recognised as a permanent entity and was mandated "to examine methods of procedure to prevent any activities from abroad designed to overthrow established governments or provoke instances of intervention or aggression". The committee was also asked to study "the relationship between the violation of human rights and the absence of representative democracy, on the one hand, and political tensions affecting the peace of the hemisphere, on the other", and to prepare a preliminary report which could then be commented upon and eventually implemented. Not surprisingly, Dr Castro denounced the Santiago meeting as "nothing more than a farce which looks like part of the international plot versus the Cuban revolution".

Despite the activities of the IAPC, tension between the United States and Cuba continued to mount. In March 1960 Dr Castro, emboldened perhaps by the promises of Soviet support which he had received, denounced the Rio Pact and by July had expropriated certain United States oil companies in Cuba. On 18 July Peru called for a consultative meeting of the OAS for the purpose of "considering the requirements of continental solidarity and the defence of the regional system of American democratic principles against possible threats". This meeting, it was agreed, should take place immediately after the sixth consultative meeting of the OAS at San José in August. By the time this assembled Dr Castro had suffered a rebuff at the United Nations, to which he had complained on 18 July of "United States economic aggression and intervention", since the Security Council, at the urging of the United States, decided to refer the dispute to the OAS. All that the seventh consultative meeting at San José agreed to, however, was a declaration in general terms which condemned "intervention by an extra-continental power in the affairs of the American republics". A separate resolution set up a committee of six to attempt mediation between the United States and Cuba, but Dr Castro's only reply was to tear up the resolution. The abortive Bay of Pigs invasion of Cuba in April 1961 was a shock to the OAS, but no attempt was made by President Kennedy to embroil the organisation in the affair. Nevertheless, the President made it quite clear that, if necessary, the United States would act alone in the defence of its national interests.

At the consultative meeting of the OAS at Punta del Este in January 1962 Brazil's proposal for "finding a basis for co-existing with the Castro government" failed to win support and unanimous votes, except for those of Cuba, were given to a resolution declaring that Marxist-Leninist principles were "incompatible with those of the inter-American system". Sixteen of the delegations present agreed to suspend their trade in arms with Cuba, but only a bare two-thirds majority was won for a resolution "to exclude the present government of Cuba from participation in the inter-American system"; Argentina, Brazil, Chile, Ecuador and Mexico were among the dissenting states. It is possible that this United States-sponsored effort to have Dr Castro thrown beyond the pale was one of the factors driving him into the arms of the Soviet Union, since the immediate aftermath was the crisis of October 1962 which sprang from the dispatch of Soviet missiles to the island. During this crisis the OAS supported President Kennedy's stand, recommending on 23 October that "all measures be taken, including the use of force, to ensure that the Government of Cuba cannot receive further military aid from the Soviet Union". Bolivia, Brazil and Mexico, however, made clear their minority position by saying that they would not countenance any armed invasion of Cuba. The fact was that the threat of the Soviet missiles to the security of the United States was so great that the OAS had no alternative but to follow in Washington's footsteps.

On the one hand, therefore, the OAS cannot be said to have "solved" this dispute, in so far as it stemmed from Cuba's policy of fomenting revolution from below amongst her neighbours, since Dr Castro is still in office and does not appear to have abandoned the larger aims of his policy. Nor can it be said, on the other hand, that the OAS, as distinct from world opinion in the wider sense, has in itself dissuaded the United States from removing Dr Castro's regime by force.

In the Panama Canal dispute in 1964, however, the OAS was able to play a modestly useful role, although this was largely due to the United States' decision to regard Panama's grievances as inspired by nationalism rather than Communism. Once President Chiari of Panama had been dissuaded from pressing for satisfaction through the UN Security Council, both sides accepted assistance from the IAPC, though that body's efforts to mediate at first foundered on Panama's refusal to negotiate on the basis of the existing treaty. On 4 February 1964 Panama summoned the Organ of Consultation of the OAS and a five-nation sub-committee appointed by that body prevailed upon the two sides to negotiate, a joint agreement being reached on 3 April. This involved a plan to build a new canal and the drawing up of a fresh treaty to govern the existing canal with recognition of Panama's sovereignty over the Canal zone.

At the other extreme, the Dominican crisis in 1965 provided striking testimony to the United States' dominant position in the OAS. The Trujillo dictatorship in the Dominican Republic had been the focus of much tension in the Caribbean, culminating in the decision of the sixth consultative meeting of the OAS in San José in August 1960 to impose economic sanctions on the Republic and break off diplomatic relations with it under the terms of the Rio Pact. After Trujillo's assassination the OAS further helped to keep the temperature down in the friction between the Dominican Republic and Haiti in 1963. A crisis was caused in the organisation, however, by the dispatch of United States marines to the Republic on 28 April after the *coup* in that state four days previously. President Johnson excused his action by reference to the Punte del Este resolution which declared that Marxism-Leninism was incompatible with the inter-American system.[8] But this, in the opinion of many Latin American states, did not justify the President's omission to consult the organisation before calling in the marines. A five-man conciliation commission sent by the OAS to the Dominican Republic in May 1965 achieved very little and on 6 May a dramatic step was taken when an Inter-American Peace Force (IAPF) was voted into existence. Chile, Ecuador, Mexico, Peru, Uruguay and Venezuela, however, feared that this would set a precedent for collective intervention in their own affairs and eventually only Brazil contributed substantially to the force.

The IAPF's sole function was to cooperate "in a spirit of democratic impartiality in the restoration of normal conditions in the Dominican Republic and the inviolability of human rights, and the establishment of an atmosphere of peace and reconciliation that will permit the functioning of democratic institutions". The force was, however, disliked both by the rebels in the Dominican Republic, led by Colonel Caamano, and the loyalists under Wessin y Wessin, and they appealed to the United Nations on 25 June for its withdrawal. Nevertheless, the force can be said to have helped to maintain the peace and under its auspices a three-man OAS Mediation commission, which spent two months in the Republic, was able to work for an acceptable solution. The fact that the United States

[8] See above, p. 263.

representative on the commission, Mr Ellsworth Bunker, was part of an inter-American team cooled some of the anger aroused within the OAS by the United States' unilateral action in sending the marines in April and also made the commission's work more palatable to Caamano and his supporters, although Wessin's eventual acceptance of the ten articles of the ultimate agreement was more due to Washington's threat of a withdrawal of aid if he refused. There is no doubt, too, that the presence of the OAS in the Dominican Republic in the form of its observation mission served to make the elections of July 1966 fairer than might otherwise have been expected. The OAS may therefore be described as having provided a cover under which the United States could contract out of a commitment which it had assumed through imputation of a Communist character to the Dominican rebels. At the same time, the episode showed how a regional organisation, even one which includes vocal critics of its Great-Power member, can be swept aside by that Power when it is consumed by fear as to the security of the region in which it is situated.

Finally, in Cuba's disputes in the early and mid-1960s with other Latin American states, notably Bolivia, Colombia and Venezuela, the OAS has served as a means for organising collective action against an allegedly subversive state without in the process doing much to remove the real causes of the friction. The brief history can be recounted in four stages. Firstly, in December 1963 Venezuela appealed to the Council of the OAS against alleged Cuban intervention and aggression; in February 1964 a seven-nation fact-finding committee appointed by the Council to investigate this complaint, formally indicted Cuba for sending arms to Venezuelan rebels, training guerrillas for action in Venezuela and seeking to overthrow the Venezuelan government. Secondly, at the ninth consultative meeting of the Council of the OAS in July 1964, all members agreed to suspend commercial and diplomatic relations with Cuba and urged countries outside the region to cease trading with that country. By the end of 1964 only Mexico maintained diplomatic relations with the Castro regime. The third phase came with the capture of a small force of Cuban guerrillas as they landed on the coast of Venezuela in May 1967. Following this incident, the Foreign Ministers of the OAS charged Cuba with aggressive activities and voted for a new inquiry into the real, ascertained and serious danger to all Latin America. When a report issued from this inquiry it disclosed that Dr Castro was stepping up his allegedly subversive activities, but there was no support for the idea of an OAS police force in the two countries to which it was most likely to be sent, Bolivia and Venezuela; once more, fear that the force might set an undesirable precedent for intervention operated against it. The fourth and final stage of this problem (at least for the time being) came in September 1967 when an OAS Foreign

Ministers' meeting decided to refer the question to the United Nations in the hope of winning more universal support for sanctions against Cuba. Since the Communist states now accounted for some 80 per cent of Cuba's trade, it was never likely that such a move could be successful.

To sum up, one may say that although the OAS disposes of a comprehensive and elaborate set of procedures for dealing with disputes and has been fertile in developing expedients for pacification, such as the IAPC and the IAPF, these procedures have been fully effective in only a minority of the cases of dispute with which the organisation has had to deal. The enormous disparity in strength and wealth between the United States and other OAS members has tended to encourage Washington to take unilateral action without always following the OAS "rules of the game". At the same time, the OAS has served to make United States' action somewhat more palatable to other member-states of the inter-American system. Otherwise, the OAS has on the whole been more successful in drumming up support for particular forms of action against offending individual member-states, notably Cuba, than in tackling the roots of the problem of co-existing with such states. But there can be no doubt that, on the longer view, the OAS has proved its usefulness as a dispute-settling agency, as is shown by the proneness of member-states to refer their disputes to it.

The League of Arab States

The League of Arab states, or Arab League, is based on a pact signed in Cairo on 22 March 1945 by seven states, Egypt, Iraq, Lebanon, Saudi Arabia, Syria, Transjordan and Yemen, which came into effect on 10 May 1945 and has the object of co-ordinating the policies and activities of these Arab states, to which the Arab states of the Mahgreb were added as they attained independence.[9] As such the League has always tended to fall foul of the deep divisions and mutual rivalries between the Arab states, to say nothing of the frictions engendered by President Nasser's efforts to unite the Arab world under his own leadership and on the basis of a modernised, radical nationalism. The Arab League lacks much in the way of machinery for the settlement of disputes between its member-states and Article 5 of the Pact of the League, which deals with this subject, is severely restricted in its application. It merely states that "any resort to force in order to resolve disputes between two or more member-states of the League is prohibited", and then goes on to stipulate procedures for peaceful settlement as follows: "if there should arise among (member-states) a difference which does not concern a state's independence, sovereignty or territorial

[9] See Robert W. Macdonald, *The League of Arab States. A study in the dynamics of regional organisation*, Princeton, N.J., 1965, pp. 319–26 for the text of the pact.

integrity, and if the parties to the dispute have recourse to the Council (of the League) for the settlement of this difference, the decision of the Council shall then be enforceable and obligatory". In only one or two instances of inter-Arab disputes has this machinery been put to constructive use.

In the major dispute between the Arab states and their foremost external antagonist, the state of Israel, the Arab League has been used to secure some measure of co-ordination between the policies of its members and also some degree of compromise between the positions of the more extreme Arab states, such as Algeria and Syria, which have striven to "push Israel into the sea", and those of the more flexible members, such as Jordan, which have sought terms of accommodation with the Jewish state. As for the former of these activities, it was under the League's auspices that the Palestine Liberation Organisation was set up in 1964 and in the following year the Unified Arab Command and the PLO joined forces to form Palestinian units whose motto was "we shall return". Moreover, it was through the League that the economic boycott of Israel, the concerted opposition to Israel using the Suez Canal, the refusal to attend international conferences, except for the United Nations, at which Israel was represented, and the persistent demand at the United Nations for the implementation of the UN resolution on refugees was organised. As far as the second of the above-mentioned functions is concerned, the working out of middle terms between Arab extremists and Arab moderates, the League's official neutral attitude towards the refugee problem is one example. But the League has evidently done little so far to make it easier for its members to enter into a negotiating relationship with Israel and it is upon this that the prospects for resolving the Arab–Israeli dispute seem to depend. The contrary may even be the case, namely that the more the Arab states seek to hammer out a common attitude towards the Israeli question, the more unwilling to negotiate with Israel they become, since fidelity to the Arab cause is bound to be judged, in a collective meeting-place such as the League, in terms of irreconcilability towards Israel.

In the Lebanon–Jordan dispute of 1958, however, the Arab League played a significant, if not decisive, role, though here the tendency, to which we have drawn attention earlier, for the United Nations and the regional organisation to serve as competitive agencies for the settlement of disputes was apparent. On 21 May 1958 Dr Malik, the Lebanese Foreign Minister, complained to both the Arab League and the United Nations that the rebellion in Lebanon was in essence inspired and armed by the United Arab Republic (UAR). The Security Council refrained from intervening until the League had attempted a settlement and after six days of discussion the League Council, meeting in Benghazi, agreed on a compromise resolution calling for the cessation of external intervention while the

Lebanon was settling its domestic problems. This resolution was, however, rejected by both the UAR and Lebanon and the matter went back once more to the United Nations which thereon created UNOGIL (the United Nations Observer Group in Lebanon). Then came the second phase of the crisis with the *coup* in Iraq on 14 July 1958 and the landing of British and United States troops in Jordan and Lebanon respectively. At a special emergency session of the UN General Assembly in August ten Arab countries, including Jordan, Lebanon and the UAR, agreed after private discussions on a compromise resolution which enabled Britain and the United States to withdraw their forces, an opportunity for Secretary-General Hammarskjöld to begin his mission to the area, and, most important, an Arab acceptance of the principle in this case of non-interference in other states within the Arab world. Thus, the Arab League did not directly contribute to the settlement of this problem, but the show of Arab unity which made the settlement possible certainly reflected the spirit of Arab cooperation which it is an object of the Arab League to foster.

When Iraq laid claim to Kuwait a week after Britain abrogated its protective treaty with Kuwait on 19 June 1961, the Arab League at first deferred consideration of the problem while it was before the UN Security Council. The League's Secretary-General, however, attempted mediation in view of the Soviet Union's veto both on a Security Council resolution calling on UN members to respect Kuwait's independence and Kuwait's application to join the world organisation. In the course of these mediating endeavours he visited Baghdad, Kuwait and Saudi Arabia. On 12 July the Arab League welcomed Kuwait as a member and supported its application to join the UN; the Arab states also undertook, through the League, to provide Kuwait with effective help in order to preserve its independence. On 8 August Kuwait adhered to the Arab Joint Defence Treaty and agreed to the withdrawal of British forces from its territory provided an Arab defence force took their place. In mid-August an Arab military mission arrived in Kuwait and on 10 September the first detachments of the 3,300-strong Arab League force, consisting of Jordanian, Lebanese, Saudi Arabian and UAR troops, began to make their entrance into the threatened country. It seems in fact to have been the British force which initially deterred an Iraqi attack, but the Arab League force did exert some measure of moral and political pressure and filled the vacuum after the British withdrawal. The Arab League force remained in Kuwait until February 1963, by which time the dispute had come to an end. In October 1963 Iraq formally dropped its claim to Kuwait and diplomatic relations between the two states were restored. The overthrow of General Quassim, the problems presented to his successors by the Kurdish revolt and their realisation that Iraq had aroused widespread antagonism in the

Arab world contributed to Baghdad's wish to re-establish friendly relations.

In the Yemen dispute the Arab League played a much more modest role, merely serving as an agency for the organisation of an Arab summit conference in Cairo in January 1964, at a time when President Nasser had evidently decided that his confrontation with monarchical forces in the Arab world should be ended in the interests of presenting a united front against Israel's plan to divert the waters of the Jordan. At that conference President Nasser and King Saud of Saudi Arabia held bilateral talks, and again at a successor conference in September; these exchanges ended in a ceasefire in the Yemen in November. Once again Israel provided the reason for the de-escalation of later phases of the conflict in Yemen when President Nasser withdrew his troops from that country in June 1967 as a consequence of the six-day war with Israel.

It remains to mention three other disputes affecting Arab states in which the League played either a very minor role or none at all. In the Algeria–Morocco border dispute the League Council passed a unanimous resolution in October 1963 urging an immediate ceasefire; a UAR-sponsored resolution calling for a committee of mediation was also adopted. Mediation by the League was, however, rejected by Morocco on the ground that the UAR, the originator of the proposal, was biased in Algeria's favour. Nevertheless, an Arab summit meeting in Cairo in January 1964 enabled Ben Bella, King Hassan and President Nasser to talk together, and this had some effect in lessening the tension. Lastly, in the Aden dispute the Arab League served as little more than a forum for Arab nationalism and for denunciation of Britain and the Federal rulers, while in the Muscat–Oman dispute the League contributed nothing positive towards its settlement.

One may therefore sum up by saying that on several occasions the Arab League has served as a focus of Arab unity, and this has had some effect in defending the independence of certain Arab states when threatened from outside. In one particularly favourable situation, the Kuwait crisis in 1961–63, the League made its presence felt with an effective police force. The League has, however, necessarily had to mirror the various divisions in the Arab world and in so far as it has united the Arab states against external opponents, especially Israel, it has probably done so at the cost of their diplomatic flexibility. Hence there are drawbacks as well as advantages in the existence of the Arab League as far as the peaceful settlement of disputes is concerned.

The Organisation of African Unity (OAU)

The Organisation of African Unity, established at a Conference of independent African states at Addis Ababa in May 1963, is similar to some other regional organisations in that its purpose is to strengthen the solidarity of its members against some external Power or Powers, in the OAU's case the surviving forces of white supremacy in Africa, especially as embodied in Portugal's possessions in Southern Africa and the present regimes in Rhodesia and South Africa. It is also different from most other regional organisations in that it includes no dominant state and is instead a partnership of almost equally weak equals. The combination of these two features has meant that collectively OAU member-states have been reluctant to take up a strong position on any dispute arising within independent Africa for fear of alienating one or other of the states concerned. This has not, however, prevented many member-states from bringing their disputes before the organisation for solution and, despite the delay in setting up the OAU's Commission of Mediation, Conciliation and Arbitration, various *ad hoc* commissions and committees have attempted to deal with problems presented to the organisation.

In the Morocco–Algeria border dispute Algeria was more inclined to use the OAU machinery since the organisation clearly stood in favour of the inviolability of existing frontiers; by the same token Morocco, which was seeking the restoration of Greater Morocco at the expense of Algerian territory, was hostile to OAU intervention and its signature of the OAU Charter had in fact been accompanied by a reservation stating that this should not be regarded as a recognition of existing borders or a renunciation of Morocco's territorial rights. Nevertheless, when King Hassan and Ben Bella met at Bamako in Mali in October 1963 under the mediation of President Keita of Mali and the Emperor of Ethiopia, and reached an agreement accepting a ceasefire, the establishment of a demilitarised zone and the cessation of hostile propaganda on both sides, they also agreed that the Council of the OAU should establish an arbitration commission to decide who began the hostilities and to submit recommendations to Algeria and Morocco for the "definitive settlement of the dispute". At an extraordinary session of the OAU Council on 15–18 November 1963 an *ad hoc* commission was appointed for the dispute consisting of representatives from Ethiopia, Ivory Coast, Mali, Nigeria, Senegal, Sudan and Tanganyika. The commission met frequently, moving from one African capital to another and experiencing difficulties, first over translations, then over its terms of reference; it was disputed whether the latter gave authority to arbitrate, as Algeria wished, or merely to engage in mediation and conciliation, as Morocco desired.

The Council of the OAU received reports from the commission in February 1964, February 1965 and October 1965, but when in May 1966 the tensions rose again and the commission was urgently requested to meet, the crisis had passed before, in July, it actually did so. In the event, the commission which reached agreement on a demilitarised zone was that set up by the Bamako awards, though these in themselves were an effort of the OAU; moreover, direct negotiations between King Hassan and Ben Bella at the Arab League meeting in Cairo in January 1964 greatly contributed to easing the tension, as recounted in the previous section of this chapter.[10] Thus, although the OAU played a certain role in this dispute by acting as a safety valve and a face-saving retreat for both sides, the chief contributions towards the *modus vivendi* which finally emerged were made by the mediatory efforts of Emperor Haile Selassie and President Keita of Mali, the bilateral talks between King Hassan and Ben Bella, and perhaps by the realisation on both sides that friendly relations were more profitable to their respective countries than border hostilities.

In another African dispute, that between Somalia, on one side and Ethiopia, Kenya and French Somalia, on the other, Ethiopia only just preceded Somalia on 9 February 1964 in requesting an extraordinary meeting of the Council of the OAU to consider the serious fighting which broke out early in 1964. Kenya also asked that its dispute with Somalia over the Northern Frontier District (NFD) should be put on the agenda of that meeting. Somalia, realising that the OAU was likely to be more sympathetic towards Ethiopia and Kenya, wanted the UN Security Council to deal with its complaint but was persuaded by pressures from fellow OAU members and Secretary-General U Thant to allow the regional organisation to handle the matter. When the extraordinary meeting of the OAU convened in Dar es Salaam, it called for a ceasefire and the cessation of hostile propaganda, and urged Somalia and Ethiopia to negotiate a settlement and Somalia and Kenya to take steps to settle their dispute "in the spirit of Article 3, paragraph 4" of the OAU Charter. A ceasefire was negotiated in the Somalia–Ethiopia dispute, but this was due more to the timely mediation and tactful negotiation of Lieutenant-General Abboud of Sudan than to the OAU resolution. At the ordinary meeting of the OAU Council in Lagos two weeks later resolutions on the Somali dispute similar to those adopted at Dar es Salaam were passed, though with the emphasis now laid on "respect for sovereign territorial integrity". Somalia naturally considered this as favouring its opponents and was angry that Ethiopia had been able to resist the admission of neutral observers into its territory. However, once again timely intervention by Sudan enabled the Foreign Ministers of Ethiopia and Somalia to meet in Khartoum and it was in this more intimate atmosphere that agreement was reached on a demilitarised zone, the establishment of a joint commission to supervise the withdrawal of forces and an end to hostile propaganda.

The OAU had certainly made it easier for the two sides to meet and

[10] See above p. 269.

helped to provide a suitable background, but the convening of the Foreign Ministers' meeting itself and its success was due to Sudan. Later, at a meeting of African heads of state in Cairo in July 1964, Somalia brought to the OAU's notice the dangers of bilateral defence pacts in Africa; Ethiopia and Kenya had just signed a mutual defence agreement evidently with their common interests against Somalia in mind. The OAU failed to deal with this complaint and instead passed a resolution declaring that "all member-states pledge themselves to respect the borders existing on their achievement of national independence". Somalia immediately put on record its disapproval of the resolution. When incidents again occurred in the Haud in March 1965 Somalia requested the Secretary-General of the OAU to appoint a commission of inquiry into the hostilities and the problem of refugees but there was no response.

As for Somalia's dispute with Kenya, the talks held at Arusha between representatives of the two states at the instigation of President Julius Nyerere in December 1965 and again in October 1967 were devoid of effect. But Somalia was now realising the consequences of its isolation in the OAU and Africa generally, and when at Kinshasa in September 1967 President Kaunda of Zambia offered to mediate, the Somali Foreign Minister, Mr Egal, responded with alacrity, with the result that the possibilities much improved of a settlement over the NFD and even the Haud. In this area of Somalia's foreign relations, therefore, the OAU may be said to have provided the incentive for negotiations and enabled President Kaunda to extend his offer of mediation at the Kinshasa meeting. But the chief positive move came from Somalia's Foreign Minister, who, since taking office, seemed determined to settle this dispute which has so poisoned Somalia's African relations.

In the case of Somalia's grievance over French Somalia, it is again noticeable how careful the OAU was to avoid any deep involvement. Both Ethiopia and the former French West African states were unwilling to endorse Somalia's stand, and, partly for this reason, when Somalia placed the question on the agenda of the OAU summit meeting at Addis Ababa in November 1966 and pressed for an "unequivocal endorsement of independence" with a referendum for French Somalia under OAU auspices, the heads of state confined themselves to taking note of France's decision to grant the people self-determination by means of a referendum. They expressed a "fervent desire" that voting should be "free, democratic and impartial" and assured the French Somalis of the OAU's "active solidarity designed to bring about and consolidate the independence of that people".

At the Kinshasa meeting of the OAU referred to above the Federal Nigerian government did not want the issue of secessionist Biafra placed on the agenda on the ground that it was an internal problem. A resolution nevertheless did appear and was adopted; this condemned any act of secession and, having emphasised that the issue was a domestic one for Nigeria, "declared (the OAU) anxious to help a mission of consultation composed of six heads of state in order to assure Lagos of the desire of the conference to safeguard the territorial integrity, unity and peace of Nigeria". The six-man mission arrived in Lagos in mid-November 1967 and mandated General Ankrah of Ghana to mediate with the secessionist authorities. The latter, however, declared the mission "a willing tool of reactionary African leaders and an instrument of imperial and neo-colonialist intrigue". With this attitude on the part of Biafra, it was hardly likely that any mission from an organisation dedicated to respect the existing territorial integrity of African states could ever succeed in bringing that conflict to an end.

It will be clear from the above that, while the OAU has served as a useful background to bilateral talks between disputing African states, the organisation itself has been inhibited by its fear of offending the susceptibilities of its members. Having naturally put first the solidarity of its member-states and their collective protection against external dangers, the organisation has discovered that it is no benefit to itself to take up positive views of the disputes brought before it. The only exception to this, if it can be so described, is the organisation's propensity to come down on the side of the *status quo* and to give a somewhat discouraging hearing to states which argue that it should be changed.

The South East Asia Treaty Organisation (SEATO)

The South East Asia Treaty Organisation, based upon a treaty for collective defence signed at Manila in September 1954, is, despite its title, disqualified in certain respects from being included in this account of regional organisations considered as agencies for the peaceful settlement of international disputes. In the first place, several important states in the region, notably India, Indonesia and Malaysia, are not members. Secondly, some of its leading members, as for instance the United States, Britain and France, are not situated in the region. Perhaps SEATO is best defined as an arrangement for organising collective regional defence from outside, that is, from the United States, and for filling the vacuum after the military collapse in the region of another outside Power, namely France.

As a collective defence system, SEATO has played only a limited role in the organisation of deterrence and the actual use of military force to repel aggression. In two of the disputes studied for the purpose of the present book, the Quemoy–Matsu question in 1958 and the Vietnam conflict from the Geneva conference on South East Asia in 1954 until the present, the chief burden has been borne by the United States with little or no assistance from its fellow-members in SEATO. It may be that the organisation helped to draw the United States into the Vietnam conflict, but neither the principal military effort in defence of South Vietnam, nor the elaboration of peace proposals on the non-communist side has been a special responsibility of SEATO. Furthermore, in the negotiations which led up to the neutralisation of Laos at the Geneva conference in 1962, President Kennedy's meeting with Mr Khrushchev in Vienna in June 1961, the actual talks at the Geneva conference in 1962 and Secretary-General U Thant's mission to Laos all played more important parts than the efforts of SEATO. It cannot be said, either, that SEATO has been at all actively involved in disputes between its members, or between any of its members and other states in the region, or has made any notable contribution towards their settlement. The same may be said of the Central Treaty Organisation (CENTO).

The Commonwealth

The Commonwealth, having regard to the geographical dispersion of the old British Empire from which it sprang, does not rank as a regional organisation as defined in terms of the spatial propinquity of members of the latter. It is, however, an international association of less than universal membership, and the sentiments which are supposed in theory to bind its members together would seem at first sight to facilitate its playing the role of an agency for settling disputes between them. It is true that, apart from its regular Prime Ministers' conferences and its secretariat, the Commonwealth disposes of no specialised machinery for the settlement of disputes between members *inter se:* the proposal for a Commonwealth court of law, urged some years ago, found very little support. Nevertheless, the mere fact that the Commonwealth is essentially an amorphous and informal entity could be said to increase its potentiality as an organ for the settlement of disputes since such facilities for this work as there are could be easily and indefinitely expanded if the will were there.

It must be recorded none the less that, as a matter of historical fact, the Commonwealth does not appear to have made a notable contribution to the settlement of disputes between its members or between rival factions within the territory of one or other of its members. To take the two classic instances of intra-Commonwealth disputes, the Indo-Pakistan conflict and the controversy over *apartheid* in South Africa, the Commonwealth cannot be said to have contributed much towards the settlement of either dispute. Indeed, it could be argued, in the South African case, that the sense of collective strength which the Commonwealth inspired, after South Africa's departure, in the remaining Commonwealth states which opposed *apartheid* was misleading, considering the invulnerability of South Africa against the kind of sanctions the Commonwealth could muster and the determination of its white electorate to adhere to their principles. It is possible that, had the Commonwealth not existed, Britain, and even perhaps the Asian and African states, might have been willing to reach an accommodation with South Africa. It is even more probable that, without the pressure from the independent African states within the Commonwealth, Britain would have found it easier to come to terms with the Smith regime in Rhodesia. It is also evidence of the unimpressive record of the Commonwealth as a dispute settling agency that it was quite unable to offer any effective mediation in the civil war in one of its larger member-states, Nigeria.

On the other hand, it could be said, with regard to the South Africa and Rhodesia disputes, that the Commonwealth in these affairs has represented the conscience of Britain and that, while it is always easy to settle disputes peacefully if one side or the other jettisons its principles, the Commonwealth has served to discourage that kind of settlement. But this takes us back to the fundamental question which must run like a red thread through any such study as this, namely, how much sacrifice of moral principle is worth how much convenience of having a particular dispute settled? The Commonwealth certainly has no shining record of the disputes it has settled. But it has reminded us that a settlement without justice may be worse than no settlement at all.

Conclusion

Regional international organisations, which seem likely to remain a permanent feature of the world political scene, may be described as having four major functions in the peaceful settlement of disputes. First, they provide a forum of limited size and specialised experience in which the parties to a dispute, if they be members of the organisation, can meet. Secondly, like universal international organisations, they can adopt resolutions for pacific settlement in the light of which states involved in disputes can relax their rigid positions on the issues at stake. Thirdly, they can offer a range of mediatory resources more knowledgeable and perhaps more accessible than those of comprehensive and universal organisations such as the United Nations. Fourthly, parties to a dispute which happen to be members of the same regional organisation may be more inclined to heal the breach between them if they recognise the dangers to the organisation which that breach implies, given that they both wish to maintain the solidarity of the organisation.

We can lay down no general rule, however, as to the usefulness of regional organisations in the resolution of disputes between their members and *external* states. In so far as the regional organisation provides support for their members in such disputes, it may induce the external state or states to come to terms. On the other hand, it may make the organisation's member-states more intransigent in their disputes because they know they have the organisation's backing. A great deal here will depend on whether the observer who is trying to estimate the force of these contrary considerations agrees or disagrees with the moral stance of the internal and external states concerned.

The existence of regional organisations is bound to raise the question of conflicts of jurisdiction between them and the universal organs of the international community, especially the United Nations. The UN can gain from having some of its pacific settlement work devolved on to suitable regional agencies and this is undoubtedly the intention of the Charter. On the other hand, where there is a considerable disparity in strength and influence between members of a regional organisation, the possibility arises of the lesser state in such an organisation being shut off from an appeal to the larger body, the UN. There is therefore an obligation on all UN members to exert themselves to ensure that this does not occur. For example, the UN should, through its appropriate means, see to it that as far as possible the agreements setting up regional organisations do not prejudice their members' right of appeal to the larger international community.

At the same time, the experience of the regional agencies we have considered in this chapter confirms the fundamental point we must make about the general settlement of disputes through international organisations, namely that these bodies dispose of no magic means by which disputes can be swept away unless it is in the felt interests of the states concerned so to dispose of them. An international organisation, universal or regional, can in favourable circumstances increase the inducements leading states towards a settlement and provide the facilities for making one. But in the last resort even in the most highly integrated regional agencies, as those in Western Europe, the ultimate decisions must be those of the states concerned and must be arrived at on the basis of the balance of expected national gain over expected national loss. In calculating that balance, however, states must try to estimate the value of the regional agency to their general national purposes. The more useful such an agency is for a state's daily life the less inclined that state will be to allow disputes within the organisation to affect its solidarity and efficiency. The best way, in other words, in which regional agencies can play a part in the peaceful settlement of disputes is by making themselves indispensable in every way to their member-states.

12. Negotiation

I

NEGOTIATION is listed in Article 33, paragraph 1, of the United Nations Charter as the first of the methods for the peaceful settlement of international disputes to which Members are enjoined to resort before they refer them to the world organisation. Nevertheless, the existence of the United Nations and the regional organisations discussed in the previous Chapter by no means rules out negotiations between the parties to a dispute even after they have submitted it to those bodies. The late Dag Hammarskjöld considered that, so far from international institutions having rendered traditional diplomatic methods obsolete, they have rather enhanced their value. "The legislative process in the United Nations", he wrote,

> is not a substitute for diplomacy. It serves its purpose only when it helps diplomacy to arrive at agreements between the national states concerned. It is diplomacy, not speeches and votes, that continues to have the last word in the process of peace-making . . . When I speak of private procedures, I mean here the methods of classical diplomacy as applied within the framework provided by the Charter and the institutions of the world organisation. There has always been this practice of private and quiet diplomacy in the UN and there has been a marked increase in its use within the past year or two. But the need for it is not sufficiently understood.[1]

Indeed it has been argued by one writer on the United Nations that that body makes quiet negotiations on traditional lines easier today than in the past, since delegates in the UN lounges may talk over outstanding differences between their countries without arousing the public attention which, say, a visit by an Ambassador to the Foreign Ministry of the country to which he is accredited might provoke.[2]

Negotiation Defined

Negotiation has been defined as a "process in which explicit proposals are put forward ostensibly for the purpose of reaching agreement on an exchange or on the realisation of a common interest when conflicting

[1] *United Nations Review*, March 1958.

[2] Andrew Boyd, *United Nations: Piety, Myth and Truth,* Pelican Books, 1964, p. 68.

interests are present".[3] The act of negotiation presupposes the existence of an unresolved difference between states; when governments are in communication with one another without being conscious of the existence of a difference which both feel needs to be resolved, we would speak of "consultations" rather than "negotiations". Moreover, for the purpose of this chapter, the term "negotiation" is restricted to exchanges between two governments or two groups of governments. When that number is exceeded, the resulting multilateral exchanges are so different in kind as to call for discussion under a separate heading; the nature of these exchanges is partially dealt with in the previous two chapters on universal and regional international organisations. A further point to be made about the definition of negotiation is that the agreement which is sought may concern, not only the substance of the disputed questions between the parties, but the order in which those issues are to be treated, that is, the agenda of the negotiation, the rules to be applied in the negotiation and the manner of implementing any agreement eventually reached on the substantive issues. Soviet negotiators appear to place a great importance on the first two of these items while Western representatives are sometimes surprised to find them serving as sticking points.

Negotiations on matters great and small of common concern to modern governments are ubiquitous and continuous. They are one of the primary functions of the diplomatic services maintained by all present-day states. Indeed, there is hardly another method of handling international disputes among those listed in Article 33, paragraph 1, of the UN Charter, the use of which is not normally preceded and accompanied by some form of negotiation between the parties. The submission of a legal issue to the International Court of Justice, for example, requires a negotiated agreement between the parties known as the *compromis*, by which they define the point of law on which they seek the Court's judgement. States can hardly call on the services of an arbitrator or mediator without reaching a prior agreement, through negotiation, to do so. The decision of a government to submit a dispute to the United Nations, as Britain and France submitted their dispute with President Nasser over the nationalisation of the Suez Canal company to the UN Security Council in September 1956, usually, though not invariably, follows upon a failure to settle the dispute through negotiations.

Public Relations Diplomacy

There is, however, a most important difference between diplomatic negotiations in the second half of the twentieth century and those described

[3] F. C. Iklé, *How Nations Negotiate*, New York, Evanston and London, 1964, pp. 3–4.

by such classical writers as François de Callières, Antoine Pecquet or even Sir Harold Nicolson.[4] This is that the context in which proposals for the settlement of a dispute are made has widened far beyond the traditional one in which negotiations have been carried on since the origins of the international system. We are referring here, of course, to the vast enlargement of the "public relations" aspect of diplomacy which has been so striking since 1918. Of course, European governments since the eighteenth century – in Canning's day, for instance – have been concerned to extract the maximum advantage, in terms of public support at home, from their foreign policies. Moreover, the propaganda function of diplomacy has never ruled out private negotiations in the traditional manner when the states concerned deemed it to be desirable. Nevertheless, in the present century it has become common form for government spokesmen, either before negotiations begin or during their course, to make use of press conferences, broadcasts, interviews with journalists, or public or Parliamentary speeches to drop hints or convey signals about changes in their governments' position on outstanding disputes which may be pursued later in the form of diplomatic soundings by other governments.

It is well known for instance how a significant shift in the Soviet position on the Berlin dispute of 1948–49 was intimated in answers by Marshal Stalin to a journalist which omitted all mention of the quadripartite control of the Ostmark to be introduced as the currency in Berlin, the issue on which negotiations had previously broken down; how Britain, France and the United States created an opening to sound Mr Gromyko on this point at the United Nations; and how this led to negotiations which resulted in the lifting of the blockade and counter-blockade on 12 May 1949. Similarly, *pari passu* with the formal negotiations in Paris since 1968 on ending the war in Vietnam, all the parties concerned, the United States, North and South Vietnam, and the National Liberation Front, did not hesitate repeatedly to make public certain modifications in their respective negotiating positions, possibly with effect on the Paris talks, though we cannot be sure of this without access to the records of those talks. Again, it appears to have been in response to an expressed public willingness on the part of the Soviet Union to discuss "modifications" in the Berlin situation incorporated in a speech by Mr Gromyko at the Supreme Soviet on 10 July 1969, that the three Western Powers, Britain, France and the United States, addressed their notes to Moscow on 8 August proposing an exchange of views about Berlin. This is not to say, however, that genuine

[4] François de Callières, *De la manière de négocier avec les souverains*, Paris, 1716, translated as *The Practice of Diplomacy* by A. F. Whyte, London, 1919; Antoine Pecquet, *Discours sur l'art de négocier*, Paris, 1737; Sir Harold Nicolson, *Diplomacy*, London, 3rd ed., 1963.

negotiations were not desired as well, especially in the last of these cases.

These developments are part of the process by which diplomatic negotiations since the end of the First World War have been confused with "public relations", in the sense of stands taken by governments on disputed questions, not in the first instance to promote a negotiated settlement, but to impress or reassure their own people and the world, and possibly to depress, mislead or divide people in the other state. We may deplore this vulgarisation of diplomacy; Lord Strang, among others, has criticised it when he wrote that,

> There is no doubt that this public ventilation and discussion of the issues of foreign policy, often at awkward moments, has a hampering effect upon the flexibility, resourcefulness and imagination with which diplomatic operations might otherwise be more fruitfully conducted.[5]

One of the worst consequences of diplomacy practised as "public relations" is to confuse governments as to whether other governments with which they are in dispute are genuinely seeking an agreement or whether they are putting forward proposals merely for home and foreign consumption. This has been especially notable in the long-drawn-out negotiations on disarmament between East and West since 1945 in which it has always been hard to distinguish between offers of genuine negotiations and the bidding for a favourable world opinion.

To a large extent, however, this bifurcation of diplomacy into purposive negotiation, on the one hand, and public relations on the other, is both inevitable and irreversible. It is a product of the contemporary cult of "mass democracy", the principle that foreign policy should reflect the electorate's opinions and interests, the improvement in public education and development of mass communications and the resulting vulgarisation of politics, with the concurrent tendency for the professional diplomat to cede more of the limelight to the professional politician. The history of the conflict in Vietnam since the French military defeat there in 1954 has shown how easy it is for an external Great Power to become involved in a foreign civil war and to find it almost impossible to withdraw as a result of being ensnared by its own openly avowed commitments and the necessity to keep public opinion well disposed to the war by exaggerating the advantages to be won by taking part in it and minimising the cost and risks.

This new, public relations aspect of diplomatic negotiation has come to attach itself even to the word "negotiation " and the ideas its mention stimulates. On the one hand, there prevails, especially among the Western democracies, and especially when dealing with totalitarian states, a certain "guilt complex" about diplomacy, a feeling that an onus lies with one's own side never to refuse an offer to negotiate and never to break off

[5] *The Diplomatic Career*, London, 1962, p. 76.

negotiations once begun. Throughout the Berlin crisis of 1958–61, and the same is true, though to a lesser degree, of the more recent dispute over Gibraltar, the side wishing a change in the *status quo*, that is, the Soviet government and Spain respectively, have been able to exploit this "guilt complex" by publicly calling for negotiations even when it was evident that the positions of the two sides were too far apart for negotiations to serve any useful purpose. Even though, in the Berlin situation, Mr Khrushchev had himself created the crisis by his note of 27 November 1958, the Western Powers felt called upon to initiate negotiations with the object of proposing concessions in return for a Soviet commitment to respect a legal position in Berlin which the Soviet Union was already bound to respect by virtue of unequivocal wartime agreements; at the same time, of course, the Western Powers' position was distinctly precarious as the city was located within the Soviet sphere of influence, and moreover those Powers had a definite interest in warning the Soviet Union and East Germany against over-hasty moves. Similarly, once negotiations have begun, democratic governments are apt to find themselves criticised at home if the other side can make it appear that the democracies are responsible for the breaking off of those negotiations. There always exist in the Western states newspapers and other media of mass communication which can argue that, had negotiations gone on a little longer or if the other side's latest proposal had been scrutinised a little more carefully, a chink of light might have appeared. It was this circumstance which served to keep the four-Power Foreign Ministers' talks on Berlin going in Geneva in the summer of 1959 long after it was clear that there was no useful business to be done. Totalitarian states seem to have fewer inhibitions about refusing a call to negotiate or walking out of the negotiating forum, as Mr Khrushchev did at the abortive Paris "summit" conference in May before the negotiations had even begun, or as the Soviet delegation walked out of the UN Committee of Ten on disarmament in the same year. Moreover, such states are better able to exploit this public relations aspect of diplomacy because they know that the democracies have much more difficulty in putting their point of view across to the ordinary people in totalitarian states.

On the other hand, the very word "negotiations" came to acquire a pejorative connotation, especially in the United States, after the visits by the British Prime Minister, Mr Neville Chamberlain, to the German Chancellor in 1938 leading up to the Munich agreement, and the "Big Three" conferences at Yalta and Potsdam at the end of the Second World War. No doubt experiences of this kind served to reinforce much older suspicions current in the United States that that country's diplomats could never enter into exchanges with their European counter-parts without being worsted in the process. It seems that this was one of the reasons why the United States was reluctant in the 1950s to respond to Mr Harold Macmillan's and, earlier, Sir Winston Churchill's call for a "summit" meeting with Soviet leaders. This restraint on diplomatic negotiations acts, of course, in a contrary direction to the Western "guilt complex" about negotiation to which we referred in the previous paragraph. Nevertheless, they may both serve to delude the democracies as to the basic truth that neither negotiation nor a refusal to negotiate can ever be a panacea, or, as the case may be, a disaster for all states in all circumstances. Negotiation – it may be a truism but it is none the less vital to remember it – can only hope to be successful where there already exists enough common ground between the disputing states for the diplomatic process to throw a bridge between their respective positions. At the same time, it cannot be assumed that a negotiated agreement can reflect anything other than the respective strength, whether measured in terms of physical resources or the availability of alternative options, of the parties concerned. The omission to take this factor into account in considering the Yalta conference of February 1945, when the Soviet Union was in effective military occupation of large areas of Eastern Europe liberated from Nazi Germany, has bequeathed to American public opinion so many myths about the negotiating process.

There are two further aspects of present-day diplomacy which distinguish it from its traditional form. One of these arises from the alliance systems of the post-1945 world. Here we have a situation in which one bloc of states, as for instance the NATO countries, face another bloc, the Warsaw Pact states. If one group, like NATO, consists of Western democracies whose unanimous consent is necessary before a common negotiating position can be taken up, while the other group's position is determined by a single paramount Power and virtually imposed upon the others, it is clear that the former group's negotiating stand may be marked either by undue rigidity or a certain vagueness which is an inherent consequence of the attempt to satisfy all the group's member-states. This has frequently been evident in East–West negotiations over Berlin.

The other notable aspect of contemporary negotiation is the clash of diplomatic styles, not only between liberal democratic and totalitarian states – a clash which, incidentally is sometimes much exaggerated – but between "old" and "new" states. The latter often seem to have little time for traditional diplomatic rules, language or courtesies; indeed, they may not only be ignorant of these time-honoured niceties, but may even fear and despise them. Moreover, the new states are not infrequently represented by a charismatic head of state whose tenure of office may be precarious, or by diplomatic agents whose bond is readily repudiated or ignored by their political principals at home. Both these developments confront Western democratic governments with special problems.

Diplomacy, we must next note, is a form of communication, and it must therefore be presupposed that the parties are in fact in communication with each other. It is true that the absence of diplomatic recognition of, or diplomatic relations with, another government does not necessarily rule out all negotiations with it. Britain was able to negotiate with Soviet Russia on such issues as the repatriation of prisoners of war, the control of propaganda, compensation for properties nationalised by the Soviet authorities, and the terms of a loan to Russia, before the first British Labour government accorded recognition to the Soviet regime in 1924. Similarly, the United States discussed for many months in 1952–53 an end to the Korean war with the North Korean authorities at Kaesong, and later Panmunjom, and for more months still in Warsaw with representatives of the Chinese Communist government without being in diplomatic relations with either.

Indeed, it could be argued that the Warsaw negotiations, simply because they have been conducted away from the public eye, have offered more hope of a fruitful outcome than would more publicised talks between the United States and a recognised Communist government in Peking. Nevertheless, it is clear from the Arab–Israeli dispute, among many, that the absence of formal channels of communication between governments immensely hinders both negotiations and the implementation of negotiated agreements. It is no assistance to the use of negotiation in the settlement of international disputes when diplomatic relations are broken out of pique, as has been fashionable during the last twenty years, or when they are rendered impossible by one government's dislike for the ideological complexion of another. As Iklé has written,

> A history of past negotiations establishes a habit of communicating which may induce governments to keep in touch during emergencies. Such a habit is well ingrained between Washington and Moscow but lacking between Peking and Washington.[6]

It cannot be repeated too often that the purpose of diplomatic recognition is not to confer a certificate of respectability on another state or government, but to establish lines of communication with those authorities in the other country who are willing and able to assume responsibility for negotiating and implementing international law and international agreements. Equally vital is the maxim that the more threatening to the existing international order a state seems to be, the more, not less, important it is to be in diplomatic touch with its effective rulers in order, if possible, to influence their conduct.

[6] *Op cit.*, p. 45.

II

We may now consider who the negotiating agents of governments normally are and how well equipped they seem for using negotiation as a means of settling international disputes. Plainly, they are of two types: the permanent official, or career diplomat, and the practising politician, the political head of the diplomatic service, the Foreign Minister or his deputy, or the head of state or government. Both have been affected in the way they perform their work by the immense improvements in transport and communications since, say, Sir Edward Grey, the British Foreign Secretary in 1914, recalled that he hardly ever left the country on an official mission except to visit Paris with King George V in April 1914.[7] The permanent civil servant in the Foreign Office or Ministry of External Affairs or abroad on mission has had to deal with a vastly increased flow of messages from the foreign post to the home base and *vice versa;* this has called for greater energy and skill in separating the more from the less important facts of any dispute and a greater range of knowledge in understanding the immensely diverse matters covered by such communications. At the same time, with the expansion and increasing speed and comfort of air travel, the official can be expected to commute to and fro with increasing frequency between foreign posts and the home base for purposes of consultation. On his side, the political head of the Foreign Office or other department concerned, can now be at the site of a dispute in which his country is involved in a matter of hours at the most; there are accordingly obvious advantages to be derived from the resulting closer co-ordination of the work of officials and that of Ministers to offset any possible disinclination on the politician's part to leave his commitments at home to meet other politicians or Ministers abroad.

The result has been that in practice the roles of politicians and diplomatic representatives have been to some extent confused, though the distinction may still be present in the minds of both, especially in the West and certainly in the United Kingdom. On the one hand, the official, particularly when acting as a delegate to an international organisation, has found himself drawn into a forensic, or at least quasi-Parliamentary, style of debate when justifying his government's position. On the other, the politician has perforce had to act a diplomatic role when negotiating agreements with his opposite numbers at home or abroad. The dangers implicit in both these tendencies are obvious enough. The diplomat, especially if he is highly skilled in the arts of the public performer, may be tempted to emphasise the forensic side of his work in contrast to the quiet bargaining with foreign officials, or Ministers, which has distinguished the

[7] *Twenty-five Years*, Vol. I, London, 1925, Chapter XV.

classical European diplomat. The politician, on his side, may equally be tempted to regard diplomatic negotiation as an exercise in which he has to achieve a victory that will read well in the press rather than a *modus vivendi* in which both sides have to make sacrifices and in which neither can attain all that it wishes. The politician naturally wants results to advertise to his people at home and may forget that "the methods of diplomacy are those of the tortoise rather than the hare".[8]

Perhaps the most effective distribution of labour, at least in theory, though this is not always possible in practice, between these two types of negotiator is that in which the politician plays his part at the beginning and at the end of the diplomatic process while the permanent official occupies the ground between these two extremes. This is to say that, under favourable conditions, we should expect the politician to create, together with his colleague in the other country, the climate of feeling or "atmosphere" in which the approach to negotiation can take place. If, for instance, there has been in a particular dispute a long period of stalemate and relations between the states concerned have grown steadily more poisoned and devoid of hope, a meeting of Ministers, who can be presumed both to reflect and to guide public opinion in their respective countries, can make a beginning by setting the tone for a new phase of negotiations. The revolutionary Egyptian officers who succeeded King Farouk in 1952 and the successors of General Quassim in Iraq in 1962 and of President Sukarno in Indonesia in 1965, were thus in their turn able to lay the basis for better relations, with Britain in the first instance, with other Arab states which came to the assistance of Kuwait in 1961 in the second and with Malaysia in the third, from which sprang what seem to have been useful, if only, in the first instance, temporary, settlements. Then again, at the end of the negotiating process, when the minimum conditions and expectations on each side have been so defined that bridge-building becomes conceivable, only the politician, in consultation no doubt with his colleagues in the government, can determine whether the political price, in terms of the cost of making the final sacrifice to facilitate the agreement, can be paid.

In between these two functions, the creating of a suitable atmosphere for negotiation and the making of the final concession or concessions to facilitate an agreement, the permanent official may be regarded as coming into his own. He follows up the initial attempts to improve the atmosphere, given that these are successful, by defining possible solutions, estimating the costs and benefits of each to each state, explaining to his own government the legal and other implications of each of these solutions, and evaluating in so far as he is able the likelihood of the other side keeping to

[8] Lord Strang, *op cit.*, p. 80.

its undertakings on the basis of past experience of its record in dealings with other states.

The skill of both the politician and the diplomat in performing these various functions derives in the main from natural endowment, training and experience, and especially the latter. The politician who has risen to that senior position in the government which those who undertake international negotiations on their country's behalf must occupy, may be expected to have had a long experience in gauging the state of feeling in other groups or individuals with whom he does business; in knowing when to stand firm, when to give way, how to retreat with good grace from an untenable position; in exploring the weak points in an opponent's case; and in reconciling conflicting interests or viewpoints. The official, too, will generally have little but his actual experience of diplomatic negotiation to draw upon unless, as in the United States, it is customary to employ as senior diplomats people from other walks of life such as the professions, business or the armed forces. On the whole, however, it does not appear that any state systematically prepares its negotiators for their work by any special training. Moreover, the latter-day suggestions that diplomats should be acquainted with studies such as psychology, anthropology or sociology, which are now supposed by social scientists to throw light on the management of social conflict, have so far largely gone unheeded. Nor does it appear that there exists in the Foreign Office or foreign service of any country anything in the way of an accumulated repertoire, so to speak, of diplomatic wisdom or skill with which the newcomer to the art could prepare himself. Many countries now run various kinds of courses for diplomats on other aspects of their work, for instance, business and refresher courses and so on, but this is not quite the same thing.

On the other hand, it may be said in defence of official practice that there may lie here an important truth as to the real nature of negotiation or diplomatic bargaining. There are certain skills, perhaps surgery or teaching, which may be systematically acquired through the learning process; the experienced hand may communicate to novices an understanding of how he goes about his work, even though in the last resort success is a matter of native endowment which cannot be acquired by learning. It may be that the diplomatic art is not of this kind. So much depends in diplomatic negotiation on insight into the other side's mental attitudes, its fears, hopes and expectations; on appreciation of the possibilities in a given situation of bridge-building formulae which must be unique in order to fit a unique conjuncture of events; on seizure of the right, or the ripe, moment for opening negotiations, offering a concession once they are open, or theatening to break off the talks, or actually breaking them off. Possibly the experienced negotiator can perform all these tasks successfully when confronted with a determinate situation without being able to explain coherently how he does it. "Little has been written on the strategies and tactics of negotiation", writes an American student of this subject, "that would be equivalent in precision and coherence to the better studies on military defence, deterrence and arms control".[9] Yet his own book, though carefully constructed, can hardly be called a comprehensive handbook for the successful negotiator, no doubt, again, because so much here lies in the realm of art rather than science.

In all this, of course, we must remember that the negotiator has two purposes to fulfil, of which the first is in practice vastly more important than the second, though the disinterested student may wish that this order was reversed. The first task is to carry out his government's instructions and to come away from the negotiating table with the best possible bargain from the standpoint of his own country; the second, if it figures at all among his responsibilities, is to get his instructions modified if necessary so as to leave the world a better place than he found it and to contribute to peace and harmony in a general sense. François de Callières described the self-interested functions of diplomacy when he wrote in the eighteenth century, and much of what he says, with some differences of vocabulary, would stand today:

> A powerful prince who maintains a constant system of diplomacy served by wise and instructed negotiators in the different states of Europe, and who thus cultivates well-chosen friendships and maintains useful sources of information, is in a position to influence the destiny of neighbouring foreign states, to maintain peace between all states or to pursue war where it is favourable to his design. In all these concerns the prosperity of his plans and the greatness of his name depend first and last on the conduct and qualities of the negotiator to whom he entrusts his services.[10]

Admittedly, the other side will need to gain from any negotiated agreement if it is to be concluded at all and if there is to be any expectation of its durability. Admittedly, too, every country must think twice before acting so as to appear too ruthless and acquisitive in its international relations lest it discourage other countries from doing business with it. But in the last resort a negotiator's career will generally be considered successful in terms of how profitable it has been for his own country in its international disputes.

This means that the criteria by which a negotiator acting primarily on his country's behalf will be judged skilful are not necessarily the same as those which are relevant for determining a negotiator's skill in the general

[9] F. C. Iklé, *op. cit.*, p. x.
[10] *The Practice of Diplomacy*, ed. by A. F. Whyte, p. 18.

settlement of international disputes. From the narrow standpoint of a particular country it may not always be to its advantage to see disputes settled, in which case a negotiator will paradoxically serve his country best if his mission fails. It is hard to see what immediate gain would accrue to the Soviet Union, for instance, from a settlement of the dispute between the United States and Cuba, or to the United States from a settlement of the dispute between the Soviet Union and Communist China. On the contrary, it is not hard to suggest reasons why each of these countries would like to see the respective dispute continue. Similarly, there may be occasions when a country gains a definite benefit from the continuance of a dispute between itself and another country. So long, for example, as relations between the Soviet Union and the Federal German Republic remain strained, the Soviet Union is able to represent itself as the champion of all the East European states which fear a revival of German militarism. So long as the United States preserves a certain emotional distance between itself and the Soviet Union, it can count upon the continuing support of its European allies in the Atlantic pact, which otherwise might suspect collusion between the two super-Powers and hence the United States' lack of interest in their affairs.

We must therefore conclude that if disputes between states are not successfully resolved the reasons do not always lie in lack of skill on the part of the negotiators or the absence of effective conditions for negotiation. It may be, on the contrary, that the continuance of an unresolved dispute happens to be more profitable, on balance, to one or both of the states concerned than its resolution.

III

Nevertheless, there are certain general principles of effective negotiation which experience has disclosed and which may be mentioned as examples of the kind of rules which might be included in the repertoire of diplomatic practice we have referred to above.

First, there is the overwhelming importance of the states involved in negotiation gaining, or at least seeming to gain, some determinate benefit from the act of negotiation, or certainly avoiding some determinate loss. It is often said that states are more likely to continue to press a dispute if the expected outcome of a negotiated settlement appears in the form of a loss to one side and a gain to the other; in other words, a "zero sum" outcome, when the pluses and minuses are added together. No one likes to be a net loser and a potential net loser will tend to go on with the dispute even if the continuance of the struggle is likely in the short run to add to his losses. The prospect of a definite gain, on the other hand, will encourage him to come to a negotiated settlement. Thus, in the Berlin crisis of 1948–49, it seems that the loss and inconvenience of the blockade and counter-blockade of the city persuaded Marshal Stalin to end the conflict, with the highly hypothetical benefit of a resumption of four-Power talks on all-German questions as an additional inducement. Similarly, the Soviet decision in May 1955 to terminate the ten-year deadlock over the Austrian peace treaty seems to have reflected a Soviet calculation that there was more to be gained from accepting the treaty as an inducement (among other things) to West German opinion to agree to the same condition of neutrality for themselves than from a continuance of the dispute. Again, in the dispute between Somalia and her neighbours in the early 1960s, the prospect of better relations with the latter encouraged the new Somali government, which came to office in May 1967, to end what had become a stale and unprofitable dispute. In much the same way, we have seen in the previous chapter that the conclusion of the Anglo-Icelandic fisheries dispute on the basis of the "six-plus-six" formula in 1962 was by no means all loss for Britain. What it gained was the continuing goodwill of Iceland towards NATO, one of the most important sheet-anchors of British foreign policy, together with an end to the discomfort of standing out against a large body of world opinion in favour of that formula, as the Geneva conference on the law of the sea in 1958 had shown.

The gain to be derived from a successful negotiation which re-defines and modifies the *status quo* may, as in the last instance, be somewhat hypothetical as compared with the continuance of the present situation, at least for the country which is advantaged by the *status quo*. But at all costs negotiation must never aim at, or have the effect of producing, a feeling of defeat and humiliation in the other side. Even in wartime, when a dispute or complex of disputes is being pursued with the full force of one's national armed strength, it is essential to let the enemy people know that surrender does not mean their extinction as a nation, but rather the determination to have no dealings with their present political regime. This certainly seems to have been the interpretation placed by Britain, the United States and the Soviet Union on their Unconditional Surrender policy towards the Axis Powers during the Second World War. In peace-time it is even more important to leave the other side, or at least its people, with the conviction that, so far from having lost from a negotiated settlement, it has definitely gained. So much importance, for instance, has been attached by world opinion to the late President Kennedy's highly conditional undertaking not to attack Cuba when Soviet missiles were withdrawn from the island following the crisis in October 1962, that the average person today may find it hard to decide which policy suffered a defeat: Mr Khrushchev's policy of placing Soviet missiles in Cuba or

President Kennedy's policy of seeking to topple the Castro regime. This meets the ideal condition of successful negotiation; in the words of *Alice*, all are winners and all receive prizes.

The above principle is well stated in authors of old and new vintage. De Callières writes thus about it:

> The easiest way to find the right bias is to make each proposition which you put forward appear as a statement of the interests of those with whom you are negotiating, for since diplomacy is the attempt to find a basis of common act or agreement, it is obvious that the more the opposing party can be brought to see your designs in their own light and to accept them thus, the more surely will their cooperation for any action be fruitful alike to themselves and to you.[11]

Similarly, the former American Ambassador, Hugh Gibson, has written:

> In fact, victory and defeat are the negation of diplomacy. The diplomat should never forget that the problem he is working on is only of relative importance in that it is one of an unending series that must be discussed with the other party through the years, and therefore, while he must do as much as is expedient for his country it must be within such limits and under such terms as will obviate resentment and a sense of injustice in future negotiations. It is important to have everybody satisfied so that they bring to the next negotiation a desire for further agreement and not a yearning for revenge – the inevitable result of defeat.[12]

We have argued, in discussing the nature of international disputes, that what gives to a dispute its special character is the feeling of right or entitlement which the parties bring to their confrontation.[13] It is this, above all, which makes the notion of compensation, which is so essential to successful negotiation, so difficult to translate into practice. If two states both claim the same thing, and with a sense of entitlement, almost any negotiated settlement must affront the feeling of right of one or the other since the same object cannot belong to, or be at the disposal of, both parties at the same time. It may be that an important international amenity, such as a canal, is under the sovereignty of a particular country, which satisfies that country's feeling of legitimacy, and is at the same time regulated by international agreements, as the Suez Canal was regulated by the Constantinople Convention of 1888, so as to satisfy the sense of right of users of that amenity. But this does not rule out disputes as to the division of revenues from use of the amenity, provisions for its defence and policing, and the precise relationship between sovereignty over the amenity and the international rights of users. At some stage a point may be reached at

[11] *Op. cit.*, pp. 122–3. [12] *The Road to Foreign Policy*, New York, 1944, p. 77.
[13] See above, chapter II.

which the asserted claims to right of one side conflict with the asserted claims to right of the other and both cannot receive satisfaction at the same time. It is at this point that the essential principle of compensation becomes hard to fulfil. How can the claims to right of one side or the other be satisfied in such a way that it does not feel that it has been the net loser in the negotiating process?

One solution to this difficulty is known as the "package deal" or "tie-in". A number of issues in dispute, though only two in the case of the "tie-in", are joined together as part and parcel of the same negotiated settlement, and in this way the grievances of either side over its losses in one issue of the settlement are offset by the satisfaction of making gains through the simultaneous settlement of another. A celebrated example of a "tie-in" was the Anglo-French Entente of 1904, by which British paramountcy in Egypt was recognised by France in return for British recognition of French paramountcy in Morocco. The attempt to negotiate a "package deal" is illustrated by the abortive Anglo-Soviet exchanges in 1924 when the intention was to provide for British recognition of the Soviet government and a British guarantee of Soviet loans raised in the London money market as part of a "package deal" which would also include compensation to British holders of Russian bonds, payment on which had been suspended by the Bolsheviks when they came to power in November 1917. A somewhat similar "package deal" was contemplated at the four-Power Foreign Ministers' talks on Berlin held in Geneva in the summer of 1959; the idea was to secure a reaffirmation by the Soviet Union of the three Western Powers' occupation rights in Berlin and of freedom of access from Federal Germany to West Berlin in return for arrangements to meet Soviet allegations that West Berlin was being used as a base for espionage and subversion in East Germany.

The merits of "package deals" and "tie-ins" are clear enough. They deal in one transaction with a number of matters in dispute. They may provide for the cancelling out of losses in one part of the settlement by gains in another. It is true, however, that the Soviet Union, a factor of considerable weight in post-1945 international affairs, has shown no considerable liking for the "package deal". Moreover, the linking of settlements in this way can have the drawback that the whole mosaic of agreements may be placed in jeopardy if one of them subsequently breaks down or is the subject of serious dispute later. There is also a conflict of choice between across-the-board settlements of the "package deal" and "tie-in" type and the principle of tackling one issue at a time in the interests of manageability and practicability and in order to give the negotiators the confidence to go forward and settle other issues if they already have one achievement to their credit behind them.

The conflict between these two principles of negotiation has bedevilled disarmament negotiations between East and West since the Second World War. On the one hand, it has been argued that states are unlikely to disarm in respect of any single one of their weapons until and unless a universal sense of security is created by progress towards general and complete disarmament.[14] On the other hand, there is the contention that general disarmament, covering all the great military Powers and all the major weapons of war, is too vast and visionary an undertaking to offer any reasonable prospect of success during the sessions of any disarmament conference, and that the way to proceed is to single out merely one field of arms control and make progress with that first. Although the latter argument raises the question as to which field of arms control that should be, since what is acceptable to one country will probably not be to another, it must be admitted that, in all the talk at disarmament conferences since 1945, little or nothing has emerged from the various plans for general and complete disarmament; the only substantial arms control agreements which have been signed, notably the partial Nuclear Test Ban Treaty of 1963 and the Nuclear Non-Proliferation Treaty of 1968, have been essentially measures of limited scope.

The problem of compensating the side which receives the more unfavourable return from the negotiation remains, however, even with the piecemeal pattern of settlement, perhaps even more than with the "package deal" or "tie-in". As it happens, the partial Nuclear Test Ban Treaty and the Nuclear Non-Proliferation Treaty were not concluded as the termination of disputes between the principal sponsoring Powers, the United States and the Soviet Union. On the contrary, these two agreements, and especially the second, reflected some of their strongest common interests. The disputes which these agreements symbolised were in fact between the sponsoring Powers on one side and states which either did not possess nuclear weapons, or were in the act of acquiring them on the other. The fact that the second of these agreements, at least, has not yet proved the universal success that was hoped may indicate that, where a genuine dispute exists, the partial negotiated agreement may not be the best solution since it cannot deal adequately with the problem of compensation to which we have referred. What has, in fact, deterred some of the most important non-nuclear countries from signing the non-proliferation treaty so far is their feeling that it represents all sacrifice on their own side and no discernible gain, apart from the rather hypothetical benefit of an improvement in the general outlook for world peace and security. The more positive gains which the sponsoring Powers offered

[14] For the most able defence of the "general" as opposed to the "partial" arms control agreement, see P. J. Noel-Baker, *The Arms Race*, London, 1958.

the non-nuclear countries, namely guarantees against nuclear attack by third states and access to the technological knowledge acquired by the sponsoring Powers as a result of their own nuclear programmes, have not so far seemed definite and dependable enough to induce some key non-nuclear countries to sign and ratify the treaty.

In deciding between the "package deal", or "tie-in", and the "single issue" technique of negotiation much will depend upon the general character of the states concerned and the state of existing relations between them. As between states which have a lengthy tradition of friendship and a certain community of shared political or cultural values, or which belong to the same alliance, the partial agreement is perhaps more appropriate. If such an agreement leaves behind it a feeling of uncompensated grievance on one side or the other this may be more tolerable if the beneficiary state is traditionally a friendly one with which there is a likelihood of continued amicable relations such that losses in dealings with it will be compensated by gains in the future. When, on the other hand, a liberal democratic state, for example, is dealing with a totalitarian regime, the latter may be less likely to accept an uncompensated loss from a state which it classifies as part of an already moribund world; a gain for itself, on the other hand, it may not regard as an invitation to make concessions on its side in the future, but a victory in a long-term struggle which it cannot afford to lose. In dealing with a hostile or totalitarian state, therefore, a democratic country might be better advised to sound out the possibilities of across-the-board settlements in which there are neither conspicuous winners, nor conspicuous losers. But naturally, as in this whole question of conditions and techniques in the successful negotiation of issues in international disputes, a great deal will depend on the particular circumstances of the time.

Much importance, next, has come to attach to the site or venue of negotiations. Choice of site has, in fact, often provided one of the major issues in the "talks about talks" preceding substantive negotiations, of which the long exchanges between Washington and Hanoi about a venue for the negotiations about Vietnam which finally opened in Paris in March 1968 are a striking example. It would be generally agreed that, when practical considerations, such as ease of access for delegations, accommodation and other facilities, provisions for security and so on are set aside, the site itself is of symbolic value in the main; but the symbolic aspect may nevertheless be crucial. The fact that the British and French Prime Ministers went to a German city in September 1938 to sign the agreement relating to Czechoslovakia and that President Roosevelt and Mr Churchill went to the Soviet Union near the end of the Second World War to negotiate and sign the Yalta accords has added to the disfavour in which those two sets of negotiations have since tended to stand with Western public opinion. A conference site, like that of Berlin in 1878 or Portsmouth, New Hampshire, in 1905, where the Russo-Japanese peace treaty was signed, may mark the entrance of a new state into the inner circle of Great Powers. It may, like the choice of Paris for the negotiation of the 1919 peace settlement with Germany and of the Hall of Mirrors, Versailles, for its signature on 28 June, symbolise the uprooting of old grievances while planting the seeds of new ones. A further interesting example of the importance of the site for negotiations is the abortive Anglo-Iraqi Treaty of 1948 which failed largely because it was concluded in Portsmouth, not Baghdad; public protests in Baghdad against the Treaty could not be controlled in the absence abroad of all the principal Iraqi Ministers.

There are certain conference centres, such as Geneva, which have such an established tradition as international meeting places that their choice in most circumstances arouses no dissent, though for many years the Soviet government refused to send its diplomats to conferences in Switzerland owing to one of them having been assassinated there in the 1920s. On the other hand, the siting of United Nations headquarters in New York, though it anchored the United States to the organisation, has probably had some adverse effect on the warmth of Soviet and Afro-Asian feelings towards the world organisation; on one occasion Mr Khrushchev proposed its removal to Geneva, though even about that some of the developing nations may have had their doubts and Geneva in any case had, at least in 1945, an atmosphere of failure about it. The most that can be said on this subject is that, as far as possible, the site chosen should be regarded as part of that complex of gains and losses which we have described as an inherent element in effective negotiation of international differences. That is to say that a country which, on balance, is likely to gain from a negotiated agreement should not as a rule make difficulties about proposals for a choice of site made by the other side, other things, such as the practical convenience of the place, being satisfactory. Nothing can militate more against the longevity of a negotiated agreement than a sense in one of the parties to it that it has sustained an uncompensated loss from an arrangement concluded, signed and sealed in the other country's capital.

IV

Finally, we may return to our 50 case studies of international disputes since 1945 and consider the extent to which negotiations, or rather bilateral negotiations, have assisted in resolving them. The question is difficult to answer, first, because, as we have pointed out earlier in this chapter, it is almost universal for negotiations to precede the reference by the states concerned of a dispute between them to other means of settlement; and, second, because even when other means are being applied, it is customary for negotiations between the original parties to continue. Negotiation is also required for the implementation of any agreement reached by other means of settlement.

If, however, we confine ourselves to the 15 disputes which we described in chapter IX of this Part of the book as having been "peacefully solved", within the meaning there given, we find that bilateral negotiations played an important part in all of them.[15] But in seven cases (Netherlands–Indonesia, Guatemala, Suez, Lebanon–Jordan, Algeria–Morocco, Dominican Republic and Indonesia–Malaysia) armed force or the threat of it, in some cases on a large scale, had been employed before the parties resorted to effective negotiation. In two of these seven cases, Netherlands–Indonesia and Suez, economic pressures applied by the United States are generally regarded as having played a substantial part in inducing at least one party to the argument to negotiate. Moreover, in all 15 instances, with the possible exception of the West Irian, the Austrian and the Icelandic fisheries questions, third parties played significant roles in moving the conflict towards an agreed solution. In at least nine of the 15 cases (Netherlands–Indonesia, Guatemala, Suez, Lebanon–Jordan, Algeria–Morocco, Panama Canal, Dominican Republic, Somalia, Icelandic fisheries), international organisations, whether universal or regional, acted as not inconsiderable elements in the process of solution, if only as providing a forum or contact point for the parties in their negotiation.

Conclusion

We may conclude, therefore, with two general observations. The first is that bilateral negotiations in the modern world rarely ever succeed in themselves in bringing an important dispute towards peaceful settlement. Generally there are third parties waiting in the wings, available to help or to nudge the disputing states forward or to warn one or the other of them against intransigence; or international agencies provide a forum for talks or for various kinds of collective pressure to be applied. The world has grown too small for any but the tiniest states to carry on their wrangles without some intervention of outside forces. Negotiation, in other words, seems to act most effectively when it is conceived as merely one of a whole constellation of dispute-ameliorating forces.

Secondly, it cannot be over-emphasised that negotiation of its own accord can achieve little unless there is some change in the whole pattern of the interests of one or both of the parties as *they themselves* assess that pattern. External events, internal political, social or economic changes

[15] See above chapter IX, Table 4, p. 190.

in the parties themselves, or changes in the attitudes of third parties or international organisations, can effect that modification in the pattern of a state's national interests, but not, or hardly ever, negotiation. Negotiation can and must reflect a re-evaluation by the parties of what they stand to gain or lose by a continuation of the dispute or by a settlement on the most generous terms which the other side, in the light of its own pattern of interests, can afford to offer. But that re-evaluation can seldom be brought about by negotiation unaided by other resources.

13. Mediation

I

WHEN two states, or parts of states, are involved in a dispute and are unable to resolve their differences by negotiation, the occasion may arise for some third party, which may be another state or an individual, or the organ of some international association, to step into the dispute and lead the parties towards an agreed solution through compromise. This process is known as mediation. Mediation is a term often used to refer to a wide variety of third-party interventions, but it is possible to differentiate it fairly sharply from certain other forms of third-party assistance rendered to disputing states and to do so on the basis of traditional usage. For example, the expression "good offices" is generally understood to mean a friendly encouragement to disputing states to continue their efforts towards an agreed settlement or the provision of channels of communication between the disputing states when their former channels have become clogged. The mediator, on the other hand, is generally regarded as having a somewhat wider scope: his function, always provided that the disputing parties will allow him to perform it, is actually to take the thread of negotiations into his own hands; to discuss with the parties, jointly and/or separately, their proposals for ending the dispute; to act, like those providing good offices, as a channel of communication between the parties if necessary; to suggest proposals of his own; to play an active role in narrowing the gap between the two sides; and possibly even to serve as the guarantor of the settlement ultimately reached, if any.

At the same time, mediation is normally distinguished from arbitration, which is discussed in the next chapter, in so far as the arbitrator is generally thought of as proceeding "on the basis of respect for law" if not, like an international judicial agency, on the basis of rules of international law.[1] Ideally, the arbitrator should sit in judgement on any dispute by proposing solutions which do no violence to the existing legal rights and obligations of the parties, though he may very occasionally "bend" the rules in the interest of finding a settlement. The mediator, on the other hand, can afford to be somewhat more flexible in his attitude towards the relevant rules of international law. Since his fundamental aim is to work for an

[1] Article 15 of the Hague Convention of 1899 states that "international arbitration has for its object the settlement of differences between states by judges of their own choice and on the basis of respect for law".

acceptable and, if possible, viable solution, the existing legal position may, on occasion, have to be subordinated to practical convenience. To this extent the mediator may be described almost as a law-maker, or at least as one who suggests steps towards the creation of new international law, rather than an administrator of international law. Accordingly, one may expect mediation to be resisted, and a strictly legal process such as arbitration to be preferred, when one or other of the disputing parties takes his stand on existing legal rights and contends that there is nothing beyond the implementation of existing law which needs to be talked about. At the same time, since mediation is not limited to the implementation of existing law, one may expect that third parties will be all the more reluctant to undertake it simply because the scope for new law-making, with all its risks of alienating one or other of the disputing parties, is so considerable.

Two Basic Conditions

But this brings us to the two basic conditions which must exist before mediation can be employed with any effect. First, there must be qualified mediators willing and able to take up this work and the inducements to a third party to act as a mediator must be greater than the very real discouragements which function in a contrary direction in the would-be mediator's mind. It is commonly supposed that all countries, and especially the Great Powers, have a strong interest in meddling in other countries' affairs either for prestige reasons or to win some practical benefit for themselves. However, as we have already seen in this book, there are powerful forces at work dissuading outsiders from "fishing in dirty waters". In the first place, the scope of the commitment to intervene may be quite unpredictable and the motives for the original intervention soon tend to be lost to sight as the extent of the third party's involvement is enlarged. Then again, the very entanglement of a third party in international disputes tends to arouse some antagonism, either in the two states concerned in the dispute or in the world at large, and the intervening party may have to pay a high price in the form of loss of popularity or diplomatic goodwill. But when the intervention takes the form of mediation the drawbacks of attempting to fulfil this task may well exceed any hypothetical gains. The mediator, in short, runs the risk of alienating one or other, or both, of the parties as he makes his own recommendations clear. The mere fact that he is mediating between opposed parties with different views means that the compromises he must work for are to some degree unsatisfactory to both sides since they are bound to imply that neither side can achieve all it wants. This dissatisfaction commonly takes the form of resentment and antagonism towards the mediator who thus becomes the focus of hostility for both sides. Indeed, there have been occasions when mediators, like Count Folke Bernadotte in the Arab–Israeli conflict in 1948–49, have even had to take their lives in their hands when going about their work. In return for exposing himself to such risks the mediator can expect to receive certain benefits, as for instance reputation as a peace-maker or better relations between the disputing parties which may in some form be a distinct advantage to himself. However that may be, the costs of offering oneself as a mediator – and the same applies to states which act in a mediator's role – have seriously to be taken into account when we consider whether the mediatory resources at present available in the world are adequate to meet the need.

The second condition which needs to exist before mediation is even possible, to say nothing of its being effective, is that mediation and the proposed mediator should be acceptable to both parties. Unless this condition is satisfied, mediation cannot even begin its work; there is no such thing, fortunately or unfortunately, as enforced mediation. There are, it seems, three grounds on which a disputing state might object either to the principle of mediation or to the person of the mediator. The first arises where the state concerned feels it is getting all it wants, or a substantial part of it, without the need for recourse to mediation, which must have the effect of imposing some compromise. Alternatively, if the ruling authorities of a state have reason to think that the development of a dispute is working to their definite disadvantage, they may propose mediation as a means of reducing their anticipated losses or of gaining some sympathy from world opinion on account of their willingness to allow an impartial intermediary to intervene in the dispute.

Secondly, mediation may be objected to if one or other of the parties believes that any conceivable mediator would tend to be biased against itself and in favour of the other state. One of the strongest arguments in favour of the existence within the international community of states which are committed to neither side in the principal international controversies of the day is that such states are available as mediators without necessarily being suspected of bias towards one side or the other.

The third and perhaps least important of these grounds for objecting to the intervention of a mediator is that he is not well enough informed about the problem on which he is called upon to bring his mediatory influence to bear. Other things being equal, a state is likely to prefer a mediator who will lean towards its own side in the argument rather than an unfriendly but expert one. Nevertheless, it remains an important qualification of a mediator that he should be fully conversant with the local conditions in which the dispute is taking place, with the economic, social and other relevant circumstances which exist at the site of the dispute, and with the history, origins, and nature of the dispute. This observation has to be borne in mind when we are considering later the case for some sort of professional training of mediators. It is enough to say here that the mediator's knowledge and practical experience of the problem in which he is expected to work at all times form an important consideration which both sides to the dispute have to take into account.

II

Turning now to the 50 case studies of international disputes since the Second World War which form the basis, or one of the bases, of this study, we can see that they may be divided into four classes with reference to the act of mediation. First, there are the disputes in which mediation was not offered by a third party, so far as is known from published sources. Secondly, there are disputes in which mediation was offered, but was not accepted by one or other or both of the parties. The third class is made up of those disputes in which mediation was offered and accepted but did not succeed. Fourthly, and finally, there are the examples of international disputes in which mediation was offered, accepted and attempted with success or some measure of success. By way of commenting on this form of classification it is worth pointing out that in some instances it is hard to know how to describe a particular form of third-party intervention; for example, in the Anglo-Icelandic fisheries dispute in 1961 the various discussions of this question which took place within the NATO structure may be considered by some a form of mediation and by others merely multilateral or "regional" diplomacy. Again, it is not always easy to say, when a given dispute is wound up, whether this was due to mediation or how far it was due to mediation. As we shall argue later, mediation seems to be most effective when it works in conjunction with changes in the general circumstances in the dispute which tend towards a settlement.

In the first of these classes, that is, those in which mediation appears not even to have been offered by a third party, we would place some 12 of our 50 disputes or 24 per cent. The list is as follows: the Austrian question, South Tirol, the Muscat and Oman dispute, the Anglo-Icelandic fisheries question (with the reservation mentioned above), Quemoy–Matsu, the Berlin issue 1958–61, Mauritania and Morocco, the U2 affair, Angola, the Chinese minority in Indonesia, Hong Kong and Czechoslovakia 1968. It will be seen from an examination of this list that the disputes included in it fall into four different groups, a scrutiny of which sheds some light, on the kind of disputes which appear to be unsuitable (or, conversely, suitable) for mediatory treatment in the existing conditions of world affairs.

First come disputes involving the greatest Powers of the day in which there is clearly no intermediary who could take out of the hands of those Powers the responsibility for settling the issue as far as possible on their own terms. The fact that the tensions between the greatest Powers of the post-Second World War period have been related to ideological differences between distinct philosophical positions stated in absolutist terms have tended to shut these tensions off from compromises proposed by mediators. Mr Khrushchev used to say that, while there could be neutral nations, there could not be neutral men. But it is doubtful whether in the harshest periods of the Cold War there could even be neutral nations as between the great opposing ideological forces, or at least nations which both sides could agree to be neutral. Thus in the Austrian question (1945–55), the Quemoy–Matsu dispute (1958), the Berlin crisis of 1958–61, the U2 affair (1960) and the crisis arising out of the invasion by Warsaw Pact forces of Czechoslovakia in August 1968, mediation was unthinkable because one or other of the super-Powers would not allow it and there was nothing which the rest of the international community could do by way of persuading or compelling them to. Secondly, there is a group of disputes in which one of the protagonists claimed that the issue concerned domestic jurisdiction and hence was out of court as far as mediation was concerned. To accept mediation in such cases, it was argued, was to admit that the country concerned was not master in its own house and no state has been able to agree to this. The claim of domestic jurisdiction may in some of these cases have been a rationalisation hiding some less principled reason for objecting to mediation; nevertheless, the world is still composed of sovereign states and a country which agrees in a particular instance that there is really no dividing line between the domestic and the international is well on the road to denying its own essence. In the foregoing list of disputes in our first category the South Tirol dispute, which Italy claimed was a matter for its own untrammelled jurisdiction, the conflict over Angola and the issue of the Chinese minority in Indonesia are all examples of the rule that recourse to mediation is an admission of international accountability which states, jealously safeguarding their sovereign rights, are generally unwilling to concede.

Thirdly, there is one case in our list, the Oman and Muscat dispute of 1955 to 1959, which was too much of a local affair to stimulate offers of mediation, although external states, especially Britain and Egypt, were involved through their support for the opposing sides. The Sultan, with firm British support, felt that he could contain the Imam and his dissident followers without invoking the heavy machinery of international mediatory intervention and there was no-one in the outside world who felt impelled to intervene as a mediator in what was essentially a "family affair".

Fourthly, there are two instances, the Mauritania–Morocco and Hong Kong disputes in which it was felt on one side at least (and it requires the agreement of both sides to make mediation possible) that the matter was too vital to be left to mediation. In such cases, where the claim put forward by one side amounts to the total surrender of the other, the party which resists a change in the *status quo* generally considers that only force could compel it to abandon any particle of its position; and these, it must be stressed, are the kinds of dispute in which to yield even a particle is in effect to yield the whole.

Next comes the second of our broad categories, namely those disputes in which mediation was offered but was not accepted. Six, or 12 per cent, of our 50 disputes fall under this heading: in chronological order, the Tibet dispute, the South African *apartheid* question, the "two Chinas" issue, the Vietnam conflict, the Hungarian revolution of 1956 and the civil war in Nigeria. In the Tibet question the government of India applied all the pressure at its disposal in order to induce China to accept mediation but the Peking government refused. The ground for this refusal, namely that the Tibet question was purely an internal affair of China's, is another example, like the third group in the category dealt with in the previous paragraphs, of a claim of domestic jurisdiction either discouraging offers of mediation or causing their rejection if made. The same applies to the South African *apartheid* problem, South Africa having rejected a United Nations good offices commission in 1952 and the UN Secretary-General's mediatory efforts in 1960, and to the Nigeria–Biafra conflict, in which Nigeria on the same grounds refused the many mediatory attempts of the Commonwealth and the Organisation of African Unity; or refused them on any other basis than recognition of Nigeria's sovereignty in the disputed area.

In these two cases, however, the basic issue aroused such emotional feeling in many parts of the world that countries felt an obligation to try to bring the matter to a peaceful conclusion by offers of mediation. The "two Chinas" question probably falls into this category too as being, like the Hungarian revolution, an affair of one or other of the major Powers which did not brook external intervention; but also the Chinese Communists, having far-reaching claims of right both against the United States and the Taiwan regime, no doubt felt that in the course of time they would come into their own anyway. Hence Peking China rejected both the mediatory efforts of India and the Afro-Asian states at the United Nations and the mediatory proposals of the UN peace committee under Mr Lester Pearson's chairmanship, which were drawn up in January 1951. Likewise the Soviet Union refused to accept mediation from the late Dag Hammarskjöld when the Secretary-General visited Hungary after the crushing of the revolution in that country in 1956. As for Vietnam, mediatory efforts have been multiplied from many quarters as the United States became ever more deeply involved in the war, but the gap between the two sides was far too great to be bridged by mediation, or even so far by the conversations between the actual belligerents which began in Paris in March 1968.

The third major category includes all the disputes in which mediation was offered and accepted but failed or played only a very minor role in determining the eventual outcome. We propose to include 24 of our 50 disputes in this category, or 48 per cent of the whole, thus constituting it the numerically largest of our four categories. The fact that the majority of the 50 disputes consists of examples of mounted, but ineffective, mediation is highly significant in itself. The total list in this category is as follows: Poland, 1944–45; Greece, 1944–49; Indonesian independence; Palestine, 1945–49; Kashmir from 1947 to the present; Trieste before the settlement in 1954; the Berlin crisis of 1948–49; the Anglo-Iranian oil question; Guatemala, 1952–54; Cyprus, 1954–59 and 1963–68; the Suez crisis of 1956; Laos, 1959–65; Cuba and the United States, 1959–61; the Sino-Indian border question, 1959–65; Somalia's dispute with her neighbours, 1960–65; the Kuwait issue, 1961–63; Goa, 1961; the Yemen conflict, 1962–67; the Cuba missile crisis, 1962; the Aden or South Yemen dispute, 1963–67; Gibraltar; the Indonesia–Malaysia confrontation; the Arab–Israeli conflict.

It is difficult to classify the many different reasons why mediation, though attempted, failed in these 24 disputes, but in almost all of them the sheer determination of one side or the other to rely on its own resources to enforce a solution ruled out the kind of compromises which a mediator might have recommended. Thus, in the dispute over Poland at the end of the Second World War Britain, having been a guarantor of Poland in 1939, was bound to intervene as a mediator but, in the result, was unable to do more than persuade Stalin to accept the so-called Curzon line as Poland's eastern frontier; on the crucial issue of the composition of the Polish government, on the other hand, neither Britain's intercessions nor those of Mr Harry Hopkins, who went on a mediatory mission to Moscow in May and June 1945, were able to affect any change in Soviet policy. In the Greek civil war in 1944 to 1949 the attempted mediation by the United Nations Special Committee on the Balkans (UNSCOB) was less effective in causing the conflict to subside than United States' aid to Greece and Stalin's determination not to overstep the mark in the support he gave to the Greek Communists. In the struggle for Indonesian independence (1945–49), the Indonesian rebels asked for a mediator but the Netherlands refused. The UN Good Offices Commission representing Australia, Belgium and the United States, enjoyed some success in negotiating the Renville agreement, but it was largely the probable economic cost of a prolongation of the war to the Netherlands which finally caused that country to bow to Indonesia's secession. In the Palestine question (1945–49), the UN Special Committee on Palestine and Count Folke Bernadotte played mediatory roles without much tangible success, though the UN Conciliation Committee met Arab and Jewish representatives at Lausanne in April 1949 to deal with the problem of refugees and the status of Jerusalem. Similarly, Dr Gunnar Jarring's mediatory mission to the Middle East in accordance with the Security Council resolution of 22 November 1967 has not, at the time of writing (summer 1970), brought the two sides nearer together. Again, in the Kashmir dispute, the mediatory missions of Sir Owen Dixon and Mr Frank Graham had evidently little effect in promoting a viable settlement, which has not even yet been reached.

All the disputes in our list of 24 which fall into this category could be examined in the same way *seriatim*, but the general pattern is already clear. When a state regards the question in dispute as an important one the losing of which would be harmful to its interests or honour, a mediator or even an international organisation acting as a mediator can achieve little. Not until something occurs which causes a change in the pattern of the state's interests is mediation likely to be effective, and then only perhaps as a means of keeping negotiations moving forward until a settlement is reached, perhaps by the ordinary processes of diplomacy. The mediator, after all, usually has no coercive capacity behind him to enable him to put his recommendations or decisions into effect, nor as a rule economic or other benefits to confer which might ensure that a state which loses certain policy objectives in accepting the compromise he offers will be compensated for its losses. The mediator, when all is said, is only one man, or at most a small committee representing an international organisation strictly based on national sovereignty, doing his or its best within perhaps a few decisive weeks to come up with a solution satisfactory to the two sides, which may regard each other as the personification of evil; and unless the solution offered is satisfactory to both sides, in the sense of promising more gains than the expected benefits to be derived from continuance of the dispute, we may be sure it will not be implemented. To which must be added the fact that the opening for successful mediation may be fleeting and overtaken by shifts in the attitudes of the parties concerned.

Finally, we must consider the relatively small category of disputes in which mediation was attempted and was successful. Before doing so, however, we must notice that certain disputes in the previous category which eventually enjoyed a peaceful termination were helped along, so to speak, by mediation even though this cannot be said to have played a major role in the settlement. Thus, in the ending of the Trieste dispute in 1954, mediation by the Western Powers played a major part in preparing the way for the bilateral negotiations which finally resolved this dispute; similarly, United States intervention helped with the final settling of the Anglo-Iranian oil dispute in 1954, just as American and United Nations efforts with the resolution of the Suez crisis in 1956, and the friendly intercession of the ruler of Kuwait played some part in the reduction of tension over Yemen. Sometimes it happens, too, that mediation has the effect of bringing hostilities to an end though without resolving the basic issues in the conflict. Thus the mediation of Sudan on behalf of the Organisation of African Unity in Somalia's disputes over borders with her neighbours led to a ceasefire with the dispute still unresolved, and the Great Powers, and especially the Soviet Union, intervened to stop the fighting between India and Pakistan in 1965, which led to the Tashkent conference in January 1966 in which Mr Kosygin played an intermediary role. Only perhaps in the case of Trieste can mediation be said to have had a major influence in resolving the dispute definitely.

The case is different in our fourth category; here, not only was the dispute resolved, but mediation by a third party can be described as having been instrumental in achieving this result. The seven cases, or 14 per cent of the 50 disputes, are as follows: the first phase of the Indo-China dispute, that is, from the end of the Second World War until the Geneva Conference of 1954; the Netherlands dispute with Indonesia over West Irian; the Lebanon and Jordan crisis of 1958; the Congo crisis from 1960 until 1963; the dispute between Algeria and Morocco; the Panama Canal question in 1964 and the Dominican crisis of 1965. It will be seen even here, however, how other circumstances had to exist and supplement the efforts of the mediator, and how the dispute itself was, so to speak, tending towards a solution before mediation was able to do its work. In two cases, Indo-China and the Congo, the military defeat of one of the two parties to the dispute preceded mediation; mediation was in effect part of the process of peacemaking. In the Indo-China situation the decisive French defeat at Dien Bien Phu in March 1954 and weariness at the cost of maintaining her position in South-East Asia laid the basis for the mediatory efforts of Britain and the Soviet Union at the Geneva conference on Korea and South-East Asia in July 1954, of which both those states were co-chairmen. Similarly, the defeat of the secessionist policies of Moishe Tshombe of Katanga during the Congo crisis of 1960–63, a defeat in which United States military equipment and facilities played a signal role, likewise preceded and laid the basis for the mediatory efforts of the United Nations which paved the way to the pacification and reunification of the Congo. In a somewhat similar way, in the Netherlands–West Irian and the

Lebanon–Jordan disputes, the precondition for the success of mediation was the sharp pressure applied by the United States in favour of a termination of the crisis. In these two sets of cases, therefore, military defeat in the field, on the one hand, and, on the other, pressure applied by the richest and most powerful state of the day acted as the catalyst which brought the problem to the point at which mediatory activities could do their work.

The liquidation of the other three disputes in this category, the Algeria–Morocco and the Panama and Dominican Republic disputes, illustrates the value of regional organisations as providing instruments through which mediation can be applied. In the first of these, the mediation by Emperor Haile Selassie of Ethiopia, with President Keita of Mali at Bamako, which was at once personal and in the name of the Organisation of African Unity, led to the ceasefire accepted by both sides. In the case of the two Latin American disputes, over the Panama Canal in 1964 and the politics of the Dominican Republic in the following year, the readiness of the United States to allow the regional organisation to which all the parties belonged, the Organisation of American States, to exercise a conciliatory role was the key to the successful acts of mediation in these cases. What appears to be significant about the disputes considered in this paragraph is that mediation was offered by states, or by organisations representing states, with which the disputing parties were already both dealing on a day-to-day basis over a wide variety of matters of mutual concern. Perhaps this is one clue to the way in which confidence is built up in a mediator by states which have recourse to his assistance. A mediator from a distant country, appointed, as he must be, on an *ad hoc* basis, seems somewhat less able to command confidence than an old and tried partner in other diplomatic activities. But here again it is noticeable how important factors other than the mere act of mediation played a part in creating an appropriate atmosphere in which a final settlement could be worked out. In each of the two Latin American disputes mentioned in this chapter, it was not so much the availability of mediatory organs within the OAS but the willingness of the United States to listen to and take account of OAS opinion which played a vital role in the mediator's success. To summarise, these are all examples of mediation being a secondary, or perhaps highly contingent, means of alleviating international disputes. We must always be on our guard against considering it as some kind of international panacea.

The Limitations of Mediation

We are now in a position to draw certain general conclusions concerning the act, and art, of mediation from our analysis of the foregoing experience.

Our first observation must be that mediation, however sensible and convenient it may seem at first sight, suffers from certain drawbacks in the resolution of international disputes. To begin with, it seems to be the exception rather than the norm for disputing states to agree to third-party mediation in their affairs. In the early stages of a dispute they are inclined to believe that they will derive more substantial benefit from keeping the dispute under their own control than from resigning any part of this control of it to a mediator. Possibly the need to offer continuous public justification of their position in a given dispute encourages governments to believe that they should rely on their own unaided efforts rather than call in aid some mediatory agent from outside; they come to regard their cause as so strong that it needs no outside support and certainly no outside judgement.

For this reason a great deal attaches to the correct timing of a mediation offer. If an offer of, or proposal for, mediation is made too early, while one or other of the states concerned may still be confident of having its own way or keeping the threads of the dispute firmly in its own hands, the rebuff may be such as to discourage similar efforts in future. If, on the other hand, the suggestion of mediation is made after the critical moment for it has passed the dispute may be settled by other means, as for instance by force. It is a curious fact in international affairs that, while a state may have an interest in keeping a dispute in which it is involved at a pacific level, sometimes the only way in which mediation offers can be encouraged is by adopting a belligerent posture as though war over the issue was only just round the corner.

Another inherent drawback in the mediation process is the possible reluctance of a mediator, whether a state, an international organisation or individual, to associate himself with policies or attitudes which may lower his standing in the diplomatic world without bringing countervailing benefits. The relatively few examples we have given of successful acts of mediation in the post-Second World War period are hardly an encouragement to would-be mediators, especially when we take into account the time and trouble involved in the mediator's work. One can well understand the reluctance of many countries and individuals to adopt the mediator's role in an international dispute considering the discouraging and unenviable nature of this work.

The record of mediation in the last twenty-five years also underlines the point that mediation by itself has scant power to resolve the sort of disputes which occur in the contemporary international system. It is when combined with other agencies and external pressures, and, more especially, when the basis for a settlement has already been laid by the military defeat of one of the parties, or some other factor leading to a revision of hopes and expectations of the parties, that mediation meets with some success. Mediation rarely succeeds on its own; the position is much more favourable when there exists a concatenation of circumstances which are already in operation as tending towards an improvement of the situation.

III

Turning now to the qualifications and recruitment of mediators and the question of their training for this work, anything which can be said under this heading must be subject to the overriding principle that, in the first and last resort, a mediator must be acceptable to the parties concerned in the dispute. This means that there is little to be gained by outlining in the abstract suitable qualifications of a mediator or the requirements of any system for the deliberate training of mediators, or by having the UN Secretary-General, or some such person, draw up lists of mediators available for use by states when involved in disputes with each other. The mediator who is acceptable to both parties in a dispute is bound, in existing circumstances, to be chosen on an *ad hoc* basis and hence generalisations about the requirements of a mediator are largely out of place. Nevertheless, in the light of the increasing activity of international organisations, universal and regional, in the mediatory field, it is worth asking whether our present method of recruiting and training mediators is as efficient as it might be.

In the first place, it may be noted that, as far as is known, no Foreign Office or Ministry of External Affairs in the world does anything to equip members of its staff for the work of mediation. Apart from what he may pick up in the ordinary course of his political or diplomatic career, the mediator who has been active in international disputes since 1945 has normally undergone no special training. The same would seem to be true of members of the United Nations Secretariat who, again, have only their daily practical experience to draw upon to equip them to perform their role as mediators. It could be said, however, that in addition to the traditional qualifications mediators have revealed in the past, such as intelligence, practical experience of international affairs, diplomatic skill and tact, together with intimate knowledge of the disputes with which they are called upon to deal, certain other skills may under modern circumstances be included in the list.

A mediator, for example, would seem to need some knowledge of the social structures of the different countries for which he acts in order to understand better the kind of internal pressures which lie behind a government's demands and objects in a dispute in which it is involved. Nor need this knowledge be confined to a particular country for whose problems a mediator is called in aid. The student of social structure, such as we are suggesting that the mediator might usefully be, should be able to apply general sociological methods of analysis to any country in the disputes of which he may be asked to intervene.

Some have also argued the possibly more doubtful proposition that the mediator should have some understanding of modern psychological theory in order to be able to appreciate the manner in which the parties to a dispute are visualising the issues between them. We do not in this study accept the now fashionable notion that disputes are "all in the mind", rather than conflicts of objective interests. Nevertheless, there is a case for saying that no-one who has to deal with quarrels between organised groups can fail to realise the vitally important psychological forces which can and do affect the manner in which parties to disputes perceive their mutual relations. A mediator cannot but profit from a better understanding of such forces up to the limit of what modern psychological ideas have to offer.

IV

Finally, there are certain observations to be made about the manner in which the mediator or the mediating organ goes about the work in hand. Are there any methods of mediation which experience has shown to be more productive of result than others? First, as we have already pointed out, the timing of a mediatory intervention is of the highest importance. There is danger in attempting such an intervention before the moment is ripe. On the other hand, there is a tendency for the international community to drag its feet until a dispute has entered upon its violent or near-violent phase, when offers of mediation tend to come in droves. On balance, it is perhaps preferable that an offer of mediation should be made a shade too late than a shade too early. A premature attempt at mediation may lead one or other of the disputing states to set its face against such intervention as long as the dispute lasts. If the appropriate moment has passed, on the other hand, the states concerned may grasp at a belated offer of mediation lest the point of no return come at which there is no avoiding violence. But this is a rule which can only be observed after careful scrutiny of the individual case when it occurs.

Secondly, it is clearly advisable that the mediator should, if possible, dispose of some specific inducement, apart from the general advantage of settling a dispute rather than leaving it unsettled, to persuade the disputing states to sink their differences. A classic, though in the nature of things rare, example of this was the mediation offered by the International Bank for Reconstruction and Development in the Indus waters dispute in 1961.[2] Here the disputing states, India and Pakistan, were given to understand that the Bank's financial assistance would not be forthcoming unless the dispute was settled; hence in this case mediation was fortunately combined with strong inducements to accept it. When the mediator is a single individual, unless he has the backing of some national or international organisation behind him, this method is not usually available. Hence there is a strong case for trying to build up the resources available to the mediator, especially through the instrumentality of the United Nations and its specialised agencies.

There are, among others, three ways in which these international organisations can use their resources to strengthen the mediator's bargaining position *vis-à-vis* states involved in a dispute in which he is intervening. First, the world organisation, the United Nations, could consider whether it is not possible to provide some assurance to a state involved in a dispute that it will not suffer, as far as its security is concerned, if it agrees to accept the principle of mediation or a particular mediator's recommendations; in other words, something in the nature of a guarantee against armed attack could be given to a state if it accepts mediation in a dispute. So stated, the proposal may seem utopian and there are some obvious practical difficulties. It should be remembered, however, that under the nuclear non-proliferation treaty opened for signature in July 1968 the three nuclear Powers sponsoring the treaty, Britain, the Soviet Union and the United States, made declarations of intent to assist non-nuclear countries which were the subject of aggression and which had deprived themselves of the capability for nuclear retaliation through signing the treaty. This is, in all conscience, a somewhat weak and unreliable form of guarantee, but it is worth asking whether something of the same sort, if possible in more automatic form, could be worked out as some assurance to states, especially to weak states, as an inducement to them to accept mediation and its results.

Secondly, thought could be given to the various technical assistance programmes of the United Nations to see whether some of them could be managed with a similar end in view. The main object of the exercise is to persuade states to accept third-party intervention; or, in other words, to regard the rewards of a peaceful settlement at least as high as the gains a state may expect to make from the unilateral pursuit of its own interests in a particular dispute. There is certainly no moral, or even practical, argument against the use of United Nations economic and, to a less extent, technical assistance for this purpose, though care would have to be taken

[2] This dispute is not included in our fifty case studies, though the background of Indo-Pakistan conflict is covered in our study of Kashmir.

to ensure that the poor countries, who rely on such assistance, were not prejudiced in the operation of some such scheme, as compared with the rich nations, who do not.

A third and somewhat more negative possibility is that a state which refuses mediation should be threatened with some of the sanctions which the world organisation, in theory at least, has at its disposal. The repertoire of such sanctions is very wide indeed and includes such far-reaching measures as the concerted interruption by member-states of trade with the recalcitrant state and even its expulsion from, or suspension of membership of, the world organisation.[3] It is otiose to say that everything under this heading would depend upon the attitudes of member-states, as far as both the adoption of the relevant resolutions and their implementation is concerned, when such drastic remedies are contemplated.

Needless to say, a threat of sanctions should not be made unless it is credible; in practice international sanctions have not been a success and their future credibility is not impressive. Nevertheless, if the states of the world are serious in demanding more success in the peaceful settlement of international disputes, they must will the means as well as the end. For there are surely no two ways about it: either mediation must continue to take its place as merely one of the available techniques for peaceful settlement and must await a change in the perceived interests of the parties to a dispute if it is to be successful; or, alternatively, means must be found to heighten the attractiveness of mediation as a means of peaceful settlement, and this must depend upon a revolutionary change of attitude on the part of states towards their obligations and responsibilities within the present international system. The latter in its turn will depend to some degree upon how far the UN Secretary-General can instil this feeling into them; this fact underlines once more what the world lost in the death of Dag Hammarskjöld in 1961.

At all times, however, and even in the most favourable circumstances, mediation must remain for the most part a slow, tortuous and time-consuming process, with many setbacks and often little to show for all the effort invested. What this means in terms of the personal qualities of the mediator is clear enough. But the question has also been raised as to whether the international community does not have to face the problem whether mediation should be made a full-time profession rather than relying upon the *ad hoc* reference of disputes to mediators whose main occupation lies in some field outside that of the settlement of international disputes. There are, it may be argued in favour of professionalism, risks in a situation in which the mediator has his loyalties divided between his

[3] See Article 16 of the Covenant of the League of Nations and Articles 6 and 41 of the United Nations Charter.

work as a mediator and his work in his ordinary occupation. It may also be doubted whether a mediator who spends most of his time in some other occupation, especially, as many mediators do, in a political calling, can command the necessary credibility as a third party in a dispute. Difficult as it may be to frame proposals for the recruitment, training and financial maintenance of a corps of professional mediators within, say, the Secretariat of the United Nations or some other international organisation, the case for full-time professionalism is a strong one. It seems, too, that full-time professional mediators might be more likely, after a period in their posts, to acquire a reputation for judgement and impartiality than the mediator drawn on an *ad hoc* basis from some different walk of life.

After weighing the case for and against professionalism in mediation, however, we conclude that the drawbacks exceed the possible advantages. Unless the demand for mediators were heavier and more continuous than it is, it is difficult to see how a full-time corps of specialists numerous enough to cover the different varieties of disputes on which to exercise their skill could be provided with enough work. Moreover, the case for professionalism does not dispose of the basic principle of all mediation in the field of international relations, namely the primary acceptability of the mediator to the parties, without which there can be no mediation; the professional mediator, simply because he is a professional, is not necessarily more acceptable to the parties than an amateur. One of the most important reasons which might give a mediator some chance of success would be a reputation for experience in the international field. This could only be acquired in many different activities over a considerable spell of time and one cannot imagine someone beginning life as a potential mediator; the mediator's experience, not his commitment to the career of being a mediator, makes for his success.

14. *Arbitration and Adjudication*

I

DURING the twenty-five years since 1945 which this study more particularly covers there has been an undoubted decline in the role of adjudication, though to a less extent in that of arbitration, as a means for the settlement of international disputes when compared with the situation between the two world wars. This decline is evident in the mere titles of recent articles by authoritative writers on this subject, as for instance "The decline of the Optional Clause" by Sir Humphrey Waldock[1] – written, incidentally, in the mid-1950s, when the family of states was much smaller than it is today and hence tending to understate today's position – and "The present stagnation of inter-state adjudication" by Professor J. H. W. Verzijl.[2] C. Wilfred Jenks has written that "since the Second World War remarkable advances have been made in virtually every sector of international organisation except the judicial sector". He continues: "there has been no comparable advance in international adjudication; on the contrary, there have been no major innovations in the competence, organisation, procedure and effectiveness of the International Court of Justice during the last quarter of a century".[3]

The evidence for this relative decline, or at least stagnation, may also be found in a few random statistics. First, the number of cases considered by the International Court of Justice since 1945 has been no greater than that of those considered by the former Permanent Court of International Justice from its foundation in 1921 until the outbreak of the Second World War. Secondly, although the number of states in the world has more than doubled since the inter-war-period, and the same applies to the number of states which are adherents to the Statute of the International Court of Justice (ICJ) by virtue of their membership of the United Nations Organisation, the number of states accepting the world court's compulsory jurisdiction under the so-called Optional Clause consisting of Article 36 (2) of the Statute has remained virtually the same. The comment of Professor Waldock on this is that "the historical record does not . . . justify any great optimism that by degrees the Optional Clause may bring about a general system of compulsory jurisdiction". "Today", he continues, "despite the almost universal support for compulsory jurisdic-

[1] *The British Yearbook of International Law*, Vol. 32, 1955–56, pp. 244–87.
[2] *International Relations*, October, 1963.
[3] *The Prospects of International Adjudication*, London, 1964, p. 1.

tion at the San Francisco Conference, fewer than half the Members of the United Nations are adherents to the Optional Clause and of these many have qualified their acceptance of the Optional Clause by the insertion of numerous limitations, reservations and conditions in their declarations".[4] Or, as another authority, Charles de Visscher, has written, "the reality is that today, as formerly, the international tribunal is generally only given jurisdiction of minor conflicts where the interests involved are limited".[5]

The third quantitative indication of how resort to international courts and tribunals has tended to lag behind the use of other means for settling international disputes since the Second World War is the fact that requests for Advisory Opinions from the ICJ have not markedly increased despite the increase in the number of bodies which are now competent to ask for such Opinions within the United Nations scheme of things. Under the Statute of the old Permanent Court of International Justice only the Council and the Assembly of the League of Nations were entitled to ask for Advisory Opinions from the Court; under the United Nations Charter all the major organs of the United Nations are likewise entitled and so are all the United Nations Specialised Agencies if they are so authorised by the General Assembly. Yet during the life so far (1970) of the world organisation only eleven Advisory Opinions of the ICJ have been requested by and given to the United Nations General Assembly and only two given in response to requests by other bodies. It is remarkable, taking into account the many legal issues inherent in the successive international problems considered by the Security Council, that that organ has only once so far approached the Court at The Hague for an Advisory Opinion despite its being expressly authorised by the Charter (Article 96) to do so. This record is meagre by any test and would seem to betray a marked lack of confidence in the judicial process on the part of the world organisation of which the Hague Court is an integral element.

We shall see in a later section of this chapter that this stagnation of the judicial process in the settlement of the legal differences between states is further illustrated by the incidence of judicial or arbitral[6] proceedings in

[4] *Op. cit.*, p. 246.

[5] "Reflections on the Present prospects of International Adjudication", *The American Journal of International Law*, July, 1956, p. 471.

[6] In the present work the words "arbitration" and "adjudication" are both assumed to refer to the settlement of legal issues in an international dispute by reference to the rules of international law as interpreted by qualified legal authorities. It is further assumed that the only material difference between the two processes is that arbitration is normally effected by judges of the parties' own choosing, whereas adjudication normally refers to the work of the ICJ or such similar established courts. It may be argued that the arbitrator can, at the request of the parties, go beyond a strictly legal function and apply equity or natural justice. We would ourselves regard this, however, as falling more under the heading of mediation or the work of commissions of inquiry. See *supra*, pp. 297-298.

the case studies which we have compiled for the purpose of the present inquiry. It is pertinent at the present stage, however, to try to review some of the reasons for this general decline or stagnation of the judicial process in international relations.

In the first place, the former Permanent Court of International Justice (PCIJ) enjoyed an undoubted advantage as far as the volume of work presented to it is concerned in that when it was formed in 1921 the legal structure of many parts of the world, and certainly of Europe, had been refashioned, almost *de novo*, by the peace treaties at the conclusion of the First World War. These agreements created a tension, or network of tensions, between the beneficiaries of the treaties, that is, the victors in the First World War, on the one hand, and those disadvantaged by the treaties, that is, the defeated states, on the other. The interpretation and application of this highly complex body of new rules of international law naturally became the subject of continuous international debate, not only between former enemies, but also between former allies, especially, for example, between Britain and France in regard to the enforcement of sanctions against Germany for alleged non-payment of reparations and many other questions. Since all these states, victors and vanquished, could be described, at least until the advent of National Socialism in Germany in the 1930s, as belonging to what was still regarded as a single European culture, they all believed in the relevance and usefulness of resorting to judicial machinery for the settlement of contentious legal questions arising within the new order of things created by the peace settlement. Hence it is not surprising that of the 33 contentious cases submitted to the Permanent Court during its life, 18 arose directly or indirectly out of the peace settlements concluded between 1919 and 1923.[7] None of the cases submitted to the present world court falls clearly into an analogous category for the obvious reason that so far there has been no general peace settlement with the former Axis Powers agreed and negotiated by all the major victorious states. Peace settlements, as with Italy and Japan, have been made but by no means on the comprehensive scale of the settlements at the end of the First World War.

It should be emphasised, however, on the other side of the balance sheet that in the years since 1945 the number of international treaties and attempted codifications of treaty law, though not always successful, have increased out of all proportion, so much so that international courts will probably find that conventions rather than customary international law will predominate among the legal rules they are called upon to apply. This expansion of treaty law may provide judicial tribunals with a considerable increase in their work in future.

[7] Jenks, *op. cit.*, p. 87.

If we confine ourselves, however, to the strict examination of experience since 1945 we realise that instead of the old, pre-war conflict between "status quo" and "revisionist" states, turning upon the interpretation of a comprehensive treaty system, there have been in the post-war world three main types of international disputes to none of which the judicial process as we have known it in the past is easily applicable. The first is the great "East–West" complex of disputes between Communist and non-Communist states in which ideological differences and disputes about areas in which Communist and non-Communist political and strategic influences overlap, have been peculiarly intermingled. In these conflicts the old Communist aversion to Western international law and judicial institutions (in theory at least, although in recent years the Soviet Union itself, as it becomes more of a *status quo* Power, is apparently undergoing a change in this respect) has tended to render the idea of a resort to judicial agencies to settle the legal issues within these disputes largely irrelevant. The Western Powers, for example, might have sought confirmation from the ICJ at The Hague of their legal entitlement to a military presence in and freedom of access to the western sectors of Berlin during the crises in East–West relations concerning that city in 1948–49 and 1958–61. But no one can suppose that the Soviet Government would have agreed to such a submission or would have considered the Court a relevant agency for deciding the issues. Moreover, Soviet agreement and acceptance of the relevance of the Court were necessary for such a submission to be effective, unless the Western Powers had been able to seek an Advisory Opinion from the Court through some body authorised to do so in accordance with Article 65 of the Court's Statute.

The second major type of conflict has been that between former colonial Powers and new nationalist movements seeking freedom from the colonial bond, as for instance the dispute in the late 1940s between the Netherlands and the Indonesian nationalist movement; or between former colonial Powers and ex-colonies over the efforts of the latter to shake off what they consider to be relics of colonial rule, as the dispute between Britain and France, on one side, and Egypt, on the other, concerning the latter's nationalisation of the Suez Canal Company in 1956 or between India and Portugal concerning the residual Portuguese enclaves in India. There are two aspects of disputes of this kind which tend to inhibit resort to international courts to help with the attainment of a settlement. One is the fact that here again, as we so often find in the treatment of international disputes, the disagreement is not so much about what the law is as about what the law ought to be, and no reasonable case can be made out for saying that judges, no matter how impartial or versed in the law they may be, can be accepted as authorities on the essentially political or moral question of what the law ought to be. The other inhibiting factor is the very natural tendency of non-European nationalist movements and new non-European states to consider that the rules of international law and the courts and tribunals administering those rules are to a large extent the invention of the established European Powers which are parties to the disputes which those courts and tribunals are expected to pronounce upon.

This last difficulty is evident once more when we consider the third major type of dispute in the international system since 1945, namely between new, or ex-colonial, states themselves, such as the dispute over the frontiers of Somalia, the dispute between Morocco and Mauritania or the conflict between Algeria and Morocco. There is admittedly a good deal of evidence to the effect that the attitudes of the new Afro-Asian states towards international law and the settlement of international legal questions by international courts and tribunals are by no means as hostile as they are often represented to be, and that they are becoming less hostile. These states appear in reality to have no more and no less of that jealous regard for their own sovereign rights and of that same unwillingness to allow a court of law to determine legal disputes in which they are involved without their consent than the older members of the international system from which they have broken free. Some authorities have even argued that most of the work of the ICJ in recent years has been brought to it by new states.[8] Again, in the Protocol of Mediation, Conciliation and Arbitration adopted by the independent African states in July 1964, the general rules of international law concerning arbitration as traditionally understood in Europe were incorporated. It has been forcefully argued, too, that in so far as many of the new Afro-Asian states exhibit no considerable enthusiasm for the world court at The Hague, this is because of the "availability of alternative methods which in their view offer greater opportunities for compromise in a shorter time and with less expense and which leave them a wider freedom of action if the final settlement is not to their liking", as, for instance, United Nations political organs, especially the General Assembly, regional arrangements and special arbitral tribunals.[9]

Nevertheless, when all is said, it is hard to expect the new states to make, at least in the early years of their existence, any notable contribution to the positive expansion of international adjudication. After all, the new states plead, with a strong sense of the rightfulness of their case, for a "new deal" in international relations, and for a new order, if not in relation to international frontiers and territory, at least in relation to the distribution of income and wealth in the international community; and hence they

[8] I. F. I. Shihata, "The Attitude of New States towards the International Court of Justice", *International Organisation*, Spring 1965, p. 208.
[9] *Ibid.*, pp. 217–18.

can have no especially strong affection for the prevailing legal system in the world. The International Court at The Hague, moreover, is geographically and emotionally remote from most of them; there is, it is true, provision in Article 22 (1) of the Court's Statute for the Court to move its sessions round the world according to the physical location of a particular dispute, but this provision does not seem to have been much exploited. In so far as the new ex-colonial states tend to regard the existing machinery for international adjudication as being biased towards the "West" or the "white man's world", they could hardly have been persuaded otherwise by the Court's verdict in 1966 when it decided, after four years' proceedings, that Ethiopia and Liberia were not entitled, as members of the former League of Nations, to challenge before the Court the administration of South-West Africa by the government of the Republic of South Africa. It well may be that this was the only conclusion the Court could have reached on the strict interpretation of the facts and the law of the case. No doubt, too, the duration of these abortive proceedings, as is so often the case, was due more to the time taken up by states in making their submissions then to any dilatoriness of the Court itself. Nevertheless, the outcome, especially when seen through the eyes of ex-colonial states, could not have enhanced the Court's standing in the third world.

There are further reasons which some authorities have referred to as inhibiting recourse to arbitration and adjudication in the settlement of international disputes, and these, paradoxically, have to do with changing attitudes in the international community, and especially among the greatest Powers, towards the use of force as an instrument of foreign policy. It became evident as early as the middle 1950s that the great military Powers were by no means as free to resort to armed force to settle their differences with other states as they had been throughout most of the history of the international system. The frame of mind of the international community at large, and especially among the numerous new states of Africa and Asia, the goodwill of which the great military Powers were trying to win, was against it, and so were the express provisions of the United Nations Charter, save for quite exceptional circumstances. Public opinion within the greatest Powers themselves, especially in the Western or non-Communist countries, tended for a variety of reasons to frown upon it, and in any case the great nuclear Powers became increasingly conscious that any resort to force by themselves, particularly in areas of strategic importance to each other, could have the most calamitous consequences, not only for the countries against which that force was applied, but also for the nuclear states themselves: in unleashing the whirlwind they themselves might be blown to their own destruction.

The consequences for international adjudication of this change in attitudes towards the use of force, it has been argued, were two. First, non-nuclear countries felt somewhat more at liberty to use force themselves, or at least to adopt an uncompromising position in their disputes with other states, because they no longer felt the age-old fear of being punished for misdoing by the Great Powers. Julius Stone, for example, has written that,

> When it began to appear that small states can violate with impunity the rights of big states, the interest of the small ones in third party settlement understandably diminishes. In so far as a blanket prohibition is now assumed to be placed on the use of force by any state, even to enforce its legal rights, the effect is to undermine the modest binding force which international law enjoyed in the old-fashioned days before the League and the United Nations.[10]

The other argument is that in the period between the two world wars the case for submitting international disputes, or rather their legal aspects, to determination by properly constituted judicial tribunals working with due regard to all the established legal procedures was principally that this was the only rational alternative to war, which opinion at the time regarded as capable of ending civilisation. The more evident it has become during the last two decades, however, that war in fact settles nothing because it may under nuclear conditions destroy the belligerents with equal completeness, the less obvious is the blunt confrontation between law and war.

The world has so far since 1945 discovered other ways, none of them, however, having any high degree of reliability, of coping with the presence of states armed to the teeth with the deadliest weapons and quarrelling with each other about every possible subject without actually resorting to war. It has not yet been established in any precise terms by what means, methods and rules this near-miracle can continue to be worked indefinitely, but plainly resort to the settlement of disputes by international adjudication has not been accepted as the only, or even a highly valuable, means of peaceful co-existence. The result has been to diminish somewhat the urgency for states to accept, for example, compulsory jurisdiction under the world court's Statute since there are clearly other processes and techniques by which war can hopefully be averted. The point has been stated by C. Wilfred Jenks in the following terms:

> It may well be that the lessened tendency to use force in international relations resulting from the changed political climate of our times, the increasing interdependence of nations and the difficulty of a limited recourse to force in circumstances in which any recourse to force may involve the danger of general and atomic war – a tendency which has found legal expression in, and crystallised with binding legal obligation

[10] "Law, Force and Survival", *Foreign Affairs*, July 1961, p. 553.

> as a result of, the General Treaty for the Renunciation of War and the Charter of the United Nations – has had an adverse effect on the willingness of states to submit to arbitration. In many cases the alternative is no longer arbitration on the one hand and war or other forcible measures of redress on the other, but adjudication or arbitration on the one hand and stalemate on the other.[11]

Whatever the validity of these two hypotheses in any particular instance, it remains true to say that the old belief, so frequent among Anglo-Saxon writers in the inter-war period, that the international community could somehow be transformed into a highly integrated whole by legal means, by stronger obligations being imposed on states to settle their disputes by peaceful means, such as arbitration or adjudication, by increasing in some way the scope of compulsory jurisdiction under the world court's Statute, by making more effective provision for sanctions against law-breaking states, and so on, has lost much of its plausibility. As we shall see later in this chapter, there are no doubt certain ways in which the confidence reposed by states in the existing machinery for arbitration and adjudication of their disputes could be enhanced. It remains true none the less, and this now probably represents the consensus of informed opinion on the subject, that the main burden of the settlement of international disputes must rest on political rather than legal institutions and devices; on balancing these interests against those rather than on applying the footrule of a general law; on negotiation, bargaining and the search for mutually acceptable solutions, rather than on a trial in a court of law from which one side emerges the victor and the other the vanquished. The point has been well stated by Jenks in his contention that:

> Fundamentally the problem of compulsory jurisdiction is political and psychological; legal and technical ingenuity can find a solution, and generally a variety of possible solutions, for all the technical and procedural elements of the problem, but the heart of the matter lies elsewhere.[12]

It is doubtful, however, whether Jenks is quite correct when he continues that the "essence of the question is confidence; confidence in the stability and adequacy of the law, and confidence in the integrity and predictability of the courts and tribunals administering the law". No doubt much remains to be done to increase the confidence of states and governments in the respects to which Jenks refers, but the "heart of the matter" seems to be that most of the disputes between states are not differences as to points of law, but differences about the use of resources, about rights and entitlements, in a moral as well as legal sense, about the desirable

[11] Jenks, *op. cit.*, pp. 104–5.
[12] *Ibid.*, p. 101.

relationships between organised groups of human beings. It is a misunderstanding of international relations to suggest that much more than a small, though still no doubt appreciable, fraction of these differences can be settled by law courts as distinct from the daily mutual bargaining of organised interests.

II

The point we have just been making becomes even clearer when we consider the extent to which our 50 case studies of international disputes occurring since 1945 reveal the incidence of arbitration and adjudication in present-day international relations. The historical record is not an impressive one. In more than three-quarters of these disputes arbitration or adjudication does not appear even to have been proposed by either side or by third parties as a means of settlement, leaving only 12 in which either form of proceeding was at all relevant. In one of these cases, the Netherlands–Indonesia dispute of 1945–49, arbitration was provided for by Article 17 of the Linggadjati Agreement if a mutual settlement could not be reached by other means, but no use appears to have been made of this provision on major issues between the two parties. When agreement was finally reached between the Netherlands and the Indonesian authorities on 2 November 1949, a Union Court of Arbitration was created to settle disputes arising out of the Statute of the proposed Netherlands–Indonesian Union itself, which ceased to exist when Indonesia received its full independence. In the later dispute between the Netherlands and Indonesia over West Irian, when the Union no longer existed, the Netherlands offered and Indonesia refused to have the issue referred to the International Court. Indonesia seems especially to have resented the fact that the Court supposed to decide the issue, the International Court of Justice, was situated at The Hague.

In seven further cases out of the 12 disputes in which there was some reference to settlement by arbitral or judicial tribunals the proposal was made by one side and not accepted by the other and, since in none of these cases was the principle of compulsory jurisdiction applicable, the proposal fell to the ground. In almost all these seven cases the situation was the uncomplicated one that the side proposing arbitration or adjudication was favoured by the existing legal situation while the other side was calling for a change in the law. It was left to each side as a result of the deadlock arising from differences over resort to legal tribunals to make what political capital they could out of their respective arguments. In the South Tirol question, for example, judicial settlement was proposed by Italy, the country benefiting from the *status quo*, while Austria, who wished a change in the *status quo*, was opposed to settlement by judges on the basis of the existing law. A similar case was the Netherlands–Indonesian dispute over West Irian in 1952, which we have dealt with in the preceding paragraph. Again, in the Anglo-Icelandic fisheries question, it suited the United Kingdom that the dispute should go to the world court, and this she proposed; but the Icelandic government, which was arguing on behalf of a change in the law of the sea relating to the maritime frontiers of states in which it called a "special position", was naturally unwilling. In the frontier dispute between Somalia and Ethiopia, the latter country was willing to go to arbitration since this must almost necessarily have involved deciding the question on the basis of a treaty of 1908, which clearly favoured Ethiopia. Somalia, in refusing, claimed that she could not be certain "that adjudication based on law would give priority to the right of self-determination as against traditional rules about the sanctity of dispositive boundary treaties". The conflict between law and demands for changes in the law, which runs like a red thread throughout the history of international relations, could hardly be more pointedly expressed.

The other two examples out of the seven are instances of precisely the same kind. First, at one stage of the Cuba missile crisis in October 1962 the Russians raised the question of the legality of President Kennedy's quarantine of Cuba, without actually proposing the submission of the issue to judicial testing, presumably in the knowledge that it would be hard in modern times to establish the legal rectitude of what was once called the "pacific blockade". The then British Prime Minister, Mr Harold Macmillan, brushed aside the question of the legality of the American administration's action by saying that he did not think that "this is the moment to go into the niceties of international law" and that "in new situations – and these are unprecedented situations in the nuclear world – we cannot rely on a pedantic review of precedents.[13] The United Kingdom, herself, in the second of the two cases referred to, has repeatedly proposed referring the legal issues in the dispute with Spain over Gibraltar to the ICJ, as for instance on 10 October 1966. Spain, which has not signed the Optional Clause in the Court's Statute and therefore cannot legally be forced into Court, has refused, following the normal pattern of behaviour of states which desire a change in the existing legal framework, which judges can only be expected to interpret and apply.

It is interesting to note, too, that in the Suez crisis in 1956, when suggestions were made to the British Government that it should submit the question of the legality of President Nasser's action in nationalising the Suez Canal Company to the ICJ, the proposal was rejected ostensibly on the ground that by the time the Court had pronounced its verdict

[13] H. C. Deb., Fifth Series, Vol. 664, 25 October 1962, Col. 1060.

President Nasser would have completed his *fait accompli* and nothing could compel him to undo it except military force exercised by the maritime Powers, and that if military force had to be used, it had better be used early rather than late. It seems clear, however, that the prevailing uncertainty about the legality of nationalising a concern the regulations governing which are embodied in an international convention, must also have had some inhibiting effect on the British Prime Minister as far as submitting the issue to the world court was concerned. As compared with the Gibraltar case, in the Suez instance the boot seems to have been on the other foot.

This brings us to the four solitary cases in which the arbitral or judicial process was resorted to out of our total of 50 disputes; and in each of these four cases the outcome was unsatisfactory or unfortunate in one way or another. First, in the South-West Africa case, which extended in all over 15 years of the ICJ's life, the Court first determined in 1950 that South Africa was not obliged to enter into a trusteeship agreement relating to her administration of South-West Africa within the United Nations system, but that the old mandatory system governing South Africa's administration of the territory was still in force. When, in consequence of this, Ethiopia and Liberia, as Members of the old League of Nations, sought in 1961 to have the mandate revoked and the South African administration of the territory terminated, the ICJ at length determined in 1966 that Ethiopia and Liberia did not possess the interest in the case which they claimed, though the jurisdiction of the Court in the matter was upheld. Whatever the legal correctness of this decision it could not but come as an anticlimax after so many years' litigation. It is interesting to see that the South African system of *apartheid* in South Africa, as distinct from South-West Africa, has never been made the subject of a request for an Advisory Opinion from the Court, despite South Africa's obligation as a Member of the United Nations to promote and encourage respect for human rights and fundamental freedoms for all without distinction as to race, sex, language or religion.

Secondly, in the Anglo-Iranian oil case in 1950–53, the Anglo-Iranian oil company at first suggested arbitration but Iran refused. Then, on 26 May 1951, after the nationalisation of the oil company by the Iranian government, the United Kingdom submitted the case to the ICJ, availing herself in doing so of the Optional Clause, to which Iran had also subscribed. In July, the Court issued certain provisional measures intended to keep the situation unchanged while consideration of the substance of the case was proceeding. Iran refused to comply with these provisional measures and there were no practical means to hand by which they could have been enforced unless Britain, a party to the dispute, had enforced them herself. When the International Court finally pronounced upon the case it was to declare its lack of jurisdiction, thus appearing to support what had been the Iranian government's claim from the outset, namely that the issue of nationalisation lay within its own jurisdiction.

Thirdly, in the case of Portugal's rights of passage through Indian territory to her own enclaves in India, Portugal took the question to the International Court on 22 December 1955 on the ground that India was interfering with her rights of access to her territorial possessions on Indian soil. In 1960 (the duration of the case is another example of how matters are apt to proceed before the Court), the Hague tribunal decided that Portugal had a right to free passage for private persons but not for her armed forces. The implication of this, at least in the mind of the more nationalistic Indians, was that Portugal had no legal right to defend her territory in India and hence the Court's judgement could be regarded in some sense as the immediate prelude to the incorporation of the Portuguese territories in the Republic of India in the following year. Resort to the world court may thus in this instance be said to have accelerated a solution to the dispute, but the manner in which the Indian authorities eventually terminated the question was hardly calculated to commend itself to those interested in the peaceful settlement of international disputes.

In the fourth and final of these instances of arbitration or judicial settlement, namely, that of the Algeria–Morocco dispute, an arbitration commission was set up under the auspices of the Organisation of African Unity to deal with the frontier question, to determine the responsibilities for the outbreak of hostilities and to make proposals for a settlement. The Commission met and deliberated at Bamako but failed to reach a final settlement of the frontier question which has, however, remained quiescent though unresolved. The interesting thing about this case is that it was between two African states created in the post-war period and that there occurred the sole example we have from our 50 case studies of arbitration having been attempted and having made some limited progress.[14]

By any test the above is an unencouraging record, a record of arbitration and adjudication having been ignored in the great majority of cases, where in most instances some limited resort to either was technically feasible, of their being proposed by one party to the dispute and rejected by the other

[14] It may be objected that our fifty case studies happen to be such as to exclude certain disputes which have been settled by adjudication since 1945, for example, the Minquiers and Ecréhou (Britain and France) and Sovereignty over Certain Frontier Land (Belgium and the Netherlands) cases. We have already explained the reasons for our choice of the fifty disputes (Introduction, pp. 8–9) and would merely add that cases successfully adjudicated, like the two mentioned, were not of the greatest weight in post-war international history and occurred between states whose relations were otherwise cordial and which desired a third-party settlement to keep them so.

and, where the process was initiated, of the outcome either being disappointing or making no real or tangible contribution to the final settlement of the dispute. The meaning of this, in terms of the attitudes of states towards the international judicial process, is that some states, feeling that they have a strong legal case, have seen their proposals for judicial settlement rejected by the other side; others have fought strenuously against the submission of disputes in which they are involved to the judicial process of settlement and, in conducting their resistance, have not increased their own enthusiasm for judicial settlement; and still others, having forced a rival state into court, have seen the court's decision flagrantly and with impunity disregarded by the other side, as Albania disregarded the award by the International Court of Justice of damages to Britain for losses arising out of the mining by Albania of the Corfu Channel. In summary, therefore, it cannot be said that the international community's experience of arbitration or judicial settlement has been a happy one, and, paradoxically, this applies both to states which have favoured resort to these methods of settling disputes as well as to those which have opposed it.

The above remarks suggest one possibly important factor in judicial settlement which may have played some part in inhibiting states from choosing this means of composing their disputes, namely, the impression created by legal proceedings that they are a kind of contest in which one side eventually wins and the other loses; in other words, a "zero-sum" game when all the gains and losses are added up. The Institute of International Law at its 49th session in Neuchâtel in 1959 included among its resolutions the statement that "recourse to the International Court of Justice or to another arbitral tribunal can never be regarded as an unfriendly act towards the respondent state". Nevertheless, it is almost bound to be so regarded considering that the mere style and form of judicial proceedings suggests a competition in which one state, that which takes the case to court, is seeking to demonstrate the wrongfulness of the other, and it can hardly be doubted that this endeavour, especially if it is successful, cannot but have some effect in terms of alienating the other state whereas the principal aim of diplomacy should be reconciliation on the basis of a formula which respects and upholds the interests of both states at one and the same time. Ideally both parties to a dispute should feel, when it is finally settled, that they have gained something more than the mere satisfaction of having the dispute resolved at all; only on the basis of such feelings on both sides can the settlement be regarded as likely to endure. In some cases, as for instance the settlement of a boundary question, it may be possible for a legal tribunal to resolve the issue by giving due weight to the arguments of both sides. Yet it remains an unfortunate characteristic of judicial proceedings that in the majority of cases one side or the other must "lose" in the sense of having its own interpretation of the law in the matter at issue overruled by the court. It is questionable whether this is the most appropriate basis on which international relations can be restored when the dispute is ended.

III

It is appropriate to conclude this chapter with some suggestions as to how recourse to international arbitration and judicial tribunals might be encouraged, at least in the settlement of the essentially legal issues in international disputes. This final qualification is of the highest importance. If a half-century's experience of international adjudication has proved anything, it is that courts of law cannot and should not be expected to fill the gap created by the absence of a legislature in the international community. However able and learned judges may otherwise be, it is not their function, nor within their professional competence, to give binding decisions on what the law ought to be.[15] That question can only be settled in the international system, as it is in the political system within the frontiers of states, by the pressure and counter-pressure of the organised forces in society. If the controversy concerns the question of what the rule of law is and how it should be applied, the judge's verdict is certainly authoritative. But only to a limited extent do international controversies turn upon such a question, and it is often the less important aspects of international controversies which do so turn. Having made this principle clear, we can now proceed to consider some of the ways in which more use could be made of the world's courts and tribunals in settling the legal aspects of such controversies.

First, a number of proposals have been made in various quarters for widening and broadening the employment of judicial agencies in the settlement of international disputes. It has been argued, for instance, that the rule that states alone may submit contentious legal questions for settlement by international tribunals might be relaxed, as indeed it has

[15] It should be pointed out that the present authors are acquainted with, but do not accept, the validity of arguments, as stated, for example, by Professors Richard Falk and Miles McDougal, to the effect that judges, municipal and international, may legitimately fill "gaps" in existing law or modify law in order to make it accord with changing social, technological and other conditions. It may be that in, for example, the Norwegian Fisheries case (1951) or the Nottebohm case (1953) the ICJ did exercise certain legislative functions, though even this is a matter of opinion. Our view, however, is that this is to exceed the judge's competence since there is no strong reason for thinking that judges are any more qualified than the layman to perform what is essentially a political function.

been relaxed in the jurisdiction of the European Court of Justice, the Statute of which allows individual persons to plead before it on their own account. This may be in accordance with the tendency, which has been developing ever since the Industrial Revolution began in Europe towards the end of the eighteenth century, for individuals, or organisations composed predominantly of individuals, to deal with one another across frontiers without being unduly conscious of their nationality. Hardly any of the 50 disputes selected for the present study, however, have arisen from differences between individual persons, or organisations representing them at the non-governmental level. It is hard to foresee such types of disputes becoming anything like the standard form in the immediate future.

It has also been suggested that the machinery of the ICJ could be made somewhat more flexible and informal. This might be done, for example, by making arrangements for the Court to settle more issues, and more expeditiously, by certain of its member-judges acting in chambers rather than in full court,[16] by increasing the range of nationalities represented on the bench at The Hague, though this may have the effect of making the Court even more cumbrous in its working, and by making more use of the provision for the Court to hold some of its sessions in other parts of Europe, and indeed of the world, than at The Hague[17]. The image, which now tends to prevail, of The Hague Court as an established, highly conservative body, proceeding by orthodox and time-honoured methods, and firmly oriented towards European civilisation and legal practice, does not endear it to countries and governments remote from Europe, especially in the developing world.[18]

It must be conceded, however, that these are all essentially minor proposals for change which will hardly do much to revolutionise the present practice of the international community with regard to arbitral and judicial methods of settling international disputes. They cannot touch the heart of the problem, and that heart is surely the absence in the states of the world of any deeply ingrained habits of referring to courts the legal aspects of and the legal issues in their controversies with each other. If appropriate habits of consulting law courts could be built up the practice of doing so would become automatic instead of being, as it is now, partial and intermittent.

It is at this point that the greatest responsibility rests with the wealthiest and most powerful states of the world. In such matters as the issue of declarations under the Optional Clause of the world court's Statute and

[16] Provision is made for cases to be heard in chambers in Articles 26–9 of the Statute of the ICJ.

[17] See Article 22 (1) of the Court's Statute.

[18] See Jenks, *op. cit.*, p. 762 for this and other similar proposals for reform.

the general practice of referring legal issues in disputes to courts and tribunals, the smaller countries tend to follow the example of the greater. And the example set by the latter has not always been encouraging. The Soviet Union, by virtually closing her eyes permanently to the existence of the Hague Court, has made it easier for other states to follow her example. The United States Senate, when it adopted the notorious Connally amendment on 2 August 1946, by which it reserved to the United States the right to define what were matters of domestic jurisdiction and hence excluded from the operation of the American declaration accepting the Optional Clause in the ICJ's Statute, paved the way for other countries, some of them important, similarly to emasculate their declarations; the Connally amendment has been subjected to much criticism both in the United States and elsewhere, but attempts to secure its removal, even when supported by the administration for the time being in power, have so far been unsuccessful. It could be argued that equally, when Britain in 1957 amended temporarily her declaration of adherence to the Optional Clause so as to exclude matters judged by herself to involve national security, and so forestalled any attempt to refer to the world court the question of the legality of British nuclear tests in the Pacific, she set an example which could not have been lost on other states. It should be emphasised, however, that this and other provisos have now been dropped from the latest British declaration accepting the Optional Clause and that this is now in many respects a model, not only of the kind of statement which advocates of a wider acceptance of the Optional Clause have always had in mind, but of the good example of international legal practice which we are arguing that the major states should set to the newer and lesser ones.

A further responsibility lies on the greatest Powers, as it does on all Members of the United Nations, to do what they can to ensure that the various organs of the world organisation make full use of their rights under the Charter to ask for Advisory Opinions from the International Court of Justice on controversial legal issues as these arise in the day-by-day work of these organs. Again, the power of example is a formidable one. If it could be seen that a regular flow of opinions on controversial points of law was issuing from the Court to United Nations organs, the indispensable confidence of Member-states in the Court's potential usefulness to themselves in their legal controversies with each other might be enhanced. Certainly it would seem that there is little in the way of encouragement to states to settle their disputes by arbitral or judicial proceedings if the United Nations itself and its organs make so little use of the judicial resources at their disposal when they are expressly authorised to do so by the Charter in the matter of Advisory Opinions.

But, most important of all, something must surely be done to dispel the common notion that arbitral or judicial proceedings are in some way a peaceful form of conflict from which one side must and will emerge as the "winner" and the other as the "loser". From this undoubtedly springs much of the reluctance of many, or one may say most, states to entrust their interests to the decisions of courts of law. National honour is most painfully engaged in the question and the state which "loses" a case before an international court is almost bound to feel that its self-esteem has been reduced and it may seek to appease its resulting sense of humiliation by resentment against the "winner", from which situation new sources of friction may spring up in the future. It is mainly in order to avoid this kind of embarrassment that more than two-thirds of the Member-states of the international system have so far refused to be bound to go to the International Court through having accepted the Optional Clause.

It is not easy to suggest a remedy for this psychological factor in reluctance to resort to arbitration and adjudication. It is for all practical purposes inherent in legal proceedings that the court should eventually favour one side and reject the arguments of the other. One experiment which might be attempted to counteract this is to try to ensure that as far as possible the settlement of political, economic or other non-legal issues in a dispute should proceed *pari passu* with the settlement of its legal aspects. A state which fails to establish its case in the one set of proceedings may succeed in doing so in the other, and hence "face" may be saved. It would, however, be important for both parties to manage such joint proceedings in such a way that one of the two was not the "loser" in both; the "winner" in the legal proceedings might be well advised to pay quite a high price in the non-legal parallel action and *vice versa* in order to lay the basis for better relations in future with the other state. It is admitted, of course, that any practice on these lines might demand a greater maturity of approach on the part of states than we are likely to see in the imaginable future. One further expedient would be to try to increase the number of issues coming before international courts and tribunals so that states are at frequent intervals both "winning" and "losing" their arguments before such bodies.

It could be valuable, too, to attempt to formulate a hierarchy of tribunals with a right of appeal from a lower to a higher court until the final court of appeal, the International Court at The Hague, is reached. There is a possibility in this notion that a state's resentment arising from being worsted in a lower court might be compensated by a successful appeal to a higher one. It remains true, however, that in the final resort there is no substitute, if we are to aim at more frequent and comprehensive determination of legal issues in disputes between states by international courts and tribunals, for the education of public opinion in the various states, and especially in the leading states of the world, in the necessary facts of adjudication and arbitration, resulting, as may be hoped, in the conviction that national prestige need not be involved when a state is compelled to go to court, or even when it fails to establish its case when it does go to court. What the world would seem to stand in need of is some educational effort to build up and disseminate the idea that the state which agrees to submit its legal disputes to international courts is the one which should be accorded prestige, not the state fearful that its prerogatives of sovereignty will be compromised by recourse to an international court.

We have seen that the role of arbitration and adjudication in the settlement of present-day international disputes is a modest one indeed. That is partly because an international dispute may concern not so much the interpretation of law but demands for changes in the law, and on this question no judge can be accepted as authoritative *qua* judge. But that role is also modest because the states of the world are still far from having the habit of resorting to arbitral and judicial agencies for the settlement of their legal disputes, and the more international arbitration and adjudication stagnate, the less opportunity will there be for that habit to grow. We would stress here the responsibility of the greater states to give a lead and the equal need for arrangements to dispel the illusion that the resort to a court, even a compulsory one, is necessarily a moral defeat if the end of the process is that the state concerned loses its case.

We should add the vitally important fact that if judicial means of settlement of disputes plays on the whole a minor role, this by no means implies that international law itself is not a powerful force in helping to determine state behaviour. There is not the slightest doubt that it is, and perhaps is becoming more so. All states, and possibly the "old" states especially so, are very careful to ensure that their external policies are in accordance with law, so far as contrivance can make them so, for fear, among other reasons, that otherwise they might have to face the adverse judgement of an international tribunal. International courts may therefore be said to play a negative role as deterrents to illegal state behaviour. But we believe that much remains to be done before that negative role can be given a more positive aspect and our recommendations are framed in that spirit.

15. *Conclusions*

THIS book has dealt successively with the nature of international disputes, their origins, development and solution. We have also discussed disputes within states under the same four heads in so far as internal disputes bear upon the relations between states. It is not our purpose in this final chapter to summarise in detail the drift of our argument. We intend here merely to gather together some of the main threads and try to indicate how the study of international disputes, as we ourselves see it, now stands.

The Inevitability of Disputes

In the first place, we would emphasise the point repeatedly made in this book as to the inevitability within the present global system of states of disputes and situations of friction between them as we have defined these terms in the Introduction.[1] Most people bewail what they imagine to be a dangerously high incidence of conflict in international relations; many hope, pray and search for some formula, arrangement or means for eliminating or settling international disputes which could guarantee the absence of strife between nations. We ourselves do not regard the incidence of international conflict as unduly high, though there can be no grounds for complacency in this. Indeed, considering the far from docile nature of the human animal, the need, it seems, for nations to have what Professor A. J. Toynbee once called a "devil" (in other words, an external adversary) "to keep them up to the mark", and considering above all the absence of any supranational machinery which can guarantee the peaceful settlement of international disputes, the wonder is, not that nation-states conflict, but that they do not conflict more often and more violently than they do. Moreover, as we have pointed out in an earlier passage, a high proportion of international disputes, between 50 and 60 per cent, are in fact peacefully settled or fade in time from the diplomatic agenda without force being resorted to.[2]

The difficulty about the widespread idea that somehow, by better international communication, the creation of a world Parliament with power to make law with binding effect or a more enlightened system of education throughout the different states, disputes can be eradicated from international relations is not so much that such thinking is inconsistent

[1] Introduction, *supra*, pp. 2–4.
[2] Part III, Chapter 9, *supra*, p. 193.

with the harsh facts of human nature and the international system, but that the inevitable failure of such hopes tends itself to sharpen international friction. He who entertains expectations of a world without conflict is apt to ascribe conflict, when it inevitably occurs, to the ill-will of the other side, its failure to organise its internal affairs properly or to the inordinate nature of its demands. Hence there tends to enter into human conflict the exacerbating force of the illusion that, were it not for the policies of the adversary, perfect harmony would prevail; and, what is more, that it *will* prevail once the adversary is thoroughly defeated.

As opposed to this style of thinking we would set the more realistic and perhaps more humane conviction that organised groups such as nation-states cannot co-exist for long within the same confined space without quarrelling about something. Moreover, the closer the states are brought into contact with each other by the progress of transport and communication and the more their affairs are intermingled through trade, foreign investment or tourism, the more the occasions for friction between them. Points of contact between states, it must always be remembered, are also points of friction. If the present international system, with its lack of a supreme legislature and effective machinery for the enforcement of law were to be superseded by a single world government, frictions between the then non-sovereign nations would still exist, but they would be handled differently. However, we have to concern ourselves with the world as it is, based on national sovereignty and the equality, in theory at least, of its constituent units, the states. The problem is how to deal somewhat more efficiently with the conflicts of interests, goals and values which constitute an endless contingent liability within that world.

Some recent writers on international relations insist that much, if not all, international conflict is all "in the mind", that states or groups within states quarrel, not about "real" things, but about the different "images of reality" which the antagonists hold.[3] The implication of this would seem to be that if we could eradicate distorted images of the real world from men's thinking and substitute for them an accurate perception of the real world, the conflicts arising between states would be eradicated, too. We agree with this in the truistic sense that hardly any human action can be performed without some thought or feeling, which may be unconscious, and hence that all human activity has a psychological aspect which must be taken into account if that activity is to be understood. It is obvious, too, that the physical distance which still separates many states from each other, the differences in their cultures, climates of opinion and historical experience, must colour their perception of any determinate situation before them; and since these different images of reality coincide only

[3] See Chapter 1, *supra*, pp. 28–29.

rarely and accidentally, some conflict is bound to exist in the international system, or indeed in any social system, because men are not alike and do not feel and think alike about their experience.

We would insist nevertheless that some of the most important conflicts of interests between and within states arise from differences of basic values which cannot be validated or invalidated by reference to established facts.[4] We have argued, in our discussion, for instance, of the nature of disputes (chapter II), that what distinguishes them from other forms of competition is *inter alia* a sense of justice, legitimacy, or entitlement on one or other side or both. It may be hard to determine in any given dispute whether or to what extent the appeal to justice represents a genuinely felt sense of moral entitlement; or whether it is manufactured *ex post facto* in order to buttress a claim to possess what the other state has or a refusal to yield to it something which it desires. But even if we assume the former explanation, namely that the moral basis of international claims is genuine rather than invented for the occasion, we must admit that moral differences cannot always be resolved simply by referring to the direction in which the facts of the situation seem to point. In other words, the question "what ought to be?" cannot always be disposed of in terms of what is.

A familiar instance from recent history will show the truth of this. During the Suez crisis of 1956 one of the main points in dispute was: which was the weightier consideration, Egypt's demand to be sovereign without restriction within its own territory, including the right to dispose as it willed of amenities, such as the Suez Canal, situated within that territory, or the right of the international maritime community to enjoy the use of the waterway under internationally controlled conditions? No matter how clear the perception by the opposing parties of the facts in this dispute, the basic conflict of values, or incompatible titles to justice, would have remained. Where justice is in competition with law, the issue can be resolved only by reference to value systems which rest, in the last resort, not on facts, but on faith.

Moreover, it is also true that states conflict, not so much because they fail to see the realities of their common predicament or because their value systems differ, but because they both desire the same thing, and that thing may be such that if one party has it the other must go without. In other words, we must frankly recognise that there are such things as objective conflicts of interest between states. If China enforces on India a revision of their common border to her own advantage, India must be disadvantaged. If the richer nations at UNCTAD conferences find they cannot revise the terms of trade to benefit the poorer countries, the latter will suffer, and

[4] See on this the writings of Professor F. S. C. Northrop, especially *The Meeting of East and West*, New York, 1946.

doubtless feel resentful as a result. If the United States equips itself with an anti-ballistic missile system capable of making itself invulnerable against Soviet missiles, the Soviet Union is bound to feel that much more insecure.

We cannot but agree that the well-being of the world as a whole would be enhanced if the states spent less time and resources quarrelling with each other and more time and resources cooperating for the common good. The truth remains, however, that at any given level of total world welfare and security, conflict is bound to ensue as to how that welfare and security are to be shared out. To brush aside real conflicts of interest as though they were mere hallucinations is in effect to blind oneself to the nature of international disputes. It is far more useful, having acknowledged the inevitability of conflicts, whether arising from imperception, incompatible value systems or differences of objective interests, to discover how these conflicts can be managed with the least wastage of the world's resources or, more briefly, at lower cost.

The Necessity for Statecraft

In the course of this book we have argued that the elaboration of schemes for the reform of the international system is not a hopeful answer to the problem. A central authority in a disarmed world with laws, tribunals and enforcement powers may eventually come about; but, if so, it will be built piecemeal by states over time in the course of grappling with particular situations, including particular disputes. New methods and procedures for keeping the peace must be hammered out bit by bit, in action and not in advance and in the abstract. They must be created to suit the occasion and tested and, if found successful, developed further according to the requirements of the next occasion, and so on. All this is to affirm that reform of the international system has its part to play in restraining the disputes of the world; but reform depends not upon schemes, but upon the quality of statecraft shown by states in tackling problems as they arise. Moreover, the other main aspect of restraining disputes also depends upon the quality of statecraft practised by states. A good condition of the international system helps to prevent, limit and solve disputes; what helps still more is good statecraft by those engaged in them.

If it is asked what we mean by good statecraft, we mean first of all practical skill, an innate capacity which can only be improved by experience of action. We mean, secondly, political wisdom: and with this we have been concerned in this book in so far as it can be improved by the scholar's reflections on garnered experience.

As regards the *prevention* of disputes, what is needed is understanding of what disputes are and how they arise out of judgements of interest and honour, justice and power. So far as disputes within states are concerned, certain broad principles emerge about the structure which a society needs if peace within it is to be preserved. These, which have long been known, which are reflected yet again in the case studies that we have made, and which we have tried to formulate, need continuous refinement by those charged with the management of contemporary societies. Ultimately nothing is more essential to the prevention of internal disputes than the vigour of normative political philosophy in the great centres of civilisation; for this has a deep, though indirect, influence on practical debate and action. With general understanding of how disputes arise and how they are prevented, statesmen and people are better placed to attend in good time to grievances against the structure of their own society and so to forestall or deter challenges which may destroy it.

Much the same applies to the prevention of disputes *between* states. These disputes are prevented by fear of power and willingness to do justice. Among certain groups of states, it may be that new communities will grow, superseding the present nation states; but, if so, this will require not merely the creation of links of interest between the separate societies, but also constant attention to political and social justice. The new society's structure must be not only powerful but also just if disputes are to be prevented.

In the second part of our book we said that when a dispute is not prevented it may develop, with consequent waste, damage and danger, in two senses: the scale of pressure and counter-pressure may rise, ending ultimately in war; and the number of antagonists may increase by the intervention of outsiders. Thus we are presented with the problem of the *limitation* of disputes in those two senses.

So far as disputes *within* states are concerned, the nature of the dispute may be such that it is readily contained within constitutional limits or the parties may determine that it shall be so. Where the pressures of power and force are in contemplation, however, limitation depends upon nothing else but the understanding by the protagonists of the effects of force on the life of the society and their judgement of its effectiveness in the circumstances. Similarly, as far as outsiders are concerned, the limitation of the dispute depends upon their grasp of the general considerations governing intervention and the shrewdness with which they apply these to the facts of the particular situation. Increasingly, the international community of states may organise non-partisan intervention; but this can never be mere neutral peace-keeping – it is always in some way "judicial". Above all, the considerations which govern intervention and which deter partisan and facilitate non-partisan intervention are premised upon the existence of a balance of power among states, world-wide and regionally. Unless their peoples, and particularly those of the great Powers, understand this and act upon that understanding, all other efforts towards the limitation of disputes are in vain.

As to the limitation of disputes *between* states, this same factor is of paramount importance: states are deterred from going to extremes by the equipoise of power. Yet this by itself is not enough. They are also deterred in so far as links of interest exist between them which they hesitate to sacrifice to their conflict, and in so far as there prevails in the world and in each cultural region a climate of opinion which dishonours war. Action to strengthen tenuous links and to sustain the ideals of the peaceful pursuit of conflict is a continuous necessity. Yet this again is still not enough. The balance of power may be struck at an ever-mounting level of armaments and tension. Links of interest, unless they be those of shared dispute with another, are readily swept aside in pursuit of a dispute. The ideal of peace is cogently denounced as hypocrisy by a state with a sense of grievance. What is further needed is evidence of willingness to consider the merits and needs in the opponent's case, and the knowledge of the manner of handling an opponent who will not do the like or a situation which is intractable. In short, what is finally required for the limitation of disputes is understanding of justice and of prudence and the application of this understanding in statecraft.

Finally, as to *solutions*, we have reviewed in Part III of this book the different agencies and techniques now available in the international system for the settlement of inter-state disputes. We have examined in some detail the use made of these instruments by the parties to international disputes since the Second World War and have also tried to estimate the success which has been attained, with particular reference to the experience gained in each of our fifty case studies. We have, where suitable, suggested ways in which these agencies and techniques of peaceful settlement could be improved, and have indicated the kinds of disputes which lend themselves to resolution by such agencies and those which are more intractable.

Our general conclusion is that the world at present is not lacking in machinery for the peaceful settlement of disputes if the will on the part of the disputants to use that machinery is there. Inevitably, the decision to resort to these agencies rests with the states themselves. Their sovereignty, even in this interdependent world of today, is still far more than merely theoretical: not only is this true of the greatest Powers; even quite small and weak countries have proved remarkably resistant to pressures from other states to compose their disputes speedily and peacefully. It may therefore be taken as a general rule that unless and until the parties to a dispute feel that it is in their interests to settle a dispute, the mere existence of technically adequate machinery for peaceful settlement and exhortations to settle exerted by other states are likely to have only limited effect.

Some have suggested that what the world may see is a kind of directorate of the great Powers or rather perhaps a dyarchy of the super-Powers, a return, in other words, to the primacy of the UN Security Council, as envisaged in 1945, applying their joint pressures on smaller states to settle their disputes peacefully. But the evidence of great-Power intervention in the Middle East crisis at the time of writing (summer 1970) suggests that those Powers still have a long way to go before they can act in unison as policemen of the world, even if the smaller states would accept them in that role.

There is, however, one specific recommendation we wish to make concerning the existing machinery for the peaceful settlement of international disputes before we examine further the vital question of the factors affecting the attitudes of states towards the use of that machinery. It is this: we have been repeatedly struck in the course of our research by the absence of any attempt either by governments, international organisations or scholarly institutions to draw conclusions from the world's actual experience of international disputes, especially as concerns the questions why some disputes are more easily resolved than others, why states are more willing in some conditions than in others to resort to third-party settlement and other such questions as we have ourselves examined in this book. Studies of particular disputes exist in abundance; so do theoretical speculations about international conflict in general, its cause and cure. But something, we feel, is needed in the middle ground between; namely, detailed, thoroughly researched, comparative studies of international disputes since, say, the Second World War, compiled with the object of throwing light on the question of what kind of conditions in these disputes influences their outcome and consequences.[5]

It would seem natural, and has always been considered natural, that if a community wishes to reduce the incidence of, for example, traffic accidents, crime, divorce or drunkenness, it should initiate studies of the types of conditions under which these social evils occur and, by observing uniformities or similarities in these conditions, if such exist, make recommendations as to how they can be avoided. It is a remarkable fact that nothing similar seems to have been attempted in relation to international disputes, heavier though these may be with potentially tragic consequences for mankind than the social evils we have just referred to. In this book we have made an effort, on a necessarily modest scale, to study the history of international disputes since 1945 with a view to laying a basis for under-

[5] To some extent the gap is filled by the *Repertory of Practice of UN Organs*, but this is a factual rather than analytical account.

standing their nature, origins, development and solution. But this is merely a beginning. Politics, as we have repeatedly argued in this book, is partly a creative activity, accomplished through intuitive judgement, imagination and the experienced grasp of human circumstances, for which learning can never be a complete substitute. But this is not to say that politicians and diplomats cannot gain from reliable and carefully researched case studies of international disputes in which conditions and methods of settlement are set out, compared and evaluated, an analytical compendium, so to speak, of conflicts of which the international system has had experience.

Finally we return to our basic questions. What governs the attitudes of states towards the peaceful settlement of their disputes; under what conditions are states most likely to have recourse to peaceful means of settlement; and what influences the success or otherwise with which these means are used? Firstly, we have stressed the necessity of considering the total circumstances of a state before its attitude towards a particular dispute can be understood. In contradistinction to the situation which normally prevails among individual persons, a state's disputes with its peers tend to be a function of all its international relations; a deterioration in relations between a state and one of its neighbours can often lead to an improvement in its relations with another, on the simple principle of diplomacy that it is not prudent to have many enemies at the same time. This does not mean that the best way of dealing with a state's disputes is to worsen its relations with states with which it is not in dispute. It does mean that attempts to settle disputes must take into account the whole pattern of a state's interests, as displayed in all its external relations, since that pattern has a fundamental role to play in determining its attitude towards a particular dispute.

Secondly, we would emphasise again that the state is an institution in which the supreme decision-makers, that is, the government, are responsible, or at least sensitive, to the opinions and emotions of large numbers of people. An individual in a dispute with another individual can consult his own mind as to whether he should press ahead with the dispute and when, how and on what terms to settle it. The governing authorities of a state, on the other hand, have to take up positions which command the support of others, whether these be many, as in a liberal democracy, or few, as in the totalitarian society. This simple fact creates endless difficulties in the settlement of international disputes: governments are driven by domestic opinion to assume more intransigent postures than they otherwise might do; small disputes are built up into major crises by newspapers and broadcasting organisations which thrive on the drama of conflict; negotiations on delicate and complex matters are relayed, word for word and blow by blow, to inflamed and touchy supporters behind the governments on either side. All these circumstances tend to make the process of peaceful settlement of disputes more difficult than it otherwise would be.

It is right that ordinary people should know what is being done in their name at the diplomatic level, at least in broad outline; certainly they have a right to know what their government is committing them to by agreements they reach with other states. But compromise is inherent in almost every international agreement, and compromise does not come easily to a proud people awaiting an unmitigated gain from a dispute, or to rival politicians of the existing government who are only too anxious to show up the alleged weakness of those in office. There is no magic which can circumvent this problem of the relations between government and people as affecting the settlement of international disputes. All we can say is that a duty rests with all those who have to do with educating a national people to ensure that future generations are schooled, not so much in the old-fashioned, and probably false, idea that in the last resort the interests of all nations are precisely the same, but in the need to recognise the legitimacy of the interests, motives, goals and values of other people besides their own. All nations are condemned to live on the same confined planet. Nothing can more surely bring them to destruction than the idea that Providence or some other extra-human force has ordained a monopoly of right and reason for one's own cause.

This leads us to the final point, namely, the duty of all of us continually to scrutinise the international system and to ask ourselves whether we are conducting our relations with other countries in such a way as to avoid a feeling of grievance and intolerable unfairness being bred in the minds of people in the rest of the world which will in time make them a threat to the existing system. No social order can remain secure unless it accords with the sense of justice of most of the people most of the time. We have insisted throughout this study that national governments must be expected to preoccupy themselves with their own state interests, and that their appreciation of how best to advance these interests will tend to govern their attitudes towards disputes with other states. But perhaps the world must now go beyond this, not to the renunciation of national interest in favour of some vaguely conceived international interest, but to an appreciation of how another state's interests, objectives and values can seem as meaningful, natural and precious to itself as one's own interests, objectives and values seem to oneself. Most people, when they talk of improving the state of the world, or its machinery for settling international disputes, tend to think of all this happening within a larger framework which generally suits themselves. But people must be prepared to go half-way, perhaps even further, to altering the shape of the international system, and its order of moral priorities, so as to make it seem just and fair to those who at present reject it or the policies of some of its leading member-states. And this may necessitate some sacrifice of interests, objectives and values on one's own side.

These are all modest conclusions, though of daunting complexity when it comes to furthering their implementation in the real world. As we forecast in the Introduction, we have no concise formula to offer which would at once help the nations to overcome their problems to their mutual advantage. The fact is, as it seems to us, that international disputes arise because men and nations are what they are and the international system which they comprise is what it is. We must understand the world we live in, as well as our own human nature, if we wish to understand and deal more effectively with the very human phenomenon of disputes which arise within it. At the same time, we must never lose sight of the moral aspect of the problem. Disputes, as we have argued, tend to arise because in this country or that there develops the conviction that the present state of affairs is wrong, that it offends natural justice. Sometimes this argument is no more than a cover for otherwise unadorned greed and ambition. But we are not entitled to describe it as such until we have first done our utmost to ensure that the international system is as just, in the eyes of other states as well as our own, as all our best efforts can make it.

APPENDIX

CATALOGUE OF INTERNATIONAL DISPUTES: 1945–70

1. Poland, 1944–45
2. Greece, 1944–49
3. Austria, 1945–55
4. Indonesian independence, 1945–49
5. Palestine, 1945–49
6. Indo-China, 1945–54
7. South Tirol, 1945 to present
8. Kashmir, 1947 to present
9. Korea, 1947–53
10. Trieste, 1945–54
11. Berlin, 1948–49
12. South Africa, 1948 to present (including the two issues of *apartheid* and South-West Africa)
13. China: Taiwan, the UN, 1950 to present
14. Indonesia and West Irian, 1950–62
15. The Anglo-Iranian Oil Company, 1950–53
16. Tibet, 1950–59
17. Guatemala, 1952–54
18. Cyprus, 1954–59 and 1963 to present
19. Vietnam, 1954 to present
20. Suez, 1956
21. Hungary, 1956
22. Muscat and Oman, 1957–59
23. Anglo-Icelandic Fisheries, 1958–61
24. Lebanon and Jordan, 1958
25. Quemoy–Matsu, 1958
26. Berlin, 1958–61
27. Laos, 1957–65
28. United States and Cuba, 1959–61
29. Sino-Indian Border, 1959–65
30. Mauritania and Morocco, 1958–69
31. Somalia, 1960–65
32. U2, 1960
33. Congo, 1960–63
34. Angola, 1961 to present
35. Kuwait–Iraq, 1961–63
36. Goa, 1950–61
37. Yemen, 1962–67

38. Cuba missile crisis, 1962
39. Aden (South Yemen), 1963–67
40. Algeria–Morocco, 1959–63
41. Gibraltar, 1963 to present
42. Indonesia–Malaysia, 1963–66
43. Panama Canal, 1964
44. The Dominican Republic, 1965
45. Chinese minority in Indonesia, 1965 to present
46. Rhodesia, 1965 to present
47. Nigeria, 1966–70
48. Hong Kong, 1967 to present
49. Arab–Israeli conflict, 1967 to present
50. Czechoslovakia, 1968

Index